Irrational Ravings

Pete Hamill

Irrational Ravings

G. P. Putnam's Sons, New York

Copyright © 1971 by Pete Hamill

All rights reserved. This book, or parts thereof, must not be reproduced in any form without permission. Published simultaneously in Canada by Longmans Canada Limited, Toronto.

Library of Congress Catalog Card Number: 77–163410

PRINTED IN THE UNITED STATES OF AMERICA

This book is for Jimmy Cannon

Contents

7

III. NAM, 167

IV. WHITE MISCHIEF, 227

V. POLS, 259

VI. FIGHTERS, 321

VII. NEW YORK, 349

But the most vicious attempt to transfer the blame for the Kent State student deaths that I have read was in the illiberal New York Post, *by columnist Peter Hamill. Listen to his irrational ravings. . . .*
—SPIRO T. AGNEW

Introduction

I

THERE is something peculiar and disturbing about reading through ten years' work, in order to choose some of it for preservation. Journalists of all persuasions have a common complaint and a common failing: They write too much, and they write under terrible pressures of time and space. Most of them cannot bear to read their own work when it appears the next day in a newspaper or the following month in a magazine; they know that the text has been set in type, locked up and sent out under their names, and that the rash judgment can never be withdrawn, the clumsiness of the phrase never smoothed out, the half-conceived thought seldom brought to fullness. Someone once described journalism as history in a hurry. It is a definition that suffers from the usual journalist's glibness, but there is something to it. Reporters, at their best, do write a kind of first draft of history, and in America, they have largely tried to do so with some personal honesty. Their limitations are the limitations of the form itself.

All these pieces were written swiftly, in circumstances that varied, but always under the pressures of time and space. The newspaper columns were the most difficult of all. I have always felt that the best a column can hope to do is present a fragment of an event or an idea, hope to move the reader for a few random moments, and remind him of the gathering darkness before he moves on to Rose Franzblau and Mary Worth. No newspaper columnist I know (and I certainly do not know all of them) believes that he will solve any problem in four triple-spaced pages. He goes on, because he knows that sometimes something *will* happen; I've written more than a hundred columns about the war in Vietnam, and I might as well have been publishing them in the Arctic Circle, for all the effect they had; on the other hand, I once wrote a column asking Nelson Rockefeller, the governor of New York, to let the old bank robber Willie Sutton out of jail and the next day Willie was on the street. I don't know if I really had anything to do with it, but I claimed the victory anyway. Writers don't win anything very often, so the tendency is to claim whatever plausibly can be claimed. And New York was certainly a better place with Willie Sutton out of jail.

The longer pieces in this collection differ from the newspaper columns, but reading them again is still an unsettling experience. Newspaper writing is the club fighting of journalism; you put the Indian blanket over the shoulders, walk into the arena, throw some punches, and go home. But in most of these long pieces I've been trying to work something out, to let the prose grow richer and allow the ideas, if any, some room to breathe. And yet I wish I could rewrite some of them, to soften the glib hard guy's tone in a number of them or cut away the sentimentality in others. In some of the pieces in this book, I'm a much younger man, intoxicated with the *sound* of words, and the prose is lusher than I would like it to be. There is a distinction to be made between rich prose that is bony with fact, yet enriched by nuance, texture, and resonance, and a prose that is merely lush. In the longer pieces I've tried to write richly, and most of the time I've failed. I'm lush when I should be rich. The lush stretches are a kind of prose bougainvillaea, without meaning, crawling over the page, smelling of jasmine, but without very much reason for being there. It is a sin of young writers, but nonetheless a sin.

But there is also something happening in this work that has nothing to do with technique. In the broadest sense, these fragments are an attempt to discover something about the world and something about myself.

II.

In the most crucial ways, the kind of journalism I write has been formed by my personal history. I was born in Brooklyn,

14

New York, on June 24, 1935. My parents, Billy Hamill and Anne Devlin, were Belfast Catholics who had emigrated to the United States in the 1920's. My maternal grandfather, Peter Devlin, was a ship's officer who brought his wife and two small children with him to New York when he started working on American-based ships. One morning in 1916, he fell between his ship and the dock and was crushed to death. My grandmother took the two small children back to Belfast. She died in 1928. My mother returned to America in 1929, landing in New York the day that the stock market crashed. For a few years, she was an indentured servant, working as a maid for a rich family to pay off the cost of the passage. My father's father was a stonemason, with a family of fourteen, and he lived and died in Belfast. Life in that hard Northern city was never easy, under the best of circumstances, but in a city where the Protestant majority discriminated against the Catholic minority, it was impossible. My father joined Sinn Fein, the Irish revolutionary organization, got himself into various unnamed troubles, and then suddenly left for the United States in 1923, taking a ship through Liverpool to New York. There is no way to trace either family back farther than my grandparents because all the records were apparently burned in the Protestant-Catholic rioting of 1922. Anne Devlin and Bill Hamill met in the United States, were married in the 1930's, and raised a family of seven children, of which I'm the oldest. They were poor. I had my first steak when I was seventeen.

Somewhere in the above paragraph are the seeds of the kind of writer I later became. I grew up in a state of rage. Sometimes I hid the rage; sometimes I displaced it, in long afternoons at the public library near my house, where the books of Howard Pyle, Robert Louis Stevenson, and Kenneth Roberts took me out of present time and put me into some other world where bearded pirates clashed on stretches of yellow beach, or young boys hid under bridges away from Blind Pew, or Roger's Rangers made the terrible journey to the Northwest Passage; and when there was no way to hide the rage, no way to displace it, I would explode into violence, the hands clenched into fists, hammering and battering at people I did not even know. The violence was always white and blind and savage, and when I think about the cause of it now, it always seems to involve humiliation. I remember one cold winter afternoon when I was four-teen. I had won a scholarship to a Jesuit high school called Regis, which was a long subway ride away from Brooklyn, on Eighty-fourth Street and Park Avenue in Manhattan. Most of the students were upper-middle-class, and I spent the first few months there in a state of desperate unhappiness. I was trying to learn Latin and algebra, but more important, I was looking for a school that did not exist; I had imagined Regis as a place where older boys shared a democratic camaraderie with younger boys, where you learned from one another and went to basketball games together as a body to cheer for the school team. Instead, I found a place stinking with class rank and priv-ilege, with turf reserved for seniors, smoking privileges allowed to some students and not to others, and a student body that was, in retrospect, docile and cliquish. On this rainy winter day, I arrived at school, soaked by the walk from Lexington Avenue. There were large holes in the bottom of my shoes; I did not own a pair of galoshes; instead, cardboard had been stuffed into the shoes. When I went into the locker room of the school, my shoes were squishing with rainwater. I found a piece of cardboard in a wastebasket and sat down on a bench and took my shoes off. I was tearing the cardboard to fit the shoes when I heard laughter. I looked up to see a couple of juniors snickering and giggling at my shoes. I felt humiliated and grubby and helpless. All that day, I sat in class like a bomb, and when school was over, I waited down the street in the rain in a door-way on Park Avenue, until I saw one of the young men who had laughed. I exploded in a fury of punching, kicking, and stomping and left the kid smashed and bleeding on the side-walk, before I ran off in the rain. I didn't go to school for two days, because I was frightened and somehow ashamed. Ever since, it has been impossible for me to watch a black kid walk into a white school without wondering if he had cardboard in his shoes. Ever since, I've been afraid of the murderer who lives in my body.

But there was more to the anger than poverty. There was something in me that wanted the world to be fair. I grew up hearing stories of the injustices in Northern Ireland, of what the Protestant landlords were doing to Catholic *and* Protestant

16

workers. That led to a kind of rude sympathy for underdogs, for blacks, Puerto Ricans, and Indians, for the damaged and the lost, which was further deepened by the fact that as a young man in America my father had lost a leg playing soccer. In the years when I was growing up, my father had a street fighter's sense of bigotry; he wouldn't let anyone use the words "nigger" or "spic" in the house, and once, when I was about eleven, I used the word "kike" at the dinner table, and he leaned over and smacked my face brutally and said, "Benny Leonard was a kike." I didn't know what he was talking about, I didn't know that Benny Leonard was a Jew off the Lower East Side who had become the greatest of all lightweight champions of the world, but I never used the word "kike" again. It is a simple matter to sneer at that story, at its lack of sophistication or its possibly patronizing implications. But it was the way you learned things in that neighborhood, and I thank the old man for doing what he did. He would never have described himself as "liberal." He simply hated unfairness, bigotry, and the absence of justice.

I didn't know until much later that we were "white lower middle class." I just thought we were poor. It never occurred to me that there were people who were poorer than we were. Everybody in that neighborhood seemed to be in the same jam, except for the few Irish who had more or worked harder or been luckier, or laughed less, and who owned houses nestled close to the church on the hill. I never liked them very much because they treated most of us like muckers. I didn't like the church much either. I was an altar boy for four years, and it was like working backstage at a television show. The priests seemed a gang of fakes to me, sleek fat men with smooth hands, who went through their mumbo jumbo every morning and lived off the honest labor of poor people. It seemed wrong to me that they did not work. It was even worse that their privileged position, based on craven fear of "God," allowed them to tell the rest of us what to do or allowed them to sit in judgment in the dark hole of the confessional booth. On Seventh Avenue and Twelfth Street, where I lived, people were scrambling for enough to eat; in the church on Ninth Avenue, people who didn't work were drinking wine from golden goblets. I left the church when I was sixteen and never went back. I haven't had much respect for authority since then, whether it is embodied in the person of a cop, an archbishop, or a Secretary of Defense.

And yet, despite the rage and anger over injustice, there were other things happening during those years that I remember with great affection. Some of them are in this book, in pieces done for *New York* magazine, in which I've tried to understand precisely how I felt about certain matters. I've tried not to sentimentalize that period of my life, and I certainly don't go along with the reverse snobbery that it was somehow better to have grown up poor. That is a judgment made by people who have never been poor. If you can understand the roots of anger and violence, there is some possibility that they can be controlled. Not excised; controlled. I don't think I've succeeded yet, and some of the newspaper columns are still the work of an essentially violent man. But I have finally understood that the anger and violence come from that part of me that is still fourteen years old and humiliated by holes in my shoes, yet wants desperately to believe in the golden democratic promise that had brought my people across an ocean into exile and which had too often been such a disappointment.

III.

I quit high school when I was sixteen and went to work in the Brooklyn Navy Yard. I had been writing stories for about four years then, some of them in the form of comic books, for which I also drew the pictures. One of my stories, printed in comic book lettering and illustrated with some particularly lurid drawings was submitted to my English composition class at Regis. It featured a particularly stupid detective named Chuck Taylor. The principal of Regis was the Reverend Charles Taylor. I was given an F.

But I wanted more than anything else then to be a comic strip artist, and at home, I had a tall flaking metal cabinet stacked with comic books. I spent long hours copying them, studying them, and drawing them in small 8 x 10 composition books. My favorite was *Terry and the Pirates* by Milton Caniff, and when Caniff left that strip to draw *Steve Canyon* in the *Daily Mirror,* I started clipping out every day's strip and pasting them in scrapbooks. Caniff was the best of the strip artists, a boldly original draftsman and clever writer who knew something about human character; if he had not drawn a comic strip, he might have been a great film director. One Christmas, my mother wrote to him (he lived in New City, New York) and told him about how fanatic I was about his work, and he sent me back two brushes that he had used in drawing his strip and an original drawing of Steve Canyon. That really was some Christmas.

The comics brought me to newspapers. One of my favorite books was Bill Mauldin's *Up Front*, with all the great Willie and Joe cartoons from the Second World War, and when Mauldin's second book, *Back Home*, came out, my brother Tommy and I went to a bookstore and stole it. His third book was a marvelous memoir of childhood called *A Sort of a Saga*, and Mauldin soon grew into a kind of intellectual hero of mine, the kind of man I would like to be. He could draw, and he could write; he had been poor; he had a fine disdain for authority and in his postwar cartoons he wasn't afraid to draw millionaires with shaking hands, drooling chins, and pinholes for eyes. When Mauldin went to draw for one of the successors to *PM* (it was either the *Compass* or the *Star*), I started buying the paper every day; I also discovered Walt Kelly, who was an editorial cartoonist then, and tried to understand a writer named I. F. Stone. I was working in a grocery store after school, and with what money I had for myself, I bought newspapers and books. Once I bought about thirty copies of George Seldes' newsletter *In Fact* for a dollar in a used-book store on Pearl Street; I really didn't know what on earth he was talking about, but it struck me as being vaguely antiauthoritarian, and I liked the man's tone. By the time I started work in the Navy Yard I was reading all the newspapers except the *Times* (which had no comics), I had become a retired Catholic, I was determined to be a comic book artist, and, under the influence of Mauldin, I was some sort of vague left-winger. We all have strange beginnings.

I worked in the Navy Yard for a year and then joined the Navy. It was a difficult time, because I still couldn't handle authority, and I remember it vaguely as a time of rolling around on the ground outside the roadhouse joints in Pensacola and

Mobile, trying to beat petty officers to death. But something else happened during those years. I met a guy named Duncan, who had been going to Rollins College in Florida when the Korean War started and had been pulled into the Navy through the reserves; he was the first person I ever knew who had gone to college. And I met a slightly older guy named Henry Whiddon, a painter, from Marietta, Georgia, who hated the Navy even more than I did. Duncan encouraged me to read, Whiddon to paint. I read *The Great Gatsby* and then *The Sun Also Rises*, and soon I was working my way through the base library. My letters home started getting literary in the worst way, as I tried to use words to explain what was happening to me, and I started filling notebooks with fragments of prose, words I had never heard before, poems, epigrams, character sketches, even short biographies of writers and painters, and of people I met in the Navy. At the same time, Whiddon was introducing me to the world of painting and sculpture. In his locker he had a collection of art books and small reproductions of paintings and drawings, and when I wasn't reading Hemingway or Fitzgerald or Dos Passos, I was studying or copying drawings by George Grosz, Rico Lebrun, a Japanese-American named Kuniyoshi, the great Mexicans like Orozco and Siqueiros. I responded most to the strongest draftsmen, the men with the ability to make the most direct statement and somehow transform it into art. I was working as a storekeeper at one of the tiny bases around the sprawling naval air station at Pensacola: it was dull and tedious work; but it gave me time, and I remember it now as a time of almost daily intellectual excitement, alternating with off-duty violence. In some circuitous way, I was receiving an education.

By the time I was discharged I was bursting with a desire to go back to school. I was entitled to educational benefits under the Korean GI Bill of Rights, and in the Navy I had constructed a vision of life in college for myself. The first week I was home, I went up to Columbia to apply for admission. Columbia in the early fifties was no place for a kid who had never graduated from high school and who retained the manners of the Brooklyn streets. The assistant dean who interviewed me suggested that I go to a community college and become a dental technician or something that better suited my background. I remember the man's bald head and polished fingernails. I also remember my own hurt and baffled anger as I left Columbia. There was not going to be any college, in any conventional way. I tried some alternatives. I applied for a job as a copyboy at three newspapers (the *Times*, the *Journal-American*, and the *World-Telegram*), but they weren't interested either; this was the period when the personnel director had begun to set himself up between editors and potential employees, and personnel directors understand only résumés. So I drifted around for a year, working at an advertising agency called Doremus and Company as a $30-a-week messenger. I could have gone back to the Navy Yard, of course, and made a lot more money; my relatives thought I was throwing away my life. But somehow, during those long evenings in the Navy, I had tasted steak, literally and intellectually. I wanted to take a shot at something larger.

Doremus and Company was a financial agency that produced all those "tombstone" ads on the financial pages of newspapers. For six weeks, I carried mats and plates to those newspapers that wouldn't hire me as a copyboy. Each trip past presses, teletype machines, and rooms full of typing reporters intoxicated me more, I suppose because it seemed a life that was forever beyond me. I started to talk to the one commercial artist at Doremus, and he managed to get me moved from the mail room to another part of the agency, where I became a proofreader. Within six months, I was working uptown at an agency called the Fred Wittner Company and was going to night school at Pratt Institute in Brooklyn studying advertising design.

Fred Wittner had been a sportswriter at the *Herald Tribune* during that newspaper's glory days in the 1930's and later had become a public relations man for Amelia Earhart, among other clients. His agency handled industrial accounts: chemicals, machinery, industrial processes. He was the best in his field at the time, but there was a part of him that remained a newspaperman, that would have preferred a seat at the championship fights with Jesse Abramson to lunch at 21 with a client. One afternoon, he saw me trying to plow through *By Love Possessed*, James Gould Cozzens' great bloat of a novel (it was that year's savior of American literature), and he became curious about me. From that day on, he never failed to be kind to me or to keep the dream of newspapering bubbling and alive.

Two other men were even more crucial to me. The first was Ernie Waivada, who was the art director at the Wittner agency, a superb designer, and still a good friend. He was about ten years older than I was, single, a political liberal, a good drinker, and we spent a lot of time after hours talking about art and design. He made me an assistant in the art department, first showing me the technical skills: how to handle rubber cement, how to apply fixative to chalk, how to letter, and, along the way, the most important thing of all, how to see something fundamentally first and apply detail later. I plunged into a study of the great designers: Paul Rand, George Giusti, Charles Eames, Herbert Bayer, all the men from the Bauhaus, the theoreticians like Moholy-Nagy, and dozens of others whose names I can no longer remember. I forgot about becoming a comic book artist; in a kid's brash way I was trying to learn something that had become more important to me under the influence of the people I was meeting. Ernie Waivada, who was from Worcester, Massachusetts, and had graduated from Art Center School in Los Angeles, urged me to go to art school, and I ended up at Pratt, because in night school they didn't much care whether or not you had graduated from grammar school as long as you paid your tuition. In the second semester at Pratt, I met someone else, and the pendulum started swinging back again, from pictures to words.

The first night Tom McMahon showed up to teach English composition at the night school at Pratt, he had a French cigarette dangling from his lips, and he was wearing a foreign intrigue trench coat. He eased himself into the classroom, stood for a long moment until the class hushed itself into silence, and then flipped the cigarette behind him into the hall, without looking where it was going. Jesus! It was theatrical, even hammy, but it was a sensational entrance. A few weeks later, when I submitted an analysis of the Bobo Olson–Sugar Ray Robinson middleweight championship fight as an essay for class and correctly picked Robinson by a knockout, McMahon somehow decided to teach me how to write. He started by teaching me how to read.

Until I met McMahon, my serious reading had been as disordered as the rest of my life. In the Navy it was determined by the books on the library shelf; later it was influenced by things like the design on the cover. I learned then (as I still do, in many ways, today) by experiencing things viscerally, then standing back at some distance and trying to understand them intellectually. I worked from stomach to heart to head. My formal education had been truncated, and there were, and are, large gaps in my understanding of many things. McMahon sensed that and apparently tried to devise some means of correcting it. Over the next five or six years, with time off while he went on a sabbatical with his wife to France, and I went off "to paint" for a year in Mexico, he taught me something about textual analysis and the careful use of words. We combed Hemingway line by line, to see how he managed to pack so much emotion into paragraphs whose individual components seemed so flat and spare; we studied Aristotle's *Ethics*, to see how a great thinker builds arguments (and also, I suspect, to force some ideas about behavior into my head). McMahon tried to get me to understand the British linguistic philosophers—and failed. But he did introduce me to the hard, brilliant essays of George Orwell, most important "Politics and the English Language." Orwell's influence remains all over my work to this day.

More than anything else, McMahon taught me that words meant something. They were not typographical ornaments; they were not to be slapped around the page with abandon. They were to be used with care, even love (although McMahon would probably stiffen at the use of so vague a word). He loved careful, sane writers (E. M. Forster was a favorite), but he also knew that the best American writers also had darkness in them, that Fitzgerald's romanticism was his strength and his destruction, that Hemingway's stories were not boyish evocations of sensation, but openings into the horror, that Pound had to go mad, that Eliot's retreat into Christianity was a way of holding off the demons. He didn't talk much about those matters, but I understood that behind the concern for style and craft, there was a dark knowledge of America brooding beneath the surface. There was a direct line from Hemingway's *A Pursuit Race* to Nelson Algren's *The Man with the Golden Arm*; Mark Twain was grappling with Samuel Clemens; Hawthorne would have understood *The Deer Park*. I wanted to know what was happening to me on the streets of Brooklyn; I wanted to know why so many people were caught in sorrow and defeat in the richest city on the earth; above all, I wanted to understand. McMahon taught me many things in those years, but perhaps the most important lesson was that words could be a means of understanding. He is teaching now at the University of Texas, and I haven't seen him for a long time. But there are still moments when I sit at a typewriter, exhausted by a long day's journey, afraid of emptiness, writing against the deadline's implacable demands, and feel the brooding presence of his disdain. At those moments, I feel I should be doing something else.

IV.

By the time I was twenty-five I was a partner with a man named John Snyder in a commercial art studio on West Forty-sixth Street. I had ruined my eyes staying up all night lettering six-point type with a one-hair brush, and I was more and more bored by the commercial art business. Bored, and somehow vaguely ashamed of it. After work, McMahon was setting standards of excellence, and I was becoming a well-paid hack. Jack Kennedy was making his splendid dash for the White House, the Eisenhower years were almost over, and America seemed to be moving into a period that promised style and spirit and the redemption of the old by the young. And there I was, in the business of putting shabby goods in pretty packages. I was working twelve to fourteen hours a day, and it just didn't seem worth it.

One of the accounts I had brought to the studio was a Greek-language monthly magazine called *Atlantis*. It was owned by a decent old guy I always called Mr. Vlasto, but it was edited by his son, James, who is now one of the finest political public relations men in the business. Jimmy Vlasto and I were the same age, and spent much time in the magazine's office on Twenty-third Street and Tenth Avenue laughing over what we were doing. I couldn't read Greek, of course, but neither could Jimmy, so every month it was a sheer guess about what story was appearing under what headline or what, in fact, we were even publishing. I would lay out the magazine, paste up forty-four pages of mechanicals, and get paid in two and a half days. And then Jimmy and I would go drinking.

Jimmy knew that I was interested in writing, that, in fact, I would rather work for a newspaper than be a commercial artist, and one day over drinks, he said casually that I should start writing for the magazine. He wanted to try to broaden the magazine, get some of the younger Greek-Americans to start reading it, and if I wanted to write for it, the space was there. A month later, somewhere in the winter of 1959, Jimmy published my first story, which was about William Saroyan. I wrote every month after that; it was a better early apprenticeship than I could have obtained going for coffee at the *Times*.

Through the second half of the fifties, while McMahon was trying to educate me, I had never lost the urge to be a newspaperman. Waivada had started me reading the *Post*, and every day I would rush out at lunchtime to read Murray Kempton and Jimmy Cannon in the first edition. I didn't always understand Kempton, but there was something both elegant and passionate about his style that moved me and fed my angers. He had refined the great weapon of the fifties—irony—into something private and supple. But it was Cannon who made me want to be a newspaperman. He wrote a sports column, but it was always more than that. In some ways, the hero of the column was its style, an undisciplined personal mixture of New York street talk, soaring elegance, Hemingway and Algren, deep Celtic feeling, city loneliness, Prohibition violence, and a personal belief in honor. Years later, I was sitting up one night with Jimmy Breslin, at that hour when men tell each other the truth, talking about how Jimmy Cannon had affected one-half a generation of American newspapermen and Red Smith had influenced the other half. "Cannon was it," Bres said. "There was nobody else." Breslin, Gay Talese, and I (along with a number of others) were influenced by Cannon in ways that we no longer recognized; anyone who goes back and reads those Cannon columns would see it immediately.

Because of Cannon and Kempton, the *Post* became a very special newspaper to me. In early 1960, I wrote a long letter to the editor that was more a manifesto about ruined youth than a letter; it was published. A few months later, Jimmy Wechsler, who was then editor of the paper, published a book called *Reflections of an Angry Middle-Aged Editor.* I bought it and read it through that night. The next day I sent Wechsler a long, impassioned letter about the book, the world, and the state of American journalism. A few days later I received a brief note from him asking me to come down to the *Post* for a talk. I showed up one late afternoon, walked nervously through the city room to his office in the back, and went in to see him. He offered me a chance to try out as a writer on the *Post.* I don't remember anything else about the day.

V.

The *Post* became the great democratic school I had always longed for. I knew nothing at all about the mechanics of newspaper writing when I arrived, but there were teachers everywhere. A young guy named Ed Kosner (now a senior editor at *Newsweek*) took me over the first night and showed me how to slug a story and something about compression. A brilliant tortured man named Fred McMorrow started bringing my stories back from the copy desk, where he worked, to show me what I was doing wrong and how to correct it. The managing editor was a whirlwind of a man named Al Davis, who had a first-rate story sense, and a passion for literary style, and a wild sometimes destructive temper; he shouted at a lot of other writers, but he never shouted at me. Offstage, working on the day side, was Paul Sann, the executive editor, setting the standards for all of us.

But most important were the writers on the night side. I worked nights for the first year and a half, abandoning the commercial art business after the first three months. The other night-side writers then were Gene Grove, Normand Poirier, and Betsy Luce, and all night we were usually graced with the presence of Alfred G. Aronwitz, who was finishing some series against a deadline or pushing one last ounce of life into a story that other writers would have long since abandoned. At eight in the morning, when the shift was over, Betsy Luce would go home, and the rest of us would retire to a saloon called The Curb, around the corner from the old Post Building on West Street. McMorrow would come in at nine o'clock with the first edition, and then we would rehash the whole paper, rewriting leads in our heads, finding second-day angles, laughing at material stolen from the *Times*. Everything was new and bright and possible. I was learning from the best teachers around, and it was all free.

The pieces in this book come from the ten years that followed. I left the *Post* after the 108-day strike in 1962–63, went to Europe as a contributing editor for the *Saturday Evening Post*, and wrote a lot of slick stories about movie stars, mostly because the editor I knew at the *SEP* was in charge of entertainment. I didn't like writing the pieces, but I was seeing Europe for the first time and being paid for it rather handsomely, so I didn't complain. I came back to America at the point when it was becoming a darker, bloodier place; the promise of the Kennedy years was shattered in Dallas; I couldn't concentrate on the magazine articles I was writing and I was unhappy away from newspapers and their immediacy and speed. Then, in 1965, Paul Sann asked me if I wanted to come back to the *Post* as a columnist. I started the following week.

I suppose I would have become another kind of writer if it hadn't been for the war in Vietnam. Jimmy Breslin made a tremendous impact on New York journalism with his column for the *Herald Tribune*, and a lot of people mistakenly felt that my column would be the *Post*'s version of Breslin (Jimmy and I were friends, and when I started the column, he was, as usual, generous with advice). The subject was New York, the city I loved more than any other, and I suppose I would have become a kind of minor-league Damon Runyon if the bodies hadn't started coming home from Asia in the rubber bags. The killing in Asia made it impossible to be Damon Runyon, and I started warring with myself in the column, torn between descriptive narratives and polemics. Looking through those early columns, I'm struck by how callow so many of them were, how derivative, how influenced they were by other writers, including Kempton and Breslin. I was learning how to handle the form, and the results were uneven. But it was the thing I wanted to do more than anything else on earth, and I worked on it with all the energy I possessed. Today, when I fall on my ass, it's *my* ass. I've spent some time away from the *Post*, writing briefly and unhappily from Washington for *Newsday* and wandering for six months without writing at all after the murder of Robert Kennedy. I've published a novel, written screenplays, been married, fathered two daughters, been divorced. I still waste too much time in saloons, I still smoke too much, and there is a lot of work that I would like to do before dying. But as I write, the sun is shining brightly, I love a good woman, the days seem longer than they used to be, I hear music playing somewhere, and I want to get on with the next ten years.

P. H.

Brooklyn, New York
April 1, 1971

I. Brooklyn

ONE reason why I never became a painter was a concern that began to grow in me during my early twenties. It was a concern that bordered on obsession, and it was about time. As I acquired the mechanical skills of drawing and painting, the form itself became more and more static to me, two-dimensional and constricted. Very early, growing up where and how I did, I began to sense that time did something quite profound to human beings. It tamed them or defeated them or destroyed them. Kids I grew up with became alcoholics or heroin addicts, disappeared for long stretches in prisons (where they "did time"). Others, filled with joy and exuberance in adolescence, turned into dull, conventional, sometimes bitter and more frequently frightened men as they grew older. I saw time working on my mother and father and wondered about my four dead grandparents and how they had already arrived, played their parts, and left. In my early thirties, I started to sense what time was doing to me.

Writing seemed a better way to deal with those concerns than painting, and after I started writing for the *Post*, I never went back to painting. Today it all seems much more complicated to me than it did when I was starting. Journalism (or nonfiction, or the essay—the name of the form seems as complicated as everything else) can do certain things better than fiction. It can be direct, hard, concrete; it can also evoke real places, the effect of actual events on individuals. Most of the time, however, it cannot get into the head or the heart of human beings, certainly not with the precision of first-rate fiction; whenever some of my more confident colleagues claim that the "new" journalism has supplanted fiction, I think of Proust and laugh. At this point of my life, film excites me more than any other medium. Movies also do certain things better than any other form (weather, the movement of humans and horses, the extraordinary complexities of the human face, the effect of light on place), and writing screenplays has been an experience that is as rewarding as anything I've ever done. In the end, however, writing is writing, and the form you choose should be the form that best expresses the thought or the feeling that you are trying to unload.

The pieces in this section are part of an attempt to understand some of the effects that time had worked on me and some of the people with whom I was young. That meant trying to understand Brooklyn. So these pieces are about Brooklyn and about the fifties, written in the late sixties and early seventies. The word "pieces" is an accurate description because they are really only fragments; I was trying to return to matters that were once important to me and to describe them as accurately as possible. Understanding the place and the period might also explain the distance I'd traveled from both. The results remain tentative, to be explored more deeply and, I hope, with greater perception as I grow older. The form won't really matter.

The Seventeenth Christmas*

I

The Greyhound roared up the Jersey Turnpike in the rain, its fierce power leaving the cars behind, the thick wheels ripping through the gathering pools of water with the driving stateliness of a cruiser. The bus that was carrying us home for that 1952 Christmas smelled of stale smoke and damp wool; on that detail, memory does not fail. Sailors stood in the aisles, soldiers dozed in their seats, and all the racks were heavy with duffel bags and seabags. Across the wide back seat there were four paratroopers who had come on board at Philly, and they were singing with the help of a bottle of Four Roses. The darkness was punctuated by struck matches or bright explosions of white light from cars passing in the other lanes, and we stared out at the rain-glossy roads, past the small neat towns and the clumps of dark forest, out past the neon of roadside taverns, past the blue-white glare of gas stations and the bright wilderness of those first crude shopping centers, to the place where our girls were.

I was in love then with a girl named Kathleen Q., and I sat at my window seat, watching the raindrops carve small rivers across the glass and trying, as young men have always done, to conjure her face. Stuffed in the waist of my Navy blues was a wallet that contained photographs of her: an angular girl with thin legs and wrists, wearing a long dark coat, standing in Prospect Park with benches curving around behind her in the direction of Monument Hill. Her face had a look of wan sadness. All through boot camp in Bainbridge, I had looked at those gray sad pictures at random hours of the day or while standing guard duty at garbage dumps at night or whenever I tried to match the neat, precise Catholic girls'-school handwriting of her letters to someone who actually existed. But after a while

* Originally published as "Christmas with the Old Man"

she had become those photographs, and in the darkness that night, going home at 60 miles an hour after three months away, I tried to remember the texture of her skin, the timbre of her voice, the sound of her laughter, and tried to control what was happening in my stomach as I fought off the anxious knowledge that she might no longer be there.

At some point the paratroopers started to sing Jo Stafford's "You Belong to Me," a big song that year in the Navy bases and the Army camps, because it was about women promising fidelity to men who were going away. We were boys, of course, but we were trying very much to be men, and a lot of us were going away to die in Korea. As we approached the flats of Jersey, they were singing about the pyramids along the Nile and the jungles when they're wet with rain and how you should remember, darling, all the while, that you belong to me. I moved deeper into the seat, thinking about taking Kathleen Q. home to her house on Seeley Street the night before I went away, sitting with her on the porch, talking about the great cities of the world and how I wanted to see them all, while she looked at me with puzzled blankness; thinking about that September night and its sense of fracture; thinking about how I was seventeen and a half now and on my own at last; and always thinking about her and how I was coming home for Christmas with its promise of warmth and snow.

II.

The bus dropped us off at the old terminal on Thirty-fourth Street. The place smelled of gasoline fumes and frying hot dogs and too many people. I remember a blond girl breaking from a crowd and rushing to a guy in an Army uniform; a group of guys in wraparound coats and what we used to call gingerella hats grabbing an Italian guy and hoisting him into the air as if he were Audie Murphy and had just captured the whole Chinese Army; a silent chorus of blacks in civilian clothes waiting for buses bound for the South; several older women crying as other young men boarded buses for departure—all of it played against the harsh mechanical roar of engines and city noise and a jukebox playing somewhere.

32

Nobody was there to meet me. I hadn't really expected anyone; we had no telephone at home because we could not afford it; even if we could, I would not have had the money to call from Maryland with the exact time of arrival. I told myself that it didn't really matter. As I stepped into that bus terminal crowd at midnight, it seemed to matter more than I ever thought it would; even today, after a thousand airports, some trace of that first empty return stays with me. When I arrive somewhere late at night, a part of me always hopes that a girl will call my name.

I went out onto Thirty-fourth Street, with the seabag on my shoulder, and walked to Eighth Avenue to take the subway home. Suddenly, a drunk lurched across the wet street and a taxi screeched to a stop in front of me. "Dumb son of a bitch," the cabby yelled; the drunk spun away like a stunned dancer, and I started to laugh. I hadn't seen a drunk in three months, and I knew I was back in New York.

At Jay Street–Borough Hall I crossed the platform and got on the D train. That was *our* train, the one that serviced the neighborhood, the one that took the young guys to their first jobs as messengers on Wall Street, the one where you might see a familiar face. But I didn't recognize anyone, and as the train pushed through the tunnel, making the hard metallic turn at Bergen Street and out onto the high trestle over the Gowanus Canal, I wished I had arrived earlier and that I could have called Kathleen. Below me, the Gowanus looked like a smear of fresh tar, and the Kentile sign burned against the sky, and in the distance my slice of Brooklyn lay in brooding darkness.

When I got out at the Seventh Avenue stop, the rain was over. I looked through the window into Diamond's Bar and Grill, but my father wasn't there. He wasn't in Fitzgerald's either, and before going up to the house, I crossed the street and looked into Rattigan's. Someone waved from the bar and I waved back, but I didn't see Billy Hamill anywhere.

We lived at 378 Seventh Avenue between Eleventh and Twelfth streets. There was a small butcher shop to the left and Teddy's Fruit Store on the right, and when I went in, I saw that the mailbox was still broken and the hall smelled of backed-up sewers and wet garbage. There were, of course, no locks on the doors, and I stood for a moment in the yellow light of the 30-watt bulb, shifting the seabag to the other shoulder. Two baby carriages were parked beside the stairs, and in the blackness at the back of the hall, I caught a glimpse of battered garbage cans with their long day's cargo. I started up past the apartments of all the others: first floor right, Mae McAvoy; on the left, Poppa Clark; second floor right, Anne Sharkey and Mae Irwin; left, Carrie Woods. Carrie was a tiny sparrow of a woman who kept dogs and drank whiskey, and the dogs began a ferocious attack at the locked door, trying to get at me as I passed. There were traces of dinner smells in the hall. It was almost three.

Our door was not locked. I dropped the seabag in the hall and went into the darkness, groping for the light cord. I found the cord, and a transformer hummed for a few seconds, and then the round fluorescent light on the ceiling blinked on. The room was as I remembered it: a white-topped gas range where the old coal stove had once stood against the far wall, the sink to the left beside the window that had never been opened, a Servel refrigerator with a broken handle next to the bathroom door, a closet beside the front door with a curtain covering the disorder within, a table in the center of the room, linoleum on the floor, and a clothesline running the length of the room because we had no backyard. Roaches scurried across the table, panicked by the harshness of the sudden blue-tinged light. I could hear movement in the darkness of the railroad flat, and then my mother was coming through the rooms.

"Oh, Peter, you're home," she said, and embraced me and hugged me. And then she stopped and stepped back and told me how good I looked and how I had put on some weight and what did I want to eat. The tea kettle was on before I could answer, and then I started asking about my brothers Tom and Brian and John and Denis, and my sister Kathleen, and my mother asked me about boot camp and what it was like and where I was going when Christmas leave was over and how she hoped it wasn't to Korea. The tea was strong, served Irish-style with milk and sugar, and my mother said they had waited for me to come home before getting a Christmas tree. Behind us in the darkness, there were sounds of people sleeping and the sweet smell of children and milk and diapers.

"Where's Dad?" I said after a while.

"Oh, he's sleeping."

"Sleeping one off?" I said.

It must have seemed cruel, but she ignored it.

"He waited up for you," she said. "But none of us knew what time you'd be coming."

"Tell him to wake me when he gets up in the morning."

Later I lay under a blanket on the living-room couch, listening to the familiar sounds of home and safety, of forms breathing in the darkness, steam hissing in radiators, and the buses moving heavily on the street outside. I started to doze and was banged awake by the scream of fire engines hurtling down Eleventh Street to some random tragedy. I lay there for a long while, thinking about how uncomplicated and simple a matter it was to love my mother but how my father was another matter. I thought again about Kathleen Q., uneasy still, and somewhere near dawn I fell asleep.

III.

Christmas really did mean something in that neighborhood, if you were poor and Irish. The Depression was still a fact there, lingering like the roaches after the rest of the town had raised the money for an exterminator. My mother had arrived in America on the day the stock market crashed; my father came in 1923, on the lam from anti-Catholic bigotry in Northern Ireland. They were the Irish without property, and in that year in the early fifties, there seemed little hope that they would ever really own anything. Food always came before possessions. So Christmas became one of those brief seasons of celebration, when you held back the dark with tinsel and laughter and noisy evenings and cheered the fact that you had moved through another year.

At lunchtime the next day, my father came home; he worked across the street for the Globe Lighting Company, on the third floor of the old Ansonia Clock Factory, which had been for a while the largest factory in America and was now a dirty red-brick pile. I could hear him coming up the stairs, one step at a time, humming quietly some fragment of an old song. He was a

35

short, compact man then, with glossy black hair, and there was a picture on the wall of one of the bedrooms that represented all the mystery of him to me. The photograph was brown and beginning to fade, and it was a group portrait of young men in soccer uniforms who played for a team of Irish exiles called St. Mary's Celtics. One of them was my father.

In 1951, I had worked for a year in the sheet metal shop at the Brooklyn Navy Yard, and men there told me about how good my father had been, when he was young and playing soccer. He was fierce and quick, possessed of a magic leg, moving down those Sunday playing fields as if driven by the engines of anger and exile, playing hardest against British teams, the legs pumping and cutting and stealing the ball; hearing the cheers of strangers, and everybody drinking after the games until the late hours in the speakeasies, singing songs they learned across an ocean. Until one day, in one hard-played game, a German had come out of nowhere and kicked, and the magic leg had splintered and my father fell as if shot, and someone came off the bench and broke the German's jaw with a punch, and then they were pulling slats off the fence to tie against the ruined leg and waited for an hour and a half for the ambulance to come from Kings County Hospital while they played out the rest of the game. The players and the spectators were poor; no one owned a car. And then at the hospital he was dropped in a bed, and there were no doctors, and across the room detectives were questioning a man whose stomach had been sliced open in a fight, and the ceiling reeled and turned, and there was no feeling left in the magic leg. When the doctors finally showed up the next morning, the leg was thick with gangrene, and they had to slice the football boot off with a razor, and in the afternoon they took the leg off above the knee. When he talked about it later, he never mentioned the pain. What he remembered most clearly was the sound of the saw.

And so I had grown up with his presence in the house but never had the kinds of things other kids had with fathers. We never went out to play baseball or kick a football around a field. He was a stranger I had come to love from a distance. He drank a lot in Rattigan's across the street, and at night he would come in with some of his friends and they would sit in the kitchen and talk about fights, with my father illustrating Willie Pep's jab on the plastic knob of the lamp cord or throwing Ray Robinson hooks into the wash on the kitchen line. He loved to sing, and I always liked the outrage and the passion that he would force into the lines from "Galway Bay," about how the strangers came and tried to teach us their ways, and scorned us just for being what we are. . . . We were what we were in that neighborhood, and we didn't care what the strangers thought about us. I loved that hard defiance, and I would lie in the next room listening to them, as they brought up the old tales of British malignance and murders committed by the Black and Tans. But I didn't really know him; he had left school at twelve to work as a stonemason's apprentice and had struggled for a while at night school at Brooklyn Tech; but he didn't really know how to deal with me when I tried to do homework, and in many ways he was still Irish and I was an American. I loved the way he talked and the way he stood on the corner with a fedora and raincoat on Sunday mornings, an Irish dude waiting for the bars to open, and I loved the way he once hit a guy with a ball-bat because he had insulted my mother. I just never knew if he loved me back.

He came in that day and said, "Hello, Magee," and shook hands and embraced me, and then sat down to tomato soup and cheese sandwiches and talked about how that son of a bitch O'Malley was talking about taking the Dodgers out of town and how Archie Moore was fighting Joey Maxim for the light-heavyweight championship that week and how Eisenhower looked like somebody's aunt. I didn't have much to say, and after lunch he went out, telling me he would see me later.

I put on a pair of pegged pants and a zipper jacket and told the kids I would be back in a while but that I had to make a phone call first. I went over to Mr. B's to call Kathleen, because that candy store had a booth with a door on it. Her mother answered. She said hello, but the tone was evasive and cool, and something moved and flopped again in my stomach, and I thought about how her letters had come every day for a while and then had tailed off and become ambiguous. I hung up and went out to get the Seventh Avenue bus down to St. Joseph's to see the girl I thought was mine.

IV

The funny thing now is that I have no idea why I loved that girl; all I can remember was breaking up with her. I waited for her outside that school, which was in downtown Brooklyn. There were Christmas decorations everywhere, sponsored by the big downtown department stores, Christmas music blared from Davega and Modell's, and I stood there rehearsing things to say, wondering what I should do. I suppose all of us were the same in the fifties: Would we kiss her or waltz her away or come quietly to her and surprise her? I never knew how to handle such things and still haven't mastered the craft. It didn't matter because suddenly she was there, in a swirl of girls in green uniforms, and she was awkward and shy and perhaps a little ashamed, and I knew it was over.

We went home together on the D train and walked through Prospect Park toward her house, and she tried to tell me how it was better this way, how I was in the Navy, and she, after all, was still in high school, and wouldn't it be better to wait for everything until I was discharged? I said that would be three and a half more years, and I didn't want to wait, and didn't she understand, and a lot of other things that I can't remember now. We sat on a bench in the cold, looking out over the lake in the park, the whole area deserted and gray, and the heights of Monument Hill rising behind us, while thin shelves of ice gathered at the edges of the lake, like frost on a window.

Was there another guy? I asked. And she sat there quietly while I shivered in the zipper jacket, and she tried to tell me how I could finish high school in the Navy and later go to college and how she loved to read my letters and how good my drawings were. But she never answered the question, and then she was saying good-bye. I left her on the corner of Seeley Street, feeling cold and desolate and went down the block to a bar called the Parkview and started to drink beer with the bricklayers. Someone made Moore a lock over Maxim and talked about this kid Floyd Patterson beating both of them, and then two ironworkers started to argue over the best way to operate a crane, and around seven-thirty I was pretty drunk. I called her on the telephone, to tell her I loved her and that I wouldn't go back to the Navy if that was what she wanted. I would go AWOL, maybe I could change my name, and it would all be okay. She hung up on me, and I walked out into the night.

I couldn't call home and wanted badly to see my brother Tom. But I went instead to a place called Boop's on Tenth Avenue and Seventeenth Street, where all of us used to drink with someone else's draft card and where the bookmakers watched the fights and where there were a lot of Italian hard guys I liked a lot. I called Timmy Lee and he came up, and then a few of the others showed: Tommy Conroy, Joe Kelly, Joe Griffin from the Gremlins, Vito Pinto, Jack McAlevy. Most of us were home on leave, and we were all happy to be together, playing boss and underboss with the Italians, listening to the jukebox and bragging about imaginary sessions with imaginary women in the towns where there were no neighborhood witnesses. Around midnight, Joe Griffin said to me, "Hey, I hear Kathleen is going out with Tommy Twiggs. What happened?" And I said I didn't know about it; when did that happen? He shrugged and said forget it, forget her, there's more than enough ass in the world. But she's not ass, I said, and Joe, who was a happy short guy with a great smile, said something about how they're all the same under the covers and ordered another round.

Around three o'clock I took a guy named Porky into the back room for a talk. I was bleary with beer. Porky was one of the older guys, hard if he wanted to be, the biggest Joe Miceli fan in the world, and I liked him a lot. I asked him if he could get me a gun.

"Hey, whatta you want wid a gun, kid?"

"I want to kill someone."

"Don't be ridiculous, kid."

"He took my girl."

"You are seventeen, eighteen. Girls, there's millions a girls. You're, what, in the Navy? See the world. Forget this bitch, whoever she is."

And I thought after a while that Porky was right, and we went back to the bar, with Porky draping his arm around me, and I guess he told the other Italian guys to take care of me, because for the rest of the two weeks' Christmas leave they treated me as if my closest friend had been hit by a truck. That night we closed Boop's, the beer clouding my grief, and Timmy Lee and Joe Kelly and I left together, to go back to the Seventh Avenue end of the neighborhood. I woke up in the morning with a thick tongue and dirty fingernails, and my shoes were spattered, and I couldn't remember coming home. There was someone I was supposed to call, but I couldn't remember who it was. It certainly wasn't my lost girl.

v.

We bought the tree all right, with my brothers Tommy and Brian and me going down to the main neighborhood shopping street of Fifth Avenue, arguing with the guys selling the trees out of stake trucks like hot suits. We didn't have money for lights, but there was a lot of angel hair and aluminum streamers and gaudy balls from other Christmases and that crepe paper in a brick pattern to plaster all over the chimney.

On Christmas Eve my father was out, and the children had gone to bed early. I sat for a while in the kitchen with my mother. Christmas was always the most difficult time of the year for her, because she wanted so much to make her children happy and didn't have the money to buy anything very fancy. She made do with stockings filled with tangerines and walnuts, bought on credit at Jack's grocery store, or managed to stretch her credit at one of the department stores, but every subsequent Christmas there seemed to be one more child to please, and it wasn't very easy. The women like her waited until Christmas Eve and headed for the stores on Fifth Avenue to get the remainders at cut rates.

"I'm going out to do the last-minute shopping," she said. "Is there anything you want?"

"No, get some stuff for the kids. I'm okay."

She shook her head slowly over the cup of hot tea, looking quite sad in the land where the streets were paved with gold. I told her I still had about $20 from my leave pay, but she told me to keep it, that she had enough to manage. But then she started quietly to cry. "God," she said, "I just wish I could do everything right. I just wonder what God is doing this for." I didn't know what to do or how to react; she had always been the strong one in the family, the one who didn't drink and who helped us to survive. I left $15 on the table and went out into the night.

I decided it was time to drink for the first time in Rattigan's. There were strict unspoken rules in that neighborhood; if you were under age, you did not drink where your father did his drinking, because he should not be responsible for what you might do. I was still under age, but they knew I was in the Navy and I decided to go in. Rattigan's was a dark place with an unused food counter to the right and a long mahogany bar across the far wall, with a lot of whiskey bottles piled in rows, a television high over the left, and Schlitz signs bubbling against the back mirrors. My father was sitting on a stool near the entrance to the back room, sipping a beer and talking to some friends. I went right to him.

"Hello, Dad," I said.

"Hello, Magee," he said, and he seemed genuinely pleased to see me. I put the five on the bar. "You drinking?" I said casually. "Of course," he said. And George Loftus, a short, wizened bartender, pulled us a couple of drafts. My father started introducing me around. I remember meeting a huge cabdriver named John Mullins, a guy named Johnny the Polack, a cop named Joe Whitmore. The place filled up, as men relieved of children came in for some solace. Near the windows at the other end of the bar there were three guys in their twenties drinking whiskey.

After a while, my father started getting boozy and sentimental. He had his arm around me and started telling me how proud he was that I was serving my country, and when I sat on the stool beside him, he squeezed my left leg. "Christ, I wish I had your legs," he said, and that reminded him of something, and he started to sing. The other guys loved to hear him sing then, and he did "Patty McGinty's Goat" and "O'Hara from Tara, McNamara from Mayo," and the "Green Glens of Antrim." He was into "Galway Bay" and had reached the point where the strangers came and tried to teach us their ways, when one of the younger guys at the other end shouted down the bar.

"Hey, knock it off, I can't hear myself t'ink."

The bar went suddenly silent. My father got off his stool, the song snapped shut, and stared down the bar. "Who's the wise guy?" he said. The three guys were laughing now, and one of them said, "I'm terrified."

That was all my father needed. He went down the bar, limping heavily on the wooden leg, and as the first of the young guys turned, my father hit him right on the chin with a hook, and the guy went down. The one next to him turned, ready to punch, and I hit him with a right hand, and he went down. The third guy put his hands out, palms forward, placing himself out of it, and the first guy got up, and my father knocked him down again. Together we beat them a little more, and then we dragged them out the door and left them on the sidewalk. The noncombatant member of the trio went out the back door. It was just like a western, and my father and I went back to the bar together with our arms around each other, joined in a union based on drinking and violence that we had never had before.

"Where was I, Magee?" he said.

"The strangers came and tried to teach us their ways. . . ."

Before he resumed the song, he turned to Joe Whitmore and said, "This is my son Peter. In whom I am well proud." I don't know where he got that line, but we closed the place, singing together into Christmas morning. When we got back upstairs to the kitchen, he showed me what Moore was going to do to Marciano, throwing the short right hand at the lamp cord, the way he used to do it with his friends, and after a while we went to sleep.

When I went back after New Year's on the bus, there were more soldiers and sailors than before. They talked in the quiet night, about going to Korea and their girls and what they had received for Christmas. I didn't care that much about Brooklyn now, with my girl gone and most of my friends in the service; in some odd way, I felt free, as the bus moved west to Oklahoma and other strange and exotic places. I hadn't received much for Christmas in any ordinary way; but my father loved me back, and there was no other gift I wanted.

December 7, 1970

The Neighborhood Girls

It is always a Friday night in a place like the Caton Inn on Coney Island Avenue, with the booths in the back room full, lit only with little candle-shaped red bulbs, and people standing three-deep at the bar, with the bartenders watching them get drunk before copping their change. All of us have money in our pockets, in some vague year in the fifties, squashed up against the wall in the crowd, watching the swinging doors open and close, while the Coney Island trolley moves along outside with a metallic slicing sound. We are all unsuccessfully disguised as Arab princes: dressed in maroon wraparounds or Ripley suits, or pants with a 13 peg and a 33 knee, with a four-inch rise over the beltline, laced with one of those thin plastic belts they used to sell in Royal Tailors on Fifth Avenue, a high shine on the thick Flagg Brothers shoes and the hair heavy with Vitalis. We are talking about prizefighters and ballplayers or about the jobs we had taken after dropping out of high school, feeling the evening move on toward midnight, while Ray-Ray Grillo, the bouncer, tells us to keep the glasses off the jukebox. The jukebox is six for a quarter, and the music pours out over the two rooms, lush with violins. Billy Eckstine:

> The night is like a lovely tune.
> Beware, my foolish heart
> How white the ever-constant moon;
> Take care, my foolish heart. . . .*

The place begins to fill. Wimpy, Noona, Danny Mac from the Tigers. A guy named Lar. Denny Moore. A few guys from the South Brooklyn Boys. Eddie Norris and Charlie Regan from the Gremlins, away in the back under the TV set. Somewhere out in Brooklyn now, the movies are breaking. There is a human flood on the sidewalk in front of the Brooklyn Para-

* "My Foolish Heart," ©1949 by Anne-Rachel Music Corp.

mount and the Loew's Metropolitan, and people are climbing into cabs and buses. And in minutes, the girls start to arrive.

There's a line between love and fascination
That's hard to see on an evening such as this,
For they both give the very same sensation
When you're lost in the magic of a kiss. . . .

The girls are moving around against the far wall, in groups of threes and fours. There are red plastic-covered stools, and some of the girls sit down, while an occasional gallant surrenders his stool and starts to talk.

"Hey, Rosie. Howya bin?" he says.

"Awright, Joe. Ya lookin' good yisself."

"Wanna dance?"

"Sure. Watch my pockabook, will ya, Betty?"

The girls are drinking rye and soda, and most of the guys are drinking beer. The only scotch drinkers are the ironworkers, who make the most money. It doesn't make any difference. To the guys. The girls have already started making judgments. They are all eighteen, and they want a guy who has a car and a reasonably steady job.

"Where ya workin', Joe?" she says.

"Wall Street."

"Oh, that's a drag, I bet."

"It's steady."

"Well, ya always get a bonus."

"Yeah. Pretty good ones too."

They are in the back room now, with the floor crowded, the sanded wood gritty with pebbly wax. Wimpy is next to them, dancing with a girl whose eyebrows are arching toward her hairline and who is wearing a black dress with thin shoulder straps and high Cuban heels. The dress is covered with sequins, and every time they take the light, the sequins glitter.

"I heard you gotta car, Joe," she says.

"Yeah. A heap. A forty-seven Chevy."

"Well, it's better than nothin'," she says.

"Yeah."

"You still goin' with Ellen?"

"Nah, we broke up."

44

"That's too bad."

"Maybe we can go down to Nathan's later," he says, tentatively.

"Maybe," she says.

When they get back to the bar, after the first cha-cha starts, Betty is all alone. Nobody will ask her to dance. Her boyfriend is in Korea. She sits alone, drinking a Four Roses and soda. There are a few other girls like her around the bar, and there is an unwritten agreement that while their guys are away at the war, nobody will bother them. That winter there is one steaming neighborhood romance: a guy who came back from Korea with a bride he acquired somewhere in the South; he meets his old girl, leaves his new wife, and they spend all that winter in the Caton Inn. In the spring, his old girl goes into a convent. The wages of sin.

> . . . For this time it isn't fascination,
> Or a dream that will fade and fall apart.
> It's love,
> This time, it's love,
> My foolish heart.

Moving to the end of the night: into cars parked near the big lake in Prospect Park, or down the deserted side streets near the piers, or to the backs of tenement halls. Some have peeled off earlier, to sit in the back rooms of bars where they are not so well known: Lyons' on Cortelyou Road or McCabe's in Coney Island. There, sitting alone, trying to overcome embarrassment or urgency, the lies would flow, and occasionally some truth. Mostly it was lies.

We knew nothing, of course, about those girls. Growing up in that neighborhood, working-class white, most of us Catholics, we never really thought about women as complete, rounded human beings. Moving around this past year, I'm not sure that the situation has changed much. It's better, but not by much.

We believed, as men seem to believe in most Catholic countries I've visited in the years since, that there were two kinds of girls: good girls and whores. A good girl was one who kept herself icily aloof, went with one guy, and who didn't, as we used to say, "put out." Usually she had met her guy in high school. They "went steady" for a couple of years and then got engaged, and when he had finished with the Army (very few went to college), they would marry. Most of those girls were rather docile in the sense that they accepted, even embraced, the role that the men had assigned to them. They were Somebody's Girl, and that meant they must accept the whole package. They were never to go to bars, or even to the movies, unless accompanied by other girls, who were to act basically as chaperones. They were supposed to accept the fact that the guys had their own private male pleasures: a night at the fights or certain nights when they went drinking with the boys. If the guy and his friends arrived at a place like the Caton Inn and the girl was dancing with someone else, this was a major crisis. And the crisis was caused by the disruption of the idea of inevitability.

And that was what their idea of love was all about. We believed then, as nobody I know believes anymore, that life moved in a straight line. You met a girl, "fell in love" with her, married her, and lived happily ever after. There was, of course, little consideration given to some rather important matters. In that neighborhood, for example, sex and love were separate parts of life. "Good girls" were virgins; "whores" were girls who pushed out past romance and actually went to bed with guys. A "good girl," of course, might commit a variety of venial sins while laughing and grabbing with her boyfriend late at night on the couch in the darkened living room. But Alvera the Bush, for example, was up on the roof taking on the Tigers.

A lot of this could be traced, I suppose, to the effects of a Catholic education; all those speeches about "purity" and the immaculate conception and the fires of hell had to have some effect. But I think it was more complicated than that: Alexander Portnoy, after all, wasn't an Irish Catholic. If there was a single symbol of what was wrong with growing up in any white working-class neighborhood in the 1950's, it was the dried-up unused Trojan which had stayed so long in the wallet that it left a permanent oval ridge in the imitation leather.

It was probably all more complicated than we thought. To begin with, it was the Eisenhower era. Politics was dead, and nobody much cared who was in office. I can't recall a *single* political conversation with any girl I ever grew up with, and aside from Ireland and Italy, the only foreign country many of them had heard of was Korea, because that was where their boyfriends had gone. The result of this was that the normal quotient of human passion became self-centered and parochial.

Unfortunately, this self-absorption wasn't accompanied by much questioning. Most of us didn't know anything about ourselves, and so it shouldn't have been so surprising that we knew nothing about the women we thought we loved. We came to them through a gauze of romantic mush; they were extensions of the movies we had seen and the love songs we played on the jukebox. Betty, sitting alone at the bar, untouched and virginal, became some local version of June Allyson, faithful and true, sitting home to knit while Jimmy Stewart battled the Yellow Peril. That girl you took home at the stroke of midnight before spending the rest of the night drinking with male bravado in the bookmaker's place on Seventeenth Street was Debbie Reynolds. They had a ceramic purity or a touching loyalty, but we really had no sense of them in any more complicated way. They were objects, not subjects, and I suppose we were the same to them. If they met a man with a reasonable job, with some consideration for what the neighbors thought, with no inflated ideas of his own possibilities, then they could buy the whole glossy varnish of romance.

And romance, rather than love, was what it was all about. Most of us were inarticulate about anything abstract, so those songs we played late at night did the job for us. "Because of you," Tony Bennett sang, "my romance had its start." . . . Or the Four Aces would shuffle onstage, singing "Is it a sin, to love you so? To hold you close, and know you are leaving?" The songs were basically trash, but they were the most important expression of that time, because they established our myths. Most of them were about separation and loss, and that should have been no surprise, since so many guys from the neighborhood were leaving for the Army or the Navy every week. The worst thing that could happen to a guy who might be going off to die (the romantic impulse again) was for him to feel betrayed. It happened to a few guys. I remember one night in the Navy, after receiving a "Dear John" letter from a girl I thought

47

I loved, going wild with grief and rage and breaking up a bar in Pensacola, Florida. It doesn't matter that I can no longer remember her face, or that I was chasing various ladies around Pensacola; what mattered then was betrayal.

There was, of course, always a barely submerged impulse toward violence in all of us then. We were, after all, only kids, and because we had no real sexual outlet, violence was probably inevitable. The girls, as I remember them, even encouraged it. And in that sense, they really did embrace the vision of themselves we had created. If you really were an object, then you could be owned, and you would be owned because a man had assigned you some value. To have men fight over you because they thought you were valuable was just another way of proving themselves to you. I remember one night in the Caton Inn, when my right hand was already heavily encased in plaster from being broken a few weeks before. I was going with a girl named Catherine Rogan then, and at one point, after I came back from the jukebox, she whirled on her stool and told me that some guy standing behind her had goosed her. It never occurred to me that she might have imagined it; I hit the guy between the eyes with the five pounds of plaster, and he fell backwards like a tree, his head landing on the toe of a guy named Frank Christie. Christie's toe was broken, and the place later erupted into a minor riot, because the guy I hit was some minor-league thug from South Brooklyn, whose friends arrived later in a fruit truck. It didn't much matter to me, because by then I was gone with my girl. It is still referred to as the night Pete Hamill broke Frank Christie's toe with a punch.

So there was that *macho* thing, along with everything else. And a pattern of sexual frustration that still affects many of the people I grew up with. Most of us believed one of the great New York myths: that you could never make it with a neighborhood girl, that you must go outside the neighborhood to find girls who were interested in sex. This might have been true, but it never seemed to occur to many of us that our girls might be doing the same thing. We didn't really know, because we didn't really know our girls.

When I was twenty-one, I escaped to Mexico. By the time I came home most of the people I knew had married. There were

48

weddings in Holy Name Church or St. Saviour's, and wedding receptions at Prospect Hall or the McFadden Brothers American Legion Post, and then honeymoon trips to the Poconos or Bermuda. One morning all the girls were five years younger than those of us who were left, and we started moving on. Now, looking at the others in old photographs, I realize how terribly young they were and how terribly careless and how most of them were virgins.

It was very late at night, a few weeks ago, and I was standing at the bar at Farrell's in the old neighborhood. With me was an old friend, a fireman now. We had been in boot camp together and traveled across many boisterous nights; we went different ways as we grew older, but we still enjoyed each other's company.

"It's weird, isn't it," my friend said, "how things turn out."

"It sure is," I said.

"I mean, look around the neighborhood. Everybody we grew up with is getting fat and out of shape. They can't stand their wives. They read *Screw* in the bars and then talk about how morals are being corrupted. They stand around here and bitch about how long the kids wear their hair. It's weird. It's like they were never young."

That is probably true. The women especially were oddly old before they should have been. They settled into their lives after marriage without much argument, and running into them now and then, I'm always struck by how narrow the results were after such romantic promises when they were all eighteen. They have settled for making oatmeal in the morning and getting the kids out to school, cleaning the apartment, putting quilts on the bed, going out to Safeway or Bohack for the shopping, and all the rest that goes with it. I remember talking with one of those girls a couple of months ago. She had recently been divorced, something that would have scandalized the neighborhood in the fifties, but which was no longer very extraordinary. She told me which marriages were on the rocks, who was separated, who else was divorced, who had remarried.

"And you know," she said, "almost every time it was the guy's fault. The guys just couldn't face reality."

And I suppose that was true. One guy I knew didn't see his wife naked for the first eighteen months of their marriage; they went to bed clothed and made love in the dark. Another girl I knew had been married to a guy for six years, and the only time he made love to her was when he was drunk enough to face her. (This is not, of course, a situation peculiar to the white working class.) A lot of the girls just shut off that part of their lives and concentrated on the children. At twenty-two they acted as if they had been married for twenty years.

What remains remarkable about those women is how very complicated they were and how seldom the men rose to those complications. They had qualities that many women (and men) don't have: fortitude, a kind of crazed courage, a special kind of dignity. But they also had (and have) a very human warmth that is oddly missing in many of the men. I really don't know why, although I suspect that it is because the women faced "reality," in the worst sense, and accepted the role of raising children and being housewives; the men, many of whom were working at jobs that bored or brutalized them, seemed to feel more trapped: into jobs and families and time itself. They look around today, at the eighteen-year-olds of my brother's generation, and they see kids who are enjoying sex, who probably won't have to marry out of some biological need, who have incredible freedom of choice and movement. When they were eighteen, they had to construct some cotton-candy vision of the future, where June Allyson took care of the kids and you lived a full, rich, romantic life, filled with certainties. It never happened that way, for an awful lot of them, and I find that sad and oddly disturbing, for all of its inevitability. Love might be a genuine emotion or the greatest hoax ever invented by Western culture. I don't pretend to know. But the girls and boys I knew in Brooklyn were human beings who were damaged by the tawdry popular myths that surrounded them, who believed in love and knew more about what they wanted than they ever knew about each other. We were all quite ignorant then, and there is no way to rejoice because you escaped the worst of it. The songs of those years were rich with violins, but they led to a lot of gray and sour mornings. There is no moral here, especially from the likes of me. But those people I used to know did at least have an

incredibly romantic couple of years when they were young. Maybe it was worth what followed, although I doubt it.
February 16, 1970

Brooklyn: The Sane Alternative

One cold spring I found myself alone in Rome, in a small room high up over Parioli, trying to write. The words came thickly, sluggishly, and none of them were any good. I quit for the day. For a while I read day-old copies of *Paese Sera*, the Communist daily, and the Paris *Herald*, and then, bored, I turned on the radio, lay down on the lumpy couch, and, half-listening, stared out at the empty sky. The music was the usual raucous Italian stew, mixed with screaming commercials, and I fell into a heavy doze. Then, suddenly, absurdly, I came awake, as an old song started to play. "She kicked out my windshield. She hit me over the head. She cussed and cried. And said I'd lied. And wished that I was dead. Oh! Lay that pistol down, Babe. . . ." It was "Pistol Packin' Mama," by Tex Ritter, and how it came to be played that afternoon, twenty years after Anzio, I'll never know. But I did not think about the hard young men of that old beachhead, or about their war, or even about cowboys in flight from homicidal girlfriends. I thought about Brooklyn.

When I was a kid growing up in Brooklyn, "Pistol Packin' Mama" was the first record we ever owned. My brother Tommy and I bought it for a dime in a secondhand book-and-record shop on Pearl Street under the Myrtle Avenue El, and we played it until the grooves were gone. The week before we bought it, my mother had arrived home with an old wine-colored hand-cranked Victrola, complete with picture of faithful dog and master's voice, and a packet of naillike needles. It was given the place of honor in the living room, in the old top floor right at 378 Seventh Avenue—that is, it was placed on top of the kerosene stove for the duration of the summer, and it was almost as heavy as the five-gallon drums we hauled home in the winter snow to feed the stove (steam heat, then, was a luxury assigned to the Irish with property). We thought that phonograph was a bloody marvel.

The purchase of "Pistol Packin' Mama" was something else again. We did not really lust after hymns of violence; we weren't country-and-western buffs (we always preferred Charles Starrett, the Durango Kid, who was all business, to the saps like Roy Rogers and Gene Autry, who played banjo as they rode after outlaws). It was something more complicated. We bought "Pistol Packin' Mama" because it was the first hard, solid evidence we had until then about the existence of the world outside Brooklyn.

We studied geography in school, of course, with all those roll-down maps of the world, those dull figures about copra production, the uses of sisal, and, of course, the location of the Holy Land. But Brooklyn was not on those maps. *New York* was, but to us, New York was some strange, exotic city across the river, where there were people who rooted for the Giants and the Yankees. Brooklyn was not there. Even Battle Creek, Michigan, where we sent a hundred Kellogg box tops, was on the map. Brooklyn was not. The people who secretly ruled the earth did not recognize us, and we did not really recognize them. So to own a copy of that awful record was like establishing diplomatic relations with the rest of the world; "Pistol Packin' Mama" had been a *hit*—broadcast from a million radios—and for Tommy and me to have a copy of it, to hold it in our hands, to turn it over (the flip side was something that went "Rosalita, you are the rose of the baaaanjo!"), to be able to play it at our leisure and not wait to hear it at the whim of those people who secretly ruled the earth—that was breaking out.

Lying on that couch in Rome, I had already learned that you never break out of anything, that it was ludicrous to think that you could solve anything by setting out on journeys. The last time I had gone there, Brooklyn had seemed shabby and worn-out: not just in the neighborhood where I grew up, but everywhere. There was something special, almost private, about being from Brooklyn when I was growing up: a sense of community, a sense of being home. But I hadn't lived there for a long time, and when I did go, it seemed always for a disaster: to see the corpses of men, baked by the heat, being carried out of the *Constellation* as it burned in the snow at the Navy Yard; to visit, like a ghoul, the mothers of dead soldiers; to cover the latest hostilities between the Gallo and Profaci mobs; to talk with the father of an eight-year-old boy who had pushed a girl off a roof in Williamsburg. Only the dead know Brooklyn, Thomas Wolfe had written. For a while it seemed that way. The place had come unraveled, like the spring of a clock dropped from a high floor. Nevertheless, that night in Rome I started getting ready to go home.

The Brooklyn I came home to has changed. For the first time in ten years, it seems to have come together. In Park Slope, people like David Levine, Jeremy Larner, Joe Flaherty, Sol Yurick have moved into the splendid old brownstones; the streets seem a bit cleaner; on some streets, citizens are actually planting trees again, with money they have raised themselves through block associations and block parties. Art galleries are opening. Neighborhoods like Bay Ridge and South Brooklyn now have boutiques and head shops. People who have been driven out of the Village and Brooklyn Heights by the greed of real-estate operators are learning that it is not yet necessary to decamp for Red Bank or Garden City. It is still possible in Park Slope, for example, to rent a duplex with a garden for $200 a month, a half block from the subway; still possible to buy a brownstone in reasonably good condition for $30,000, with a number of fairly good houses available for less, if you are willing to invest in reconditioning them. Hundreds of people are discovering that Brooklyn has become the Sane Alternative: a part of New York where you can live a decent urban life without going broke, where you can educate your children without having the income of an Onassis, a place where it is still possible to see the sky, and all of it only fifteen minutes from Wall Street. The Sane Alternative is Brooklyn.

Impressions can be backed up by any number of statistics. Today Brooklyn is the fourth-largest city in the United States. It has more people than 26 states, contains 1 out of every 65 persons born in this country. For thirty years there have been jokes about the tree that grew in Brooklyn; in fact, the borough contains 235,000 trees, which is a hell of a lot more than you will find in the high-rise ghettos of the Upper East Side. Brooklyn's purchasing power in 1968 rose to $6,600,000,000, up $347,000,000 over the previous year. In 1967, wholesale and retail trade in the borough amounted to $5,400,000,000; there was a payroll of $2,400,000,000 for 704,800 jobholders. In a study called "The Next Twenty Years," the New York Port Authority predicts a 7.7 percent growth in jobs by 1985, while population will grow at only 2 percent. According to a 1965 Dun and Bradstreet report, Brooklyn is now the nation's fourth-largest industrial county, third-largest food consumer, and fourth-largest user of goods and services. The median income ($5,816) is still $175 less than that in Manhattan, but the median age of the 2,627,420 citizens is 33.5, lower than New York City's as a whole (35) and lower than the median (34) in the metropolitan region that includes Westchester, Rockland, Nassau, and Suffolk counties.

But no set of statistics can adequately explain what has happened to Brooklyn in the years since the end of the Second World War. They don't explain its decline. They don't explain its renaissance.

For me, Brooklyn is the great proof of the theory that many of the problems of the American city are emotional. If you were born in Brooklyn, as I was, you learned something about this quite early. Through most of its early history, Brooklyn was really a kind of bucolic suburb, dedicated to middle-class values, solid and phlegmatic. Its citizens owned small farms. They opened small manufacturing plants, especially on the Manhattan side of Prospect Park, which is the section of Brooklyn that today most resembles the dark industrial image of the nineteenth century. When the subways pushed out past Prospect Park into Flatbush and beyond, Brooklyn became the bedroom for the middle class. Its first period of shock and decline came after the 1898 Mistake, when the five boroughs were united into Greater New York under the supposedly benevolent dictatorship of Manhattan. Until then, if we are to believe old newspapers, Brooklynites were proud and industrious citizens who planted their own trees, who gloried in their independence.

Most of them opposed the 1898 Mistake, but the deal was pushed through the state legislature by the Republicans, who thought that the large number of Republicans in Brooklyn would help them wrest control of the entire city from Tammany Hall. (In those days, of course, Republicans were in the tradition of Lincoln, not Goldwater and Thurmond.)

After the 1898 Mistake, some sections of Brooklyn started to change radically. In the nineteenth-century part of town, the poor Irish and the poor Italians started moving in; they filled the old-law cold-water-flat tenements; they ran speakeasies during Prohibition; some of them learned how to make money with murder. The poor Jews moved into Williamsburg and Brownsville, where they also learned something about the rackets. The respectable people, as they thought of themselves, fled to Flatbush and Bensonhurst and even out into the wilds of Flatlands. But there was a long period of stability that almost lasted through the Second World War.

The first cracks in that stability showed up during the war, when a lot of fathers were away fighting and a lot of mothers were working in war plants. Some Brooklynites had been shocked at the revelations about Murder, Inc., the brutal Brooklyn-based Jewish-Italian mob whose members killed for money. But when the teen-age gangs started roving Brooklyn during the war, then some citizens thought the end was near (you could abide Murder, Inc., of course, if your other institutions—family, church, jobs—remained stable). In Bedford-Stuyvesant, the first black gangs, the Bishops and the Robins, began to assemble; down on Sands Street the Navy Yard Boys were already rolling sailors and shipyard workers; the Red Hook Boys came out of the first projects and the side streets around the Gowanus Canal; the Garfield Boys, from Garfield Place in South Brooklyn, expanded into the South Brooklyn Boys, and became the training ground for many of the soldiers who are now in the Brooklyn chapters of the Mafia. In my neighborhood, the Shamrock Boys became the Tigers, and they fought the South Brooklyn Boys with an expertise in urban guerrilla warfare (on both sides) that the Black Panthers would be advised to study. I don't know if there ever really was a gang called the Amboy Dukes (I am told by buffs that there was), but

Irving Shulman's *The Amboy Dukes* became the bible for a lot of these kids; they studied the sayings of Crazy Shack the way the motorcycle gangs later studied Lee Marvin and Brando in *The Wild One.*

The gangs were wild, often brutal; there were more than a few knifings and gang rapes, and a number of killings, especially after the war, when veterans started bringing home guns as souvenirs; in shop classes in the high schools, students spent more time making zip guns out of pieces of pipe than they did making bookcases or pieces of sinks. The gun—especially if it was a *real* gun—became a thing of awe. The first time I ever saw Joe Gallo (they called him Joe the Blond in those days) he was in the Ace Pool Room upstairs from his father's luncheonette on Church Avenue; someone, I think it was an old friend named Johnny Rose, whispered to me, "Don't ever say nuthin' about him: he's *packin'*."

The gangs started breaking up in the fifties. First, the Korean War took most of the survivors away, all of those kids who had been too young for the Second World War. By the time they came home they were sick of fighting; they married, and some of them moved away. But while they were gone, something else had arrived in Brooklyn: drugs. What the Youth Board and the cops had not been able to do, heroin did. More of them died from OD's than ever died in the gang wars. Prison took a lot of them, and for some odd reason, the ones who had managed to escape arrests and habits became cops. Only two really new gangs started in the fifties: the Jokers and a gang from my neighborhood which called itself Skid Row. The Jokers lost a lot of members to drugs, and a few of them were involved in a brutal stomp killing. I still see some of the Skid Row kids around. My brother Tommy was a member for a while; by the time he was in CCNY three of the gang were already dead from heroin.

The whole terrible period of the gangs, followed by the introduction of heroin, changed a lot of citizens' attitudes about Brooklyn. Those who had escaped the Lower East Side now started talking about escaping Brooklyn. Events seemed to have moved beyond their control. You could do the best you were capable of doing: work hard, hold two jobs, get bigger and better television sets for the living room, watch steam heat replace kerosene stoves, see the old coal stoves in the kitchens dragged out to be replaced by modern gas ovens, and still people in their teens were found dead in the shrubs of Prospect Park, their arms as scarred as school desks. "We gotta get outta Brooklyn." You heard it over and over in those days. It wasn't a matter of moving from one neighborhood to the next; the transportation system was too good for all that; it was out "to the island" or to California or Rockland County. The idea was to get out.

Leaving was made easier by four central factors in the period of postwar decline in Brooklyn. All, in their special ways, were emotional. The four factors: (1) the folding of the Brooklyn *Eagle*; (2) the departure of the Brooklyn Dodgers for California; (3) the long years of insecurity about and the final folding of the Brooklyn Navy Yard; (4) the migration of Southern Negroes, most of whom settled in Brooklyn, not Manhattan.

The *Eagle* was not the greatest newspaper in New York in its day; there were, after all, eight others (the *Times, Herald Tribune, News, Mirror, World-Telegram, Post, Journal-American,* and *Sun*), and for years Brooklyn had two other papers—the *Citizen* and the *Times-Union.* But the *Eagle* was a pretty good paper for what it was attempting to do, and all it ever really attempted was to cover Brooklyn. I used to deliver it after school, which is why one shoulder is lower than the other, but along with a lot of other people I used to read it. I don't have the slightest idea what its editorial policies were, though I imagine they were conservative, since its owner eventually folded it up instead of submitting to the Newspaper Guild. I used to read the comics and the sports pages and odd features like "Uncle Ray's Corner," which was all about the life-style of the mongoose, and other matters. The best comic strips were *Invisible Scarlet O'Neil,* who had some kind of special vein in her arm which she pressed to become invisible, and *Steve Roper,* which was about a magazine reporter. Of the sportswriters, I only remember Harold C. Burr, who had a gnarled face pasted above his column and looked something like Burt Shotton, who was interim Pope of the Dodgers while Leo Durocher sat out a suspension, and Tommy Holmes, who joined the staff of the *Herald Tribune* after the *Eagle* folded.

But even though the *Eagle* was not a great paper, it had a great function: it helped to weld together an extremely heterogeneous community. Without it, Brooklyn became a vast network of hamlets, whose boundaries were rigidly drawn but whose connections with each other were vague at best, hostile at worst. None of the three surviving metropolitan newspapers really covers Brooklyn now until events—Ocean Hill-Brownsville, for example—have reached the stage of crisis; the New York *Times* has more people in Asia than it has in Brooklyn, and you could excuse that, certainly, on grounds of priorities if you did not also know that this most powerful New York paper has three columnists writing on national affairs, one writing on European affairs, and none at all writing about this city.

Without the *Eagle*, local merchants floundered for years in their attempt to reach their old customers; two large Brooklyn department stores—Namm's and Loeser's—folded up. If you were looking for an apartment or a furnished room in Brooklyn, there was no central bulletin board. School sports are still largely ignored in the metropolitan papers; as Pete Axthelm once pointed out so vividly about the great Boys' High team, Boys' High is in Brooklyn, for God's sake, in *Bedford-Stuyvesant!* How could you expect to get your reporter back alive? But the *Eagle* covered school sports with a vengeance, and the rivalries between various high schools were strong and alive. Today they don't seem to matter much; hell, even the old ladies who used to yank the *Eagle* from my hand to read the obituaries don't have that consolation anymore.

Nobody really covers the Brooklyn borough president's office anymore (as I suppose nobody has covered the Bronx borough president since the absorption of the Bronx *Home News* by the *Post*). Nobody covers the borough as a whole. When Hugh Carey announced that he was running for mayor, not many New Yorkers knew who he was, despite the fact that he is one of the most important members of the New York City Congressional delegation and comes from the borough with the strongest Democratic party machine. He is from Brooklyn; nobody knows his name. (The void left by the loss of the *Eagle* has been increasingly filled in recent years by the weekly neighborhood papers, of which the *Park Slope News-Home Reporter* is by far the best I've seen. During the school strike, it ran the single best account of the anger and bitterness on local levels of any paper in the city.) In any other city its size, there would be at least two newspapers. Brooklyn has none.

The loss of the Dodgers was an even deeper emotional shock to the people of Brooklyn, because it affected so many more people than the *Eagle*'s demise did. Kids, for example. I remember an afternoon in the fall of 1941, when I was six, sitting in the midst of a crowd of thousands on the steps of the just-opened central branch of the Brooklyn Public Library. A few days before, the Dodgers had won the National League pennant. All through the thirties they were the clowns of the league: An outfielder named Babe Herman had been hit on the head with a fly ball; three Dodger runners once ended up on third base at the same time; a player named Casey Stengel once came to bat, tipped his hat, and a bird flew out. But in 1941 they won the pennant, and Brooklyn welcomed them home like champions. All the schools were closed. There was a motorcade from the Brooklyn Borough Hall right up Flatbush Avenue to Ebbets Field, and in the huge crowds people were laughing and cheering and crying, lost in that kind of innocent euphoria that always comes when underdogs win out against all odds. (Imagine what will happen in this town when the Mets finally win a pennant.) All of them were there: Kirby Higbe, Hugh Casey, Dolf Camilli, Durocher himself, Pee Wee Reese, the great and tragic Pete Reiser: all of them smiling and waving in the bright sunshine. I was six, and even I knew who they were.

Well, they lost the World Series that year to the hated Yankees, when Mickey Owen dropped a third strike. But nobody gave up on them. "Wait till nex' year" became the perennial battle cry, and for the next fifteen years they were one of the finest baseball clubs in the country. Then suddenly, with the stealth of a flat thief, Walter O'Malley took them away. They were still making money at Ebbets Field, despite the old ball park's rickety condition and despite television. Dodger fans, after all, were *loyal.* But the Dodgers, in O'Malley's opinion, were just not making *enough* money. One barren spring, Ebbets Field was left empty and dark, the dugouts abandoned, the infield turning to brittle dust, the great greensward of the outfield gone brown and mottled, the bleachers, where so much laughter, joy and sorrow had been staged, whipped by a cold wind. Today the old ball park is gone. Still another housing project is planted on its site, with only a brass plaque to tip a chiseled hat to a rowdy and innocent past.

The operative word in the whole matter of the Dodgers is "innocent." Baseball was a sport then, and if you came from Brooklyn, baseball meant the Dodgers. There were always some nonconformists; I remember a guy named Jackie McEvoy who rooted for the Giants and Buddy Kelly, who later died in Korea, rooting for the Yankees. But the Dodgers really were "The Pride of Brooklyn," and Dixie Walker really was "The People's Cherce." This vast confraternity of baseball maniacs held that borough together in a very special way; first, they provided common ground: Italians, Irish, blacks, Jews, Poles—all went to the games. Second, they provided something to talk about that did not involve religion, politics, or race. And most important, they helped refute the canards about Brooklyn that puzzled so many of us when we were kids: the tree, the Brooklyn accent, the William Bendix type in all the movies, etc.

Dodger fans believed in myths. They were romantics, of course, hoping that the impossible could be made possible, but often they settled for small victories. If the headline on the back page of the *Daily News* said FLOCK BEAT JINTS 3–2, then all was well with the world. It was no small surprise that when Bobby Thomson hit The Home Run off Ralph Branca to win the 1951 pennant for the Giants, several people in Brooklyn committed suicide.

I suppose that such emotions over a group of grown men playing a boy's game seem rather ludicrous today. But the people of Brooklyn had this one thing, this one simple belief: that ballplayers were the best people on earth. And in the evenings, thousands of fans, literally, would walk across Prospect Park to the night games, past the Swan Lake and the Zoo and out onto Flatbush Avenue, joined together by this odd faith in people named Snider and Furillo and Campanella and Cox. They were *part* of an experience larger than themselves, something that involved gray scoreboards, Red Barber, peanuts, special cops, the Brooklyn Sym-Phony, the crowds on the streets outside, Gladys

Gooding at the organ, the roar at the crack of the bat, Pete Reiser breaking his skull against the concave outfield wall, Snider dropping home runs into the gas station on Bedford Avenue, black men laughing with white men in the bleachers when Robinson took his jittery lead to second, beer, hot dogs, laughter. Laughter. The Dodgers were called Dem Bums, and the laughter came in part from knowing that they were not.

And when they left, the people of Brooklyn were shocked. As deeply shocked as they had been by almost any other public act in their time. They had given the Dodgers unquestioned loyalty. They had given the Dodgers love. It never mattered to the fans that the Dodgers also made a lot of money. Hell, they *should* make a lot of money. The important thing was the game, the field of play, the heroes. But O'Malley took them away. For money. Nothing else. Sheer, pure greed. And for a lot of people that was the end of innocence. Romantics are always betrayed in the end, and O'Malley did a savage job of betrayal.

The Brooklyn Navy Yard was crucial to Brooklyn for at least one very good reason: It gave us work. It even gave me work. In 1951, during the Korean War, I went to work at Shop 17 in Building 63 of the Navy Yard as an apprentice sheet metal worker. The number of men working there had declined from a peak of 70,000 during the Second World War to about 40,000, but the Yard was still the largest single employer in the borough. I hardly know the boy I was then; in memory it was a rough wild time, with a lot of drinking in the saloons of Flushing Avenue, much laughter with welders, and kindness from various people who said I was a bloody fool to be working with my hands when I could still go back and finish high school. I had one great job, with a thin, coughing black man who was a welder-burner and who stopped working every half hour to drink milk. He said it coated his lungs against the filings of burned metal. He coughed a lot anyway. We were working on an aircraft carrier named the *Wasp*, which was being refitted to accommodate jet aircraft. All the old bulkheads had to be removed, to be replaced with sturdier walls. His job was to burn around the edges of the bulkheads with an acetylene torch. My job was to pile into the bulkheads with a huge 20-pound hammer and knock them flat. It was an orgy of sheer animal fury, setting yourself, swinging ferociously, beating and smashing those bulkheads until they fell, while the thin black man coughed and laughed. "You some crazy white boy," he would say. "You some crazy white boy."

But all of us working there, even in the early fifties, knew that the Navy Yard could not make it. To begin with, it was not a very economic place to build ships. It could be used for repair work, of course, but the big jobs—the new carriers, the atomic submarines—almost all went to private industry or to shipyards where the workers were a little hungrier. In the Navy Yard you were a federal civil servant; it was very tough to get rid of you over small matters. The professionals at the Yard did a good day's work, but for a lot of the people who saw it as a day's pay, there wasn't much work done at all. At Shop 17, they would punch in at 8 A.M. and immediately dash to the men's room on the second floor. They would then grab an empty stall (not an easy matter), put an arm on the toilet-paper roll, and pass out for an hour. Later they would go down to the floor, check out to the tool room, and spend an hour smoking. There might be a little work done, but by 11:30 it was back to the men's room to start washing up for lunch. After lunch, the pattern repeated itself, except that washing up to go home often started at 4 P.M., a full hour before checking out. There was something beautiful about the sheer audacity of those malingerers, but it also spelled the doom of the Yard. The 70,000 dwindled to 10,000 and finally to none. When Robert McNamara finally ordered the Yard closed, there was great public hand wringing; nobody who ever worked there was at all surprised.

In addition to the loss of immediate jobs, there were other things involved for the people of Brooklyn. Many small factories and businesses lived off the Yard as subcontractors. In the immediate vicinity of the Yard there were bars, gas stations, naval outfitters, whose lives were intimately involved. In the long years of rumor and uncertainty, many gave up and moved on. The workers themselves were wary of signing leases, buying homes, purchasing anything on credit; they simply did not know when the ax would fall. A number of smaller businessmen in Brooklyn felt that if the Navy Yard could not make it, with its natural advantages, its federal subsidy, then *they* never could make it. The Navy Yard, in the years of its decline, became still another emotional symbol. Brooklyn without the Yard was not Brooklyn. It was as simple as that.

The black migration hit Brooklyn harder than any other part of the city. There were pockets of Puerto Ricans in Brooklyn, clustered around Smith Street in Boerum Hill, around the Williamsburg Bridge, and out in Sunset Park. But the really large numbers of Puerto Ricans had gone to East Harlem and the South Bronx. The Southern black man came to Brooklyn.

There were several reasons for this. It was far more difficult for a badly educated rural black man to get an apartment in Harlem than it was in Bedford-Stuyvesant. Harlem was a society, the black capital of America, with its already well-defined institutions: churches, numbers runners, landlords, restaurants, artists, after-hours places, con men, musicians, etc. Bed-Stuy was much looser, much less structured. In Bed-Stuy you didn't have to be hip.

Bed-Stuy was also easier to block-bust. A number of black real estate operators (in addition to whites) made fortunes busting Bed-Stuy. They often employed white salesmen, who would purchase a house in a white street, move in a black family, and then start calling up everyone else on the street. Since many of these areas had two-family houses or old elegant brownstones, this was much easier to do in Brooklyn than it was in Harlem, where old-law tenements were the rule. Less money was involved, and more heartbreak, especially for the unfortunate hardworking black man who thought he had escaped the ghetto only to find that it was coming out behind him.

So Bedford-Stuyvesant exploded. Whites began leaving by the hundreds. In places like Brownsville, they left because Brownsville had almost always been a slum, and the second generation that was making it did not see any need for further loyalty. Others simply saw the whole thing as hopeless: Brooklyn, which in their youth had been the city of trees and free spaces and security, was being torn apart by drugs and gang wars. The *Eagle* was gone; the Dodgers had departed: *Take the money and get out while you can.* There was racial fear involved, of course, but it would be too easy to explain it all away that way. It was race plus despair plus insecurity about money plus desires for the betterment of one's children plus—the most important plus—the loss of a feeling of community.

As Bedford-Stuyvesant expanded (any street that was occupied by blacks became Bedford-Stuyvesant, whether it was in Clinton Hill or Crown Heights), fear expanded. In Park Slope, across Flatbush Avenue from Bed-Stuy, real estate operators started breaking up the fine old brownstones into black boardinghouses. Most were occupied by transients, as boardinghouses have always been occupied, and they simply didn't care what neighbors thought about them. The streets became littered with broken bottles and discarded beer cans, the yards filled with garbage, drug arrests increased, hookers worked the avenues; there were knifings and shootings, and soon the merchants on Flatbush Avenue started folding up and moving away. No insurance could cover what they stood to lose. When the Peconic Clam Bar on the corner of Flatbush and Bergen Street closed up because of too many stickups, the game looked finished. The Peconic Clam Bar was across the street from Brooklyn Police Headquarters.

And then, suddenly, Brooklyn seemed to reverse itself. You still cannot get a taxi to take you from the Village to any neighborhood remotely near Bed-Stuy. But the borough has halted its own decline, stopped, brought the panic and despair almost to an end.

Again, the reasons are complicated and have certain emotional roots. The wound of the Dodgers' departure seems finally healed; the arrival of the Mets gave the old Dodger fans something to cheer for, and there are no more of the old *Brooklyn* Dodgers now playing for the Los Angeles team. Baseball itself has declined in interest: It's slow, dull, almost sedate these days, especially on television. Pro football excites more people in the Brooklyn saloons, and it is a measure of the anti-Establishment, anti-Manhattan feelings of Brooklynites that they all seem to root for the Jets (not all, of course, not all, but the romantics do).

Word also began to drift in from the suburbs: Things were

64

not all well out there. Those who left Brooklyn because the schools were overcrowded soon found that the schools were also overcrowded in Babylon. Those who fled the terrors of drugs soon found that there were drugs in Rahway and Red Bank and Nyack, too, and that flight alone would not avoid that peril. There was cultural shock. A childhood spent leaning against lampposts outside candy stores could not be easily discarded, especially on streets where there were no candy stores, where the bright lights did not shine into the night, where the laughter of the neighborhood saloon was not always available. People started longing for the Old Neighborhood. "These people can't even make a egg cream right." "I tried to get a bits-eye-oh out here, an' it tastes like a pair a Keds." When I would go out to California on various assignments, I learned that I would be serving as a courier from the Real World; guys who had gone out to Costa Mesa and San Jose and LA twenty years before wanted me to bring *veal,* real-thin-honest-to-Jesus veal cutlets so they could make veal Parmigiana the way it is supposed to be made. In the suburbs late at night, people would sit in their living rooms and talk about boxball, devilball, buck-buck-how-many-horns-are-up? (called Johnny Onna Pony by the intellectuals), ringalevio, and always, always, stickball. Remember the time Johnny McAleer hit three spaldeens over the factory roof? Or the time Billy Rossiter swung at a ball, the bat flew out of his hands, hit an old lady on the head, and went through the window on Twelfth Street? Remember the Arrows, and the great money games they had on Thirteenth and Eighth? Nostalgia worked its sinister charms. The Old Neighborhood wasn't much, but it wasn't this empty grublike existence in the suburbs, struggling with mortgages and crabgrass and PTA meetings and water taxes and neighbors who had never shared one common experience with you. A little at a time, people started to drift back. It was not, and is not, a flood. But it has begun.

For younger people, the suburbs seemed to hold a special horror. If you were a writer and you were faced with a move to the suburbs, you would rather go all the way into exile: to Mexico or Ireland or Rome. You could not live in the Village or Brooklyn Heights, because the real estate scoundrels had made those places special preserves for the super-affluent (you *could* live in those places, of course, but the things you would have to do to afford it would make it impossible to live with yourself). Younger people started looking over the neighboring terrain. They cracked Cobble Hill first, reclaiming a number of fairly good buildings. Then Park Slope started to open up; the boardinghouses were bought for as little as $14,000, cleaned out, rebuilt and rewired. That was only four and five years ago. Today the prices are slowly being driven up, and the great fear is that the real estate people will take over this place, too.

The New People, as they are called, saw Brooklyn fresh. They had not known it before, so they knew nothing about its decline. Most important, they carried with them no old emotional wounds. Instead they saw it as a place with great broad boulevards like Eastern Parkway and Ocean Parkway (once, my brother and I walked out Ocean Parkway all the way to Avenue T because we read in the papers that Rocky Graziano lived there; we sat around on benches for hours, but we never saw Rocky, who was the middleweight champion of the world). They recognized that Greenwood Cemetery, which contains the bones of such diverse worthies as Boss Tweed and William S. Hart, was one of the great urban glades, a spot with lush foliage, sudden hills, bizarre statuary (at night, when we were kids, we would sneak into the cemetery to try to catch the giant turtles which lived in its ponds; the ghosts sent us running). They know that the Brooklyn Museum is one of the finest in the country, with a great collection of graphics, a splendid African collection, some superb American Indian pieces, and paintings by Ryder, Jack Levine, etc. (we went there to see the mummies, to walk into the bowels of the mock pyramid, dreading the Pharaoh's curse, remembering every terror of that great picture *The Mummy's Hand*). They know that Prospect Park is a masterpiece of landscape architecture, the park that learned from the mistakes of Central Park, which by comparison is bland and flat, and they know that during the Revolutionary War, George Washington had a command post in its hills (but they've never been inside Devil's Cave, nor did they know what happened in the night in the shrubs along the Indian War Path, and they don't know the spot where Yockomo was shot to death near the Swan Lake by Scappy from South Brooklyn, and they weren't there the night that Vito Pinto dove into the Big Lake at three in the morning and found himself wedged in the mud three inches below the surface, and they never saw Jimmy Budgell come tearing down the horse path on a strawberry roan like one of the Three Mesquiteers). They know that the great arch at Grand Army Plaza contains a fine piece of sculpture by Thomas Eakins, that there is an abandoned tunnel under the Plaza, that the main branch of the Brooklyn Public Library is one of the best in the city (and when I was a kid I used to look up at the carved legend on the wall that begins HERE ARE EN-SHRINED THE LONGING OF GREAT HEARTS . . . and spent one long summer hoping that someday I would be a Great Heart too and that maybe books were the key). They saw Brooklyn in a way that we had not seen it when we were young, and they saw it in a way that Brooklyn had not seen itself, perhaps, since the years before the 1898 Mistake. I just wish that they could have been there that afternoon at the now-shuttered 16th Street Theater, when Tim Lee (now at the *Post*) and his brother Mike were taken by their mother for the usual Saturday matinee of three Republic westerns. At one point, a *Superman* chapter came on, and Mike Lee stood up, and shouted at the top of his lungs, "Hey, Ma! I can see the crack of his *ass!*" His mother beat him mercilessly with a banana that was part of the lunch and then took them all home.

The New People are part of the emotional cure. There are other, more practical cures under way. For one thing, the migration of Southern blacks seems to have come to an end; it has at least been reduced to a trickle. More important, Bedford-Stuyvesant has been developing its own institutions. Quietly and steadily, the Bedford-Stuyvesant Restoration Corporation, which was started through the efforts of Robert Kennedy, has been working very hard at bringing jobs to the area. IBM has already announced that it will build a manufacturing plant there. Plans are under way to build a new Boys' High. The city has committed itself to building a community college in the area. Through one of the two corporations set up by Senator Kennedy, a $75,000,000 mortgage loan fund has been put together and a job-training program for 1,200 persons is under way. With federal help, three firms (Advance Hudson Mounting and Finishing Co.; Campus Graphics, Inc.; Day Pac Industries, Inc.) have begun a $30,000,000 project of plant construction that will employ 1,435 people. Say what you will about the Black Panthers, they probably have a small point to make about ghetto businesses owned by whites; through reform of the insurance laws, more and more black businesses are starting in New York, the vast majority of them in Brooklyn. The development of the Black Pearl taxi system is an example of the building of institutions; let the white cabdrivers bitch and complain and issue dark warnings about cabdrivers in "gypsy" cabs who might have criminal records. The fact is, the Black Pearl cabs (and others not connected with Black Pearl) have made it possible for black residents of Bedford-Stuyvesant to travel the way a lot of other New Yorkers travel, and the money is staying in the area.

In addition, thousands of Puerto Ricans have settled in Brooklyn, in flight from the urban demolition that passes for slum clearance in Manhattan and the Bronx. There are now more Puerto Ricans in Brooklyn than in any of the other four boroughs, and they have brought with them their many virtues: the instinct to open small businesses, the almost visceral need to hold a family together, a sense of community. Sure, the Puerto Ricans play their radios loud, they play dominoes in the street, and they drink a lot of canned beer wrapped in one-pound bags (at a party once, someone asked my friend José Torres to go out for "twenty-four bags of beer"). But for me, that has made Brooklyn a more exciting, more lively place. You can measure a city by the life in its streets, and the Puerto Ricans have brought life with them: abundant, rowdy, and baroque.

It is true that parts of Brownsville now look like Hamburg in 1945. Entire blocks have been abandoned to the rats and the wind. Old temples from the days when this was a Jewish area are now boarded up or have given way to Baptist churches. The gym at Georgia and Livonia, where Bummy Davis used to train while the Murder, Inc., goombahs looked on benevolently, is now gone; a big sign saying FORTUNOFF'S FOR MAH-JONGG SETS covers the windows, and you wonder how many people in the neighborhood play mah-jongg these days. (Milton Gross from the *Post* lived around that neighborhood, and I wonder if he was there that day twenty-five years ago when my father took me out to watch Davis with a bunch of other fight buffs in somebody's old Packard.) Near P.S. 174, there is one of those Mondrianesque cityscapes—blue, yellow, pink squares that were once the walls of kitchens and bedrooms, where people loved each other, and quarreled late at night, and cried angrily at the meanness of poverty, and then moved on. You can still see an occasional dairy appetizing store out there, and Carlucci's on the Brownsville end of Eastern Parkway is still one of the best Italian restaurants anywhere. But there remains this feeling of walking through purgatory. Street after street has been leveled. Only later do you discover that much of this demolition is part of a Model Cities plan and that those streets will again be alive with children and perhaps even trees. (But where are all the people now? Where on God's poor earth did they go?) In Ocean Hill-Brownsville (the school district, not strictly the neighborhood) there is a revolution of sorts under way. It is led by people like Rhody McCoy, his governing board and the Reverend John Powis of Our Lady of Presentation R.C. Church. They are working at the hardest part of any revolution: the part that goes beyond posture and mere defiance to accomplishment. They understand what the Board of Education and various other bureaucracies staffed by suburbanites don't understand: that the key is community. If they lose, Brooklyn loses, the city loses, we all lose.

The Brooklyn Navy Yard seems to be on its way back. A group called CLICK (Commerce, Labor, Industry Corporation of Kings)—started by people like Stanley Steingut, Brooklyn Borough President Abe Stark, and Congressman Hugh Carey—has joined the City of New York (mainly the Economic Development Administration, with the help of another Brooklynite, Commerce Commissioner Ken Patton of Park Slope), to bring the Yard back to life. They hope eventually to provide between 30,000 and 40,000 jobs in the Yard by attracting civilian investment. They have signed a contract with Sea Train, Inc., which will employ more than 3,000 workers in its first eighteen months. The Yard, which covers 170 acres, already houses several small companies, such as the Rotodyne Manufacturing

Company, which employs 130 workers building industrial ovens. The city is processing dozens of other applications. It might not come back to even the last payroll (1963: $201,000,000) for quite a while. But the beginning has been made. The governing factor in the city's decisions to rent space is that the space must be used for jobs. They will not rent space for warehouses and have already turned down one request from the Federal Bureau of Prisons, which wanted 12 acres for a jail.

Not far from the Yard, the Pratt Center for Community Improvement is drawing plans for the revitalization of the entire neighborhood near the Yard: Fort Greene, Williamsburg, Bedford-Stuyvesant. Among many other plans, they hope to set up a series of nurseries along major bus routes leading to the Yard, so that working mothers from Bed-Stuy will be able to drop off small children on their way to work and pick them up on the way home.

Out in Flatlands, a new industrial park is being built on 96 acres, to provide 7,000 jobs, and three plants are already under construction. The Brooklyn waterfront continues to outstrip the Manhattan waterfront in construction of new piers and rehabilitation of old ones. Two new department stores are planned for downtown Brooklyn, and the Brooklyn store of Abraham & Straus has now passed Bloomingdale's in net sales. The Downtown Brooklyn Civic Center is now complete, and if the architecture rather resembles Abe Stark Stalinist in manner, it is at least new and it functions. Coney Island seems to me to be in decline, with the amusement area shrinking, old saloons like Scoville's gone, the old bungalows on the side streets battered away, many proud houses gone seedy and squalid. But I'm told that last year Coney Island had its best year financially since 1947. The 12-acre site of Steeplechase Park will become a public park backing on the beach, and the aquarium is planning a 5,000-seat whale and dolphin area.

The Brooklyn Academy of Music has gone through a real rebirth in the past two years, something that startles old Brooklynites who thought of the Academy as a shambling pile located down the street from the Raymond Street Jail and given over to travel lectures about the sex life of West Papuans. Today the Academy has become the dance center of the United States, possibly of the world. And it is avoiding the Lincoln Center aura of gilded society and class distinctions by giving special rates and tickets to poverty agencies, so that young people from all over the city can see modern dance, often for the first time. For those of us who used to go downtown to meet friends coming out of jail, to pick up girls at the dances at the Granada Hotel or to box at the YMCA gym on Hanson Place, it all seems very strange; not many of us ever thought that the Academy would be thriving and the Raymond Street Jail would be closed.

There remain real problems in Brooklyn. There is still desperate poverty in the slums. Many urban renewal projects are still exercises in urban demoliton. There are still too many decrepit, aging public schools, and the parochial school system remains a fragmenting anachronism. Eugene Gold, the Brooklyn district attorney and one of the best of a new breed of elected officials in Brooklyn, told me that drugs and violence remain major problems. "I would say that drugs contribute in one way or another to about fifty to seventy percent of the borough's crime," Gold said recently. "I don't mean simply arrests for pushing or possessing drugs. I mean, in addition, drugs as the cause of other crimes: burglaries, stickups, muggings and the rest. We have a drug problem in *every* part of this city. When I go into Bedford-Stuyvesant to talk to people, as I do as often as I'm asked, they have one concern: how to stop crime. How to stop drugs. It's a real problem."

My own observation is that heroin seems to have declined. Most of the old junkies from my neighborhood are either dead or in prison, and the ones who remain are thought of as freaks. But marijuana is everywhere, and pills are easily available. Unfortunately, this is not just the problem in Brooklyn. The suburbs have the problem, too. Last year, when I was spending some time in good old right-wing conservative Orange County in Southern California, drug arrests among young people had gone up almost 50 percent in one year. There is no way to escape drugs by moving out. In California, they even arrested Jesse Unruh's son on a pot charge.

It seems to me that despite the problems, Brooklyn has become the only sensible place to live in New York. Much has changed since I was a boy, but what the hell. If you consider jars of mixed peanut butter and jelly as the final sign of the decline of a great nation, people my age think the same thing about that modern abomination, the manufactured stickball bat. It is, after all, a terrible thing to deprive a kid of the chance to acquire lore, and the lore of the stickball bat is arcane and mysterious. Nevertheless, on the first day of spring this year, with a high bright sun moving over Prospect Park and a cool breeze blowing in from the harbor, I bought one of the abominations and a fresh spaldeen and talked some of the local hippies into playing a fast game. It was the first time I had played since moving away from Brooklyn, and in one small way I wanted to celebrate moving back.

We played in the old skating rink at Bartel Pritchard Square, and the young lean kids with the long hair simply could not hit the ball. They might have been playing cricket. But the first time up, I smacked one long and high, arcing over the trees, away over the head of the farthest outfielder. On the old court at Twelfth Street and Seventh Avenue, it would have been away over the avenue, at least three sewers, and probably more. Standing there watching the ball roll away in the distance, I realized again that despite all the drinking, sins, strange cities, remorse, betrayals, and small murders, there was still a part of me that had never left Brooklyn, that wanted desperately to stay, that was still fourteen years old and playing stickball through long and random days and longing to be a Great Heart. I hoped that Carl Furillo, wherever he was, was shagging flies with an honored antique glove and hearing the roars in his ears from the vanished bleachers.

The next time up, I grounded out, but it didn't really matter.
July 14, 1969

II. Clubfighting

THIS selection of newspaper writing is, of course, not even remotely complete, nor should it be. A newspaper column is as ephemeral as the newspaper itself; the man who writes it lives with the knowledge that by the following afternoon his work might be lining a birdcage or wrapping fish. The deficiencies of the form appear obvious to me.

So this small collection of columns is not truly representative of the style, thrust, themes, or texture of the actual day-to-day columns I write for the New York *Post* or even the pieces I wrote for the *Village Voice.* Some of the omitted columns have such a specific reference to politics in progress that they would require footnote explanations almost as long as the columns themselves. Others are variations on continuing themes—the war in Vietnam, the relationship between New York City and New York State, the struggle between the boroughs of New York and Manhattan, the racial argument, etc. They are fragments of something larger and don't really belong in this collection. Others were discarded because I went off half-cocked and wrote about things I did not understand. Still others were simply botches. I think of a column as a letter to someone I respect; I don't ask that the person who receives that letter agree with me, but I at least attempt to be direct. And all collections of letters are uneven or contradictory.

I do hope that the columns I have chosen to include are still worth reading. Some have personal meaning: the column entitled "The War" ran on December 21, 1965, and was the first column I wrote about Vietnam (I had started writing the column in October). If it seems rather innocent now, it was because I was naïve and ignorant then about the war and its origins. The article about Arthur Goldberg caused an uproar in New York; it was unthinkable then even to talk about the possibility of war crimes trials for those who were in any way responsible for Vietnam policy; to suggest that the sainted Arthur Goldberg should be in the dock with the others, if trials took place, was considered evidence of the "irrational ravings" that Spiro Agnew spoke about in another context. After the column appeared, Goldberg announced from Olympus that he would not run for governor; he was coaxed back, proved to be the dull candidate I thought he would be, and was demolished in the 1970 election by Nelson Rockefeller. As I write, a lot of people who are more respectable than I am are talking about war crimes trials.

There are columns here that alternate from the giddy elation of New York the year the Mets won the pennant to the deaths of some good men. Some people thought my piece about Mendel Rivers was unnecessarily harsh; but Rivers was a malignant man in life, and there seemed no reason to say nice things about him just because he did us the favor of dying. I have never been able to stomach the official obit that begins: "Though Adolf Hitler was a dictator, he loved flowers and small children. . . ."

The pieces for the *Village Voice* were written during a strange, empty period of my life. I had left the *Post* in the fall of 1967 to go to work for *Newsday,* a Long Island newspaper that was then one of the best in the country. Bill Moyers had left the Johnson administration to become publisher of *Newsday* and had called me to see if I would become a Washington columnist for his paper. I loved working for the *Post* and the people who worked there with me, but I was in terrible financial difficulties at the time. When Moyers offered me more money, I thought about it for a few days and decided it was time to move on. There are very few *Newsday* columns in this book, because they were all written against a background of deep personal unhappiness and a growing sense that America, as I thought I knew it, was beginning to disappear. We were sinking deeper into the Asian swamp, and Lyndon Johnson seemed to be acting crazier and crazier; Robert Kennedy was holding back from a direct challenge to Johnson, because of innate caution and the urgings of some of the more conservative members of the New Frontier, who had grown fat and sleek in the years since Dallas. Johnson seemed certain of renomination and reelection, and Eugene McCarthy's candidacy still seemed a quixotic personal adventure. When an editor killed one of my columns for being too strongly anti-Johnson, I quit.

I went to Ireland and finished a novel that I had been fiddling with for a year and returned in the middle of March when Robert Kennedy sent me a telegram asking me to come home and work on his campaign. I took the family to California, but I never did go to work for Kennedy; there were too many of the old hands around, too much of the mechanical business of politics for someone like me to handle, and I could not feel entirely comfortable acting as a kind of ventriloquist for another man. I stayed in California for a while, enjoying the sea, the great dashes down the freeways, the roaring vulgarity of LA, the comforts of the sun. But at the same time, my marriage was becoming a desert.

I remember sitting out on the balcony of the house in Laguna one afternoon, looking at the Pacific, feeling quite lost. I didn't know until then just how much journalism had become a part of my being, how much I needed to make human contact, even through the written word, even with strangers. My daughters were too young to talk to, and I could no longer talk to my wife. One evening Jack Newfield called from New York and asked me if I wanted to write for the *Village Voice*. I told him that I did, and a few weeks later I started writing again. A few weeks after that, Robert Kennedy was murdered in the Ambassador Hotel, and some of the pieces here were an attempt to channel my feelings in the week after the killing. I took the family on a long circuitous trip through the Southwest and into Mexico, hoping to find some solace in a place where I had once been twenty-one years old and happy. And then, with a few casual exceptions here and there, I simply dried up as a writer. By the time the year was over, my marriage was finished and I was living alone, trying to make something of the wreckage. That, of course, is another story, and it is not in this book.

75

One further note about writing for newspapers. The columns have always been the most political of my work, but there has always been some confusion about my personal ideology. Some readers apparently think that my true editors reside in Hanoi, Peking, or Moscow; the "radicals" call me a fascist pig. It's really a lot simpler than that. I started out as a liberal member of the Democratic Party and haven't really changed much. In general, my sympathies are with underdogs and against abstraction, authoritarianism, and unnecessary cruelty. And yet I never believed that the Black Panthers were going to save either black men or America, I opposed the warped children who went around blowing up buildings as a form of therapy, I think welfare is eating the heart out of American cities and should be abolished, and I don't think you have to burn the Tintorettos just because Peter Max has made the cover of *Time* magazine. In short, I believe in tradition when it is valuable; I believe in change when it is thought out carefully and when its purpose is pragmatic. Vietnam showed us that a strong central government, with enormous power invested in the President, could be a malignant force in a democracy; the conservatives understood that years before the liberals did. The collapse of the old Tammany Hall structure in New York showed me that "reform" was not the solution to everything, that destroying the political party as buffer between government and citizen and replacing it with a bureaucracy has been a disaster. I think of myself as a democratic socialist, if such categories any longer have meaning. But to paraphrase one of Lyndon Johnson's airier statements, I am a free man, a New Yorker, a Democrat, and an American, in that order. And I would gladly give up the last three descriptions to retain the first.

The War

You hear it everywhere in this town now. You hear it in over-heard fragments of talk, in mumbled conversations on subway trains, in the small talk of saloons. You hear it in the halls of our great universities, in the lobbies of our theaters, in street-corner gatherings in the slums. You hear it, as I did yesterday, while standing in the wind-tossed glare of Union Square or in the dark, sweat-smelling corners of the Gramercy Gym; you hear it in the flaking racks of the Fourth Avenue bookshops or in the booths of luncheonettes. It will not go away. You hear it from women with frightened eyes, from men with fear-baffled faces, from children whose language speaks only of betrayal. It is our refrain this winter, snaking its way through everything we do, poisoning and corroding the fabric of our lives. You hear it everywhere in this town now. We are at war.

This filthy war in Vietnam has been with us a long time, but until now we have muffled it with lies, the way we might ease a toothache with whiskey. It took slaughter to force us to stop lying to ourselves. Until last week we could believe the plat-itudes; we could mouth the wormy rhetoric of the cold war, comforting ourselves with the grand abstractions of liberty and freedom, with smug piety, as advisers. But last week, in a place called the Ia Drang Valley, 240 of us were slaughtered while dispensing advice with carbines. The headlines told us what the government will not. We are at war.

And so, between the time I finish writing this and the mo-ment you begin to read it, men will die in Vietnam. They will die in the most terrible way it is possible to die in our time: as abstractions fighting other abstractions over abstractions. Some will die heroes; others will die running. Others will only be crip-pled for the rest of their lives. But most of those young men, I suppose, will die because they were just unlucky.

It is the worst of all luck to be young in a bad time, because the young men always fight the wars. For twenty-five years now old men have been teaching young men how to kill other young men in all the countries of the world. The young men have been given guns and slogans and told that what they do is fitting and noble and will further the cause of human freedom, or the cause of Communism, or the honor of one's country. And then the young men march off to die.

They are dying right now, in places with names like Dak Sut and Hiep Duc and Plei Me and Chu Pong and Quin Nhon. The generation before them died in places called Bataan and Anzio and Salerno and Omaha Beach and Iwo Jima and Guadalcanal and the Yalu Basin. This generation cannot even remember that generation's names. It hardly knows its own.

Does anyone remember, this moment, the names of Peter Hunting, Joseph Grainger, Joseph Bailey, Bobby Swanson, Rafael Berlanga, Charles McManus, Glenn Mann, Thomas Henson, Joe Minnook, Ned Loscuito, Charles Ianuzzi, Bernard Birenbaum, Harold Scott or Dominic DeAngelis? They all died last month in Vietnam.

I know this is no simple matter. I know that for all the napalm we are dropping on the innocent, the Vietcong are murdering others. I know that when the Marines murder prisoners, it is because the Vietcong are murdering theirs. I have heard the theories about falling dominoes, about the loss of Southeast Asia to Communism. I know that to live under Communism is not to live really at all.

But I wonder how many poets we have lost in anonymous jungles and on forgotten beaches in our time. I wonder if in the Ia Drang Valley the worms are eating at the body of a man who might have cured cancer, or written a symphony, or run for President, or played shortstop for the Mets, or painted a masterpiece, or even simply loved somebody else truly.

I wonder how many wished in the last minutes of their lives that just once more they could have seen the earth break forth in another spring, or ridden a horse across a mesquite prairie, or walked a great city in a snowfall, or watched the leaves come off the forests in autumn. I wonder how many longed for the companionship of men in Saturday night saloons or the way the girls look on the first day of summer when their coats come off and they walk free down the great avenues.

I wonder how many died with pictures of girls in their pockets. I wonder if a man is dying this minute without ever having seen his daughter learn how to walk.

But my language is too general. We are supposed to talk these days of "kill ratios" and "search and destroy missions" and "village pacification." All else is mere sentiment. We must concentrate on the long view, when the blood of slaughtered men will have converted Vietnam into the earthly paradise, free from want, free from Communism, free to rule itself.

I wish I could believe it, but the contamination by lie has been too general. All I know is that something is terribly wrong. You: out there, dressing for the theater, turning on the TV, waiting for dinner, worrying about your analysis, arguing about Andy Warhol, you, remember: Tonight, young men are dying in a place called Vietnam. We are at war.

December 2, 1965

The Reporter

Let's get this straight: Harrison Salisbury is (1) a Communist dupe; (2) a fellow traveler; (3) a naïf; (4) a running dog; (5) an agent of the imperialists; (6) a nervous nellie; (7) a stooge for Robert Kennedy; (8) a tool of the New Left; (9) a hater of the American way; or (10) a traitor.

All these charges, in various forms, have been leveled against Mr. Salisbury because he did his job. He happens to be an assistant managing editor of the *Times,* but sometimes he is sent to unpleasant places to report on rather unpleasant occurrences. He happened to be sent to North Vietnam. In North Vietnam, he discovered that, from 30,000 feet, it is sometimes difficult to distinguish between an arms factory and a school. The Communists have a regrettable habit of constructing each with four walls and a roof, and occasionally a 750-pound bomb might miss the gun factory and land in a geography class. That's war.

Salisbury's dispatches revealed absolutely no major surprises.

Since the Spanish Civil War, we have all known that aerial bombing kills civilians. The Nazis perfected it on Coventry, and no one remembers today what strategic values that town possessed. After three months of bombing, everyone knew that civilians were dying in North Vietnam; there simply couldn't be that many bridges in the country.

But the Pentagon and the American government as a whole were saying that such things did not happen. That is why there is now so much argument about Mr. Salisbury. No one likes his lies exposed in the New York *Times.*

The arguments against Mr. Salisbury seem to go like this: The United States is at war with North Vietnam. Any reporting from the enemy camp must give aid and comfort to the enemy. Therefore, there should be no reporting from North Vietnam.

This is, of course, nonsense. To begin with, we have never declared war on North Vietnam, and North Vietnam has never declared war on us. In this country, a declaration of war still must come from Congress. This war, which now involves 430,000 troops and support forces, is being fought by executive decision, by a neat sidestep of the Constitution. It is all very technical if you are eating C rations in Bong Son or riding the flak over Hanoi. But Salisbury, as an American citizen, had just as much right to go to Hanoi as William Shirer had to be in Berlin in the 1930's.

The rest is more crucial and has a lot to do with the function of the press in this country. According to people like William S. White, American reporters should cease reporting if their discoveries do not serve the national interest. If United States policymakers claim that we are not killing civilians, we should not look for dead civilians. Instead, reporters should line up at the Pentagon press offices, take the press releases, and print them with a minimum of quibbling. This is known as a free press.

Now the North Vietnamese certainly did not allow Salisbury into Hanoi (with others to follow) because they are believers in a free press. Ho Chi Minh runs a Communist state, in the familiar pattern of totalitarian governments. That means his reporters line up at their government's offices, take the press releases, and print them intact. If they started acting like Salisbury, they might be taken out and shot.

But American reporters are a different breed, and it is beginning to look as if for the first time in many years—if ever—they might be affecting history. In the Dominican Republic, people like Tad Szulc of the *Times,* Dan Kurzman of the Washington *Post* and a number of others saved our national reputation. If they had not blown the whistle, we almost certainly would have General Wessin y Wessin or Tony Imbert or some other ribbon-festooned military man running the country like a plantation.

In Vietnam, the reporters are at least keeping the government relatively honest. A week ago, for example, the Saigon briefing produced a hair-raising tale in which the Vietcong lined up women and children from a small village, used them as a human shield, and caused great loss of life. Tom Buckley of the *Times* then went out to the village and discovered from American officers in the field that the official story was a lie and that South Vietnamese artillery had caused all the deaths.

The point should be this: Reporters are not cheerleaders. If they were, they would leave the trade, become press agents, and make a lot more money. More than anyone else in this country, they have the duty to police the government. No government can long function if its postures, actions, and sense of purpose become enmeshed in a tissue of half-truths, distortions, and outright lies. It does not really matter if Lyndon Johnson tells us with a straight face that his great-grandfather fought at the Alamo. It matters greatly if the same man is asking young men to die for their country in a war whose current explanation is a tragic cover for old blunders.

So it is up to reporters to tear away the cover stories. Nobody else will do it. Salisbury might have been used by the North Vietnamese propaganda machine. But if the buildings had not been bombed, if the evidence was not before his eyes, if we had not, in fact, done what the North Vietnamese claimed we had done, Salisbury would have sent back travel pieces. But he's a reporter who did his job, and for that we should all cheer.

January 24, 1967

The Bombing

Aerial bombardment for the purpose of terrorizing the civilian population, of destroying or damaging civilian property not of a military character, or of injuring non-combatants is prohibited.— Article 28, Part II of the Rules of Warfare. Adopted by the great powers, 1922 Washington Conference on the Limitation of Armaments

We've come a long way from 1922, of course. Aerial bombardment no longer involves a lot of dashing college boys, with scarves blowing in the wind, dropping hand grenades from open cockpits. It's bigger now, like everything else, and nastier, and more cowardly. A man fighting another man in the street with his bare hands must find something within himself that allows him to go on. The man in the cockpit 30,000 feet above the clouds need only avoid flak. The man in the B-52 and the man operating the SAM missile site are brothers; their problem is mathematics.

We've resumed the bombing of North Vietnam, and there is no longer any complexity to our reasons. We are bombing the North as a means of punishment. It is as simple as that. We are punishing the North.

We are not, of course, punishing Ho Chi Minh or General Giap or Pham Van Dong. They are like leaders everywhere. They plan the wars. Other people get killed in them. So we are punishing the North Vietnamese people. (If the Communists have not appropriated the phrase.) We are showing them that if they do not quit to us, we will, in the words of our beloved General LeMay, bomb them back to the Stone Age.

Perhaps Lyndon Johnson, Dean Rusk, and Robert McNamara have secret means of communication with the North Vietnamese people and that revolution against the Communists is imminent. Perhaps. I doubt it. I doubt that Lyndon Johnson understands anything about those people. Lyndon Johnson, to begin with, has never been bombed. He might feel some personal pain about the bombing, but as long as it is happening to someone else, he will sleep well nights.

There was some hope last week that something was really changing in the war situation. But domestic politics mangled it. Johnson apparently could not bear to think that Robert Kennedy might receive some credit for unfreezing communications with the North Vietnamese government. So he called in his valet, Mr. Rusk, and Mr. Rusk said that all talk of peace was wishful thinking, that there would be no Munich, that this was Czechoslovakia, and all the other useless blather that has been woven around this war like strands in a gooey cocoon. Next month another American reporter will arrive in Hanoi, and we will discover that negotiations were about to start until Rusk opened his yap, and we will moan and wonder, and drop another hundred thousand pounds on Nam Dinh.

The heart of the matter now is that the war has become simply another nagging problem, like poverty and the lack of taxicabs at 5 P.M. We don't even seem capable of revulsion anymore, and the polls tell us that the American people want more bombing, not less. A leader of courage, of course, would move against the current and inspire change; Lyndon Johnson couldn't inspire Jimmy Wechsler's dog.

The terrible thing is that we will be paying for this war for the rest of our lives. I don't mean economically, although the desperate situation of the cities and the poor will certainly not be helped. But this is the war that finished us as a nation capable of high moral posture. We are down among the street fighters now, and we can't play Lancelot to the world anymore.

I suppose the war will end some day and we will set up the Mekong Valley Authority and dispatch AID teams to North Vietnam and sell wheat to China and send cultural exchanges back and forth across the Pacific. But those people can never stop hating us. The Mexicans still hate us, and it has been more than 100 years since we burgled half their territory. And we never bombed them; we never used napalm on them; we never came on like missionaries with them. All we did was insult and rob them.

The pilots operating over Vietnam are probably brave men, and certainly have no control over what they are doing. But I wonder what it must feel like to be riding the sky, free of gravity and geography, watching the skies and the horizons change, and know that before your day's work is over you will have killed people. The people you kill are strangers. You admittedly have nothing against them. It is their cruel, despotic leaders you are against. So you are told that the only way to defeat the cruel, despotic leaders is to kill the people who have nothing to do with the war the leaders are waging. It has a beautiful logic to it, but it eludes everyone except pilots, and the people who talk to George Gallup.

The truth is that we are one of the most violent people on earth. Our heroes are western killers, mass murderers, generals, and hoods. Faced with a problem, we kill to solve it. It would be interesting for a change, though, to see us pick on someone our own size. But I suppose they don't fight that way in Texas.
February 14, 1967

Going Away

The kid's name was Johnnie, and he was seventeen years old, and in another hour he was going away. He would walk out of the second-floor apartment in Brooklyn and out of his childhood, leaving all of it behind. There would be no telephones ringing anymore, no girl's voice in the evening, no radio murmuring the news in the morning while the coffee bubbled richly and the bacon crackled on the pan. He was going away. In a couple of hours, this seventeen-year-old kid would be in the Army.

"Do you want coffee, Johnnie?" his mother said.

"Yeah, OK, coffee." He poked at the grapefruit, his handsome face tired and worn from the long farewell party the day before. There had been beer and whiskey and food and noise, and people arguing with him to stay, and some people crying, and all of it a mess. But he wasn't changing his mind. He had volunteered. He was seventeen, and he was going away.

"They think I'm crazy," he said the day before. "They don't understand."

It's always like that when you're seventeen and trying to be a man. Nobody understands being seventeen. They just stand there and look at the kid's face and remember him, six years old, playing alone on the roof of the old tenement on Seventh Avenue, with the rain running across the rooftops, making boats out of cardboard and mountains out of cork stolen from the factory across the street. They remember that and the time he started something called the Straight Shooter's Club, password "No Girls," and how excited the kid was when he first read Hemingway, a long, long time before, when he was twelve.

"They think I'm crazy, especially because I want to be a medic," the kid was saying. "But what's the use of explaining? I did everything else about the war. I marched in the antiwar parade a couple of weeks ago, and what did that get us? It didn't stop the war. All you got was a bunch of dummies calling us Communists. You can't beat them that way. You have to say you were there. You have to go. At least, being a medic, I can help save people. I won't have to kill anyone."

"You've got to serve your country," his father said.

"It's not that," the kid said. "It's something else. I can't explain it."

Now he was in the kitchen for the last time, dressed in brown corduroy pants and a denim jacket, the flight bag with the toothpaste and the shaving gear parked at the door. He was picking at the grapefruit while his mother worked at the stove, sniffling and wet-eyed. Johnnie was the fourth of her sons to go; there were two more behind him, but when the others went off, it wasn't like this. This was the sweet kid, the tender one.

"Nothing will happen to me," he said. "I won't get killed. I'm Irish."

"Right," his father said. "You've got a good education. They'll send you to a hospital somewhere. Maybe even California."

And someone remembered how the medics dashed through

the murderous scrub in that valley near Bong Son, racing for the Medevac, carrying a kid on a stretcher, and how none of the reporters would fly with them because they only went where people were dying. He remembered that and the way blood leaves a gummy film on metal and how easy it is to be killed, even if your luck gets you through the day, even if you're Irish.

"I'll write a novel about it," the kid was saying the day before. "I mean, someone has to write a great novel about this war." And you thought, yes, maybe he could, because this kid could really be a fine writer; you knew he had everything the first time he flunked plane geometry. When he flunked it the third time, you thought you had found Tolstoy.

And then you thought about his face the year he was fourteen, brown from the sun and the beach at Coney, and the way he forced himself to play football and how important he thought it was to learn how to fight and curse and smoke and how to do all the other things you seem to have to do to become a man and you could only think: To hell with the novel, to hell with literature, let the kid stay a kid.

"I've got to go, Pete," he said. "I've got to stand on my own two feet."

This was the kid who wanted to be an archaeologist in the jungles of Yucatán, who talked a lot to me about going off to Australia to work for a year on a ranch, who wanted what most kids should have and never get anymore. He wanted some adventure. He wanted to run away from home.

"Do you want me to go with you?" someone said.

"Nah, I don't want any fuss. I'll go out there alone."

"It's getting late."

"I'd better go," he said. So he stood up, the tall kid with the dark-brown vulnerable eyes, promising to write, shaking hands, bound for the Induction Center at Fort Hamilton in Bay Ridge. And his mother was really crying now, and his father was bawling, and he stood there, telling them to stop, that they couldn't do anything, because he had to go.

"I'll be all right," he said. "I'll be all right."

And then he was gone, alone, carrying that little flight bag, walking down the stairs into the gray morning, to grab a bus that would take him out of his childhood and into the big world

where people shoot each other with real guns. You must excuse me if I say the kid has more guts than most of us, but he's my brother, you see, and I've known him all his short young life.
May 9, 1967

The Killers

And so it appears, as we move into the seventies, that we have learned something about ourselves that is large and dark and final. We, all of us, sitting here in our small comforts, worrying about inflation and schools and the coming of winter, preparing for a night at the theater or a short passage with the Knicks, getting our cars repaired, swapping small talk at lunch, making Christmas lists, marrying and divorcing, wrapped in ourselves and our banalities, all of us must sleep tonight in the knowledge that we share in mass murder.

Can we look deep into those photographs by Ronald Haeberle of the Cleveland *Plain Dealer* and deny what they tell us? That girl with straight clipped bangs: She is about ten, and terrified, hiding behind a shrunken woman. In a moment, she is to be liberated forever by the guns of Americans. We don't know her name; we don't know the names of those in the other photographs, piled in a field like cordwood, and we'll never know. They were "slopeheads"; therefore, we can kill them.

One justification for the destruction of Song My is that the villages there were "unfriendly" and had been in the control of the Vietcong or the Vietminh since the 1940's. But we must remember several things: The Vietcong were the only government that many of those places had had since the Japanese left after the Second World War. And more important, the Vietcong are Vietnamese, before anything else. If the United States were to break into civil war, and 6,000,000 Chinese troops arrived to fight for one side (using the same ratio as that of American troops to South Vietnamese citizens), we would be unlikely to be friendly, especially if they seemed to spend much of their time bombing, shelling, mortaring, shooting, and burning. You cannot expect people to believe your noble intentions when you shoot ten-year-old girls to death.

Ah, but "these things happen in war." Yes, and when a stickup man shoots a grocer in the belly, we could say that those things happen in armed robberies. A guy blows his wife's head off with a shotgun; those things happen in domestic quarrels. A girl is raped and strangled; those things happen in an urban society. Lidice was one of those things that happened in a war, and we hanged people for it.

The Army will court-martial a number of people over what happened that March day at Song My. The defense will be the old one; they were acting under orders. But there will be other issues involved in that trial. Would they have killed those people so easily if they had been in Sweden? If you continually call a man a "gook" or "Charlie" or "slopehead," he is on his way to becoming an object and not a subject. He experiences no terror, no exaltation, no love; he doesn't sweat, feel hunger, suffer remorse; he doesn't care about seasons, or children, or home. He is an object who lives in a "hooch"; he is a kike, a mick, a guinea, a polack, a spic, but he isn't human, and you are free to obliterate him.

There is another issue. Can a man legitimately defend himself by saying he was "under orders" if the entire action—in this case the war itself—is illegitimate? We seem to forget that the war in Vietnam was never declared and is clearly illegal. We have something in this country called the Constitution which reserves to Congress the right to declare war. Our contract with the President uses the Constitution as its basis; every day in Vietnam, the terms of that contract are being violated.

But even worse, the contract we have with each other is being violated when something like Song My happens and we do not rise in outrage. This country was supposed to have a kind of fundamental decency at its heart, but we seem to have become at least as calloused as the Germans did. It is easier to forget it all, or blame David Brinkley for inventing it, or claim that "the liberal Communists" (to borrow the phrase of the wife of our Attorney General) were behind its exposure, or simply follow the example of the President and sit down and watch a football game.

But I hope that after this is over, we can remember some of the words of Sergeant Michael Bernhardt, who was at Song My. "We met no resistance," he said, "and I only saw three captured weapons. We had no casualties. It was just like any other Vietnamese village—old papasans, women and kids. As a matter of fact, I don't remember seeing one military-age male in the entire place, dead or alive. The only prisoner I saw was in his 50s." Were the dead members of the Vietcong? "Some of the people were not old enough to walk yet, so I couldn't see how they could be Vietcong."

But the government shouldn't get away with sentencing a handful of men and letting the others escape. The others are not those baffled young men who were conscripted and sent to Asia. The others include everybody who had anything to do with sending them there: Lyndon Johnson, Hubert Humphrey, Walt Rostow, the Bundys, and all the rest. Democrats and Republicans, from three different administrations and seven Congresses. Throw in the people who make napalm, M-16's, and the other instruments of liberation, and we might have a trial that is logical and goes after the real villains. I know just the place to hold it. It's a town called Nuremberg.

November 24, 1969

The Last Press Conference

> If the French withdraw, Indochina would become Communist-dominated within a month. The U.S. as leader of the Free World cannot afford further retreat in Asia. It is hoped that the U.S. will not have to send troops there, but if this government cannot avoid it, the Administration must face up to the situation and dispatch forces. . . . If to avoid Communist expansion in Asia and Indochina we must take the risk now by putting our boys in, I think the Executive has to take the politically unpopular decision to do it.
> —VICE PRESIDENT NIXON, *April 16, 1954*

The country might indeed be gone. There are four dead Americans on the campus of Kent State University, gunned down by other Americans. Tear gas seeps through the air of a half dozen campuses. Mass rallies are building. The Senate Foreign Relations Committee wants to go right after the executive branch and take back its constitutional power; the fear among my friends is general about a possible military coup.

From Indochina, we hear news, as we have for so long, from Peter Arnett of the Associated Press. The forces of what is laughingly referred to as the free world are moving into Cambodia, burning and shooting and destroying. Kids from Iowa are asked to distinguish between Cambodians and Vietnamese. Artillery is fired at moving human beings. The B-52's fly from our privileged sanctuaries in Thailand to churn up the earth. Here we come, Cambodia: Stick with us, and let us give you freedom. At seventeen rounds a second.

And in Washington, Richard Nixon stands on the same corrupt language that he gave us sixteen years ago. The President, we are cautioned, Has Facts That We Don't Have. One wonders: What are the facts? Have the Vietcong finally built an airplane? Has Vincent Price built them a laser beam that will drill through the earth and destroy Palo Alto? Or did we discover that those gooks, dinks, and slopes were determined to fight on and that they did not need Marx and Engels to provide them with reasons?

It is typical of a man whose closest friend is a bonds lawyer that he has no real care for language. If you can get young Americans to think of people as dinks and slopes, you can persuade them to kill those dinks and slopes. When you call campus dissenters "bums," as Nixon did the other day, you should not be surprised when they are shot through the head and the chest by national guardsmen. Nixon is as responsible for the Kent State slaughter as he and the rest of his bloodless gang of corporation men were for the anti-integration violence in Lamar and for the pillage and murder that is taking place in the name of democracy in Cambodia.

There was always this doubt about Nixon: He seemed a neuter, a man of no strong ideas or feelings, who had tried to fill his emptiness with glib anti-Communist rhetoric. His crusade against Alger Hiss always seemed to be not so much based on deep convictions as on the visibility it would give Nixon himself. He had come from obscurity, and Alger Hiss was a way to prove his own existence. Nixon lusted after power and when he got it, there were still men who refused to give him proper respect.

Some of them were Asian peasants. Others were students. Others were newspapermen, elected officials, and even members of his own party.

Now he is striking out at all of them, in the largest and grandest Last Press Conference of them all. Longhairs, Senator Aiken, Senator Fulbright, editorial writers: You won't have Richard Nixon to kick around anymore, gentlemen, after he's through with this country. If those "bums" get out of hand on the campuses, then go along with Ronald Reagan. Only a couple of weeks ago, Reagan called for a "blood bath" to solve campus disorder; well, now he has it, committed at the hands of the draft dodgers in the Guard. Nixon and Reagan: a fine pair, a fine madness.

Perhaps it is now time really to find out why Nixon visited a doctor—a shrink—during the years he spent in New York recovering from the 1962 humiliation in California. Was it his manhood, as the rumors had it? His actions since the defeat of Harrold Carswell make one wonder. Is he proving his masculinity at the expense of Asian peasants? Is he showing what a *macho* he can be by unleashing the ugliest barroom instincts in Agnew, Mitchell, national guardsmen, and the American populace? We should know, because we simply can't afford two and a half years of a President who might have those problems. We don't need therapeutic foreign policies. Not with our sons, he can't. Not with our brothers.

There are several conventional political courses which can still be followed before we end up in a state of domestic barbarism. The Senate can take the money away from the executive branch by repealing the Tonkin Gulf Resolution and by demolishing the defense budget. That won't do it all. But it might bring Nixon his senses.

If it does not, then there is one further course. Nixon can be impeached. I realize that this might leave us with Agnew. Well, then do it again to Agnew. The Congress kept Carswell out of the Supreme Court, after first keeping out Clement Haynsworth. Why not make the same kind of parlay out of Nixon and Agnew? There is no way this country can live when it has two neuters commanding power, devoid of true compassion or true ideas, dedicated to the eradication of opposition, domestic and foreign.

This country was the creation of brave men. In the past few years, we have seen our soldiers machine-gun girls and babies and old women. Some of us were insulated from that by distance or because the dead were Asians. Now the dead are Americans. At Kent State, two boys and two girls were shot to death by men unleashed by a President's slovenly rhetoric. If that's the brave new America, to hell with it.

May, 1970

The Time of Our Life

We needed a poet at Shea Stadium last night. An old one, a romantic one, a poet who could fashion tales of flight through dark woods to places where the heroes lived. He could tell about Donn Clendenon and Gary Gentry, and he would treat mightily of an old fellow craftsman like Ed Charles.

But more than that, since heroes of games are still only men, he would have to deal with the town that invented them. It was our night, a New York night, wild and sweet and riotous: a night of confetti drifting through the night air, bugles blowing from the roaring stands, firecrackers exploding like flak, streamers arcing from the upper decks in left field, middle-aged ladies with beer in buckets, hot dogs, and organ music and triumph.

He would tell about that, and tell about the people, all 56,587 of them, locked in communion, rising like a multicolored wall above the green glade, the people of New York. They were there because they knew how far they had come: from defeat and humiliation and the betrayal by the Dodgers and Giants. They had come all the way back, losers turned winners, all the way to that top of the ninth inning when all of it was put together in the largest and grandest way of all.

That was the inning when Lou Brock of the Cardinals led off with a hard smack behind second and the ball was thrown past Clendenon at first; it was not scored an error, but the throw was one for the old Mets, for Choo Choo and Elio and Marvelous Marv, for the years when nothing ever went right, when Roger Craig was losing ten games a year by one run, when nobody here could play this game. We needed that throw to remind us of where we had been, and we needed Davilillo's follow-up single to make it look close, but that was it. Vada Pinson struck out, and then Torre hit into a double play at 9:07, and then, for what seemed like hours, the place went completely insane.

The stands roared for the victory, and then a flood rushed out onto the field, racing after the vanishing Mets to the dugout, more people following, the dust of the infield churning high above them, people leaping over the boxes, and all of us following into a kind of urban Brueghel. It was as if Woodstock had been declared for the night: People dug tufts of grass from the outfield; the bases vanished; the rubber mats of the on-deck circle were pried loose; the mound was gone, the crowd in a delirium of excitement. A group of forty, mostly young, held hands and began to dance in a circle. A black man holding the stadium grass in each hand sang and cried.

This was the night to grab a homely girl and kiss her as hard as you could. It was a night for middle-aged men to kick off the gray dead accumulation of years and talk again about Cookie Lavagetto's arm or the fast ball that Branca threw to Bobby Thomson.

So our old versemaker could get all that in, and get in these three thirteen-year-olds from Rego Park named Seth Hyman, Walter Neale, and Alan Levitt, who were dancing and happy together, and mention that one of the kids was black. Tell about Rodney Johnson and Willie Gaskin, also thirteen, from the United Action team in Bed-Stuy, and how Johnson kept saying in wonder, "I stepped on a major-league field. I stepped on a major-league field." And how an old fat guy asked him if he would like to play some day on that field, and the kid said, "Don't you worry, man, we're gonna be there."

Get that in, and that strange moment in the last of the eighth inning when Gary Gentry came to bat, and the torn paper came pouring down, and beyond the paper, white in the glow of the arc lights, you could see a large flock of birds. They came over the park on the third base side, crossed high over the field, turned on the first base side, and flew back again, to disappear into the darkened sky. And some of the old guys remembered how the Dodgers were once called the Robins and the headline writers called them the Flock and how maybe you could after all believe in ghosts, and the birds were not there last night by accident.

September 25, 1969

Just Friends

It is always late at night, in some dark place where men go to deal with loneliness. The bartender is quiet and tired. Outside, a hard rain falls steadily, and there is a cop in a slick raincoat standing in a doorway across the street, watching the last tired hookers heading for the hotels. The ice clunks in the glass, the lights bubble on the Schlitz sign, a finger traces designs with coins in the wetness on the bar, and then, a woman gone, a friendship smashed, a cold bed beckoning, someone walks down the bar to the jukebox and plays Sinatra.

It was always Sinatra, because he was the special American prince who understood the terrors of the dark. It was in the songs he chose, in the dark and somber tones of his orchestrations, in the neurotic timbre of the voice itself. Sometimes the songs were celebrations, of a new girl, a bright new morning; but they were always informed by something darker, a tearing quality that led to some private place at three o'clock in the morning where you had to deal with loss and loneliness.

He was the mirror behind the whiskey bottles on the other

side of the bar, the man who was willing to explain, and in some odd way, those songs and Sinatra's singing of them became a form of consolation. Along the way he taught a couple of generations of Americans how to feel.

Now comes word that he is ending it, that Sinatra is retiring from show business and public life, and that all that he meant will be taken with him behind the doors of the house in Palm Springs. Something is wrong; it will not be the same America if Frank Sinatra will never be seen again on a public stage, with his elegance and grace, to move those of us who are strangers to him. And yet perhaps this was the only thing he could do. Some people are now asking: What's the matter with Frank Sinatra? The real question might be: What is the matter with us?

Because somewhere in the past five years, Sinatra and his America began to drift apart. Once the country had forgiven him everything: the rumors about mob links; the stupid brawls with photographers; the glasses thrown in saloons at waiters; the bodyguards; the surliness. People who move around at night understood something about all of that, knew that demons don't rise at noon, they are the snakes of midnight. It was as if Sinatra could no longer bear some terrible private pain and had to lash out, to find release, to establish contact, no matter how violent, with some other human being.

And yet there were so many other angles to his style: the generous man, moved by people who were jammed up, sending gifts, singing at benefits, calling friends to give people jobs; the Godfather, arbiter of personal disputes, father to his own children; the New Deal liberal, supporter of the Kennedys, worshiper of FDR. How could he have supported Ronald Reagan for governor of California last year? It remained a mystery, because he also raised $100,000 for John Tunney and made clear that he was still a Democrat.

And yet the Reagan Thing, as it was called, seemed to have a lot of angles in it: his disgust with the glib contempt that seemed to have become the basic style of so many of the young; the resentment of a self-educated man against people who declared universities to be the enemy; a drift into a kind of natural conservatism that comes with age. If the country could change, why couldn't Sinatra? It was as if the Reagan Thing were prelude to final withdrawal. It was even possible that, having done it, he felt ashamed of himself.

Increasingly in the past few years, there was a sense that something was becoming unravelled. He was briefly married to Mia Farrow, but she was a child; what, after all, could she possibly have understood then about the dark night of the soul? In Vegas, a casino executive knocked his teeth out, and Sinatra snarled about vengeance, but when it was over, Vegas was still there and the casino man was still alive.

He kept making films, but all the years of carelessness seemed to be catching up to him; the promise of *From Here to Eternity* and *The Man With the Golden Arm* was never kept; a Sinatra film never reached down into the darkness, the way the songs did, and after a while, people didn't go to see the films much because they had been cheated once too often. No matter what he did anywhere else, he never cheated on the songs.

And now he has asked America for a divorce or, at the very least, a separation. The best years of the relationship, the mid-fifties to the mid-sixties, were years when a lot of people were starved for belief in size; they believed in the Kennedys, and they believed in Sinatra.

In some ways he was living their lives for a lot of people, especially in cities; around the prince were the Clan, the beautiful women, the dual Ghias, Dean and Sammy and Jilly, all of them moving through Vegas, the town that Bugsy built, as if it were a private playpen. Drink all night. The best broads. Action. Sinatra, with his flinty integrity, did it all. His way. Guys dressed like him, moving through the midtown joints of Manhattan and Queens and Chicago in imitation of the prince. Only in the songs did Sinatra indicate some private knowledge that in the end he would be alone.

And yet it doesn't seem right that he should have departed this way. A statement issued from Palm Springs isn't the way to go out. This isn't Vic Damone; this is Sinatra. I wish he'd give us one for the road. In spring, in New York where it started, at Madison Square Garden now that the Paramount is gone. Just one more time let him come out on a bare stage, elegant and

96

proud, to sing the Jimmy Van Heusen songs or about Nancy with the laughing face, and give us one final chance to thank him, before he leaves forever with his style and his sorrow.
March 30, 1971

Bugsy's Dream

Las Vegas was Bugsy Siegel's dream, a private slice of the big action, and in the end it cost him most of his pretty face and all of his life. It's too bad. Bugsy would have loved the way Vegas turned out.

Because Vegas really has nothing at all to do with the sixties. This gaudy, money-obsessed town comes right out of the thirties, a grand, half-mad extravaganza dreamed up by people who had survived a depression.

It is like Bugsy himself: the Bugsy who shot his way off the Lower East Side to become a hard guy on the West Coast; that Bugsy who walked around Hollywood with George Raft, and ate dinner with Jean Harlow, and wore monogrammed silk shirts, and had a bulletproof limousine. Bugsy was one of the first gangsters who imitated art; when he showed up in Vegas during World War II, he seemed more like a contract player from Warner Brothers than a cold-blooded killer.

Bugsy's dream was to carve out a private sheikhdom in the desert, a sheikhdom where gambling, not oil, brought in the money, and whose palace would be the Flamingo Hotel. This hotel would have everything: beautiful women, men in tuxes, gambling casinos, gorgeous bars, a nightclub, a swimming pool, everything. He hired the Del Webb Construction Company to build it for him, and into it he threw every touch of grandeur he had ever seen in movies: chandeliers and marble and gold leaf and rich, thick rugs, and toilets with private sewer lines. Class. Real class. A $6,000,000 hotel! Call me Mr. Siegel, please.

There were troubles, and a false start, but three weeks after the Flamingo finally opened in 1947, the money started to roll in. Modern Las Vegas was born. Three months after the grand opening, someone shot Bugsy's face off while he was sitting on a couch in his home in Beverly Hills.

And yet today Bugsy's spirit is still everywhere.

"I wish Bugsy could of seen the Strip," an ex-fighter who works in one of the big joints told me. "I bet he didn't know what he was startin'."

So all over Las Vegas there are men in their forties and fifties, their faces too tanned, their clothes expensively gaudy, smoking cigars, making cool plays for the younger dames and acting as if nothing has ever really happened to them since they were young. They are, for example, obsessed with the word "class." That show at the Dunes has class. This singer has class. That is a very classy dame. They never stop using the word. And, after all, why should they? They come out of the thirties.

That is why Vegas strikes so many younger people as a big nothing. The shows at the big joints are baroque versions of the kind of shows that used to play at the Copa and the Latin Quarter in New York: girls, brassy no-biz-like-show-biz scores, comics, a singer who sticks to standards.

Part of the litany is the bit about the Big Bands. The Big Bands are Coming Back. Buddy Rich is at the Dunes. Harry James is back in town. Real Music. They don't seem to realize that the big bands are never coming back, that Las Vegas is merely the place where they've all gone, a kind of elephant's graveyard of old styles. In ten years, they're sure to book the Rolling Stones.

Then there is the Sinatra hang-up. It is impossible to go any-where—literally anywhere—without hearing someone talking, in deepest baritone and closest familiarity, about Frank. Frank's in Europe, no action in town. Frank was here with Dean last week. They were going to Jilly's for breakfast. Chairman of the Board, that's Frank. Frank's got class.

Sinatra might really be too fine a popular singer to turn the kids on anymore, but in Vegas it's as if he's still on that stage rising out of the Paramount orchestra pit, with Tommy Dorsey smiling coldly behind him. When the people who go to Vegas are not talking about what gangster was hit in the head by whom, they talk about Frank. They try to dress like him, they try to say things like ring-a-ding-ding (honest), and they always order Jack Daniels. Ah, well, it's one way of living the only life you'll ever have, but it will always remain a mystery to me.

There is little doubt that business in Vegas is booming, despite the airline strike. Last year's gambling receipts, before the mob guys touched a cent, were $300,000,000 and new hotel-casinos are going up everywhere. Every bus and plane brings new loads of girls trying to break into the big time, and the nickel-a-play one-armed bandits are there to accommodate the older dames who never quite made it, but stayed on anyway.

The reason Las Vegas exists, I suppose, is to provide a place for certain middle-aged people to act out fantasies. Most of them had no money when they started and, now that they do, cannot quite make it in Biarritz. But in Vegas, they can stand at the same table as a well-known murderer and crap out with as much ease. They can douse themselves with cologne, pull on silk underwear, a monogrammed shirt, and a tux, and let their money do their talking for them. Maybe, if it's a good night and the place swings, maybe Frank will come in with Mia or Dean or Sammy, and maybe he'll nod hello, and maybe then you can hit twenty-three straight passes and have Jack Entratter pat you on the back. It's a beautiful place, Vegas. Real class. It's just too bad Bugsy had the accident. He would have loved it.

August 9, 1966

Free Willie

Dear Governor Rockefeller:

We, the undersigned, feel that the time has come to let Willie Sutton out of jail. He is now sixty-eight years old and has spent thirty-seven years of his life in various prisons. He is suffering from hardening of the arteries and needs cardiovascular surgery; he might not live another year. The state parole board has turned down his latest appeal, and he cannot legally appear before another board until August, 1971. That might be too late.

We know what Willie did, but then he never made any secret

of it. He held up banks, he once said, "because that's where the money is." When asked for an occupation, he once told a judge: "It was of an illegal nature. It was bank robbing." There were times when he was less than cooperative with authorities, but this was at least based upon principle.

Willie Sutton was one of the best bank robbers who ever lived. He planned his jobs with care and precision and posed at various times as a policeman, a bank guard, a postman, and a window wiper to gain access to the banks. In his extracurricular activities he was always a gentleman, a suave dresser, an expert on psychology, Irish history and chess, and a gallant with women. He had an aversion to steam-table food, to be sure, and three times broke out of jail. And when they put him away the last time, in 1952, he was locked in Attica, that most gloomy of all New York fortresses.

We remember Arnold Schuster, too. This young man turned in Willie Sutton in 1952 and—eighteen days later—was murdered on a Brooklyn street. This vicious act, according to Joe Valachi, was committed at the whim of Albert Anastasia. Willie Sutton knew nothing about it. In all the years he spent sticking up banks, he never once committed an act of violence. He carried guns, but they were more props than anything else. In fact, when he was arrested for the last time, Brooklyn detectives spent an hour with him before discovering that he was carrying a .32-caliber automatic. There is no known record of violent activity by Willie while he has been in jail.

The point is this: Willie Sutton has paid for his crimes with most of the years of his adult life. He is now an old man. If he were set free, there is little chance that he would stroll into Chase Manhattan with a pistol looking for some walking-around money; if anything, the lecture circuit would provide him all the money he would ever need; you might even make him a consultant to the poverty program, since nobody knows more about the instinct toward larceny than Willie Sutton.

If state prisons are anything, they must be institutions which go beyond punishment. There is much lip service to this concept these days; acknowledging that this man had paid for his crimes would be a chance to show it. If Willie Sutton had been a GE board member or a former water commissioner, instead of the son of an Irish blacksmith, he would be on the street now. There are some of us today, looking at the mortgage interest rates, who feel that it is the banks that are sticking up us.

This is frankly an appeal for mercy and human feeling. Willie Sutton should be able to sit and watch the ducks in Prospect Park one more time, or go to Nathan's for a hot dog, or call up some old girl for a drink. As governor, you have the right to overturn the decision of the parole board. Letting Willie out won't gain you a vote, but it would be a hell of a thing if the old bank robber could take a look at the Christmas tree in Rockefeller Center for one last time.

Respectfully yours, The Free Willie Sutton Committee. (John Scanlon, Charles Monaghan, Joe Flaherty, Joel Oppenheimer, Pete Hamill. In formation.)
December 23, 1969

No Sad Songs

Mendel Rivers will be safely tucked into the earth today, accompanied by the usual gushy salutes and the familiar lying rhetoric of death. There is a convention, rigidly adhered to by politicians and editorial writers, that says one must speak only about the nobility and goodness of the dead, no matter how rotten, dangerous, or disgusting they were in the flesh; it's as if death and its attendant mysteries could suddenly cleanse a man's history.

Richard Nixon's eulogy of Rivers is a masterpiece of the genre and seems taken from unused drafts of his celebration of Everett Dirksen, on the occasion of that old fake's demise. "I have lost a friend," Nixon tells us. ". . . South Carolina has lost one of the most distinguished men in her history and America has lost a patriot." In two sentences Nixon thus manages to demolish all previous ideas of human friendship, genuine distinction and true patriotism.

The truth was that Rivers was a common drunk and a nasty,

willful, power-dazed man who obtained great power in Washington because of the vile anachronism of the seniority system. As chairman of the House Armed Services Committee, he knelt before the admirals, generals, and defense contractors for more than five years. He was such a great patriot that he managed to avoid military service through all his sixty-five years.

But it was Rivers' sense of his personal mission that was the worst thing about his tenure. He once told his fellow Representatives that his committee was "the only voice, the official voice, that the military has in the House of Representatives." Even granting that Rivers might have been half in the bag, this was an astonishing description of the committee's function. Representatives are elected by civilians to represent civilians; under our system of government the military is controlled by civilians; and for a civilian like Rivers to say that a committee of the legislative branch is a mere press agent for a section of the executive branch is to say that the Constitution is dishwater.

Under Rivers, no questions of importance were ever asked of the military. In fact, it was while he was chairman that the military moved more strongly than ever before toward becoming a separate national entity, not answerable to civilians, like the army in a banana republic. If Rivers had been scrutinizing the military, instead of blowing kazoos at its parades, there would have been no military "intelligence" units gathering information about American civilians, their loyalty or lack of it. We found out about that little caper without Rivers' help; God knows what else is going on deep in the Pentagon, among those people who refer to the Washington *Post* as *Pravda* and the New York *Times* as *Izvestia.*

Rivers gained personal rewards from his position, although most were ceremonial rather than financial. There were hundreds of foreign junkets paid for by us. And the Air Force would fly him home to Charleston, at taxpayers' expense, whenever he cared to go. But the best of all was for Rivers to sit around with his cronies, belting down the sauce, saying things like: "I've made a lot of millionaires in my time, and I'm going to make a lot more."

A lot of that kind of money went to the Congressional district which elected him to sixteen straight terms. Visiting Charleston today is like flying into one of Ron Cobb's cartoons of the Pentagon: Jets scream through the air every five minutes; civilians salute each other; highways are marked with as many military installations as there are Stuckey signs. In the three-county Charleston area, employes at military installations will earn $329,600,000 this year—almost 35 percent of the area's buying power. No wonder they named a highway after Ole Mendel.

But the people who really loved Rivers were all those sleek generals and admirals, all those procurement officers who bought tons of military junk from arms manufacturers and retired the following year to go to work for the people they'd just rewarded with contracts. Rivers never questioned any of this; after all, it was all to make America the toughest honcho in the saloon.

Rivers is now supposed to be succeeded by Representative F. Edward Hebert (D-La.), at sixty-nine another aging hero; he says that we would have won in Vietnam five years ago if those damn civilians had only let the military do what Hebert and Rivers had suggested: Kill everybody. In other words, he is another agent of the military, taking over a committee whose basic function should be to police the military. It's as if David Rockefeller became chairman of a banking committee. If there were ever a case for destroying the seniority system, this is it. Meanwhile, there should be no sad songs for the passing of Mendel Rivers. He's gone, and we're better off without him.
December 30, 1970

A Death in the Family

Nobody really knew very much about Billy Donnelly, except the people who loved him. I used to see him around with my brother Brian, laughing at the bar in a place called McCauley's on Tenth Avenue and Sixteenth Street, in Brooklyn, a good-looking, well-built kid with blond hair and a quiet style, groping his way, as we all do, toward becoming a man. He had just about made it when, early Monday morning, he died. He was twenty-five.

He wrote no novels, composed no symphonies, built no grand buildings; but to his friends, his death was quite large and quite final. He grew up on Twelfth Street, between Sixth and Seventh avenues, next to the old garage where we used to store the wood for the great Election Day bonfires. From the window of 396 Twelfth Street, he could see the sewer that served as home plate for the stickball court, and like all kids in that neighborhood, he grew up with a dream of play. He was a southpaw and one of the great hitters, and that was no small thing on Twelfth Street.

His closest friends were Donald O'Connor, Tommy Lenahan, and my brother Brian. They remember odd things about him now: how there were always chocolate chip cookies in his house; how he had a boxer dog named Randy that they all used to torment; how they would sit through summer evenings on the stoop in front of the Aladdin Carpet cleaners singing their version of "In the Still of the Night" until even the drunks from Unbeatable Joe's saloon complained. They also remember how, for the first time, they started to go away: Billy Donnelly to the Marines, Donald O'Connor to the Navy, Brian to college, Tommy Lenahan into marriage.

I remember one afternoon about five years ago on the island of Vieques, off the coast of Puerto Rico. José Torres was the light-heavyweight champion then, and he went over to Vieques to box an exhibition for the Marines stationed there. I went with him, and when Joe stepped out into the glare, someone started whistling and yelling louder than anyone else, and it was Billy Donnelly. Later we took him with us to the officers' mess, and he seemed embarrassed, locked into the rigidity of the Marine Corps. He seemed like a very young kid that night, and a few weeks later he was in Vietnam.

In Nam, he was stationed somewhere near Da Nang, and every month or so, the letters would come back to Donald O'Connor and Tommy Lenahan and my brother. The letters were filled with a kind of stunned alarm; they weren't political;

they were just a young man reacting to death and killing and maiming that he really had nothing to do with. He came out of it intact, after a bout with malaria, and when he got home, they all went drinking together, with their lives apparently spread out before them. If you are in your early twenties and have made it through a war, everything seems possible.

They all went through some boisterous years after that: They went to Woodstock, they marched in antiwar demonstrations, but most of all, they enjoyed each other. I remember a night in McCauley's, with all of them there, when someone threw a glass of water on Billy and Billy threw a glass back, and then someone poured a pitcher of water on Billy, and he stripped to his waist, and then water was everywhere, glasses, pitchers, barrels, while the bartender threw his hands in the air, and nobody ever got mad. It was a mad night to me; ordinary to them.

Then last April, Billy married a pretty girl with a great smile named Marie Italiano from DeGraw Street. They were married in St. Augustine's Catholic Church, with Donald O'Connor as best man and Billy shaking and nervous. Afterward they all went out to a reception at a place called Lisa Terrace on Flatlands Avenue. After the singing and the laughter, the boys went back to the neighborhood, and it was time for Billy to go to work on the rest of his life.

He was working on Wall Street and had moved into a new apartment out near Bay Parkway, and his life seemed finally to have settled. Then, a couple of months ago, he began having stomach pains. He mentioned it a few times and someone said it must be ulcers, and someone else said he should go to see a doctor, and for a while, he shrugged it off; young men have a way of believing that their bodies are indestructible.

Then, about five weeks ago, he finally checked into the Methodist Hospital. They opened him up. When his friends came to visit him, he told them it was his appendix, because that was what he thought it was. His father's grave face said it was something darker.

About three weeks ago, my brother Brian told me that Billy Donnelly had cancer. It's something that always happens to someone's aunt, or to some ancient statesman in the newspa-

pers, or to girls in fairy tale movies. It doesn't happen to your
friends. It doesn't really happen to someone who is twenty-five.
Not here. Not in the real world.

But it had happened all right. Big Casino. And Tommy Lenahan and Donald O'Connor and Brian went around to see him,
as the hard young body began to be eaten away, arriving with
tales of laughter and golden times, with Billy still laughing his
great laugh, until finally they were not allowed to visit him anymore. There was nothing more his friends could do except wait
for the phone call.

Last Sunday night, Marie Donnelly went to see her husband
for the last time. She told him that she was two months pregnant and the ex-Marine, the three-sewer hitter, the kid with the
great smile, struggled up from the bed to embrace her and tell
her how happy he was and what a fine child it would be. A few
hours later he was dead.

They waked him at Lyman's Funeral Parlor at Fourth Avenue and Thirteenth Street. Donald, Tommy, and Brian were
there, but there really isn't much you can say when there's a
death in that special family called friendship. They stayed as
long as they could and then went across the street to a bar
called Tom's, to drink awhile, filled with the knowledge that
their friend was forever gone and that they would never again
be able to think of themselves as young.

February 18, 1971

Requiem for a Revolutionary

The revolutionary that I remember from my childhood impressions walked with a .45 pistol in his waistband, and wanted to live
on his reputation. He had to be feared. He was capable of killing
anyone. He came to the offices of the high functionaries with the
air of a man who had to be heard. And in reality, one asked oneself, where was the revolution that these people made? Because
there was no revolution, and there were very few revolutionaries.
—FIDEL CASTRO, 1960

All evening long, the slick black limousines pulled up before the Bolivian Embassy on Massachusetts Avenue, dropping off the elegant passengers and vanishing again into the tame drizzle. Inside those doors lay the tinkling world of Washington receptions. The guests were from the approved list—part of the furniture of diplomacy and money, as familiar as the silent waiters, the sound of ice clunking dully in whiskey glasses, the muted talk, the rich bindings on the books, the feel of polished wood and oiled banisters. It had nothing at all to do with a man carrying a gun through jungles, cut off and beyond salvation, being hunted down and killed like a rabid dog. It seemed to have nothing at all to do with the death of Che Guevara.

And yet it had everything to do with it. While those guests of the Bolivian ambassador were drinking and chatting and looking over the new wife of the governor of Puerto Rico, Bolivian Army soldiers in a remote mountain town called Villa Grande were guarding what was left of Che Guevara. Castro was right: There were indeed very few revolutionaries. But Guevara was one of them, and now he is almost certainly dead. Almost as dead as the Cuban revolution. The Bolivian government can relax.

Che was gunned down by the troops of the country whose per capita income is $100 a year, where life expectancy in the central plateau is thirty-two years, where in some parts of the country two-thirds of all children die before the age of two. The soldiers who hunted him down are fed on sixteen cents a day as privates, which gives them bread and coffee for breakfast and a bowl of soup in the afternoon and nothing else. No wonder there was a sense of quiet exultation at the Bolivian Embassy reception. No bearded wild men would ever dirty those thick carpets with their muddy boots.

Che Guevara was a Communist, of course, and he helped his friend Fidel turn Cuba into a dreary Russian colony. Yet of all those brave and erratic young men who made and then betrayed the Cuban revolution he was the best. It was Che Guevara who wanted to stand and fight to the death after the yacht *Granma* landed in Cuba on December 2, 1956, with Fidel and eighty other men on board. An Argentine citizen, part Spanish, part Irish, Guevara stood on Cuban soil that day with a machine gun chattering in his hands as Batista's troops moved in. He was wounded in the neck before being carried off by another guerrilla to the Sierra Maestra to make the revolution.

In the Sierra Maestra, it was Guevara who built the bakeries so Fidel's soldiers would have fresh bread. It was Guevara who opened a school to teach peasants how to read and write and then read to his men from the work of Cervantes, Robert Louis Stevenson and the Chilean poet Pablo Neruda. It was Guevara who led the armed column down from the mountains, through a fierce barrage from Batista's fighter planes, machine guns and tanks, to take the town of Santa Clara, cutting Cuba in half and sending Batista to exile.

He was a superb guerrilla fighter, a brave man, and one of the few Communists ever to come equipped with a sense of irony or humor. He used to tell the story of the day Fidel ended a cabinet meeting by saying, "By the way, I had to fire the head of the National Bank today. Anybody here an economist?" Che shouted, "I am, Chief." "All right," said Castro, "you're president of the bank." After the meeting, Castro stayed behind to talk to Che. "Say," he said, "I never knew you were an economist." Guevara was shocked. "Economist!" he said. "I thought you said Communist!"

Guevara did not like Americans very much, and his reasons were only partially ideological (his grandmother was a girl from California.) He was in Guatemala City in 1954 when the CIA overthrew the elected government of leftist President Jacobo Arbenz by force and violence (F-47's with U.S. pilots strafed and bombed Guatemala City). In Cuba, where American investors owned one-third of the largest crop (sugar), he and Fidel were fighting an army equipped with American planes, tanks, mortars, guns, and ammunition.

So it was no surprise that he was tracked down last weekend by Bolivian rangers who had been trained in counterinsurgency by a sixteen-man team of U.S. Green Berets. Bolivia has received more than $400,000,000 in U.S. aid in the last decade; its president is an air force general named René Barrientos Ortuño, who proudly wears U.S. Air Force wings, earned at Randolph Field, Texas, and Enid, Oklahoma. Barrientos became president in a military coup in 1964; naturally, we support him. Bolivia seemed a perfect place for a guerrilla with a sense of the enemy, who had grown bored with the routine of peace.

And yet none of it worked out the way it should have for Che Guevara. Che was the great champion of peasant participation in revolution, yet the Bolivian peasants betrayed him to the army. Guevara believed in slow, careful preparation for revolution, yet seven months after arriving in Bolivia he was already fighting and losing. And now he's dead.

Yet one cannot rejoice. A few years ago, Barnard Collier visited Fidel Castro at the old Castro family farm in Cuba. On one wall there was a montage of the four most important figures of the Cuban revolution. Beneath each photo there was a playing card. Under Fidel, the ace of spades. Under his brother Raul, the ace of hearts. Under Camilo Cienfuegos, the ace of diamonds. Under Guevara, the ace of clubs. Nobody explained the significance of the cards.

Now Fidel Castro is alone. Camilo Cienfuegos is dead; some say he was thrown from a plane into the Caribbean. Raul Castro has not been heard from in months. And the ace of clubs lies high in the Andes, which he once said would be the Sierra Maestra of the Americas. Fidel Castro holds an empty hand, and the old gaudy promise of the early days of his revolution has been ruined beyond repair.

And yet . . .

And yet, why did some of us feel so badly when the news about Che first came over the wires? The last revolutionary was finally dead. We would never again see that fine, ironic, mocking smile and his tense, bold swagger. And the terrible thing was that his death did not teach Bolivian children to read. It did not give them shoes. It did not send Indians to the universities. It had no meaning at all, which was its real tragedy. Ola, Guevara: You were my enemy, but you were the only Communist I ever liked, and you were never a corrupt thug. I'm glad you died, as they used to say, with your boots on. *Vaya con Dios,* soldier. Go with God.

October 12, 1967

Murrow

I remember . . . the big raid of December twenty-ninth when the city burned, and as I walked home at seven in the morning the windows in the West End were red with reflected fire and the raindrops were like blood on the panes. That was the Christmas you sang carols in the shelters. And you were living a life, not an apology.

That, of course, was Edward R. Murrow. The year was 1946. He was saying good-bye for a while to the people he loved more than any other on earth, except his own, and in that year after the war, the future was spread out before him. Murrow had told us one thing: that you can call the British decadent, middle-class, or, as so many did, a nation of shopkeepers. But you must always give them one thing. You must always give them 1940.

And so today, when you look at TV or listen to radio, and your instincts tell you to curse them for their shabbiness, their commercialism, and their timidity, you must also give them their one thing, too. You must always give them Murrow.

Edward R. Murrow improved radio the day he showed up, and he practically single-handedly invented TV news broadcasting. There are some of us who simply have never accepted the fact that when we turn on Channel 2 at night, we will never see that long, somber face again, never see those bushy brows or that brooding, melancholy strain of exhaustion just below the handsome surface or hear that textured roughage in the voice.

He has been dead eighteen months, and he was gone for almost five years before that. When he came into broadcasting in the thirties, he was one of the brilliant young men who were creating a medium. He ran the European bureau and hired people like Charles Collingwood and William L. Shirer and Larry LeSueur and Richard Hottelet and Eric Sevareid; this was a crew of reporters, not announcers, and Murrow and William

Paley set them loose. They chased Hitler and Mussolini around a continent, telling America that war was coming. And when war did come, they put on helmets and fatigues or, as Murrow did, flying suits, and went off to cover the killing.

No one ever covered a war better, and if you doubt me, go out to a record store this afternoon and pick up a copy of a Columbia album called *Edward R. Murrow. A Reporter Remembers. Volume One: The War Years.*

It's all there: the evacuation of children from London, the air raids, Churchill, Dunkirk, Christmas in 1940, North Africa, the arrival of the Americans, D Day, the march into Germany, the obscenity of Buchenwald, V-E Day in Piccadilly Circus. And Murrow is reporting it; from rooftops in blazing London, from the sidewalks and bunkers, from the site of the ghastly camp midst the ruined bodies and the stench of death.

There was more to Murrow than that, of course. He took on Joe McCarthy when only a few lonely voices (including this newspaper) possessed the courage to do so. He took on McCarthy not because he was an especially flaming liberal, or even because he was so much a champion of civil liberties. More than anything else, he challenged, and eventually helped destroy McCarthy, because he believed this was a country built on due process of the law.

"I believe that I have learned the most important thing that has happened in Britain during the last six years," he said in that farewell broadcast. "It was not, I think, the demonstration of physical courage. That has been a cheap commodity in this war. Many people of many nations were brave under the bombs. I doubt that the most important thing was Dunkirk or the Battle of Britain, El Alamein, or Stalingrad, nor even the landings in Normandy or the great blows struck by the British and American bombers. . . . I am persuaded that the most important thing that happened in Britain was that this nation chose to win or lose this war under the established rules of parliamentary procedure. . . . It feared Nazism, but did not choose to imitate it. . . . Do you remember that while London was being bombed in the daylight, the House devoted two days to discussing conditions under which enemy aliens were de-

111

tained on the Isle of Man? Do you remember that two days after Italy declared war, an Italian citizen, convicted of murder in the lower courts, appealed successfully to the highest court in the land, and the original verdict was set aside? There was still law in the land. . . ."

In New York, Murrow remained an independent operator. When someone else at CBS fired a friend of his, Murrow would put him on his own payroll. When the hallways and corridors began their long relentless capitulation to the networks' vice-presidents, the affiliates, and the sponsors, Murrow insisted on the right to be independent. He was cut down, of course, because TV is not a place for free spirts anymore, and when he moved on to the USIA when John Kennedy called him, he must have known the future at CBS was already behind him.

And yet it is difficult to believe that the country could not have used him better and honored him more. He was smoking his cursed cigarettes almost to the end, and they cut one lung out of him and took a piece of another, and still you hoped he would make it. How we could have used him now. Murrow lived a life, not an apology. But he's dead. We must make do with what we have.

As for me, I never knew him. But there was this radio in the house on Thirteenth Street, next to the factory in Brooklyn, and you had to hold a frayed strip of wire in the back to hear anything, and what you heard in the evenings was Murrow. It was the voice on the album, and if you've never heard him, at least give him a chance.

"*This* . . . is London," it begins. . . .

December 3, 1966

El Men

A tall blonde in a red sweater walked up the side aisle, and three guys stood up to look her over. Somewhere on the left an infant wailed, and behind us a mother smacked a kid loudly across the face and told him to stop asking for a soda or she would break his rotten little neck. The special cop under the glowing red exit sign yawned. It was just another night at the Jefferson.

The Jefferson Theater is on Fourteenth Street, sandwiched between a villainous-looking saloon and a couple of orange juice stands, and for my money, it's the greatest movie house in America. The whole show is in Spanish, but it doesn't really matter. Two hours in the Jefferson and you forget wars, Communists, napalm, Sargent Shriver, and daytime television. It's out of sight.

To begin with, you have the movies. They are all terrible. They are so terrible that sometimes you can't get into the place, even when the movies are playing for the third time around. They run a lot of spy movies and murder movies, like the rest of the movie business. But they have other things too. There is for example the Estella Dallas genre. This usually involves an old item, played by Libertad Lamarque, who has fallen on evil days. In her youth, she was a great singer and beauty, but ended up doing piggy things with some mustached bounder and the result was little Jorge. Now it is like twenty years later, and Jorge is singing at La Scala. She hasn't seen him since he was two.

"Hijo mio," she says, standing in the snow outside the opera house, staring at the billboard. "My son, my son." She's tap city and can't make it to the kid's debut. Then, from out of the raging storm, a Cadillac pulls up.

It's the mustached bounder, played by Arturo de Cordova, and somewhere in the wreckage of Estella Dallas, he spots the young girl he once ruined. Their eyes meet. The old dolls in the audience start to sob quietly. He slips her a fin; she stuffs a Playbill into her shoes and goes in.

Meanwhile, Jorge has a case of the opening night glaums. When it's his big moment, time for a solo, he falters. And then Estella stands up, starts singing something like "Adios, Pampa Mia," the kid hears his mother's voice for the first time in like eighteen years, and he starts belting them dead with his voice. He comes down off the stage, and he and his mother embrace. The audience is wasted. Women are on the floor, soaked in tears. Kids are hugging their mothers. Young guys are promising their girls they wouldn't do anything like that rat Arturo de Cordova. It's all beautiful.

Then comes the stage show. And if you're lucky, the way I was the other night, the star will be a guy named Johnny El Men. Johnny El Men's real name is Miguel Angel Alvarez, and he is to New York's Puerto Ricans what Cantinflas is to the Mexicans. The character he plays is a con man and hustler in a gold vest, wearing a practically brimless hat, carrying an umbrella.

"This guy has learned what every Puerto Rican learns two weeks after he gets here, man," Johnny El Men said. We were sitting backstage. A gorgeous Mexican singer named Lucha Villa was sharing some birthday cake with the Lucha Villa Fan Club. A dozen *mariachis* were standing under the no smoking signs, smoking. "This guy has learned how to survive."

Johnny El Men survives through guile and con, but there is no malice in him. He is a true New York Puerto Rican, and he speaks the language people talk after they've been here awhile. This is what the purists call Espingles. "*Abre el* window," he says. "*Me voy al rufo* . . . *Vamanos, chica, al* nightclub and we'll have a good time, *entiende,* baby?

"Puerto Ricans laugh at their problems because they don't have any choice," Johnny El Men says. "I can do bits about welfare or the airplane, and they laugh like hell. They laugh at themselves. You know, when I start talking half English, half Spanish, they laugh because they know that's what's happening to them. They're half New Yorkers and half Puerto Ricans, and they know it."

A lot of Johnny El Men's jokes can't be printed, but you have to see him work. The eyebrows arch; the eyeballs roll; the comedy is broad and wild. The other night, he went through a bit with a straight man whose wife walks in her sleep. The straight man says that if you wake up the wife, she'll die, so you have to give her everything she wants while she's sleeping. She starts going through Johnny El Men's coat pockets. The first thing she takes out is a chicken. A whole chicken.

"Hey, that's my lunch for a week, man," he yells. She goes off with the chicken. She comes back, reaches into his coat pocket

114

again, and comes out with a roll of toilet paper. Of course. Then she takes his coat and ends up with his pants. His shorts are covered with patches, and the audience breaks up.

"You know, we only got a few things we can laugh about," Johnny El Men was saying. "We can laugh at sex, because we know that it's really funny. We can laugh at pretensions—the worn-out drawers under the pressed pants—because everyone has to have their front. The poor gotta have laughs, man, or they die."

Out front, the audience was falling on the floor over a midget *mariachi* player. It didn't seem like winter in New York.
January 31, 1967

El Barrio: The Line

The line was drawn in heavy white chalk, moving erratically through the bits of smashed glass and the flattened beer cans, and it said almost everything you had to know about the small war in East Harlem. There was a kid with a white dress shirt standing on the line, shouting at us, and pointing at the words.

"Puerto Rican border," it said. "Do not cross, flatfoot."

That was all of it: We have become a nation of borders, and the kids on the street knew it, and the cops knew it, and the people on the other side of the border knew it most of all. There were thousands of cops in East Harlem last night, doing their best to keep the violence contained. They didn't want it to spill south of 96th Street, where the people with long black limousines and fancy rents and credit cards live. They wanted it bottled up. Before the night was over, they would discover that it would be no easy thing.

"You stay over that side," the kid in the dress shirt yelled. "You stay there. This is ours over here. This is ours. We're taking it."

The line was drawn across Third Avenue between 110th and 111th streets, and on the other side of the line, at the corner of

111th Street, across from the Gulf station, there was a crowd of 1,000 listening to a short, dark-skinned kid with wavy hair who was standing up on an overturned garbage can.

"Where is Lindsay?" he was shouting through a bullhorn, while cops peered at the line of the roofs and kids played with glass in the gutters. "He said he would be here. He said he would come up here. Where is he? Where is Lindsay? It's the same old bull——! He promised, and he broke the promise. Why didn't he keep his promise? Why? Why?"

The crowd was made up of young kids in colored T-shirts, loose-fitting sport shirts, pipe-stem trousers, and it was a crowd in a different mood from Sunday night. There was nothing of a violent fiesta to these kids. They were seething, ready to be unleashed, and some people were trying very hard to unleash them.

"The only way we gonna get any respect is to break this place into little pieces," the kid with the bullhorn said. "Let's go!"

The kid threw a bottle at the gas station and jumped off the overturned trash can, and that was that. It had started, as we knew it would start, and within the hour the violence had spread all over *El Barrio.* Bottles flew through the air, as if fired from mortars. The first Molotov cocktail came scudding from a doorway, breaking into a splashy orange trail like napalm. It was to be a bloody evening, and death was moving down those littered streets.

In a minute, there was a mob, part of it moving north to 112th Street, part of it breaking and rushing down 111th Street, others massing behind a mustached kid carrying a Puerto Rican flag. About six kids smashed out the windows of the Gulf station and tried to pull over the gasoline pumps out front. Smoke rose into the darkened sky from piles of burning garbage. A young girl ran, tripped, and fell on her face in a pile of broken glass.

There were Puerto Ricans frightened of the mob, too, and they ran into doorways as its southern end moved on 110th Street. Bottles rose in high arcs from the mob. Cherry bombs came down from the windows of the tenements, popping and exploding. A dozen kids tried to stove in the plywood boarding across the front of the A&P. There were more cherry bombs and then pistol shots. On this night, someone was sure to get killed.

"How many men do you have?" said Chief Inspector Sanford Garelik, wearing a white safety helmet and dark suit. An aide walked with him. "Where are they? Bring them up quick."

Dark-green police buses pulled into the side streets, and lines of uniformed men piled out and started edging down the avenue. More bottles flew from the darkness, and someone on 109th Street heaved a garbage can from a rooftop. The cops charged across the street. A kid in a pink shirt walking with his mother was caught in the club-swinging assault in front of the JAE Furniture Store.

"Get moving!" a young cop shouted.

"What's going on?" the kid said. "I didn't do nothing."

"Just move it," the cop said. "We gotta get this place cleared."

The kid's mother, a short stunted woman in a wrinkled yellow skirt, was crying, terrorized. The cops helped the woman and her son down the block to the safety of a doorway.

"Come on in here, mother," someone shouted from the dark alley of 109th Street. "Come and get it, flatfoot. Come on, come on."

It was like that all through the night, all over East Harlem. Everywhere you went last night and this morning there were sudden scenes of violence, threats, the language of desperation.

At Third Avenue and 103d Street, there was the burned-out shell of an ABC-TV car which a mob had overturned and set on fire. Store windows were broken.

In one sleazy furniture store on Third Avenue, someone had deposited a garbage can, an act of esthetic comment more than anything else.

Away down the avenues you could see a blaze rising furiously against the night sky, and hear the scream of fire engines and snapping of small-arms fire. The cowardly bums who shoot at firemen were bringing their talents to this long night's journey into day, and there was no way at all to bring any understanding or pity to them. People who shoot firemen in the back are beyond redemption.

"It's terrible, it's terrible," said an old man named Julio Montanez who has lived in *El Barrio* for thirty-one years. "I can't believe it. I don't want to believe it. They are destroying every-thing. They are destroying everything we worked so hard for in this city. People were changing about Puerto Ricans. We were getting jobs; our kids going to colleges. *El Barrio* is no place to live very nice, but this won't help."

But the kids were beyond persuasion. All through the violent evening, José Torres, the former light-heavyweight champion, moved around the neighborhood, trying to talk to the hard-eyed young kids who were doing most of the damage.

"They really think they are doing something," Torres said. "And once they get that in their head you can't stop them. One kid said: 'I'm doing this to help all the Puerto Ricans.' The place was wrecked, and I said it seemed a stupid way to help Puerto Ricans. He said the colored people don't get anything until they commit violence. So the Puerto Ricans wouldn't get anything unless they commit violence, too."

At one point Torres was talking to a number of kids on a stoop on 111th Street when cops came piling down the street. One cop slammed a kid on the head with a pistol butt, and the pistol discharged. "That's the kind of thing that just causes more trouble." Torres said. "If the bullet hit someone and killed him, they would have stomped the cop to death."

On 112th Street between Second and Third the street was a battlefield. There were twenty-one trash cans stretched across the street and garbage littered everywhere. Halfway down the block, a group of people sat on the stoop of 226, staring at the rubble, watching the police at either end of the block and point-ing at the spot in front of Our Lady Queen of Angels school where a kid had been shot down earlier in the evening.

The people were talking about police brutality, and there was little doubt that some cops had really gone to work on people without specific provocation. Garelik and the police brass had tried almost desperately to keep the men under control, but per-son after person brought up specific cases. This, after all, was not a race riot; it was a fight between the police and the people of East Harlem.

Torres was talking to people on 112th Street, where the heaviest fighting of the night took place, when a police car, No. 1816, came by slowly, making crunching sounds as it rolled over beer cans and litter and bulling its way through the overturned garbage cans. A cop in the front seat trained his pistol on us and shouted, "All right, throw the first bottle."

It was needless and stupid, and one kid reached into a trash can for a bottle.

"No, no, don't," Torres said. He took the bottle from the kid. "That won't solve anything." Then, a few minutes later, a line of TPF troops started moving into the block in single files on each side of the street. There was no noise, no bottle throwing, no obscenity. Yet they were walking in there like a search-and-destroy mission going out to draw fire from the Vietcong.

Torres and a young politician named Joe Erazo walked down to meet them. They persuaded the TPF leader to keep the men on the other side of the street. Then they came back and warned everybody on the stoops to let it pass, that it meant nothing. This time nobody threw anything. If they had, people would have been killed.

"This is some crap," said a young man named Miguel Neves, who was discharged from the Navy three months ago. "I spend four years serving my country, and I come back to this crap? Look at this place. Just look. And what about those guys in Vietnam? They are over there fighting for a bunch of bastards who hate our goddamn guts, and over here we are treated like animals. What is this? This is crazy, that's what it is. This whole country is crazy."

Cruising the area, it certainly sounded like that. The Puerto Ricans are people who came here to work, who have opened more than 5,000 small businesses in this city in the last ten years, who would almost certainly rather live in a place where the sun is warm in winter than in the frigid prison of a slum. They have never really rioted until now. But the old rules are going. The old structures are disintegrating.

At 102d and Lexington at one fifteen, a dozen police cars roared up and men with helmets and the police equivalent of flak jackets jumped out.

"They got a machine gun up there," one of the cops yelled.

Then blam-blam-blam-blam—the shots crashed out. The cops were aiming at some shadow on the roof, and then it was suddenly over.

"This is a war, Pete," Torres said very softly. "It's a war."

For people like him, who had spent two evenings trying to get people to stop killing each other, that was a statement made in sorrow, and you knew that he had finally come to believe that there was no longer a solution, except in further killing. God help us all.

July 25, 1967

El Presidente

The room was long and crowded, filled with cigar smoke and the smell of cologne. Three uniformed men with pistols on their hips stood at the door. A central casting Latin American secret agent stood under a bad patriotic painting, the bulge of an automatic showing under his white suit. It smelled of red plush and corruption. We were all waiting to see Joaquín Balaguer . . . the president of the republic.

"Only one way to treat these students," said a narrow, yellow-faced man, lighting a cigar with a gleaming Ronson lighter and making short chopping motions with his right hand. "Bap-bap-bap. . . ."

"I'm building these houses, just like in Puerto Rico," the little man with the green eyeglasses explained. "Chase Manhattan is putting up most of the money and the government the rest. It's like a Dominican FHA. . . ."

The talk moved on. At the far end of the room, a guard stood before the first of two opaque glass doors leading to the president's office. It looked like the waiting room in U.S. Grant's White House.

The president was very busy. Wherever we talked to businessmen and members of the middle class, they talked a lot about how hard Joaquín Balaguer works. He arrives at eight in the morning and leaves at ten at night. He handles every detail of government himself. It was now seven thirty and we had been waiting two and a half hours.

Balaguer was talked of with contempt in all the poorer districts in Santo Domingo, and with a certain fondness elsewhere. He is a slippery man, who has learned how to survive. He is a professor, writer, lawyer, and historian, who once served Rafael Trujillo with fidelity. He was vice-president under the old murderer and in 1960 became president to lend respectability to the regime, which had been isolated by the OAS. He was president in 1961, when Trujillo was assassinated, and did not protest when the dictator's son, Ramfis, went on an orgy of murder and torture before stealing $70,000,000 from the national treasury.

Balaguer did respond to pressure from President Kennedy after Ramfis' departure and ordered Trujillo's brothers, Hector and José, out of the country before they could grab what few dollars were left. As head of a seven-man council of state, Balaguer turned demagogue, handing out Trujillo properties to workers and peasants and buying taxicabs with government money to hand out to cabdrivers. This only saved him temporarily: He was thrown out of the country in 1962 and did not return until last year, when he ran for president and won.

Now he was in his office, as the parade of visitors came in and out in a steady procession.

At nine thirty we were ushered in. I was with José Torres, the former light-heavyweight champion, who is writing a series of articles for the Spanish paper *El Tiempo.* A uniformed colonel stopped us, heavy with menace in a comic way. His name was Nival Seija.

"No interviews," he said. We were there by appointment to interview *El Presidente.* Nival Seija stared at us. He looked as if he wished he could get us in the cellar and go to work on our fingernails with some pliers.

"Well, what are we doing here?" Torres said.

Suddenly *El Presidente* came out of a small room in the corner of his office. He is small and prissy and was carrying his hat in his hand. Perhaps he thought it was the new ambassador. He stuck out his hand. A flashbulb went off. Torres shook his hand and smiled hello. So did I. Then we saw it. We had been used.

On Monday morning, the Dominican papers would have a

picture of the president with a smiling prizefighter for the masses and a smiling American reporter for those who were worried about his connections in the United States, or his respectability.

He said good night and marched down the empty stone corridors of the national palace, flanked by soldiers, a hero of the fatherland, off for evening vespers. Torres and I drove through the empty, darkened streets of the town, smelling the sea on the breeze, our laughter echoing down the bloodstained alleys. It's not often that you are taken by an artist.

January 16, 1967

Riding South in the Country of the Dead

The sea was behind us, and we pushed east through climbing pine forest, and into a region of rough chaparral, through small dusty hamlets made of Richfield gas stations and Coors beer joints, with the carcasses of smashed jackrabbits lying on the asphalt. Nothing moved in the heat. A woman with stringy hair and pallid face stared at us through a torn screen window. There was nothing on her face or in her eyes, no past, no history, no desire. We were in the country of the dead.

"I was yew, wouldn't try that desert till nightfall," said the fat man in the Boulder Oaks gas station. He had three "For Sale" signs planted in the dust around him. "Two girls found dead out there yestidy. The wife seed it in the paper."

A guy came out of the gas station. He had a can of Coors in his hand. His face was flat and creased, like a lifer in the Army.

"Where y'all goin'?" he said.

"Just going."

"Got room for another passenger?"

"Jesus, we're filled up. You can see."

He squinted into the car. It was filled up. He looked at us. The face was made of verticals and horizontals. They moved against each other. His eyes looked as if someone had washed socks in them.

122

"You could fit another, if you wanted."

"Sorry," I said. "We got a long way to go."

He was standing next to the pump as we pulled away. When strangers talk in America, the possibility of murder always lurks somewhere.

High in the mountains, we stopped to eat in a rest area. A door creaked on the wooden john. Barbed wire separated us from the scorched earth beyond. Horseflies feasted on three spilling garbage cans. We had to eat in the car with the windows closed. Outside, all was silent, except for the gluttonous humming of the horeseflies, and the tearing sound of a passing car.

The country started falling away, and we moved through canyons stark with black shadow and then through hills made of millions of boulders and rocks. The glare was very bright on the northern side of the hills. A snake lay on the side of the road. We passed a shattered house—had someone lived there once, alone in the furious silence?—and saw graffiti a foot high painted on its eastern wall: "Zog," "Love," "El Centro Sucks."

El Centro was a garish frieze of cold neon, motels, chicken shacks, gas stations. It was 110 degrees. Signs shouted: ICE COLD BEER. SHRIMP IN A BASKET. TACO BELL. BURGERS. ICE. MOTEL. We were glad to be out of it and into the desert which was scraped and clean, rough and fundamental.

The car was not as happy as we were. Detroit builds cars with air conditioners that cannot be used. If you use them, the car overheats. American craftsmanship. We came into a place which seemed covered with snow. The sign said PLASTER CITY. No human thing moved in it, no face appeared. Every surface was covered with this fine white dust. A sign proclaimed it the territory of the United States Gypsum Company. Huge sheds stuck up from the dust, crowned by electronic towers, and you felt that someone, in a cabin in a pine forest, was operating it from a panel board, like a man with a Lionel train set.

By the time we got to Seeley the car seemed ready to explode. We pulled into a Texaco station, its apron already busy with boiling automobiles. A man in faded navy dungarees came over, opened the hood, and started dousing the radiator with a hose. Behind him a woman with a handsome face and heavy arms leaned against a doorway. Beside her were two Coke machines, blanched white as bone by the desert heat.

"This gon' take a while," the attendant said. It was dark now, but still the heat poured off the desert.

"Gimme the wrench, Jess," the woman said. She clamped it on the radiator cap, her other hand still holding the Coke. She jiggled it a few times.

"Gah damn, Louise, ya got more guts'n I got."

She smiled thinly at him.

"I got burned last Sattidy," the attendant said to me. "Some feller with a jeep."

The woman took the cap off without an explosion. She looked at Jess coldly and handed him the wrench. Then she went back to the station's office. I walked across the street into the See Lee Café.

The place had two yellow lights at the entrance and, inside, blue lights against the walls. A cluster of men were standing at the bar. A fat Indian hooker sat at a table drinking beer. Webb Pierce was singing from the jukebox. It was air-conditioned and very cold after the desert.

"A Coors, please."

"Yes, sir," the bartender said. "Good 'n' cold."

I drank the beer down and had two more. The jukebox stopped for a moment, and I could hear the three men down the bar.

"Well," one of them was saying, "what would *you* do with the greasers?"

"Send 'em all back to Mexico, that's what."

"George Wallace'd send the niggers with 'em, too."

It was the first political talk I'd heard in two days, and it was just about on the national level. The jukebox came on again. I finished the beer, picked up my change, and went out to get in the car and push on to Mexico.

June 27, 1968

Mexico City: Where the Air Was Clean

The Paseo de la Reforma was a slithering jam of immobile, angry automobiles. The air, infected with grassy filth, made the eyes burn and water. Teams of men laid orange tiles on the old hard-packed earthen walks. The great screen of trees over the eight-lane boulevard wilted and drooped, the leaves mottled and turning brown in the noxious caldron. There was no escape: Jackhammers tore at the side streets; Avenida Insurgentes was blocked by the helmeted men and pile drivers building the new subway. An ambulance screamed for passage, but nothing moved; the plea for help was answered by a mocking chorus of busted mufflers. Where were the girls in the starched spring dresses, who ate ice-cream cones at dusk? Gone, old buddy, like everything else. The loveliest street in the Western Hemisphere was a disaster area.

If you care at all about a city, you can make excuses for her. Mexico City has her excuses. In the past ten years, 2,000,000 people have poured in from the barren provinces, all of them poor. The prosperity of the central city, built on the backs of the new arrivals, has brought the automobile with it—a guarantee, as any New Yorker knows, of a city's destruction as a city. There are, to be sure, antinoise regulations and laws against defective mufflers, but one can hardly put an ordinary citizen in jail for such offenses when the city's buses pour tons of filth into the air every day. Mexico City is built on an old lake, and the soggy subsoil has made a subway impossible until just recently, when new engineering techniques were developed. But the construction crews keep running into archaeological finds, and the first spur of the subway will not be completed until 1970 at the earliest. Meanwhile, a city of 7,000,000 without a subway or a well-developed freeway system is going to choke to death—especially if, like Mexico, it is hemmed by high mountains. On the weekends, the rich flee to Acapulco or Puerto Vallarta; the middle class get down off the mesa into Cuernavaca or Puebla. The children of Sanchez stay home and drink pulque. The birthrate is not declining.

But the city is still exciting, in the way that New York can still be an exciting city; it is not like Los Angeles, which seems to reinvent itself every day, but it retains a sense of surprise, of hidden places which must be looked for before the city can be understood. To understand Mexico City, you have to go down past the Zócalo and out through the dusty side streets toward the Penitentiary. You have to go out and wander around the

Pedregal and try to see the houses of the rich behind their high fortress walls. You have to read *Esto* and *Ovaciones,* the sports papers, and go to a dance hall, and spend at least one night belting pulque in a cantina. You have to read Octavio Paz and Carlos Fuentes, but you also have to read *Alerta* and *Alarma,* the goriest crime papers in the hemisphere (AT THE END OF THE FIESTA, THEY GAVE HIM A BULLET, says a headline in the current *Alerta.* "Pedro Garcia Gerardo," says the caption under a photograph of a guy who might shine the shoes of tourists in the Alameda Park, "who was brutalized by alcohol and drugs, demolished with kicks his little daughter, Amalia, because she was late in serving him dinner. Information on inside pages.") The inside pages make the *Daily News* read like Ronald Firbank.

There are other things, too. The Museum of Anthropology in Chapultepec Park is just about the finest museum, architecturally, in the world, making the Louvre look like a frumpy relic and the Museum of Modern Art like some dull Bauhaus exercise; it has mass, proportion, texture, and life; have you ever heard water playing in the Met or seen sandaled peasants in the Prado? As for content, there is no way to visit this museum without trying to figure out how to rob it.

The new Mexican painters, whose work can be seen in the galleries of the Zona Rosa, are doing more interesting things than most American painters. They have not eliminated the human image from their work; they have not made it into a fag joke either. José Luis Cuevas is a better painter than anyone in the Warhol school, because in the end he really believes in men and is not frivolous. Cuevas, Rafael Coronel, Arnold Belkin, and the other younger Mexican painters have fortunately chosen to follow the paths opened by Orozco, rather than the dismal road of the editorial cartoonists like Diego Rivera (if they can be said to follow anyone) and their work is informed by a dark knowledge that somehow seems more Eastern European than anything else. If you can afford a gas mask, you can still walk the city and find magnificent pieces of architecture in the more prosperous areas; this is architecture which is still adventurous, which has social rather than strictly commercial or, worse, strictly cultural use, and there is absolutely nothing like it in New York. (And of course, architecture, like sculpture, must be experienced, or it is nothing; you can't really feel Candela's work from a photograph in *Architectural Forum* or *Domus*.)

This year, of course, the Olympics will be held in Mexico City, beginning October 12, and the Mexicans have added a new dimension: They are holding a concurrent Cultural Olympics, with a continuing program of international folklore shows, poetry recitals, theater, dance, even opera. Drawn from the best available troupes in the Olympic countries, the idea is to revive the ancient idea of the Olympics, when Pindar and associates would declaim to the assembled athletes at Olympia.

The idea came from Ramírez Vásquez, the man who designed the Museum of Anthropology and who took command of the whole Olympic operation after former President López Mateos had a stroke.

Ramírez Vásquez is spending money on projects that would make Robert Moses turn to drink. The Olympic architecture itself is really first-class: Candela's Sports Palace, holding 23,000, is a gem—a concrete shell on steel supports covered with copper-sheathed plywood. It was built in eighteen months for an incredibly cheap $8,000,000. The Sports Palace and the housing for athletes will all be used after the athletes are gone. But Ramírez Vásquez also understands the value of "useless" art too. He has commissioned sculptors like Alexander Calder, Herbert Bayer, and Constantino Nivola to create a series of pieces which will line the *periférico*, Mexico City's beltway. Their scale will resemble the magnificent cluster of five brightly painted towers now planted on the road to Querétaro; designed by Mathias Goeritz, the tallest rises 190 feet. Calder's black spider will be seven stories high. I don't know what they will look like when erected, but they won't be the Tishman Building.

Predictably, the United States does not seem much interested in the cultural side of the Olympics. During the games, all advertising will be banned from the city's billboards, to be replaced by messages on the theme of peace; no American advertising agency or government agency has yet come up with a contribution. There will be a children's Art Olympics, with 250 children from all Olympic countries competing outdoors in Chapultepec Park. Some forty countries, including Japan, the

127

Philippines, Australia, Poland, and Czechoslvakia have already held competitions to choose children for the contest. The United States hasn't bothered; The National Education Association (NEA) said it wasn't interested in mounting a competition. Yevgeny Yevtushenko read his poetry at one of the already-completed events, to a turnway crowd from every economic bracket; I was told that one American poetry association wouldn't send representatives because the theme (peace) was Communist propaganda. There will be an Olympic camp for world youth, but no one has been able to find the money to send any young Americans to it ($200 plus travel costs). We can always raise the money to send a kid off to get slaughtered in Asia, but forget anything else. The function of American kids seems to be to shoot other people—not, by God, to enjoy themselves. And especially not to learn anything, particularly that other kids from Communist countries might not have horns and cloven hooves.

No, Mexico this time wasn't the Mexico I used to know, the city where the air was clear, where you could walk in the evenings along the hard-packed earth of the Reforma and smell that blend of eucalyptus trees, charcoal fires, carbon stoves, and flowers that you smelled nowhere else on earth. That's gone, fouled by the automobiles, and it won't come back. Neither will the Banos Jordan, where Joe Medel trained, or the Super Gimnasio, where Tim Lee of the *Post* belted around a tough kid one afternoon and was asked to turn pro. That year we ate onion sandwiches waiting for the GI checks, and talked a lot about painters and Camus, and drank Don Quixote beer, and smoked Negritos, and had a lot of laughs in the 30-peso whorehouses. All that is gone.

The other day I read in the list of Olympics events that the Moscow Circus was in town. The Americans were still building their contributions: a space exhibit from NASA, an atomic energy exhibit from the AEC. So I took my daughters to see the circus. On the way, I picked up *Esto,* the brown gravure sports paper, and remembered a cool morning a long time ago when Timmy and I rushed to get a copy early in the morning. The paper said that Floyd Patterson had knocked out Archie Moore in the fifth round at Chicago and was the new heavyweight champion of the world. Floyd was twenty-one that year, and so were we, and I suppose we thought we would be that way forever, and Floyd with us.

I walked down Bucarell, past the newspaper offices and the taco stands, and tried to explain to my older daughter who is six, that Mexico wasn't always this way. She didn't understand, and we went into the Arena Mexico together, with the noise hammering behind us. The circus was excellent, if you like circuses. Halfway through I remembered that nobody was heavyweight champion of the world this season, and I decided then that we would leave in the morning.

July 18, 1968

Ireland: Shadow of the Gun

On the night the government fell, the Paisleyites lit bonfires on the Shankill Road. Women with glittery eyes, children twitching with excitement, tough young men with hard faces and rough workmen's boots, all were there: the sort of crowd that used to attend lynchings in the American South. They seemed to seethe with their small victory, while the bonfires burned garishly against the night sky. Bigotry and stupidity had triumphed again over the twentieth century.

About a mile away, in the tiny brick fortresses where the Catholics live on the Falls Road, people watched the news on television, and sipped tea in front of coal fires, and hoped that the night would pass without murder. Some remembered the terrible rioting of 1920–21, which left 400 dead, when the Murder Gang would come up the Catholic streets and shoot people in their beds. Or they would talk about the riots of 1935, when the Orange Order put a stop to a Protestant-Catholic coalition of the unemployed by raising the issue of popery, and set workingman against workingman, while the landlords who owned Northern Ireland sat back and smiled their wolfish smiles. It was coming again. It was coming.

"God save us all," a Catholic woman who remembered the old terrors said. "They'll be out for blood now."

To any outsider, the old bitter argument seems absurd. Writing in 1922, Winston Churchill said:

> Then came the Great War. Every institution, almost, in the world was strained. Great empires have been overturned. The whole map of Europe has been changed. The position of countries has been violently altered. The modes of thought of men, the whole outlook on affairs, the grouping of parties, all have encountered violent and tremendous changes in the deluge of the world. But as the deluge subsides and the waters fall short we see the dreary steeples of Fermanagh and Tyrone emerging once again. The integrity of their quarrel is one of the few institutions that has been unaltered in the cataclysm which has swept the world.

The integrity of that quarrel, between Catholic and Protestant, endures to this day. Last night, someone threw a fire bomb at the home of Ivan Cooper, a Protestant MP who has been fighting for the civil rights of Catholics. There has been a run on the gun stores. The landlords who run the Unionist Party have destroyed Captain Terence O'Neill, the Prime Minister who tried in his own peculiar wan style to bring some sense to this quarter-country of 1,500,000 people (two-thirds Protestant). A demagogue named Ian Paisley sits in a prison cell in the Crumlin Road Jail, while the Union Jack flies proudly over his church, a lurid signal of victory over O'Neill. The country is sick.

Very sick. Sicker in its own demented way even than the United States, because the integrity of this quarrel is lost in such distant and ugly memories. In the United States, the disease of race at least has the virtue that skin color is its own identity card. Here everyone is white. So that in downtown bars all talk is in whispers, because one does not know the religion of the next man. When the crazed Paisley followers ambushed civil rights marchers at the Burntollet Bridge last year, smashing women in the head with bricks, trying to drown injured men in an adjoining stream, stomping on the heads of students, they found it necessary to tie white handkerchiefs to their arms to tell friend from foe. When a Catholic here applies for a job, he is not asked for his religion; he is asked what schools he attended; there are no neutral schools. (They all tell the story of the Yank in Belfast who is asked his religion. Atheist, the Yank replies. Yes, says the Belfastman, but are ye a Catholic atheist or a Protestant atheist?)

A country is sick when you walk through its swinish chilling slums and find huge fresh-painted portraits of William of Orange on the walls, 300 years after his death, as if King Billy could bring running water to the foul cribs of Sandy Row. It is sick when the words "Remember 1690" show up everywhere, in memory of some forgotten Protestant victory over Catholics at the Battle of the Boyne, or when you can stand at the bar in the Bee Hive on the Falls Road and hear Catholics talk about Cromwell's massacre of the 3,500 men, women, and children of Drogheda as if it had happened last week, instead of 1649. The ads in the newspapers still ask for Catholic or Protestant families only. Bands of hard-faced punks still stop five-year-old Catholic girls on the street and make them shout "Fuck the Pope." You can still be driving through the lush moody countryside, a place where anything can grow, where birds whistle in the dawn, country that could be a natural Eden, and then, in a town like Moira, in foot-high letters on a brick wall, you can see "The Coming of the Lord Draweth Nigh," a stark and terrible warning from the minds of human beings who worship death, not life, bitterness and the strangled heart over the possibilities of human joy. In places on the Shankill Road, grown men still mutter darkly that it was a sin and a disgrace for the voters of Belfast to have allowed children the use of playground swings on Sundays. In the old days, they will tell you, this was a Christian country; children were locked in their rooms on Sunday to read the Word, not allowed to romp in the fresh clean air.

The sickness has been here since the seventeenth century, when the first Scotch Protestants were "planted" by an English king on land that was stolen from the Northern Irish. Today the Unionist Party that rules the North has been torn apart. O'Neill was the target, because he was a moderate; the left saw him as the classic "white liberal," who thought change could be effected through the rhetoric of reason and decency, without corresponding action. The right saw O'Neill as soft on Popery, a man whose lack of "firmness" (*i.e.*, his lack of the will to machine-gun civil rights marchers), was leading to anarchy and chaos. Yet this superficial analysis cannot fully explain the forces that led to his defeat.

The truth is that politics in Northern Ireland are inextricably involved in religion and, so far, show no sign of getting themselves out of the sectarian bind. The Unionist Party has ruled the North for the entire forty-seven years since Lloyd George partitioned the country. The Unionists are the Protestant party and are actually the political arm of the Orange Order, a semisecret organization with lodges throughout the country. If a Unionist Prime Minister tries to make policies with which the Orange Order disagrees, he cannot survive. O'Neill, by opening up contact with the twenty-six-county government in Dublin, having his picture taken with Catholic Cardinal Conway, by urging moderation, and finally by agreeing on the mild principle of one-man, one-vote, had outraged the Orange Order. The purpose of the Orange Order, despite high-minded claims of belief in religious freedom, is to maintain Protestant privilege. Since Catholics have more children than Protestants, the only way to maintain the two-thirds, one-third population ratio is to force Catholics to emigrate; if the choice is starvation, National Assistance, or emigration, they emigrate. In Derry, where Catholics have a two-thirds majority, the discrimination is worse, because true electoral freedom (not just one-man, one-vote, but the abolition of gerrymandering) would mean a Catholic mayor in the North's second largest city and the end to Protestant privilege. When the 90 percent Protestant police charged into the Catholic ghetto of Bogside two weeks ago to beat Catholics with Chicago-style ferocity, they were doing it on behalf of the affluent Protestants who still own Derry.

The task of the Orange Order was made much easier by the emergence six years ago of the Reverend Ian K. Paisley, an Elmer Gantry-style revivalist preacher whose "Free Presbyterian Church" became the fountainhead of Protestant extremism. Paisley received his Doctor of Divinity by mail from Bob Jones University, a bizarre Fundamentalist college in the

American South, where, one presumes, the curriculum includes Biblical Calculus, Biblical Geography, and Biblical Accounting. Paisley hated Catholics, pure and simple, and made religion the basis of one's allegiance to Britain. His hate sheet, the *Protestant Telegraph,* carries regular articles by "Dr." Carl McIntire, whose *20th Century Reformation Hour* is broadcast all over the United States. McIntire is part of the nut right, an admirer of the Minutemen and the Birchers, and when Paisley made a fund-raising tour of the States a few years ago, McIntire helped arrange it. Paisley's wife, an attractive thirtyish woman, does not appear to have a head full of dragons until she opens her mouth.

"Shortly after he came into power," she said recently, "O'Neill smuggled across the border Sean Lemass [former Prime Minister of the Irish Republic], and Sean Lemass was a would-be murderer of the people of Northern Ireland in the troublous times in the past. My husband at that time stepped in, and we made our protest, and a lot of people were awakened to the true position. Then again he brought up Mr. Lynch [successor to Lemass] from the South, and once more my husband stepped in, and I believe he was the person used, under God, to prevent our being handed over earlier to the Republic."

What this gibberish translates into is relatively simple: many Protestants fear the idea of a united, thirty-two-county Ireland, even though one small island with an industrial north and an agricultural south would appear to make more sense than the present irrational structure. But the South is 90 percent Catholic, and the fear is that a merger would evaporate Protestant privilege at best or lead to an anti-Protestant bloodbath at worst.

The radicals in the Civil Rights Association and the student-dominated People's Democracy are not, however, asking for a United Ireland, at least not until the Republic to the south makes some essential changes (the institution of a National Health system, legalized divorce, freedom to purchase contraceptives, removal of an absurd system of film and book censorship, and the elimination of the influence of the Catholic hierarchy on the government). But for his own reasons Paisley refuses to listen to the people in the civil rights movement, who include a good number of young Protestants from Queens University, Belfast. When Bernadette Devlin went to see him to try to work out a coalition of Paisley's working-class supporters and the working-class supporters of civil rights, Paisley told her: "I would rather be British than just." Paisley has painted the civil rights people as Papists *and* Communists. The result has been more violence and bitterness than at any time since the 1920's, including the murders of several Catholics by inflamed Paisleyites.

Starting from almost nothing, Paisley is now one of the most powerful men in the British Isles. His candidates polled more than 20,000 votes in last February's Northern Ireland elections, and every weekend you can see parades of his followers marching up and down the Irish countryside. Last weekend I saw about 3,000 of them in the town of Armagh, marching to welcome home three Paisleyite leaders who had served a month in prison for disturbing the peace. (Paisley himself is doing three months, for refusing to sign a two-year guarantee that he will not disturb the peace or incite to riot.) The Paisleyites marched around the great green mall, beating drums, playing flutes, dressed in Orange sashes, carrying ceremonial swords, and wearing bowler hats that gave them an oddly pathetic look: these rough Irish faces donning the costumes of the masters. They looked like any other group of parading Irishmen, except that they insisted they were British. One of them carried a sign reading: "Wake Up Protestants, You Are Being Sold Down the River. Romanising Clergymen Call It Moderation." They marched up to a platform in Gaol Square, chanting "O'Neill Must Go" and "We Want Paisley." A clergyman took over the microphone and, in a loud Belfast accent, asked all to bow their head in prayer and then, in a booming, unmusical voice, which reminded me of people I used to hear in saloons in my neighborhood, started singing "The Lord is my Shep-Hard, I shall not want . . ." When he had finished, another man of God started shouting about "the dark black unchanging hand of Popery" which was behind the civil rights movement, and explained how the Pope had given his personal blessing to the men who took part in the 1916 Rising in Dublin (this is, of course, a lie; the hierarchy of the Catholic Church was on the side of the British in 1916, and many of the rebels were excommunicated). It reminded me of some graffiti reported on the wall of a Belfast lavatory: "The fear of the Lord is the beginning of Wisdom. Fuck the Pope!" Later that night, after the men of God had whipped the passions of the crowd into sufficient fervor, there was a riot. Four Catholics were arrested.

But Paisley's followers did win the victory over Terence O'Neill, who has now been replaced by his cousin, James Chichester-Clarke, a forty-six-year-old Tory. They won because the Unionist politicians who rule through the rump Parliament at Stormont, outside Belfast, did not really have enough guts to stand up to them. O'Neill has gone, but the trouble remains. The people of the civil rights movement have accomplished more through nonviolence, so far, than the IRA did in forty years of blowing up bridges and mailboxes. But they have also unleashed the power of a generation that will no longer live the old lies. If the new Prime Minister and his Cabinet do not listen to them, if they give in to Paisley's demented Christians, then the land will be drenched in blood. The young people here have said that it is their country, that they will live in it, and that they will not let a privileged few play the Orange card every time there is a call for justice. If they lose, and the Paisleyites win, then only one thing is certain: The shadow of the gunman will be again upon the land.
May 15, 1969

Ireland: The Killing Would Be for Christ

On a dark Tuesday afternoon, with a hard spring rain lashing the Crumlin Road, the Reverend Ian Paisley walked out of prison. The deal was made: a general amnesty, freeing Paisley and clearing the slate of all charges against his opponents in the civil rights movement. Paisley was now free again to resume the Great Crusade: to smash Popery, to destroy ecumenicism, to keep Ulster British, to maintain the Union Jack in the firm right hand of the Lord. Most of all, he was free to resume his two-a-day show at the Ulster Hall, where the faithful arrive each Sunday to be whipped into the true Christian condition of mindless ugliness and to be relieved of their money through that other great Christian tradition: the Silent Collection.

"The time has come," Paisley said, standing under a reporter's umbrella, flanked by the Union Jack, "for the Protestant people of this country to stand firm and make the province the kind of place we want it to be."

Beside him, Major Ronald Bunting nodded. In the film of the Northern Ireland conflict, Bunting would have to be played by Terry-Thomas; he is clean-shaven, to be sure, but he has that great quality of stunned dumbness that approaches innocence. One is sure that Bunting felt like a great Christian on the day of the Burntollet Bridge ambush, when his legions of shining Protestants unloaded stones, bricks, and slabs of mortar on civil rights marchers and then, as the wounded staggered into fields with blood running from their heads, unleashed a second ambush, which involved the attempted drowning of schoolgirls. But then Bunting, the pop Cromwell, must have a stomach well gilded by righteousness. Anyone who can spend as much time with the likes of Paisley as Bunting does must have a strong stomach indeed.

Paisley is a large man, with close-cropped thin hair, lips that move vertically to reveal long hard teeth, and an extraordinary pair of closely set eyes. The eyes are the color of slush, and convey at once a knowledge of sin and murder and the various regions of hell and the slick cold vastnesses of the boardroom. His father had worked for other men in a draper's shop in a provincial town, and there remains in Paisley's eyes the old resentments of people whose meals have depended on the whims of strangers. No matter what else happens—assassination, or prison, or exile—Paisley seems to be telling you from those eyes that he will never go back to where he started; it is no accident that the pale thick flesh rising up from the clergyman's collar speaks of a familiarity with pleasure.

Paisley and Bunting were released in a general amnesty that was one of the first acts of the new government of Major (everyone in this Christian country seems to have a military title) James Chichester-Clarke. It was a clever political move in the short run, because it puts the burden of responsibility for disorder on the civil rights people. On the previous weekend, during a long meeting at the City Hotel in Derry, leaders of the civil rights groups had agreed to begin a campaign of civil disobedience, placing pickets at airports, border posts, public buildings, etc. They almost certainly would have been subject to physical assaults by the Paisleyites and harassment of various kinds by the police. By releasing Paisley and Bunting, and ruling that all pending civil rights prosecutions were to be canceled, Chichester-Clarke hoped to start his administration with a relatively clean slate.

In reality, he simply moved the game back to square one. Paisley is not about to retire to the desert, to eat honey and communicate with his God. When he was released, the bonfires blazed in the Shankill Road and Sandy Row, where the bulk of his Belfast supporters live, and they started to sing: "Paisley is our leader, we shall not be moved. . . ." They see this as a capitulation to their cause, brought about by political pressure and by prayer. They also know that if the civil rights people go on with their campaign (as they must), then the government can strike hard against them, claiming that the chance for civil peace had been given and that the civil rights people were simply not interested in the common weal.

In that sense, it was a beautiful move. But it will not solve anything. The grievous problems remain: The districts are still gerrymandered at a local level to deprive Catholics of power; the one-man, one-vote measure has yet to be debated at the Northern Ireland Parliament; the Public Order Act, which is intended to fill the gaps in the already vicious Special Powers Act, is seen likely to pass; public housing is still allocated on a segregated basis, insuring that the Catholic and Protestant ghettos will remain ghettos for the rest of the century; young Catholics are still being forced to emigrate at the rate of 7,000 to 10,000 a year because they can get no work; the Protestant upper classes still rule the country like a private fiefdom.

In other words, the country remains in the same condition it was in seven months ago when the civil rights movement started in earnest. Last October 5 the civil rights people held a march in Derry to protest the lack of jobs and housing and the ugly gerrymandering which was at the heart of the problem. The then Minister for Home Affairs, a particularly thickheaded member of the Orange Order named William Craig, ordered the march dispersed by force. Police moved in with clubs and bats, lashing out at everyone in sight, mopping up the remainder with water cannons mounted on armored cars. Three days of rioting followed, as the jobless people of Derry's Bogside roared through the streets.

On October 9, as students arrived for the beginning of the fall term at Queens University, Belfast, they were handed leaflets informing them that a new group called the People's Democracy was being formed at Queens, to support the civil rights movement. They met late that afternoon at the Student Union. There was an overflow crowd. People's Democracy was (and remains) an exercise of sorts in the possibilities of political anarchism. There are no leaders (though much of the organizing was done by Michael Farrell, a lecturer at Belfast Technical College, and Kevin Boyle, a graduate student). There are no membership lists, no dues, no committees of leadership permitted to make decisions in the absence of others. It is assumed that all members are free spirits. Every public pronouncement of the group, every decision to hold a demonstration must be ratified by all members after full debate. This can lead to occasional bouts of chaos, of course, and one recent meeting that I attended had its share of speakers on ego trips. But it is remarkably democratic, and its members seem to abide by the decisions of the majority.

The People's Democracy decided to march on City Hall, in a show of solidarity with the civil rights people who had been bloodied in Derry. The most natural route takes them along University Road through Shaftesbury Square. But Shaftesbury Square, for some reason, is thought of as "Protestant territory" (presumably because the working-class Protestants of Sandy Row live within walking distance). The police would not allow the PD to march through the square. They were rerouted through back streets, emerging at Linen Hall Street, which feeds into the City Hall beside the International Hotel (in the Belfast loony bin, the International is thought of as a "Catholic hotel" and has had its windows smashed a few times by pious

Paisleyites). The police refused to allow the PD to march around City Hall, on the grounds that the Paisleyites were waiting for them, and there would be certain bloodshed.

"I was there," said a second-year Spanish student named Rita Kelly, "and the only Paisleyites I could see were about ten raving women."

The PD sat down in the street. They stayed until late that night, making speeches to each other and to passersby, singing the old songs of the American freedom movement, and finding in each other a kind of sweet solidarity. For an American to move among these people now is odd; they are a bittersweet reminder of our own moment passed, of those days in the movement when everyone was rather nice to each other. These kids have yet to go through the cycle of killings, betrayals, broken promises, thwarted dreams that turned so many young Americans sour and violent. I suppose that will yet happen, in a shorter time than it took in the United States; a lot of these kids are reading Malcolm X and Eldridge Cleaver now, and the similarities to their own conditions cannot elude them.

But for now, the PD contains some of the best people you will meet in this country. They want almost desperately to explain that theirs is not a Catholic movement, that they are working for the civil rights of all working people (and, indeed, there are a number of Protestants in the PD). Most of them consider themselves Connolly socialists—followers of James Connolly, the great Irish socialist (born of Irish parents in Edinburgh, Scotland), who went to work at eleven, served seven years in the British Army, spent a number of years in the United States, where he helped organize the Wobblies, and then went back to Ireland. He worked with James Larkin on the great Transport Strike and Lockout of 1913 and took part in the 1916 Rising. He was wounded during the fighting and had to be tied to a chair when he was executed by a British firing squad. His last words were: "It has been a full life, and isn't this a fitting end?" Connolly remained a Catholic all his life, and it is his own special brand of Catholic Marxism that is so attractive to many of these young people.

One problem with a group that is so open, however, is that it is also open to infiltration. The PD people know that there are members of the Special Branch at every meeting (the Special Branch are the secret police of Northern Ireland). But more dangerous is that the Protestant extremists are also compiling files. Most prominent of the extreme groups are the Ulster Protestant Volunteers (UPV), whose leader is Major Bunting.

The UPV is the Protestant equivalent of the Irish Republican Army. The IRA has so far stayed out of the present struggle in the North; the UPV have been heavily involved and, under Bunting's directions, pulled off the ambush at the Burntollet Bridge last January 4. The UPV is a secret organization, whose membership is now about 10,000, with another 10,000 sympathizers, and growing rapidly. At the beginning of the year it had thirteen branches; it now has twenty-five in Northern Ireland, plus three in Liverpool (where the emigrating Irish have transferred their quarrel through the years) and three in Scotland. They operate out of Orange Order lodges, and though some Orange leaders have been urging moderation, the UPV is not listening; if anything it is rapidly taking over the Orange Order itself. Already, according to the London *Sunday Times,* it has instituted a system of kangaroo courts in the North; dissenters from its policies are tried by these courts and can be punished. If the Orange Lodges function as the Irish equivalents of the White Citizens Councils, then the UPV are the Ku Klux Klan.

The IRA, however, is not dozing. I spent an afternoon with an old IRA man in Derry. He told me that the IRA position so far has been "support, but no participation." But he says that might not last indefinitely, "especially if they start killing our people." The UPV might be compiling lists, but the IRA has lists of its own. "We've been at this a long time," the old IRA man said. "Longer than the UPV. If it comes to the crunch, we won't be silent." When three main sources of Belfast's water supply were blown up several weeks ago, there were few people who blamed the action on the IRA. Most people I talked to, on both sides of this quarrel, agreed that it was more likely that members of Bunting's UPV did the job, hoping to resurrect the old bogeyman of the fanatic nationalist in the trench coat. It seems clear that the only thing that will bring the IRA into this with its full power would be a really wild campaign of anti-

Catholic, anticivil-rights violence by the UPV and its allies among the B-Specials.

There are still a number of young people here who think that the Northern Ireland situation can be sorted out short of violence. They think that world opinion, especially since the advent of television, will prevent a really murderous pogrom, which was always the solution in the old days (violent anti-Catholic rioting has taken place in Belfast alone in 1857, 1864, 1872, 1886, 1893, 1898, 1920–21, and 1935). This could be temporarily prevented by the intervention of the British government at Westminster. But if the Wilson government falls and is replaced by a Conservative government, it is unlikely that such a move will take place. (The British Conservative Party controls the Unionist vote at Westminster; at present there are ten Unionists in Westminster, and two anti-Unionists; if a Conservative government were elected with a slim majority, the Conservatives would need those ten votes desperately.)

The only lasting solution would be a thirty-two-county republic, with a federal system allowing the Protestants to function with complete freedom. The present six counties in the North call themselves Ulster, but they are not even that; the original four provinces of Ireland are Ulster, Munster, Leinster, and Connacht, but Ulster contained nine counties. Three of those counties were given to the Republic under the Home Rule Act, because a nine-county Ulster would have had a Catholic majority who might have voted themselves into the Republic.

Men are still being beaten, humiliated, and driven into exile because of that crude piece of Orange Order politicking. Today the landlords of the six counties want to maintain the status quo. They even subsidize two school systems, separate but equal, Catholic and Protestant, to keep their citizens apart. If the people in the civil rights movement are successful, there would be a thirty-two-county republic eventually, even if they did not ask for one (and they are certainly not asking for it now). If they fail, a lot of people will die. All in the name of Christ. Of course.

May 22, 1969

A Cannon in Derry: Civil Rights Revolt

The long black cannon is called Roaring Meg, and it had been used in defense of the city in 1689. Today it stands on the double bastion of the old walls of this city, aimed at the heart of the Catholic slum called Bogside. Standing beside it, you can see row after row of dirty weather-battered brick houses, their blue slate roofs spiky with TV aerials and spattered with bird droppings. Off on the right is the gray concrete slab of a dance hall called the Stardust Club, and beyond it the dark ominous spire of St. Eugene's Roman Catholic Cathedral, the tallest structure in the Bogside, standing bitter and defiant and remote. On a hill rising in the distance, set among swards of green open land, is a graveyard. By the time this quarrel reaches its natural end only the graveyard might emerge victorious.

For Derry has become the heart of the civil rights struggle in Ireland, and if the quarrel is not sorted out peacefully here, it will almost certainly end up being settled by the gun. The civil rights people, led by, among others, a heavyset pleasant man named John Hume, can be found most evenings in the lounge of the City Hotel, a block from the docks which have taken so many bitter young men off to exile around the earth.

All of them, and most emphatically Hume, tell you that they want desperately to avoid violence. But they also know that if the Unionist government at Stormont does not move swiftly on reforms, many of the young people in the movement might take more drastic steps. They know that the border separating the Occupied Six Counties from the twenty-six-county Republic of Ireland is only three miles from Derry. They know that if the right-wing Paisleyites start shooting down Catholics, then the IRA would have to move in, and the men in the trench coats—who have stayed conspicuously, and sensibly, out of the civil rights movement here—have at least 2,000 guns stashed away in various parts of the island.

"I'd like to have hope," says Hume. "And I still do have hope that we can make the reforms work. But the new government doesn't give much hope that the reforms will take place fast enough."

The new government of Northern Ireland is headed by Major James Chichester-Clarke, whose first interview session on TV the other night was greeted with loud laughter in a pub in Armagh, where I watched it. Chichester-Clarke is almost a stereotype of the landed gentry, complete with diffident English accent, bumbling vagueness, and absolute fidelity to the landed upper classes from which he springs. One of the terrible inequities of the Northern Ireland situation is that 90 percent of the land is owned by 5 percent of the people, all of whom are staunch members of the Orange Order. Through the Unionist Party the Orange Order runs the country from the Parliament at Stormont, a massive pile of stone and interior decoration just outside Belfast, and Chichester-Clarke is at least somewhat acceptable to them. After all, his ancestral home covers 500 acres. That should qualify him to lead the government of this tormented little province.

And yet it seems unlikely that Major Chichester-Clarke will ever really understand the anger and bitterness of the people who live in the Bogside in Derry. He was asked the other night whether he would visit the slum and replied, "Rather depends on the people of Bogside, doesn't it?" It does, of course, but it also depends on how much courage the new Prime Minister possesses; if he makes the reforms, if he attempts to conciliate the people of the Bogside all over the North, he would probably not last very long because he would lose the right-wing support he so desperately needs.

"It's the same old thing," said an unemployed carpenter in the Bogside the other day, standing on William Street, near the site of the major rioting that took place a few weeks before. "He's got a bit more right-wingers in the Cabinet now, but basically the whole lot are the same pack of Orange landlords."

The Bogside was built on an old marsh below the walls of the city, and today it is crowded with buildings that were slums when Charles Dickens was alive: dark narrow alleys; homes with neither running water nor inside toilets; streets covered with rubble; houses being battered by the swinging iron ball of progress; others with their windows bricked up like the eyes of blind men. On Nailor's Row, just below the city walls, the windows of the occupied houses are covered now with chicken wire mesh because the Paisleyites would come in the night and heave bricks, bottles, and rocks through the windows, hoping, one presumes, to fracture the skull of a child or an old woman to prove one's fealty to the living Christ. Down the hill, men in heavy army greatcoats and caps pulled down over their eyes talk darkly, members of the 17 percent of Derry's adult population which is unemployed. One walks away, into the Lone Moor Bar for a drink. At Fox's Corner, another group, younger, with harder, more desperate faces, stands in front of a wall with a large sign saying: YOU ARE NOW ENTERING FREE DERRY.

Derry has become the heart of the civil rights revolt here because the situation in Derry is one of the worst in the country. There is a large Catholic majority: 59 percent of all voters in the city, 63 percent of the population. But the city has been ruthlessly gerrymandered, so that the Catholics are always in the minority (12–8) on the city council. The city council (called the Corporation) was recently abolished and replaced with a commission picked by Stormont. There are five Protestants on the commission, and four Catholics, all of whom are conservative businessmen in no way connected with the civil rights movement. (The rights people call them "Green Tories.") The gerrymandering has led to a continuing ghettoizing of the city; when a new housing development is opened, it will be almost entirely Catholic or Protestant and set in already existing Catholic or Protestant ghettos. The Unionists claim that they must gerrymander the city because the Catholics are unreliable; if they took control through a democratic vote, they might fly the tricolor of the Irish Republic over the Derry Guild Hall (city hall) and declare the city free. Or they might do to the Protestants what the Protestants have done to the Catholics for three centuries (in the Guild Hall, for example, not a single employee is Catholic). In addition, owners of property and employers are entitled to more than one vote; a man running a business that employed twenty people could vote twenty times (these really blatant cases are not very frequent). If you own no taxable property, you do not vote in local elections.

This led to the initial thrust of the civil rights organizations here; that is, the principle of one man, one vote. The former Prime Minister, Terence O'Neill, finally agreed to this principle, and his government fell; Chichester-Clarke has agreed to the principle; but it still has not been passed into law, and there will probably be sustained pressure against it from the Orange Order. The owners of property are almost entirely Protestant, and they want to maintain the present system for the material benefits it provides them. The civil rights people, however, will not be satisfied with one man, one vote unless it is accompanied by reform of the gerrymandering system. It is doubtful if the Unionists who own Northern Ireland will dilute their power. Either way the result could be real trouble.

But if there really is trouble, the Unionists will have great physical power on their side. To begin with, they have the Special Powers Act, a piece of repressive legislation in the great tradition of our free world allies. Under the provisions of the Special Powers Act, a citizen can be arrested without warrant, imprisoned without trial or recourse to habeas corpus or a court of law. The citizen's home can be invaded without warrant, and with force, at any hour of the day or night. A citizen can be punished by flogging. He can be denied a trial by jury. He can be arrested and forced to answer all questions, even if they are self-incriminating, and can be punished if he refuses to answer. Inquests can be prohibited if a citizen is mysteriously killed. A citizen can be arrested for spreading false rumors by "word of mouth"; the circulation of any newspaper can be prohibited; a citizen can be arrested for the possession of any forbidden film or phonograph record. And finally, he can be arrested for any offense "not specifically provided for in the regulations."

The Special Powers Act has never been used against the Paisleyite extremists, as far as anyone here can tell. Its avowed purpose is to stop the Irish Republican Army, which is outlawed on both sides of the border. But basically it is used to prevent anyone from talking publicly about an alternative form of government; specifically, a thirty-two-county republic. Thus, you can be arrested for flying the tricolor of the Irish Republic, you can be arrested for singing the "Soldier's Song," the Irish national anthem, you can be arrested for selling the *United Irishman,* the newspaper of the Republican movement. It is against the law to include the word "Republican" in the name of any organization; presumably, if a group of American students at Queens College, Belfast, were to start a Young Republican group, adorned with photographs of Spiro T. Agnew, even they could be arrested. You could sit here and spend three weeks laughing at the lunacy of the place, except for the very real fact that before this is over, some people are going to get killed.

The right-wing Protestants are in good shape if it comes to killing. In addition to the 3,500-man Royal Ulster Constabulary (only 10 percent of whose members are Catholics), there is another legally armed group called the B-Specials. To join the B-Specials, you must be of age, without a criminal record, and Protestant. The new B-Special earns $18 a year, plus $1 a day when called in to work. He is given a uniform. And he is given a gun, which he is allowed to take home. Today in Northern Ireland, there are about 10,000 B-Specials, and though in theory they are supposed to be a supplemental police force, in fact they are the armed vanguard of the Orange Order. When the B-Specials were called into action several weeks ago, civil rights leader Austin Currie described the move as "an act of insanity." The Orange Order obviously disagrees; they see themselves being threatened by all these requests for justice, and they are keeping their guns oiled.

The civil rights movement actually grew out of the work of a little-known country doctor named Con McCluskey, of Dungannon, and his wife, Patricia. In 1964 the McCluskeys and some friends started a small group called the Campaign for Social Justice, whose major purpose was to document cases of discrimination against Catholics. For years, Catholics had felt discriminated against, especially in the crucial areas of jobs and housing, but oddly enough, until Dr. McCluskey came on the scene, there had been little hard research. Then, in 1966, an old-line Communist named Betty St. Clair founded a group called the Northern Ireland Civil Rights Association.

Both developments added something new to the old quarrel. First, the new people did not concern themselves with reunifying the country; they were not interested in making a thirty-two-county republic and limited themselves to demands for full justice under *British* law. Their demands were made out in the open; their meetings were public; they could hardly be accused of treason.

In the old days, the Unionists could pounce on any serious opposition, invoke the Special Powers Act, and imprison the leaders, with no interference from the British government in Westminster (where the ultimate political power in Northern Ireland resides). The demand for civil rights was basic and, in the age of TV, explosive. The government of Harold Wilson, which depends so heavily on the votes of exiled Irish workers in Great Britain, could not sit on its hands and explain that the Irish were all crazy.

When the first civil rights march was held last August 24, some 4,000 people showed up, including students from Queens University, Belfast. That was the real beginning. The police cooperated, with their apparently universal instinct for the wrong move, and prevented the marchers from entering Dungannon. When that scene was shown on the TV screens of Northern Ireland, thousands of people began flocking to the civil rights bandwagon. It hasn't stopped rolling yet.

May 15, 1969

Goldberg

Any edition now, depending upon communications with Olympus, we apparently shall hear that Arthur J. Goldberg has finally surrendered to our deepest longings and will do us the favor of running for governor. Some New Yorkers I know are so touched by the prospect of Goldberg leading us into the seventies that at least one girl has decided to leave the country. It was an understandable decision.

One of the great mysteries about the whole Goldberg candidacy is why it should even be proposed. Has everyone already forgotten that Arthur Goldberg spent more than two years trying to make Lyndon Johnson and his filthy war respectable? Those years at the United Nations were not made any more edifying by the stories we always heard that in private Goldberg disagreed with Johnson's policies. The fact is that in public he was pushing the whole discredited line. If there ever were another War Crimes Tribunal, Goldberg would be in the dock, along with Rusk, Rostow, Humphrey, and the rest of the Johnson claque.

It was Goldberg who led the Great Flying Peace Offensive in 1966, hopping from one European capital to another in what we learned later was only a massive publicity stunt. It was Goldberg who said, on July 12, 1966, "It is Hanoi's aggression which is the only reason for United States air strikes against military facilities in North Vietnam." Most civilized people at that time were opposed to the bombing of North Vietnam because it was killing civilians; Goldberg blamed the whole thing on Hanoi, with occasional swipes at Peking, and to read his UN speeches today is to be reminded of how morally gutless those years were. Supposedly decent men were so trapped by their own rhetoric and love of career that they lied repeatedly, most frequently to themselves.

But Vietnam is not the only reason for objecting to Goldberg. To begin with, he is sixty years old and wants to be governor without ever having governed anything. New York City is a place oppressed by its rulers in Albany; if the city is to survive, it will need someone who thinks more about the people on the city's streets as people, and not as contracts to be settled in conference rooms.

The meeting Goldberg attended at Averell Harriman's home last week is typical of the kind of government we might expect from Goldberg. There were no young people, blacks, or Puerto Ricans in attendance, if we can trust the New York *Times*. There were no representatives of the Kennedy-McCarthy followers in the New Democratic Coalition. There was one woman, although Mrs. Anna Rosenberg Hoffman could hardly be described as in the vanguard of any women's political movement.

What was there was the tired old combination that has turned the Democratic Party in this state into a creaking, lifeless shambles, sneered at by young people and ineffective, to say the least, in elections. There they were: Robert Dowling, George Backer, Arthur Krim, John Burns,* Eddie Weisl, Joe Crangle, Jacob Potofsky, and so on. These were the people who gave us Humphrey in 1968, who opposed Robert Kennedy and fought Eugene McCarthy. One of the few old Kennedy men at the meeting was Democratic National Committeeman Jack English, and he had to invite himself.

What was there, of course, was money. These people still think that you win elections by putting together a glittering financial committee, buying up what you need, and going ahead. That is why the candidates we get are usually so mediocre.

And despite Goldberg's reputation, there is much feeling that in the end, he will be a mediocre candidate. To begin with, he is probably the worst public speaker in the state, with the ability to turn the most critical political issues into exercises in tedium. A long campaign, with repeated TV exposure, might turn Goldberg into the largest bore since the last dynamic Democratic candidate hit the state. In addition, Goldberg's stands on state and city issues are vague at best; his whole style is based on being diffuse, on leaving openings that result from the ambiguity of his language. If ever we had a period which demanded clear talk from politicians, this is it. There has been little indication so far that Goldberg has that talent in much abundance. There is more evidence of his own enormous self-esteem.

One member of the progressive wing of the party told Goldberg recently that he couldn't surround himself with the people who were at the luncheon, because the association would create an image that would make it difficult for the liberals to work for him. Goldberg reportedly replied in high-handed manner: "If you don't realize I'm my own man in this thing, then you don't deserve a candidate such as me, and I very well may not run."

There is one other aspect of Goldberg's candidacy that deserves attention. It is the condescending assumption on the part

* Mr. Burns *was* a Kennedy man, and I apologized to him later.—P. H.

149

of Goldberg's advocates that the Jewish community in this city is monolithic, and that as soon as Goldberg announces, thousands of happy, laughing Jews will be dancing in the streets. That assumption is obviously revolting. For me, though, the issue remains Goldberg's complicity in the Vietnam mess. Every day, Americans are still dying out there, and Goldberg must live with the part he played in sending them there.
December 8, 1969

The Best Americans

A frail rain was falling on Forty-first Street, as the cabs pulled up and their middle-aged passengers hurried for the shelter of the Paradise Restaurant. Their wives were with them, and they wore heavy coats against the Saturday night weather, and when they took off their hats, their hair was gray with years or beginning to vanish. They greeted each other with *abrazos,* with the hearty goodwill of an evening out, and being watched, they looked no different, really, from the people you see at conventions or at union meetings. They went upstairs to a large bright room, and drank a lot of whiskey at the bar, and there was nothing at all to indicate that they were the best Americans of their generations.

They were the veterans of the Abraham Lincoln Brigade, and to be able to say that about yourself might be the only badge of honor that is worth having. Three thousand of them went to fight. Fifteen hundred came out alive, and 90 percent of the survivors were wounded. They came from everywhere, but a lot of them were tough Jews out of Brownsville and the East Side, young men who understood better than their elders what Spain meant in 1936, men who were willing to die for what they believed. We haven't had many like them since; we might never see their like again. In the thirties, when it was put up or shut up, the men of the Lincoln Brigade put up.

And so there was a strange quality of youth and joy about them, as they moved through that room at their annual dinner the other night. It was as if they were all still twenty-two, and they had made it through the Jarama, as if it were only last week that they beat back the Italians at Guadalajara, only last month that they boarded the ships and forfeited their American passports to fight for the Spanish Republic, only last year that they lay in the trenches beside the Ebro, to sing songs about freedom.

At one point, a man came up to the table behind me and embraced a white-haired man, tears in his eyes, his body trembling with emotion. He felt he had to explain himself and said, "This man saved my life. If it wasn't for Doc Kraus, I wouldn't be here." And Mark Kraus seemed embarrassed, because he is just a doctor now, and when people see him walking on Rutland Road in Brooklyn, they don't know about the splendid years of his youth; he is just a white-haired man on the streets of New York. Like all the others in that room, though, he knew what he once did; he served with the Lincoln Brigade, and that says it all.

It has been a lonely time for them in the years since Franco's legions finally marched into Barcelona. Never have so many good men been treated so badly by a supposedly civilized nation as the Lincoln Brigade veterans were treated by America. A lot of them were Communists, of course, but that was a simple choice to make in the 1930's if you were twenty-two; the Communists were fighting the Fascists, and that was that. But when Spain was over, and after a lot of them fought again in the Second World War, the pressure started. They were called "premature anti-Fascists." A lot of them were hounded out of jobs; the FBI tracked them everywhere; some, like Steve Nelson, the old Communist, went to jail. They had gone to Spain because they loved America and wanted its honor preserved; when they came home, America kicked them in the teeth.

"It was tough for a lot of the guys to adjust to that," one of them told me. "If you've had that experience at twenty-two, where do you go from there?"

I suppose you just go to work and hope for the best. The men there were middle-aged, and I suppose they talked about the things middle-aged men always talk about: their children, their grandchildren, money, the passage of time. But when the writer

Tana de Gamez stood up to speak, and addressed them as "my beloved Lincolns," my friend Curly Mende started to cry quietly, and the room was hushed and it was as if nothing at all had happened since 1939: The United States had not climbed into bed with Franco; the dictator's handpicked successor had not been entertained at the White House; the United States had not assumed in Indochina the role that Germany played in Spain. It was as if all the old words still had meaning, as if freedom and liberty and human decency had not been debased by bad usage, as if the ideals so many good men died for had indeed triumphed after all. It was as if they had shouted *"no pasaran"* and no one had gotten past them.

When the evening was over, they exchanged addresses and phone numbers, and collected the coats and went back into the strange country that America had become in the years since they were young. That country had done badly by them, but honor is not something that is pinned on you by the likes of Richard Nixon. Honor is something you earn by actions, and the men of the Abraham Lincoln Brigade are all honorable men. Outside in the rain, looking for a cab, I remembered the man who had come up to me and asked me if I was related to the Hamill who fought at the Jarama. I really didn't know, but, by God, I'm going to claim him.

February 15, 1971

March Against Death

From the Arlington Memorial Bridge, we could see the first marchers moving out of the sprawling canvas tents in the distance, their candles bobbing like trained fireflies in the darkness behind them. The broad mass of the Potomac slid by silently, like a strand of glossy tar in the night. Above us, helicopters with blinking red lights churned their way across the night sky.

The marchers approached the bridge in single file, all of them very quiet, almost reverent, and most of them young. They had come to the capital of their country prepared for the worst and were dressed that way: in combat jackets, and rough trousers, and high, bridgemen's shoes. There were a lot of beards and a lot of hair, but there were also many people in sleek clothing, the middle-class joining its children, and all of them wore the special talisman of this evening: a two-foot-wide shoe of cardboard on a string around the neck, bearing the name of an American who had been killed in Vietnam.

The cards were to be carried past the White House, where the names were to be shouted in the night, and then on to the Capitol, where they would be placed in twelve plywood coffins for later delivery to the President.

"My husband once wrote to me that we should not get out of Vietnam tomorrow, we should get out of Vietnam today," said Mrs. Judy Droz, who led the march, carrying the name of her husband, Navy Lieutenant David Glenn Droz, who was killed last April 12.

She read earlier from a prepared statement: "We have already waited too long for those tomorrows. There is no light at the end of this tunnel, only the darkness which enveloped my husband."

Behind Mrs. Droz, was Mrs. Anne Balsan, from Great Kills, Staten Island, a pretty brunette whose brother, Private First Class Walter L. Nutt 3d, had been killed in Dong Tam, Vietnam, on April 28, 1968. Filing out behind them were thousands more, led by seven drummers beating black crepe-paper-covered drums. They stopped before a wall of reporters and photographers, and talked briefly, and then started out across the bridge. Halfway across, a brace of strobes lit up, and you could see Dr. Benjamin Spock, tall and white-haired, walking with his placard bearing the name of Jimmie B. Taylor. He was asked if he knew who Jimmie B. Taylor was.

"All I know," Spock said, "is that he was from Alabama and he was killed and he was killed for no good purpose."

It was growing colder, and the weather report had threatened snow, but still the marchers came, always with the muffled drums away off, and occasional cars loaded with the enraged passing by. "Hey, ya buncha nuts," someone shouted from a passing car, and another car, driven by a young man, went by with its horn jammed down hard, as anguished in its own way as the marchers were in theirs.

When the marchers had crossed the bridge, they went silently. It had been announced earlier that no marchers would speak until they reached the Capitol, because they wanted the tone of the march to be funereal. It was funereal all right, as the lights fluttered and went out in the wind, and falling leaves were crunched in the darkness, and photographers and reporters bumped into each other, while high up on the right a tiny group of spectators watched in the brightness of the Lincoln Memorial. There was no chanting, no bravado, no obscenity, not even any hot anger. Just an eerie silence. And the drums.

As the line passed the low, three-story munitions buildings, you could see black men swabbing floors, and guards staring out with puzzled faces. At the Navy Department, a lone sailor watched from behind the locked doors. Someone had pasted a sign on the wall saying: "Support America, not Hanoi." The line crossed Constitution Avenue at Seventeenth Street, with the Washington Monument to the right, and someone looked up at its chiseled peak with the red lights blinking to ward off airplanes, and said: "God, it looks like a monument to the Ku Klux Klan." That was a line from a citizen of a broken country. When a car backfired a block away, one's first impulse was to look for someone who had been shot.

Nearing the White House, the march was picking up stragglers at the front, instead of the rear. On the right in the distance was the Executive Office Building, a brooding vulgar pile, with lights burning on the first few floors, and then pinching off into darkness at the top, like the eyes of its major occupant, Spiro T. Agnew.

At the corner of Seventeenth and Pennsylvania Avenue, local police in white riot helmets checked credentials at a barricade, while the drums approached in the distance. At 7:17, after turning into the glare of strobe lights, the first marchers went past the northwest gate.

You could not see the White House very clearly, because banks of blinding lights had been turned in the direction of the marchers from the White House lawn.

But the marchers didn't seem to care: They went by and spoke out the names of the dead: Wayne Collins, Melvin Baker, Geronimo Lerma, Joseph Aragon, Edward Lentz, Bill Moschetti, Donald Schaefer, James P. Delaney, Joseph Santos, Robert Levin . . . one after the other, on and on and the names from the state of California seemed endless: More than 3,000 from California were dead, and it would take awhile to speak all their names. They moved on to the Capitol, and as I write this, you can still see the line of candles filing down the streets around it.

It was all symbols, of course, but perhaps that is what we've come to. Agnew's assault last night on the First Amendment was a symbol. So was Strom Thurmond, getting up in the Senate to say: "I submit that the New Mobilization Committee and its present activities are part of the international Communist movement, no matter how sincere some of the participants may be. . . ." So was the presence of the Eighty-second Airborne and units of the Marine Corps hiding in Bolling AF Base and the Old Soldiers Home, while others waited at the Anacostia Naval Station, Fort McNair, and Fort Myer. They were symbols, as were the members of the Washington police who were photographing the marchers as they went by, the oldest tactic in the Southern sheriff's handbook.

Richard Nixon's trip to Capitol Hill for an unprecedented visit to both houses of Congress was a symbol: He did not, after all, tell them anything new, and was hustled in a side door to stay away from the 150 Congressional employees who were standing in silent vigil on the Capitol steps. It was a symbol of something broken that 200 people were arrested here yesterday for the terrible crime of holding a mass in the Pentagon. I suppose Attila the Hun wouldn't have permitted such vicious activities, either.

And yet the young people on the line of march were a promise of something better, if we survive the next few years, or even the next few days. It is possible that the Crazies and the Weathermen might turn it all to blood and steel, and there are some people in the administration who would welcome that opportunity.

But even if this March of Death does not go violent, then it cannot be ignored. Yesterday's Gallup Poll showed that doves now outnumber hawks 55 percent to 31, with 14 percent uncommitted.

Say what you will about polls, that number must indicate something. And the young people here are *here:* not in Sweden, not in Canada, not in Yucatán. They are Americans come to say something to their government. The most terrible tragedy of all would be if the government has already decided that it can lose an entire generation.

A lot of Americans are knocking on the White House door today, but for the moment at least, nobody appears to be home.
November 14, 1969

The Boy Revolutionaries

The day had started in a way that was oddly beautiful. All day long, these girls in yellow ponchos and boys with rain beading in their matted hair kept up their mournful file, locked together in silent witness, carrying with them their hope, their youth, and the names of the American dead.

They moved past the muted doors of the White House, and around the Treasury Building, and down the great stone gully of Pennsylvania Avenue, with the Capitol Building always there before them, like the establishing shot in every bad Washington movie they had ever seen. By nightfall it had turned ugly and violent, and gas seeped through the streets of the capital, and convoys of troops moved past them silently, heading for possible conflict with other Americans.

"It could turn bad," Adam Walinski said in late afternoon, in the chaos of the eighth-floor offices of the Moratorium Committee on Vermont Avenue. "We hope not, and we've been talking all day to those people. We'll just have to see."

These people were the boy revolutionaries, a sect of romantic middle-class children who yesterday were calling themselves the Revolutionary Contingent in Solidarity with the Vietnamese people. The sect has many splinters, of course, and yesterday

156

these included the various subsplinters of SDS, the Mad Dogs, the Crazies, Youth Against War and Fascism, and the Weathermen.

They had called a rally at DuPont Circle, in the center of an area where most of Washington's hippies have gathered for the past several years. The purpose, theoretically, was to march down Massachusetts Avenue about six blocks to Sheridan Circle, where the South Vietnamese embassy was located, and present an "eviction notice" in the name of the Vietcong-National Liberation Front. But that was not the real purpose. Everyone knew what they wanted: bloody, violent combat with the police and the National Guard, which they hoped would lead to the radicalization of all the others who were arriving for today's mass march.

"I called a guy named David Livingston from RM II Newsreel, one of the radical groups," a guy I know told me. "I told him I had a busload of people from Chicago, and I wanted to know whether they should go to DuPont Circle, whether it was going to be peaceful. He told me that they would march, and if the police asked them to stop, they would disperse peacefully and go back to the circle. He was lying."

So about 2,000 people assembled in the circle about 8 P.M. to listen to the harsh and rasping speeches of whoever had possession of the bullhorn. And then they set off down Massachusetts Avenue. Along the sidewalks were larger numbers of curious young people; when the boy revolutionaries told them to come out into the street, they did not go. Then the boy revolutionaries broke into a run, heading for the embassy, and the police stopped them with tear gas. That was to be the pattern through a long and ugly evening: It was not to be a Chicago, filled with beatings and blood; the police here were to try to do it with gas.

They came back along P Street, filing into the circle, which is the Parisian-style hub of at least five main streets, and several smaller ones. They were shouting: "Ho, Ho, Ho Chi Minh, NLF is gonna win." And they were carrying Vietcong, Cuban, and Algerian flags. One kid came up to me and said he was from Brooklyn and asked me what I thought would happen. I told him to go home. Just then, another band of about 150 marchers came into the circle, and a short-legged kid with a lumber jacket, a bandanna on his head, and the hard agate eyes of the true believer grabbed a bullhorn and shouted, "We're just regrouping here! We're not giving up now!"

Behind him, the Weathermen, wearing dark helmets and face masks, were flexing their muscles. There were about 60 of them. They were waving their black flags and their red flags and the flags of countries which stink of the grave, and they were spoiling for a fight. Around the edges of the crowd, the shaved heads of the Hare Krishna kids bobbed and moved, while some of them asked for money for the work of God.

Then suddenly, coming up past the People's Drugstore, were the police. A rock came out of the mob, and then everyone was running; about 20 of the young people stopped at a vacant lot at the corner of Nineteenth Street and loaded up with broken hunks of brick. A group of them went storming down Nineteenth Street, and I suppose it says something about them that the first brick they fired went through the window of a liquor store owned by a black man and the other went through the window of a bookstore.

Then they started to drift back into the circle. I looked up at the clock on the Guardian Federal Savings Bank; it was 9:13, and 37 degrees. Across the street, in the trampled grass and mud, the kids were soaking handkerchiefs in the water of the public fountains. Then there were sirens again, and more running. A kid heaved a brick through the window of the People's Drugstore on the far corner, and then a volley caved in the other windows, and then four trash baskets were lugged into the street and set on fire. A medical truck from the Seventh-day Adventist community services came to a stop at the burning baskets, and now there was a heavy roar of police sirens.

The gas came with a dull thump, exploding in blue clumps in the center of the plaza, and rising on the hard wind, the plumes looking strange against the black sky, and then we were all in flight. Not, as in Chicago, from the swinging bats of a punishing police force; this time it was from the corrupted air. I had a gas mask, but it didn't work; surplus, of course, from a government contractor. My skin was burning, and in flight, Connecticut Avenue became a white, brilliant blur, while all around me I heard very young girls screaming: "Gas, gas, go back, it's gas, they're gassing us. Oh, my God, they're gassing us." The wind was blowing behind us with the gas always somewhere ahead.

I ran into a place called the DuPont Villa, where the owner was locking the door against the kids with beards. Inside, people were calmly eating veal Parmigiana and lasagna. At the bar, a dozen guys sat on barstools watching a war movie.

I went into the men's room and washed my eyes with water. Outside, a waitress gave me a soaked napkin and a bottle of Schlitz, and through the drawn curtains I could still see people running. Nobody stirred from the bar. It must have been some movie.

And so it went through the evening: the kids falling back before the gas, then regrouping, and the gas coming again. At 10:10 there was a mild barrage of tear gas canisters, arcing high through the air in every direction, before us, around us, in front of us, as indiscriminate as the air itself, and all of us were running again.

After a while, it finally grew tedious. I grabbed a cab and went down to the White House. The long line of kids was still moving around the place where Richard Nixon sleeps the sleep of the just, their candles blowing in the wind. I suppose they hadn't heard yet what had happened. They were doing something of beauty and value, and not far away, a pack of swinish children was doing its best to prove that the likes of Agnew, Mitchell, Kleindienst had been right. But this one thing should be made very clear: If you read in the underground papers that the police were brutes, you read a lie. And if you read somewhere that this outbreak of a vicious little sect had anything to do with stopping the war or with the Moratorium itself, you read a lie.

The story of the Moratorium was those young people in the rain, marching toward the Capitol Building in peace. Very late last night, as a convoy of soldiers moved up New York Avenue in the direction of DuPont Circle, those other young people were still moving in silence. The boy revolutionaries had done their best to ruin it all, but there weren't enough of them. There never will be.

November 15, 1969

Ending the Sixties

Finally, on a cold bright Sunday morning, with the streets cleared of refuse and tear gas canisters, and the khaki jeeps returned to the armories, and the bitter smell of tear gas replaced again by burning leaves, the Capitol of the Republic became its old implacable self again. The great stone piles of the government buildings were quiet. Men watched football on a thousand TV sets. In isolated areas, the police were settling some last small arguments with their invaders, but to them the process was now one of fumigation rather than combat. It was over. All of it.

And it is unlikely that we shall see anything like it again. We will never see anything like that Saturday morning when we walked through the cold morning air along Constitution Avenue, with streams of children on all sides of us, heading for the Mall of the Capitol Building, thousands of them, with sweet, clear faces, carrying their ponchos, duffel bags, and youth; seven or eight deep on both sides of the streets, coming like tributaries from some secret source heading for a wild and terrible basin. They had come from everywhere, to shout out for life. You could look at them only once and know that they were not what was wrong with America.

We will never see them again precisely like this: spreading out across the Mall, their peers marshaling them with precision and manners, while in the distance flags billowed in the breeze, red and black, like the emblems of some giant Arab army in those old movies about holy wars. They moved among each other without hostility, free in some strange way from the impacted resentments of my generation. They held signs that said, THANK YOU, MR. NIXON, FOR BRINGING US TOGETHER, and FIGHTING FOR PEACE IS LIKE BALLING FOR CHASTITY, and some of them shivered under the hard blue sky, and others shared their peanut butter and jelly sandwiches, and others bobbed in a morning dance. We have always been a country devoid of gorgeous splendor, but on this Saturday they were to provide it all.

How to explain that afternoon? Details: Richie Havens singing with fierce passion about freedom; the earth, wet from the rains of the night before, turning to hard mud, and reporters clustering around hot coffee urns in a plastic tent; Peter Yarrow running the stage, and the shrill contempt-filled voices of women radicals; Paul O'Dwyer on the speakers' platform with his white hair riffling in the breeze; photographers swaying on a platform. And all the while the hill at the base of the Monument filling up, like a multicolored carpet, blotting out the green in every direction, and freshly arrived reporters telling that they were now spreading out behind the Monument, beyond our vision.

Nobody knew how many were there, neither the reporters nor the police; it could have been a half million; it could have been more. At some point I climbed up on the steel pipe structure which held the great sound system, to look; I had never seen so many people in one place in my life, not even when Lyndon Johnson's Asian clients were assembling entire nations, during one of his public relations marches through the Orient.

I remember this: David Dellinger, a middle-aged man who should know better, shouting hoarsely into the microphone, encouraging children to go to the Justice Department later, where they were certain to be tear-gassed, arrested, or worse. At his side were Jerry Rubin and Abbie Hoffman, the stand-up comics of the boy revolutionaries; Rubin, great nonconformist that he is, displayed the wig he wears to disguise the dread short haircut he received in prison. You could tell by looking at them that when the gas went off, they would not be breathing it.

I remember the boy revolutionaries crowding around the press entrance near the stage, with their flags billowing, and the rumors that they would storm the stage when George McGovern spoke, to strike down the vicious liberal enemy; the young marshals, arms locked together, holding them back, while the scent of incense drifted everywhere, and someone who had been at both places came over to say that it was two Woodstocks. Timothy Leary, his tanned face ravaged and lined, dressed in buckskin and white ducks, like some Southern Cali-

161

fornia version of Dorian Gray. Dick Gregory told Agnew jokes, and Phil Hutchins of SNCC drove off thousands with one of those endless globs of bleary leftist rhetoric about the Third World. But there were to be two superb moments which everyone there would carry forever.

The first came when Pete Seeger started to sing "All we are saying is give peace a chance." It started slowly, and then Mitch Miller was there, waving his arms to lead the crowd, and Mary Travers was beside them, and the song came chanting down, the first chant Americans have ever sung in such numbers, the crowd swaying to the music, like a rippling carpet, and Seeger saying: "Are you listening, Nixon? Are you listening, Agnew? Are you listening in the Pentagon?" and the music going on, for eight and a half minutes, everyone in the place locked into it. I ran into a tough saloon fighter I know who had tears in his eyes, who kept saying, "I've never seen anything like it. Never."

The other moment was also musical, as it had to be. Words don't mean much to a lot of these kids, and the dreary words of the rigid left must mean even less, like some odd form of static. The second moment came late in the day, when the grass was showing at the base of the Monument, and hundreds were already on the way to the Justice Department to receive their gassing for the likes of David Dellinger. The cast of *Hair* assembled onstage with beautiful Melba Moore singing out across that clamorous field, all about the age of Aquarius and then about letting the sunshine in. And the kids really joined in this one, while the stage became jammed, and someone let out a flock of doves. One dove skimmed over the crowd in a kind of salute and winged its way past them and past the Washington Monument and out into the cold city which had forced all of them to assemble here.

That last chorus said it all: Young kids, open and free about so many things, joined together, some of them swaying joyfully on each other's backs, a girl in a glossy black raincoat with her hands joined to other marshals and her head turned to watch the stage. Others crying, they were there to say farewell to the 1960's, a desperate and bloody era, one that had begun with John Kennedy standing in weather like this telling them that

162

the torch had passed to a new generation, and now, looking out at them, you remembered that when Kennedy was inaugurated most of them were only ten. The new generation was us; I wish to God we had done better.

So they had grown up with Richard Speck coming in the night window with his knife and Charles Whitman climbing to his tower; they had watched the limousine pass the Texas Book Depository a hundred times on TV, and seen Oswald's contorted face, and remembered clearly how Robert Kennedy had moved through the crowds of California and what Gene McCarthy had done in New Hampshire; they knew about that, and about Woodstock, and what the cops had done in the night in Chicago, and the way the fires had burned in Watts and Newark and Cleveland and Washington; they knew that Martin Luther King was dead and Eldridge Cleaver was in Algeria and that 12,000 miles from where they stood on the damp American earth, singing about hope, Americans were being slaughtered over abstractions.

At 5:52, on November 15, the last chorus ended, and the sixties were over. They had begun in hope, and ended with Richard Nixon in the White House and Spiro Agnew threatening other Americans with "separation," and when the crowd drifted away, there was no feeling left except remorse and loss and waste. The country had failed those children, and you could promise them nothing anymore except dark and fearful future.

November 17, 1969

Land's End

In the morning, we awoke to the sea's long deep roar, pulling at the beach, attacking and receding, punctuated by the scree of the gulls. There were no other sounds: no harsh grate of metal, no sirens trumpeting disaster, no cough of motorized exhaust. Only the Atlantic: constant, brooding, somehow defiantly

163

regal; an ocean of hard times, not a serene glassy lake like the Pacific; a sea with a history of winters, demanding nothing, indifferent, free.

That morning there was no horizon, as the fogs swirled in from somewhere beyond the sight of land. The beach was empty, desolate, covered with the tracks of birds. The wind combed the dune grass and bent the pines on the bluffs; once a boy in a red jacket appeared on the brow of the land, looked out over the sea, and disappeared. We climbed up for a better view, in a place where thorn bushes were skeletal and angry-looking, like some jagged calligraphy etched by hornets. A Tuborg beer bottle lay in the brambles, the label almost gone. Below, each end of the beach was shrouded in the fog. And the sea's bass challenge went on.

Everywhere, proud houses stood on the highlands, shuttered for the winter. They spoke of some ancient love of right angles, of wood closely fitted and joined, welded together with some confident belief in permanence, as if this parenthesis were wider than it really is, as if those houses would survive and the sea would come only so far and no farther. If Gatsby had lived, you felt sure that he would have left the tinkle of the night bands behind in the Hamptons, folded the last Chinese lanterns away in trunks, and come to live in this stillness, to forget forever the tarnished promise of the green light on Daisy's dock.

And yet, the "no trespassing" signs on the stairways leading to those houses whispered something else. There were burglar alarm stickers plastered on the windows and sheets of plastic tacked to the doors, and they seemed more than mere ritual demands for privacy from crowded summers. They were gestures against strangers coming from the city, with their cargoes of carelessness and disdain, arriving in buses and trains and rented cars. And they were more than that: you write "no trespassing" on the place in which you live when you hope to ward off a violation. It is part of the juju of a tribe that knows fear.

On the beach, solitary, removed from New York's hammering pressure, the instincts begin to relax. You watch a gull skim above the waves, with the economy of the great hunters, graceful in ways that no other living thing can be, making a slice of line against the roiled sea. And, suddenly, at the end of the arc, you see a figure in the mist at the end of your vision, coming down the beach. Fear makes its move; you keep walking, but there is no longer room for distraction; the New York instinct takes over, that tribal move that sends you to the other side of the street at night when strangers walk toward you. You do not see stones and driftwood around you; you see weapons.

And then you uncoil, feeling somehow foolish, because the figure is a thickset woman with straw-colored hair, wearing a hat that seems made for someone out of *Mr. Hulot's Holiday*. She goes by wordlessly, staring at the ground, driven by some private engine, and you think that perhaps she is quite mad. She probably thinks the same of you, standing there, lighting cigarettes, exhaling fiercely in the sea wind. A body set to smash and defend has gone suddenly loose, and why, she must think, is he trying to laugh?

We come to a sea quarry, with stones of all sizes displayed on the beach as if it were some vast tray at Cartier's. Smoothed and formed by the sea, they lie in a tumble of colors and textures: some the color of crabs, some gray with serrated edges, some the color of the ocean's dark depths. In the middle of them, the girl sees an almost perfect stone, shaped like some prehistoric egg, a pure white among the textures, the egg of the world.

Later we'll come back for it, with a bag strong enough to carry it. Sure. Yeah. Hey, that's great. But we go another hundred yards, looking at the soiled edges of the beach where fuel oil has turned the sand to the color of a bruise, looking at the great scummy clusters of undigested phosphates, when we look back and see the woman with the hat poking in the quarry. A shrug. There it goes. But on the way back, we see the great white stone rolled out on the sand, discarded, I suppose, because of its weight. It seems to be reaching back to the sea.

So we took it with us, the gritty feel of sand against its smooth whiteness making it a sensual thing. It was washed and laid out to dry on a sideboard, and it sits there now, gleaming and opaque and silent, a small trophy plundered from the sea. A bomb just blew up in the Senate, and men are dying foolishly in Asia. The sea doesn't seem to care, and neither does the egg of the world.

March 2, 1971

III. Nam

A FEW days before New Year's of 1966, I went to Vietnam, for five weeks, and the pieces that follow are the result of that trip. I knew very little about Vietnam then, nor did most Americans. I tried very hard to make the place itself come alive on the page, to say something about what it looked like and smelled like, to create a sense of its uniqueness, its shape, and how the weather was. There are few combat stories here for the simple reason that Lyndon Johnson was then engaged in his Great Peace Offensive (later exposed as a public relations hoax), and there was a virtual cease-fire on the battlefield. Most of my pieces were being mailed, rather than cabled, so the day-to-day coverage of the war remained the task of the AP and the other wire services. This left me free to move around the countryside, talk at some leisure to soldiers, look at the pacification program, and try to get some sense of the Vietnamese themselves. The pieces now seem heavy with death and an uneasy sense that the Vietnam adventure was not going to be some quick expedition into a Latin-American country, where the Marines would change the president, give the customs jobs to our supporters, build a few roads, and move on. We were in for a long season in the swamps.

The war in Vietnam forced me to question a number of loosely held personal beliefs and altered my entire approach to writing the column. In the first weeks out there, I understood that I could not cover this basically political war the way Ernie Pyle and so many other good reporters had covered the Second

World War; often the eighteen-year-old soldiers could not find adequate language to explain what they were going through or would revert to clichés from old war movies to try to express profound feelings. Increasingly, I shifted into a description of what I felt myself, because I was at least reasonably sure of those feelings. And when I got home, it was impossible for me to see the United States in precisely the same way that I had seen it when I left for my brief season at the war.

In the months and years that followed, the war seemed to touch everything. I would walk through the slums of Brownsville and Bedford-Stuyvesant and see the great complex at Cam Ranh Bay rising from the sand. I would see children stuffed into welfare hotels, eating grease, or falling down elevator shafts and remember that artillery and bombs were exploding in Asia at a cost of $30 billion a year. I had a parochial, selfish concern about New York; it was a great city, and I loved it more than any place I had ever visited. But slowly it was beginning to die. We paid more taxes to the federal government than any city in the country, but we never had enough money; the streets were dirtier, the air was poisoned, the subways were creaking into decay, the school system was a shambles, the welfare rolls were exploding, but we never had enough money. The money was going up in smoke and shredded metal in Asia.

None of that would have mattered if this had been another kind of war. I am not a pacifist; nobody with my personal quotient of violence could be a complete pacifist without being a hypocrite. The Second World War should have been fought, and if I had been old enough, I'd have gone to do what I could do. The Irish patriots of 1916 had to fight, because they had spent hundreds of useless years trying to be civilized; the Algerians were correct in using armed force against the French because it was their country, and the French wouldn't listen to talk; and later, reading about Indochina, I thought it clear that the Vietminh were right to fight the French after the betrayal of 1946. There are times when the only thing a decent man can do is pick up the gun.

But in South Vietnam, the United States had become involved in somebody else's quarrel, and probably on the wrong side. Ho Chi Minh was not about to sail into San Diego Harbor in a junk and start the rape of America. The United States itself was not directly threatened. And yet the President and his advisers were talking as if the fate of Western civilization depended upon Vietnam. They talked about "aggression" and used a variety of reasons for explaining why Americans had to die and bleed in Vietnam. None of them rang true. We were being asked to root for the upperdog, to believe that we were the offended party despite the fact that we were the most powerful military nation on the earth. In the early part of the war, the enemy was the Vietcong, a relatively small band of guerrillas without trucks, a sophisticated weapons system, or an air force; we were fighting them with artillery, B-52's, napalm, and an army of 500,000 men, along with more than 1,000,000 armed South Vietnamese. It just did not seem right.

At the same time, a lot of Americans had ceased believing in the devil theory of Communism. Joseph Stalin was long dead, and our own moral purity had long since been compromised by alliances with Chiang Kai-shek, Franco, Salazar, Batista, Duvalier, Trujillo, and a gaggle of other two-bit despots around the world. The Bay of Pigs created the first self-doubts about our sincerity; the invasion of the Dominican Republic in search of imaginary Communists heightened it; the adventure in Vietnam seemed proof of our emergence as some new kind of imperial power. We were a nation increasingly afraid of revolution, of self-determination, most specifically, of disorder; we saw the left as the enemy in every country of the world and preferred the graveyard order of right-wing dictatorships to any alternative that might promise radical social change. The Green Berets did not move into Greece when the colonels overthrew the legitimately elected government of that country. And while American energy, blood, and money were being consumed in a civil war in Asia, the cities of America were burning.

The most difficult thing about being a journalist in that period was the need to explain that one's position on the war did not spring from hatred of America, but from love. I saw it very personally and never hid my feelings about it. My parents did not choose America because it was a warrior nation; they came here to be free. And freedom was intimately connected with justice and a certain elemental decency. Vietnam soon became the focus for everything that was unjust or indecent about America. Our leaders were serving us a meal of lies, and early on, the indigestion set in. These pieces are a chronicle of a brief visit to the war. They were followed by a long series of articles tracing the American involvement in Vietnam; that involvement has been explained better by people like Bernard Fall, David Halberstam, Jean LaCouture, and others, so I have chosen not to reprint them. As I write, American troops have been reduced to the same level they were at in 1966; the South Vietnamese have left Laos at the end of a North Vietnamese boot; Cambodia is torn by war. Lieutenant Calley has been sentenced to life for slaughtering civilians at My Lai; other atrocity stories are building up in the wings, and there is much talk about war crimes trials. The Pentagon is still constructing beautiful fabrications, and the President has been on TV to explain, as all his predecessors, political and military, had done before him, that there is light at the end of the tunnel. There are more than 35,000 more dead Americans since I was there, and several hundred thousand wounded; the most conservative estimates place the number of dead Vietnamese civilians at 150,000; and nobody is sure of the number of North Vietnamese dead. The cities of America are on the edge of bankruptcy and collapse; unemployment is beginning to hit the white middle class; a lot of Vietnam veterans are coming home as heroin addicts; the Army itself is demoralized and close to rebellion. The war goes on. It might someday end, but we shall never be the same country again.

New Year's Eve in a Saigon Hospital

At dusk we rode out Cong Ly Street to the Third Army field hospital. Traffic was clotted and dusty, and away off the sky had reddened into a long, garish smear. Helicopters thrashed the air like giant birds, and as we came to the hospital, we could see them dropping the wounded at Tan Son Nhut Airport. There had been no big actions on this New Year's Eve at war, but men were still being hurt and killed in all the small ways.

Once the hospital had been a school, but in wars the mind of man is always a casualty, and the schools become hostels for re-pairing ruined bodies. We walked past a barbed-wire fence with two MP's at the gate and went with a nurse down a long white corridor to Ward 213. The walls were covered with Christmas decorations, and beneath them lay the damaged young men of the war.

A soldier lay on his back in bed, both legs swathed in band-ages, trying to read a book. His right foot was missing.

Across the aisle a thin blond kid stared at the wall, a long red tear running across his chest. A man lay unconscious with tubes running into his nose and throat, his lips parched and thirsty.

Christmas was gone, but New Year's Eve was just another evening, the men say, drinking sodas, talking softly, knowing that their bodies would never again be what they once were—and neither would they.

This hospital was filled with casualties. You could list their names, their addresses, and the brutal wounds they have suffered. You could print all of that in the agate, and there would still not be enough room in this newspaper for all of them.

But perhaps the war is really about young men like Michael Lauletta.

Lauletta is twenty-one years old, and he grew up in Elmhurst, Queens, until he joined the Army last year. He lived at 51-32 Goldsmith Street. He is a thin, narrow-faced kid with crew-cut brown hair and a nervous smile, and when I talked to him, he was reading a James Bond book in bed. His right leg was covered with bandages. He had lost four of his toes. "We were out near Ben Cat," Lauletta said. His voice is charged with the accents of New York, the quick delivery and the hard *r*, and it was wonderful to hear. "That's about fifteen miles from Saigon. We were out on this operation, and we had been out there maybe seven, eight days. Then this morning near this rubber plantation which we're guarding we hear some firing. We were around a big road, fifteen meters on each side controlled by us, and I guess there were maybe four hundred of us—what they call a reinforced battallion."

He took a fast drag on a filtertipped cigarette. "They started shooting like hell. Everybody in my platoon got shot, and then I was hit, and I said to myself, 'Well, I got mine.'

"I was still able to move, and I was lucky because the medic was right behind me, a guy named Bill Wright. He got hit, too. We were still shootin' like hell, and then I got hit in the back with a piece of shrapnel and I couldn't move."

Lauletta, who was with the Second Battalion, Second Infantry of the First Army Division, had been shot through the calf by a 50-caliber machine-gun bullet. The bullet had torn the calf right off his body, and by the time helicopters came gangrene had poisoned his leg.

"At first they thought they would have to take the whole leg off," he said. "They got some doctors here."

Like most soldiers, Lauletta talked quietly and modestly about what had happened, almost as if he were embarrassed by it. Men don't start bragging about war until they are fat and forty-five and standing in saloons. But when Lauletta started talking easily, you began to understand that like most of the others his life was changed forever.

"Oh, yeah, I miss New York," he said. "I miss the ball parks most of all. I went to Power Memorial and played a lot of baseball there and in the CYO, and I spent a year at college as a phys ed major at NYU."

He was a Giant fan, he said, and he seemed particularly pleased that he had gone to Power when Lew Alcinder had been the greatest high school basketball player in history.

172

"I guess I won't be playing much ball anymore," Lauletta said. "Not with a foot like that I won't."

On Tuesday Lauletta goes home because the war in Vietnam is over for him. He'll be going back to New York, where he'll see some old friends, guys with names like Joe Knau, Richie Miller, Bill Melnyk, Red McNulty. He'll be in the Army two years more, but he has to be ahead. He's alive.

I asked him whether he thought we should be in the war. "It didn't bother me coming over here," he said, "but I'll be glad to go home. There's too many things to worry about here. We were told not to shoot the rubber trees. If we shoot the rubber trees, we have to pay for them. It's a hell of a way to fight a war." It certainly is.

On the way out I stopped in the emergency room where all new cases are brought from the field. An Army nurse, Lieutenant Sue Brandon, was looking over a boy who had just arrived on a stretcher.

Plasma was being pumped into his arms, and thick wads of bandage covered his eyes. He had been hit in both eyes with shrapnel. Someone asked if the boy would see again. Lieutenant Brandon shrugged. He was being shipped in a few hours to Clark Field in Manila. They would do their best.

There was little noise and no celebrations anywhere else. During wars only civilians celebrate, and walking out of that hospital—the night dark, truckloads of American, Korean, and South Vietnamese soldiers moving down the dusty road—I thought of all the mangled flesh I had just seen, of the scars and the violated childhoods, and I hoped that somewhere in America tonight someone would stop at a party and drink a small toast to these children with old men's faces.

The toast should say something about the dead and something about the dying and something about the young men with ruined eyes and shattered limbs and guys like Michael Lauletta, who was luckier than most. His only problem now is that he will never again be able to move to his right for a ground ball in a safe and grassy place. I wish to hell I could tell him why.

December 31, 1966

Saigon: A Treacherous City

In the morning we ate breakfast in the My Canh riverboat restaurant. There, sitting at a wooden table, eating an omelet, sipping coffee, you felt a part of that hoked-up Orient from the old books and the half-remembered movies. Did not that sea captain with the gold earring step from some Michael Curtiz sound stage? That slender girl in the flowing *ao dai* dress—did she not come out of Conrad?

As we ate, junks moved through the muck-colored Saigon River, their tenders dressed in shorts and conical hats, paddling with even, patient strokes. Across the river, a long, jumbled row of huts was squashed against the waterline, while billboards rose above them, advertising transistor radios and lubricating oil.

The city itself was almost mournfully silent. Occasionally, the toneless boom of a foghorn could be heard from downriver, and then the steady chukkachukkachukkachukkachukk of a motorboat. Before us, the great merchant ships of the world were moored to the teeming docks, being emptied of the materials of war by scurrying platoons of Vietnamese longshoremen. The ships bent away from us in a diminishing arc, vanishing behind the bend of the river, their spiky wilderness of masts and spars forming an almost Oriental calligraphy against the foggy morning. Halfway through breakfast, we heard artillery.

Puh-phwoom! Puh-phwoom! It was coming from perhaps 15 or 20 miles away, and John Harris, an old friend from the Hearst papers, said it was probably 105-mm artillery. "I'm glad," Harris said, "they're firing that way."

This restaurant itself had been bombed by the Vietcong some months before, because it was favored by many Americans. A bomb filled with steel slivers had gone off in a corner, scattering human beings before it, and then, when the survivors rushed across the small gangway that connects the boat to the shore, a second bomb went off and killed them, too. This was, of course, an act of murder, and no veneer of political necessity could alter its basic indecency.

In Saigon today, no one ever looks directly at the person he eats dinner with; he is too busy watching the other customers. If a man walks into the men's room carrying a briefcase and emerges without it, one is advised to hit the floor. This is known as civilization.

One of the terrible things about all of this is that Saigon is a city of great physical charm, the sort of place one might visit on a vacation. It reminds me of certain sections of Mexico City and Barcelona, with broad, open avenues and squares, trees ruffled by a slight breeze from the river, flower markets, restaurants opening onto the streets, newsboys walking barefoot. The architecture is a kind of 1920's Modern gone through a sea change, with rounded "streamlined" corners, streaking concrete façades and hotel lobbies filled with bad paintings.

I have seen old photographs of the city, in the days when the main streets were covered with outdoor cafés, tables strewn across sidewalks, people sitting at them reading the papers fresh in from Paris. The French invented modern Saigon, and it is a city built for pleasure. Looking out across it from the roof of the Hotel Caravelle, with the red-tile roofs reaching through the trees for the river, you could be looking at a slice of Provence.

But today it is a city under siege, its very heart laced with treachery. No one can say precisely how many Vietcong sympathizers there are among the city's 2,000,000 inhabitants. But simply because of that, there is a sinister atmosphere about the place. Americans are the target, and you can never be sure if the shoeshine boy or the hall porter might be your killer. The Vietnamese are a people of great manners, dependent on nuance and ritual; they make most Americans feel clumsy and boorish. But walking the city, you feel more than that. In addition, you feel vulnerable, probably as vulnerable as you ever will in your life. In combat conditions, you expect to be shot at. You don't expect it while reading Malraux over your morning omelet.

This afternoon I stopped for a beer in the Imperial Bar on Tu Do Street, which under the French was the Rue Catinat, one of the most exclusive shopping streets in the Orient. The outdoor tables are gone now, and the sidewalks are filthy. Most of the great restaurants have their windows covered with wire mesh and elaborate grilles (the Saigon *Post* even contains advertisements for barbed wire, cut to your specifications). Sitting in the Imperial, sipping a 33 beer, I suddenly realized that I was drinking in a cage. No one even sat near the rim of the cage, because if a hurled grenade bounced off and exploded, fragments could still blind or maim you. The best table in the house was behind a two-foot-thick pillar near the bar. Sitting at it was a large-breasted Frenchwoman in her forties. She was the owner.

The streets come alive about ten in the morning here, though occasionally a government jeep will drive around earlier, blaring exhortatory speeches from its loudspeakers and then playing atonal music for the alleged benefit of the listeners. Some of the correspondents call this character Nguyen the K. The first time I heard it I couldn't tell whether he was running for office, shilling for a department store, or announcing a coup.

The city's tempo is swift but erratic. Each day, war or no war, everything shutters from twelve to three for siesta, and if you are looking for a high government official at those hours, you will probably locate him in a state of unconsciousness on his couch. Bicycles and a kind of open, motorized rickshaw called a cyclo are everywhere. The cyclos seem to burn river mud instead of gasoline, and between them and the hundreds of tiny blue-and-cream Renault taxis, the city is usually covered with a pale-blue exhaust fog.

There are also a lot of Vietnamese cops around, usually in pairs, dressed in white (the Americans here call them "white mice"). They watch everything, and as I write this, one of them is across the street from the hotel, standing in front of the building which the French intended as an opera house, which served for a while as the National Assembly, and which is now a kind of ghostly town hall. The cop is down there, watching me. I wave. He waves. I smile. He smiles. I suppose if I took off my shoes, he would take off his shoes.

But more than anything else, you are constantly reminded of the war. Jeeps, trucks, Navy vehicles (Saigon is 50 miles up a river from the sea) filled with soldiers and Marines whiz back and forth with great haste. The important buildings, like the

American Embassy, the USIS, and some of the hotels serving as military billets, are surrounded by cops, MP's, Marines, all of them behind a fence of round concrete blocks, three feet in diameter, strung together with lines of barbed wire. These are to prevent suicide squads from driving truckloads of dynamite to the doorstep, machine-gunning the guards, and letting the fronts of the buildings vanish in an explosion. The technique was successfully used at the Metropole Hotel a few months ago and at the U.S. Embassy last year. The Metropole is still a gutted half ruin, although the bars across the street, also damaged, have reopened.

Still, it is a pleasant enough city, and war adds its own peculiar exhilaration. This afternoon I sat in the large open-front restaurant of the Continental Palace Hotel, eating lunch. I was reading the Saigon *Post*, a newspaper of consummate style, when I saw the following ad: "Mr. Simon will offer you his Italian specialties and his famous pizza in a rustic cadre and vertimate atmosphere." How can you completely dislike a city whose advertising men write in the style of the late Colonel John R. Stingo?

The Continental Palace, by the way, is not paying off the Vietcong to keep the wire mesh off its windows. No, this hotel has the great fortune to house the Polish members of the International Control Commission. The Vietcong would certainly not want to violate the Geneva Agreements by blasting some of their fellows off the map.

January 2, 1966

The Girls of Saigon

At dusk, the sky turns mauve and sinister, with low-hanging clouds moving slowly across the surface like dark fingers bringing with them the night. In the patios of the hotels, the foliage moistens, making the plants glisten in the gloom. The great open markets cease their daylong clamor, and women with rubber shower shoes on their feet and infant children tied to their backs begin the long walk home, carrying wrinkled paper bags. The purr of bicycles is everywhere, along with the honking of taxis and the sputter of cycle drivers. Suddenly it is night, and night in Saigon belongs to Tu Do Street.

Once this was a grand street, with fancy shops and great restaurants, where the French would discuss Proust and the cotton market in the long afternoons and the merits of each other's mistresses at night. Now it is a street turning tawdry, sprinkled with bars, massage parlors, instant dentist parlors where teeth can be extracted for a dime, stores selling camera equipment and film or silk shirts in livid colors, and, mostly, a street where the lovely young girls of Saigon can be seen and sometimes bought.

They are pouring into Saigon now, hundreds of them, coming to this city where great fortunes are being made by some, and small fortunes by others. They work in the bars, some as hostesses, others as prostitutes. Most act as if there were no future. In wars, people learn to live in the moment itself, I suppose, and these girls live carefully, almost frugally, planning on opening bars of their own, but certainly not counting on it.

Walking into one of the bars is like stumbling across some Forty-second Street dream of heaven. It is all exotic-lighting, with the thump of rock 'n' roll, and gallons of whiskey and beer. And, of course, the women. There were thirteen of them behind the bar of the San Francisco Club yesterday, each with a deck of cards, each standing opposite a barstool. The girls were all dressed in the beautiful, tight-fitting *ao dai* dresses, and all were of an almost porcelain delicacy, small-waisted, small-boned, small-featured.

Bill Slocum once told me that he didn't like Oriental women because he could never tell how old they were. The one opposite me did not seem more than twelve or thirteen, and ordering a beer, I felt like a road-show version of Humbert Humbert confronting some Lolita who had just rolled in from the South China Sea. I asked her how old she was, and in a curiously baroque script she wrote the numeral 16 (the Vietnamese language has been written in a Latin script since the seventeenth century, when it was introduced by a French priest). She smiled when I raised my eyebrows, and seemed very proud.

Another girl came over and told me that she was the girl's sister, and that this was her first day on the job at the San Francisco. The little girl smiled even harder. She knew only three words in English "You." "Buy." "Drink." I've known girls in Manhattan, of course, who didn't know many more.

All over the bar, Americans were buying drinks for the girls of Tu Do Street. Beer cost the customer 30 piastres (about 18 cents). The girls drank watered crème de menthe or a concoction which one bright young lady called Saigon Tea and which turned out to be Coca-Cola. The last two cost 160 piastres, a little less than a dollar. The guy I went into the bar with kept telling the girls such stuff was bad for their teeth, but they wouldn't listen.

According to reporters who have been here a while, Vietnamese women are not in the habit of listening to anyone. They have dominated the country, in most ways, for centuries. Throughout the marketplaces, the popular novels on display all feature the ferocious exploits of their famous women. It's as if our cowboy stories were all about women. The Tran sisters, who played, in one correspondent's phrase, "a two-girl Garibaldi act," helped form the structure of the country. Madame Nhu, who arrived years later and almost succeeded in destroying it, was just a typical Vietnamese girl.

So along Tu Do Street, you can hear terrible stories of what the girls have done to American lovers who have betrayed them or thrown them off for other women or who have committed the almost unpardonable sin of wanting to leave this country. If you believe all of the stories, it would be easy to imagine nights in this town in which the only occurrences were the stabbings and mutilations of poor GI's.

On the other hand, the girls are also not about to squander their emotions. The classic case of saloon violence here involves a GI who walks into a bar at 11 A.M., buys drinks all day for his little Vietnamese barmaid, and then watches her vanish out the back door at 11:15 P.M., hop on her boyfriend's motorbike, and take off into the night. This sort of thing keeps the MP's rather busy, calming down GI's who wish only to destroy whatever steps into view.

Surprisingly, the number of American-Vietnamese marriages

is low, at least so far. It is nothing like the wave of marriages which took place in Japan after the war. One reason is that the war is just starting here; and the other appears to be the fundamental difference in character between the Japanese and Vietnamese woman.

On this one afternoon I spent several hours trying to find out something about the child sitting across the bar from me. Her name, she said, was Ahn, and she was from Long An Province, a Vietcong-ruled area in the Mekong Delta. Her sister had come to Saigon two years ago, and she had arrived three months before. She did not know what the war was about. It meant nothing. It was men's foolishness. She did not know what Communism meant. She had a brother who lived in the North. She wanted to earn enough money to open her own bar. She worked from 11 A.M. to 11 P.M., and she earned 20 piastres out of every 160-piastre drink she had bought for her, or about 12 cents on the dollar.

All of this conversation was conducted in a painfully slow manner. She spoke neither French nor English. Another girl, half Vietnamese and half French, helped translate. Other parts of the conversation were carried out in a kind of primitive pictogram-plus-sign-language routine. Looking at my notes as I read this, I realize that there are moments of idiocy in my life for which I can submit no plea before a higher judge. Those several hours convinced me that I shall never be the Oscar Lewis of Southeast Asia. The beer, of course, was a bloody marvel.

One offshoot of this great influx of girls and bars (more than 2,000 bars in Saigon now, and opening fast) is that the second-rate hotels are booming. They are not precisely brothels, although there are numerous straight brothels; they are places where the lonely GI can take his young Vietnamese girl for a few hours with no questions asked. The Vietnamese men, especially those serving in the armed forces, have not been heard from yet about the growing whoredom of their women; apparently it is just one of the fortunes of war.

The large hotels will not allow the young ladies of Tu Do Street on the premises, not because of any raging puritanical fervor, but for reasons generally of security. Last year the fifth floor of the Caravelle, where I'm staying, was bombed out and it cost $1,000,000 to repair. Women, for obvious reasons, make better Vietcong agents than men, especially for purposes of intelligence.

As I left the San Francisco, a young serviceman careened off the bar, knocked over several stools, and lurched out into the street. The thirteen barmaids giggled together. What the hell: They had his money.

January 3, 1966

Message from Bien Hoa

As you move out of Saigon into the country, the city simply peters away. It is a city under siege, but there are no walls, no wired fences, no moats.

One sees an occasional checkpoint manned by a rather sleepy soldier, but the effect is more like osmosis. One moment you are in a coughing, fume-ridden morass of cyclos, taxis, bicycles, and buses, and then you are out in the open, the country rushing past you as each kilometer brings you closer to the war.

Everything in this country is a part of the war, of course, but in Saigon the weaponry is politics and terror. The real battle is out on the face of the land. So early in the morning, if you are a newspaperman, you find yourself on the road to Bien Hoa dressed in fatigues, smoking too much, waiting to hitch a ride.

At Bien Hoa the 173d Airborne has carved a headquarters out of the red earth. It is from Bien Hoa that the troops have moved to make the first American fight for the Mekong Delta. Standing on the dusty road waiting for a lift, you know that only 15 miles from where you stand young men are being killed.

A laundry truck pulls up, and you are motioned into the back. The truck is driven by a forty-year-old Vietnamese accompanied by his eighteen-year-old sister, Li-Ly. She looks about twelve and her brother looks sixty. In Vietnam no one looks middle-aged. The young men who should now be middle-aged are all dead.

"Where you go?" Li-Ly says.

"Bien Hoa."

"Bien Hoa?"

You shout, "Yes."

She says, "Lots of luck," and breaks into almost uncontrollable laughter. The Vietnamese seem convinced that the Americans, these large strangers, are the craziest people on this earth. The girl laughed, and then her brother laughed, and then I started laughing, lying on the laundry.

I don't know what they were laughing at, but I knew there was something absolutely insane about lying on the back of a laundry truck in the disguise of war in the boondocks on the wrong side of the world. I wondered what Li-Ly would think if I tried to explain to her about Mike Quill.

The road was heavy with the traffic of war. Jeeps, trucks, military ambulances, earth movers, armed personnel carriers—all raced past us. Occasionally a creaking country bus crammed with passengers would cough by on the way to Saigon. The road was straight and good, built, I was told later, by the French. It was relatively safe during the day. At night you went at your peril.

Only occasionally would a sniper take a shot at a passing Army vehicle. (The correspondents say that the Vietnamese farmer is the only farmer in the world who works with a semiautomatic hoe.) So on the way to Bien Hoa you can sit and watch the country go by. The country was flat and broad with a regularity of landscape that reminded me of those backgrounds in animated cartoons that turn on spools to make the same drawing serve a number of actions. We passed clusters of small, thatched huts, most of them no more than cabinets 10 feet by 10 feet built with saplings. Some were hard by their private rice paddies. Others had banana or papaya trees in the yards.

Most of the clusters of huts were well back from the highway, separated from the twentieth century by fields of ripe green swamp grass. Occasionally you saw large rips in the earth flanked by mounds of rich black soil, like the droppings of some monstrous ancient animal. You could see gutted farmhouses away off, and once we passed the chimney of a burned-out building that looked like one of those lone monuments that dot the American South.

Occasionally an old farmer would stand at the edge of the highway, his wrinkled face mute and baffled, staring out from under his conical hat, as silent as the banyan trees on the horizon.

I got off the laundry truck and grabbed a ride on a jeep as we came into Bien Hoa. This is a town which now has almost sixty laundries, all servicing the base nearby. We passed the Quickly Laundry, the Ohio Laundry, the 48th Hour Laundry. Signs said, "Ice to sale here," and the servants next to me pointed out the town's most prosperous brothel, a 20-by-20-foot wooden shack. Five young girls sat in the parlor smoking industriously and drinking tea.

At the Bien Hoa air base there was tremendous activity. Jeeps raced up and down roads. Helicopters in great swarms lifted off the airstrip heading west, where the last part of an action in the Plain of Reeds was being fought. I learned later that most of the Vietcong in the area had disappeared through the night and I was a day late for seeing any action. Instead, I was taken to the Third Surgical Hospital, where I was met by Major Pete Downs of South Hartswell, Maine.

The hospital complex had sixty beds and was building more wooden barracks to house any future wounded. You could smell raw cut wood and hear hammering everywhere as the structures rose before you. Downs explained that some of the wounded are taken directly to Saigon, depending on which hospital is closest. "The medics in the field use their own judgment," Downs said. "It just depends on how really badly hit the boy has been. If he needs major surgery, he's better off in the Third Field at Saigon. We can do it here, but he's better off there."

We walked into the ward. In the bunk at the door a young Vietnamese named Thung lay staring at the ceiling. He appeared to be fifteen years old, and his left leg was amputated beneath the knee. "We're gonna make him a wooden leg all his own," a medic said cheerfully. Next to him a Negro private, Martin Davis, of Cleveland, lay with an arm in traction. "I got

183

hit ten seconds after I got outta the helicopter," he said. "It got me mad. Man, I wanted to get me some of those VC's."

Next I ran into Larry Lattanzio, who is eighteen. He was on his back on a bed across the aisle with large bandages across his shoulder. He lives at 1026 East Thirty-sixth Street in Brooklyn. He was smoking nervously. "I ain't bad," he said. "It didn't hit nothing important over there." (A medic told me later that another quarter inch and the slug that passed from right to left across the shoulder blades might have hit his spine and either killed or paralyzed him.)

"What happened was my platoon—that's the First Platoon of B Company—we came outta the helicopters and started moving at the VC down by the river. They were behind this dike dug in, like. Well, I'm running at them with this radio on my back. It ain't too easy, that radio weighs fifty pounds, when all of a sudden I feel this wallop on my back. 'Hey,' I asked myself, 'you didn't get hit, did you?' 'Yeah,' I answered myself. 'I got hit all right.'

"Imagine that? I got plugged on my mudda's birthday."

Larry Lattanzio said that he went to Midwood HS, Brooklyn College (for a while, like) and did most of his postgraduate work at Jack Cannon's billiard room on Flatbush Avenue and Avenue K.

"You gonna put this in the paper?" he asked me.

"Yeah," I said.

"Do me a favor, will ya? I want to send a message to some of the boys. The message goes to Hugo "Nose" Paulucci, Sammy "The Greek" Liounis, Sandy Golando, Curly Cafuoco, Blotchy Sepe—we call him Blotchy 'cause every time he eats he gets these blotches on his face—and Minnesota Midge Falcone.

"Tell them guys that Legar is OK. He's comin' back."

Legar?

"Yeah, you know, it's like from pig Latin. Le-Garry. That's what they call me, and Legar, that's the short version. Tell them guys Legar is comin' back."

Fellas, Legar is coming back.

January 4, 1966

184

Some Men Die, Some Men Count

In all the wars, some men die, and some men add up the losses. The footsoldier lies in the stink of the rice paddy, his feet rotting in his boots, the leeches sucking on his skin, the sweat running down the gullies of his face, feeling fear make its move in his stomach, then subside, and then move again. Sometimes, in such circumstances, death or wounding must come as a release. Then, the action over, the battle fought, the clerks move in to compile the statistics of horror, and men in air-conditioned offices in the garrison towns sit down at typewriters and prepare press releases and hope that, somehow, such statistics will dilute the brutality.

They never do, of course, but the try is always made. In this war, the try is made every day in Saigon, at 5 P.M., in the large white USIS building on the corner of Boulevard Louis Pasteur and Street of Flowers. This is a daily Saigon ritual, seven days a week, including holidays. It is called, simply enough, the Briefing, and it resembles, more than anything else, a postgame session with a football coach or a report to the stockholders of a shaky corporation.

One enters this building, after showing credentials to a Marine, and walks a short corridor to a 200-seat auditorium. On the stage are four large maps, one for each of the corps areas into which South Vietnam is divided for military purposes. At the left is a lectern bearing the seal of the United States. The lighting is dramatic.

At the door, in neat stacks, are the press releases, all in purple mimeograph ink, laying out what is known as the "day's wash." I have just left such a briefing, and the releases included news that the Korean karate team will give a demonstration in a few days, that 100,000 vitamin tablets have been sent so far to the Phu My orphanage in Saigon, and a report, complete with quotes from attending doctors, about a Claymore mine that

185

went off last night near the main gate of the Tan Son Nhut airport, killing one Vietnamese civilian and wounding five Vietnamese civilians and five U.S. servicemen. The rest concerned operations going on that day all over Vietnam. The operations read like the fight results from the AP that run in the tiniest type in the sports section.

There is, I suppose, no other way for anything as extensive as the American operation here to report such a war. There is no front in this war. There are no large thrusts to report like Patton's run for the Elbe. Nothing is neat or clean. It is really a series of skirmishes, of men being dropped into what the rewritemen call "VC-infested territory," where they proceed to kill as many Vietcong as possible and then pull out.

So, in many ways, the five o'clock briefing is a kind of grim charade. While I have attended them, they have been presided over by Harold Kaplan, who heads the press office of the U.S. Mission. He is a tall, trim man, with a sense of humor, as much candor as his position allows, and an understanding that his job of dealing out news of the war is of an almost incredible delicacy.

Kaplan's major enemy is the long history of deceit and lying that has poisoned relations between the press and the U.S. Mission here for almost four years. Under the Diem regime, the U.S. Mission was placed in a terrible position: It could lie on behalf of the head of an allied government, or it could tell the truth and watch that government crumble. For several years the American mission here chose to lie, and when Diem finally did crumble, the American public suddenly discovered that the war against the Vietcong was all but lost. Some hard-noses still try to place the blame for the swampy military situation on the reporters who were trying to report that very situation. One does not need to travel to Moscow to encounter double think in all its splendor.

Today, with the tremendous buildup of American forces and the sudden realization that we now have a growing American war to deal with, men such as Kaplan have been doing their best to get information to the public as swiftly and candidly as possible. There is still a lot of word-gaming going on. We still refuse to say how many Americans or South Vietnamese troops have been killed, except to note that "friendly forces" casualties were "light" or "moderate" (no one here has ever heard them described as heavy, even during the slaughter of the Ia Drang Valley when 240 Americans were killed and hundreds wounded). Aside from that, though, most of the information has been accurate. For that we can thank the resident press corps, which has done more than its share in keeping the American government honest.

Kaplan has some two additional problems. One is the introduction of visiting VIP's. Since I have been here, he has introduced a leader of Young Americans for Freedom, an Australian medical team, a Chinese medical team, and Teddy Gleason, boss of the International Longshoremen's Association, who had been here in an attempt to bring some order to the chaos of the Saigon waterfront. (Teddy Gleason said, among other things: "If things get worse, we'll bring over a couple of gangs and show them how ourselfs." A New York reporter suggested that he bring home a couple of hundred cycle drivers, organize them, and help solve the transit crisis. "That's not a bad idea," Teddy said. "Very good, very good.") At the most recent meeting, Kaplan told us that Jacob Javits was arriving, which kept him out of the transit situation, too.

Probably Kaplan's most sensitive problem is to maintain the façade of respecting Vietnamese sovereignty. Several days ago, the Vietnamese government announced that it would begin its own briefings, scheduled for four thirty each day, and report all the actions of the ARVN forces here. The reporters screamed. The Vietnamese government, under its last nine leaders and President Diem, was never noted for its fidelity to the truth. Kaplan said that he and others had been urging daily ARVN press conferences for some time; the reporters groaned.

But the first press conference was not the sort of exercise in wounded vanity one was led to expect. It was presided over by a rather sweaty Vietnamese general, two aides, and two young colonels who did the translations. There were not enough press releases to go around and, unlike the American briefing room, no air conditioning. Instead, we sat cramped on funeral parlor chairs with the windows open to the Boulevard Pasteur and ceiling fans beating ineffectually at the air.

187

All of the Vietnamese were nervous, except a hard-looking thirtyish major named Hong, who snapped his answers in Vietnamese with the habit of command that comes with growing up with maids in the house. The others seemed to be trying desperately to be polite and candid, and to answer as fully as possible the rather ill-tempered interrogation being heaped on them by the press corps. One thing was obvious: Most of the Americans have contempt for the Vietnamese. The Vietnamese are "they," the impersonal pronoun that can be a deadly weapon.

When the Vietnamese press conference was over, we all walked across the street to the USIS for the American briefing.

"Pathetic," one radio man said. "Just pathetic. They had all day, and they still couldn't do it right. They didn't even have enough handouts, for chrissakes."

It was pathetic all right, but the lack of handouts was not the reason.

January 7, 1966

The War's Backyard

We drove out of Da Nang in the morning, moving slowly through the clogged streets around the marketplace. Women in black satin slacks and cotton shirts argued with peddlers, their conical straw hats bobbing in a kind of staged counterpoint, like a scene from a travelogue about the lush, mysterious East. When we stopped in the jammed traffic, we could smell old fish and rotting meat and some other smell that was a compost of both. The lush, mysterious East is really like some large frightening maw filled with the taste of things long dead.

Like all the towns where the Americans have moved in troops, Da Nang is a place now booming with laundries, barbershops, sleazy souvenir stores, and places with freshly painted signs that read: "We fix and sell The Wrist Watch and the Sun Glass." In all of them, merchants bow and move nervously when the large Americans walk in, and smile in anxious collaboration when they leave. There is something vaguely disgusting about what money does to people in wars.

As we moved out of town, there were children everywhere. They stood in clusters of ten and twelve, all barefoot, all wearing shorts and polo shirts, all waving at us as we went by. The boys have wonderfully fresh faces, the only faces you will see in this country that have not yet been touched by horror.

The little girls are something else again. Everywhere you go in this country you see these small children, seven or eight years old, carrying naked infants on their hips or in their arms. In a country where all the men are gone or dead, the women must work the rice fields and the young girls must tend the children.

The roads in the north of this country are rutted and dusty, and as we moved southwest to Cam Ne, clouds of red dust filled the air. It clogged our noses and ears and left a thick coating on the hair.

"This is the wet season," said Gunner Smith, the Marine warrant officer who was accompanying me. "You should see this place in July when it gets to be a hundred and thirty degrees in the shade."

The countryside was not much different from most of the land which lies in the plains and deltas of Vietnam. Long open fields of green, filled with swamp grass or rice, extended as far as you could see. Away off, a range of mountains climbed away to Cambodia in the west. Across the land, on lonely knolls, you could see the squat concrete blockhouses and bunkers left behind by the French, and one wondered who last commanded them and in what month of what year their commanders had died.

A few miles out we started to see the marines. They were stationed every 300 or 400 feet, young boys in green uniforms. Some sat at the edge of the road, reading *Stars and Stripes*; others cleaned their weapons; some just sat in the heat, surrounded by mounds of dark-brown sandbags, watching for movement on the horizon. Away off, we could hear explosions and the sound of small-arms fire.

"That's not anything, I guess," Gunner Smith said. "Either Marines blowing bunkers, or ARVN shooting chickens."

About five miles out of town, we came to a dirt road leading off to the right. There were clumps of jungle and foliage over there, and sprinkled around the ruined façade of a house was the Third Battalion of the Third Marines. Behind them somewhere in the cluster of jungle was Cam Ne.

Everywhere you go in Vietnam, you will hear that places like Cam Ne are the only hope for any sort of victory in this war. In this small village, the Marines are operating a pacification program. This is a jargon phrase, of course, and reeks of the language of the sociologist. But what it means in short is that a strenuous effort is being made to bring the government of South Vietnam back into a village in its own country.

This village, in particular, was a tough one. The Marines fought a desperate fight to take it last year, and there was much publicity because in the process civilians and children were hurt or killed. The Marines are sensitive about it. "We were taking casualties, and the VC weren't," one major said to me the evening before. "We had to do what we did."

Part of the Marines' mission in Da Nang is to secure the great airfield there, and Cam Ne happened to fall within the area from which mortar attacks could be launched or machine-gun fire directed at airplanes. So the Marines took the village.

But one major problem in this war is that an assault force cannot merely take a village in a battle and move on. This is why there is no front in this war and no great sweeping thrusts. A battle may be fought, a new village chieftain installed, but in the night the Vietcong will walk right back into the village, murder the chieftain, and regain their control.

"If we just go around this country shooting people and moving on, we will be here for forty years," a Marine colonel working with the pacification program told me. "We have to secure these places and bring them under their own government."

The terrible thing, of course, is that for years there has been no effective government at all in these places, except that of the Vietcong. In Cam Ne, the Vietcong had been in control for twelve years. They had collected taxes and drafted young men into their ranks. Before they took the place, the village had not had any government since the Japanese left in 1945. The American task is enormously difficult and delicate. It is most likely that "pacifying" such a village will take twenty years, perhaps more.

That day the Marines of the Third Battalion were preparing to distribute clothing to the villagers. There were large cardboard containers of clothes donated privately in the United States and sacks of corn to be given out. Up and down the roads in the Village, a Vietnamese with a bullhorn announced to the inhabitants that the clothing would be distributed at one o'clock.

"Welcome to Cam Ne," a Marine sergeant said, as we climbed out of the jeep. Beyond him Marines were unloading cans of purified water and cartons of C rations. A transistor radio was blaring, and above us two jet fighter planes screamed off toward the mountains. "How about a walk around the town?" the sergeant said. Sure, I said. He strapped on his gear, picked up a shotgun, and we left to see Cam Ne.

January 9, 1966

There Are No Young Guys Here

Perhaps we, who come from the fortunate places of the earth, shall never understand about places like Cam Ne. Where I come from, a place with shattered windows and no steam heat in winter is thought of as a slum. We think it criminal if rats scurry between the walls, or if children are forced to work at sixteen, or if a man loses one shot at decency and comfort because his education was incomplete or the color of his skin was unacceptable to others.

But in the Cam Nes of the world, to live past three is a success, and to make it to thirty is a triumph. I wish I could bring you here somehow; I wish you could see the faces of the old women, the light in their eyes extinguished, their small, shrinking heads looking dumbly from under conical hats, their skin eroded, clay-dry, pitted with the half-healed gashes of the swamp leech.

When they smile, which is seldom, their teeth show tar black

191

from chewing betel nuts. If I could make that clear, make clear that these women have ceased being women at all, that their bodies have gone fallow and bone-hard like some strange new vertical beast of burden, make clear how disease has sapped them, and the filth of the rice paddies has flaked their skins, and ruined their blood, and shortened their very lives—if I could make that clear to you, you would begin to understand something about Cam Ne and perhaps about Vietnam.

You would begin to understand about Vietnam and the wretchedness of the land, if you could see the roads in the morning, clogged by people on the move, all of them old men and old women and young children. They carry on their backs all that they own: bamboo struts that make up their houses, small sacks of clothing, chickens, and an occasional pig. It is all they have. No books, no paintings, no radios, none of the soft ornaments of the twentieth century. Last year alone, 750,000 people in this country moved their place of residence, trying to keep a few hundred feet ahead of the violence. The whole country has been doing this for a quarter of a century.

But perhaps you should see Cam Ne on a trip with a couple of Marines. On this morning, I took a walk with two sergeants, Chuck Burzamato and Harold R. Hoerning. Burzamato is a short, red-faced guy, who came from Mott Street, lived in Brooklyn, and has been in the Marines for seventeen years. His wife and children live in San Clemente, California, and his parents live at 1402 East Third Street in Brooklyn. Hoerning has been a Marine for twenty-one years. His wife and four kids live in Oceanside, California, and his father, a retired New York cop, lives in Bayside, Long Island. They are professional Marines. They are also men.

We walked together down the dirt road which leads from the Marine camp to Cam Ne. The thick, gluey mud of Asia stuck to our boots and made a sucking sound as we walked. Hoerning was carrying a carbine, and Burzamato held a shotgun.

"The funny thing in Cam Ne," Burzamato said, "is that we got through to the children, and we even are getting through to the old people. But there's no young guys here. None."

"That's right," Hoerning said. "The young guys are all off with the VC."

The town is a collection of scattered huts and houses, laced with thick, crawling jungle. The Marines have been urging the people who live there to cut down the undergrowth, to clear the area of jungle. We saw an old man, with a Ho Chi Minh beard, slashing at the tangle with a machete.

"Hey, Pop!" Burzamato shouted. The old man stopped and smiled. "He's got swell-lookin' gums, don't he?" Burzamato said. We walked into the bush to talk to him. "Numbah One!" Burzamato said, using the local phrase which means something is very good. "You do number one job, Pop. You come today one o'clock, see boxie [doctor], get food! Numbah one."

The old man bowed, and shook his head yes, and said, "Numbah one, Numbah one." Burzamato gave him a cigarette and we moved into the jungle.

Everywhere in the jungle we saw trenches and long, narrow slots dug under the roots of trees. When the battle was fought here, the Vietcong were dug into the holes, covered with foliage, firing machine guns at the Marines as they moved in. "If Charlie's dug into one of those holes," Hoerning said, "you'd need a direct hit with artillery to get him out."

The jungle itself had a sinister quality. I suppose if you come from cities, there is always something treacherous about uncontrolled nature. If it is in Vietnam, the possibility of violence around each turn makes it even more so. It must have been terrible to fight here; we literally could not see 20 feet on any side of us. "You could have twenty VC in there," Burzamato said, gesturing toward a dripping dark area to the right, "and never see them."

Suddenly we came to a small clearing. On a knoll, up above a small untended private rice paddy, stood a brick house. There had once been a walk leading to the door, but it was cracked and smashed now, with scrub growing in the broken places. Bougainvillaea ran up the sides of the house, and on its porch stood a small young girl, maybe six or seven, a boy about four, and no one else. All of it—the children, the house, the small 10-foot-by-20-foot rice paddy—all seemed about to be swallowed or suffocated by the jungle.

"Hal-looo," Burzamato shouted. We walked up to the porch. The house was bare and empty. Not a single piece of furniture, no food, nothing. In one corner stood a neat Buddhist altar. The girl looked terrified. "Don't be afraid, beautiful. Me numbah one." He reached in his pocket and pulled out some candy. The little girl was afraid to take it. The boy reached out, and Burzamato gave it to him, explaining with gestures that he should share it with his sister. We started to leave when I saw something move in the corner. It was an infant, huddled in a kind of thatch nest, covered with flies. The child's skin was gray, its eyes clamped shut, its stomach swollen. It was obviously dying.

"Jesus," Burzamato said. "Jesus, Jesus, Jesus."

I thought he was going to cry.

We walked through the village for two hours. Everywhere the old people were clearing away the tangle of undergrowth, chopping away the 35-foot bamboo, taking cigarettes from the two Marines. One old man had cut away about 10 square yards, and Burzamato gave him a whole pack of smokes.

We came across one little girl whose eye had been split by a piece of flying bamboo, and Burzamato called a Marine corpsman, David Luck, from St. Paul, Minnesota, and had the eye cleaned and treated. He gave out eighteen packs of candy, and when we started back later, the children followed him all the way to the base camp. He looked like a squat, gun-toting pied piper.

At one o'clock, the people of Cam Ne had lined up, and the Marines had spread the donated clothing across sheets of cardboard. The children came into the compound two at a time, and the Marines sorted out the clothing, trying to find things of the correct size. "Lookit this," Burzamato said, holding up a sheepskin-lined jacket. "That's for when it goes under a hundred."

He took out a nightgown, made of a diaphanous material. "Just what the mama-san needs for a big Saturday night in Cam Ne." There was a lot of joking and laughter, but the children walked away from that place, past the ruined shell of the house which served as headquarters, and they were smiling.

Perhaps we do not have either a legal or moral right to be in this country, and certainly the war itself is a disgusting and abstract thing. But believe me, the Americans who are here are as

decent as anyone I've ever met. It should be unnecessary to say so, but the Marine Corps is not the Wehrmacht, and if I had my choice of dinner companions between Staughton Lynd and Chuck Burzamato, I would not be long in the choosing.
January 10, 1966

The Roots of War

We saw the cemetery at half past six in the morning, perched on a small knoll, its stone crosses jutting through the thick morning fog about 300 yards afrom the road. The driver pulled the jeep over, and we walked through the damp, wheezing earth to the front gate. Only a two-foot iron fence separated the dead from the living. We walked in.

The tombstones were in disarray, leaning at angles like monuments to cripples, and all of them were sinking slowly into the damp, black soil of Asia. Lichen spattered their faces, and snaky tendrils of wild swamp weeds pulled at their shafts. The jungle was taking them back.

There were the names—Lataud, Broussard, Michaux—and there were the years of their deaths: 1931, 1927, 1940, 1919. What had brought these men to this terrible rendezvous in a sinkhole of a town on the South China Sea? They had crossed continents and oceans to get here. Perhaps there were dreams of fortunes to be taken like plunder from the jungles and paddies. Perhaps they were in flight from some tamer place. But they had been dead a long time, and jets roared over the graves now, and in another twenty years, the crosses that marked their bones would be gone, too, swallowed by the very earth.

"Let's get the hell out of here," the driver said. "This place gives me the creeps."

We walked back to the jeep. A bent, aged Vietnamese had stopped at the side of the road, staring at us. He had seen the French die in his country, and there was something in his face that said he would see the Americans die here, too.

The French presence has not, of course, completely vanished.

You feel it everywhere, but especially in and around Saigon, which, more than anything else, is a European city clamped astride an Asian base. The French built it upon the backs of the Vietnamese, and even today it feels more like a rather large town in the south of France than a capital in the tropics.

The French, it has been said, colonized with boulevards and brothels, and in this country, at least, the saying was true. There was a time when Saigon housed the largest brothel in all of Asia, a fantastic structure called the House of Mirrors, because of the decorations in the cubicles, stocked with good wines, a good bar, and 1,200 girls. Today it is gone, but more modest brothels exist in profusion. So do the boulevards. Both, I am told, by people who remember the old days, are somewhat seamier now.

The French are most visible here in the restaurants. They travel in groups of five or six, their language utilized as a shield against the British, American, or Vietnamese around them. They sit at tables, conversation purring, talking about De Gaulle and the films of Truffaut and the currency exchange on the black market. Most of them sneer at the American effort here; after all, if France could not conquer, what possible chance could the Americans have?

There are still about 12,000 French nationals here, with a financial investment of about $500,000,000. Most of this is in rubber, and one of the minor scandals of this war is the way we have been forced to fight in the rubber plantations. Some soldiers have told me that in some rubber plantation battles, they had been given orders not to shoot the rubber trees because the United States would have to pay for them. I've asked some people in authority about this, and they have confirmed the story, but never, of course, for attribution.

The reasoning seems to be that rubber is one of the few natural resources South Vietnam can use for export purposes. If the war ever ends and the rubber plantations are destroyed, the country will be in even more miserable economic shape than it is now. So the Vietcong hide behind rubber trees, and American soldiers get their legs shot off mindful of the future economic security of the businessmen of Saigon.

Perhaps the long-range reasoning is correct, rational, and

perceptive. But it is also abstract and rather sleazy. The fact is that every French rubber plantation owner here pays off the Vietcong to stay in business. The Vietcong takes that money and buys guns which are used to kill Americans and Vietnamese. The plantations also provide shelter. A good number of the plantation employees work the rubber by day and don the black pajamas of the Vietcong irregulars at night. When large troop movements are necessary, the Vietcong can move across country almost entirely through French rubber plantations.

One military man here told me of one patrol into a rubber plantation where he came across almost 600 Vietcong, marching merrily, four abreast, through the main road of the plantation, with all the abandon of the South Hartford Marching and Chowder Association on its annual picnic and beer party. The French never said a thing. If this smells of collaboration with the enemy, well, the French have a talent for it.

The government of Vietnam, of course, should put a stop to all of this. They should either nationalize the rubber plantations or have the French shot as collaborators. They will do neither. For one thing, there are few Vietnamese in the country, I'm told, who are capable of running the plantations, so nationalization would be disastrous. Second, the government desperately needs the revenues it can extract from the sale of rubber to France. Start shooting Frenchmen, and you lose your market.

The French intellectual tradition has also held on with an iron tenacity. In the University of Saigon, the old system of the dictatorial professor reading notes and expecting to have them parroted back, jokes and all, still holds. Most of the professors hold America and its culture in contempt and assume that all literature ended with Proust. The local painters work in the tradition of the French Impressionists, rather than in any original or even Oriental tradition. The dream of most students in the universities here is to take a degree and leave for Paris. One nice thing about that, of course, is that they can beat the draft. Paris is filled with thirty-nine-year-old medieval scholars on the lam from their own country.

One should probably not be so upset over this situation. But this war did not begin in 1960, when the National Liberation Front was founded; or in 1954, with the fall of Dienbienphu; or in 1946, when Ho Chi Minh headed for the mountains after the French became the only colonial power to try to reclaim its pre-war colonies. This war began more than a hundred years ago when the French shot their way into this country. Once again in this century, the United States has come in to try to clean up the filthy moral refuse left behind by Europeans. But this time it is an even more terrible situation than ever, because this time we might be wrong.

I just can't believe that the Vietnamese peasant, over whose loyalty this war is being waged, can really tell the difference between the French legionnaire and the American soldier. Could a Red Hook longshoreman tell the difference between a Vietnamese and a Chinaman? I doubt it. That's why we're in trouble.

January 11, 1966

The Education of Huong and Luc

> We used to wonder where war lived, what it was that made it so vile. And now we realize that we know where it lives, that it is in side ourselves. —ALBERT CAMUS, *Notebooks,* 1939

We were halfway to Pleiku when Huong told me about the water buffalo, and his friend Luc, and what happened to them both that summer when Huong was eleven. We were chance companions on flight 606 to Da Nang, being carried at 10,000 feet in a C-130, one of those large freight planes that shuttle back and forth across this country every hour of the day. It had become dark, and there were troops dozing in all the seats, their hard blue metal weapons cradled in their laps. Once I looked out the small window and saw, away off, past Bien Hoa, two flares burning about the jungle and the sharp, distant flashes of artillery. Out there, men were dying.

When I sat down again, Huong offered me a cigarette. It was an American brand, with a filter tip, and I accepted. He lit it for me, smiled, and told me his name. He wore the orange beret of the Vietnamese airborne, and he had the face of a strayed angel, the features soft, the eyes those of a boy who had seen terrible things but had not yet found time to sort them all out. Huong seemed desperate to talk to someone. In the brief light of the match, I saw that he carried no weapon; he held a crutch. And then I noticed that his right leg was gone beneath the knee.

So Huong began to talk. His English was poor, mostly nouns strung together with simple verbs. He would say: "My village close Chu Lai. Marines there. Very small village. Very nice village." But listening to him was like reading James Joyce for the first time: Once you adjusted to the style it was as clear as anything could be. So we sat there, in the half-darkness, smoking and talking. I realized suddenly that he was the first Vietnamese I had really talked with since my arrival.

What Huong remembered more than anything else was the way he would ride the great water buffalo through the long afternoons. His father was gone; he knew not where then, but now, as a man, he realized that his father had probably died in the war with the French. He had never known him, so it made no difference.

He worked in the rice paddies in the village. He never went to school and did not know what a school was until the army had taken him and decided to educate him. In his village, there had never been a school.

The most fun was the water buffalo, because he was so small he could lie across the animal's back, and doze in the sun, and sometimes go to sleep. There always had been enough to eat, Huong told me, never plenty, never very much meat, but still, they had never starved. Most of it changed the summer he was eleven. He was seventeen last October.

He saw the change mainly in his friend Luc. Luc was older than Huong, by five or six years, and I thought, from the way Huong talked, that his friend was more a hero than a friend.

Luc could fight better than anyone in the village. He feared nothing and no one. Sometimes he would sit in the jungle through the long night, alone, just to prove that he could do it. He knew how to catch wild snakes with traps, and he could sit and discuss anything, holding himself well even with the elders of the village. Once, he took Huong and two other young boys for a three-day trek to the sea.

Huong had never seen anything like it before. Long, distant stretches of sand, as far as you could see, white and glittering in the sun, hurting the eyes. And beyond that, the sea itself, blue and stretching away to the end of the earth. That trip had been the greatest adventure of his life.

But then, that summer when Huong was eleven, Luc began to change. He would be gone for three or four days at a time. He would snap at the villagers when they asked where he had been. There were no more trips to the sea. And then, one day, Huong walked into Luc's house and found him holding something in his hand. He tried to hide it, saw it was too late, and then told Huong that if he said anything to anyone, he would come in the night and kill him. Luc had a pistol.

The village was never the same after that. Huong still spent hours on the back of the water buffalo in the rice paddies, and still sat by the river watching the lotus pile against the banks. But something terrible seemed about to happen—and it did.

One night, while they slept, strangers suddenly arrived in the village. They went to the house of the leader, took him outside, and shot him in the face. It was the first time he had ever heard shots fired. It was the first time he had seen a man dead. His friend Luc was with the strangers.

There wasn't much more to the story. Huong was smoking very hard as he told it. Luc, of course, had joined the Vietcong, and in six months the village was run by them. Sometimes the government would send new chiefs into the town, and at night the Vietcong would come in and kill them. The Cong put taxes on the people, and most of the young men went away with them to the forests. Luc had disappeared, and Huong now thought that he had been sent north for training, or had joined a Vietcong unit farther south.

That was about all, except for the water buffalo. Once a few years after the first killing, the government had sent in soldiers, and the Vietcong had come out of the forest at night and started fighting with them. Many were killed. But for Huong, the terrible thing was that a stray shot had killed the water buffalo, his water buffalo.

That was when he left the village.

A long blast of noise told us to fasten our seat belts. We were landing at Pleiku. No one announces such things on a military transport, but everyone knows. Several days before, a C-123 loaded with ammunition had exploded coming into this airport. Everyone was very much awake. I asked Huong what had happened to his leg.

"A mine," he said, shrugging. He said it the way a prizefighter explains that his cut eye was caused by a left hook. I asked him where he was going. He shrugged again. Maybe he could make it to Chu Lai or Da Nang. He was finished with the army now, after two years, because of his wound. They had taught him to read, and perhaps, with some luck, he could become an interpreter with the Marines. He could not, of course, go home.

The plane bumped down and screeched to a halt. The long elevator at the back of the plane dropped open, and we could see armed men standing outside, smoking quietly in the dark. Some people got off. Huong thought he would get off, too. I jumped down through the hatch, and he handed me his crutch. I helped him down. We smoked a final cigarette, and then he hobbled off across the darkened airfield. Whatever it is that makes us capable of war, it has no right to do such things to men like Huong. I watched him walk away until I could see him no longer, and I thought about the water buffalo, his friend Luc, and what happened to them both the summer he was eleven.

January 12, 1966

The War's Big Prize

From the windows of the seven-seat Beechcraft, you could no longer see the features of the earth. Banks of clouds formed a sullen floor, reaching away to the south like endless trays of soiled cotton candy. The passengers tried to read the morning papers or stared off at the grainy, red-soaked horizon, adrift in private reverie. High above us, a jet sliced a white arc into the roof of the sky. Then, a half hour from Saigon, the plane veered and dove through the wet cloud, leaving streams of moisture on the windows, and broke through to the great, rich, rolling plain of the delta.

In some ways, the Mekong Delta is what this war is all about. This wide, flat southern end of the country produces most of the rice, most of the people, and most of the bitter texture of this war. There are towns here which have been in the control of the Vetcong or the Vietminh for twenty years. The Vietcong run recreation centers for exhausted troops here, hospitals for their wounded, tax collection centers, information booths, indoctrination schools, even small-arms factories.

This is no accident. The Vietcong, as well as the government itself, know that the delta is the great, glittering prize of the war. Its black earth, thick with silt pushed 2,500 miles by the Mekong River, is so rich that it could be possible, in a time of peace, to produce three rice crops in a single year, enough to feed Vietnam and the rest of Southeast Asia as well. Instead, because men are killing each other, Vietnam imports 100,000 tons of rice a year.

We were heading for the province of Kien Hoa, whose capital is Ben Tre, located about 85 kilometers south of Saigon. It is possible, I'm told, to drive here, only with the protection of an armed guard; most people fly. We were in a plane run by Air America, which services most of the American civilian apparatus here: the embassy, the AID program, the CIA, and others. The pilot leaned out, searching for landmarks. He was drifting east, and one passenger, familiar with the area, was startled.

"Hey, man," he shouted. "Don't go over there! Too many VC's. That's a bad place."

"There ain't any good places," the pilot said.

We came down into a lumpy field, covered with smashed grass, and pulled into a concrete area where three FAC spotter planes stood in concrete bunkers. At one end, behind barbed wire and sandbags, a Vietnamese artillery crew watched over a .155 artillery piece. A corrugated iron shed served as the waiting room.

"Welcome to the Dean Rusk Memorial Airport," someone said.

And then we were in a jeep riding into town. The country down here is like that in the south of Mexico, around the Isthmus of Tehuantepec: thick dripping jungle, narrow roads, coconut trees with palms drooping when the wind dies. A sergeant next to me held a carbine.

"This is a bad time of day to travel," he said. It was about 7:30 A.M. "These bastards mine the roads in the morning, wait to hit someone, and then go back to work in the fields. This is my third time down here, and every time I come here it gets creepier." He sat in silence for a while. "I guess I'm here too long."

Then we came into Ben Tre. It is a small, clean, half wheel of a town, whose streets move like spokes from the hub of the marketplace on the north bank of the Giang River, one of the many branches of the great Mekong which traverse the delta. Thousands of people pedaled past us on bicycles, heading for the marketplace or the countryside. There were far fewer automobiles than in any town I'd visited, and the Esso and Shell stations serviced military vehicles.

Young boys shouted "ho-kay" at us as we turned into a side street. We went past armed soldiers, sandbagged installations, and more barbed wire. Then we pulled up in front of the house of Richard Burnham, who is the province representative of USOM (the United States Operations Mission, which runs the AID programs here).

Burnham is a month shy of thirty, tall, with a lean, hard face, horn-rimmed glasses, a wide mouth, and the doleful look of a young Arthur Miller. Born in Cooks Falls, New York, he graduated from Amherst and Harvard Law and entered the Foreign Service in 1962. He served as a junior officer in the American embassy in Paris and the consulate in Bordeaux and, when his tour of duty in France was over, volunteered for service in South Vietnam. He studied the Vietnamese language and the background of the country in a seven-month course at the Foreign Service Institute in Washington and took the six-week course in counterinsurgency at Fort Bragg. He has been in Vietnam since last June, and all his time has been in Kien Hoa Province.

"You eat yet?" Burnham said. We hadn't. "Let's have breakfast, and we can talk about Kien Hoa later."

We drove to a small restaurant, with rubbed, pale-blue walls and plain wooden tables, whose doors were covered with chicken wire against hand grenades. The restaurant overlooked one of those small, classically proportioned Oriental lakes so prized by photographers, and as we ate ham and eggs, watching the dragon flies pinging the surface of the water and the slight breeze feathering the trees, it was difficult to feel that we were in a country ravished by a brutal, dirty war.

Then we were joined by two American military advisers attached to the Vietnamese Seventh Regiment, and over coffee we could feel the ground trembling with artillery fire.

Later we went with Burnham on his daily rounds. His job is complex, involving the dispersal of American aid funds, checking on their use, and maintaining a kind of tired fiction that the Vietnamese government is the real power here. He is part social worker, part diplomat, part military man. Every USOM adviser in this country has a price on his head because of this. On the day we arrived in Ben Tre, the papers reported the kidnapping of one of Burnham's friends, a USOM province representative in the North. Most of those I talked to assumed that he was dead.

Our first stop was the office of the Vietnamese province chief, an army colonel named Huynh Phat Dat. Burnham was ushered into his office immediately, and the colonel came forward, with his hand out. He is a short, fat man, and it suddenly occurred to me that the only fat people I had seen in this country were army officers.

"I have a party tonight," Colonel Dat said in French. "I would like you to be my guest and come. It is a party to celebrate Tet [the Vietnamese New Year]." We said we would come, shook hands, and left.

Two doors away was the office of Nguyen Duy Phuoc, the assistant province chief, who was described to me later as "totally incompetent." He is a civil servant, the son of a civil servant, and his incompetence has brought the usual rewards of the civil servant. Among other things he was treated last year to a three-month visit to the United States as a guest of our government.

The result of this educational tour was that he has learned three or four phrases in English, or about as much as a Tu Do Street bar girl learns in a night with a paratrooper.

"You come party tonight?" he said eagerly. Burnham nodded yes. As we walked back across the dusty compound to the USOM office, we passed an ARVN soldier asleep in a jeep and a bony dog rooting around for some shade. Burnham was silent. His features were pulled tight, and he wore the look of a man who has learned that he is risking his life in a country which is ruled by the mediocre.

Perhaps Graham Greene is correct, and we Americans are the last innocents, unprepared for a corrupt world and therefore dangerous. But it would be a mistake to underestimate our toughness. When I have departed this country, men like Richard Burnham will still be here, doing what they can, surrounded by mediocrity, indifference, and stupidity. These are enemies as murderous as the Vietcong, and it takes a peculiar kind of courage to live with them.

January 17, 1966

A Boy, a Dream

In my mind, I suppose, the boy will always look the way he did the first time I saw him. He was dressed in bright-blue pajamas and running across a field of scrub with a dog nipping at his heels. He leaped and bounded, jumping across a narrow canal, his shock of straight black hair bouncing as he moved, celebrating with his body the arrival of the tall strangers. When he reached us, he stopped a few feet away, not quite knowing what to do with his hands, staring up at us with liquid, lively brown eyes. He was about ten years old, and when he smiled, his teeth were hard and white. He was a great-looking kid.

We had left Ben Tre half an hour before to spend a few hours looking around the countryside at some of the more than 300 USOM projects that have been under way in Kien Hoa Province since April. The driver, a Vietnamese named Tching, took a carbine and three clips of ammunition with him. "One is never quite sure," he said in precise, clipped English.

We saw evidence of the USOM aid (almost half a million dollars in this province alone) everywhere: maternity wards, infirmaries, hamlet headquarters, purified water systems, schoolrooms, even latrines. Tching turned down a back road, and off on the left we saw a large white building. "This is the Bach Van orphanage," Tching said. "Run by the Buddhists. We've just built a new wing for them. Would you like to look?" He pulled the panel truck to the side of the road, grabbed the carbine, and we got out. That's when we saw the boy.

He followed us as we walked into the nursery. The building was new and smelled of plaster and fresh cement and children. There were infants in all the cribs, screaming loudly, untended, even by the old Vietnamese woman, dressed in black, who was smiling gummily at us from the corner. There were no nurses. I suppose the infants are in the care of the benevolent Buddha.

It was difficult to look at the children. Their bodies were covered with sores and insect bites, and there was a feeling of pus and death about all of them. Some were turning gray, probably about to die. Some of them had bellies bursting grotesquely with disease. One had a long welt on the side of the head. Most of them had eyes running with some viscous matter like heavily sugared water. I started to back away to the door.

"Where the hell did they come from?" I asked Tching.

"The war," he said. In this country, that phrase is always uttered with a shrug. We went back into the sunshine, and I saw a small girl, the size of my younger daughter, standing alone against the wall. I squatted down to say a few words to her, to tickle her, to look at her up close. She screamed in terror, her frail body trembling with fear. I suppose that in some corridor of her young mind something told her that strangers are people who try to kill you.

When I looked away, the boy was standing there, staring straight into my eyes. He was pleading for something with his face, and it wasn't money.

We walked around the new building and past the Buddhist pagoda. This was the largest, cleanest, most solidly constructed structure in the compound. That figures. We started walking toward a collection of thatched-roof huts that I thought must be a kind of stable. I was wrong. It was the rest of the orphanage.

Walking into that building was like stepping suddenly into a dark corner of some illustration of Dickens by George Cruikshank. The place had a kind of foul intimacy. There was no electricity. The floors were hard dirt. Stacks of rice chaff were in the corners where the rats lived. Most of the children were older: a girl about seven, some stray three-year-old boys, one infant alone on a wooden platform. A young girl, her face wiped clean of emotion, held an infant on her hip; she reminded me of mentally retarded children when they grow old. In a corner, on another rotting wooden platform, a boy lay wrapped in a blanket, shivering with fever. There were food bowls scattered about, their rims scabbing with coagulated leavings. The place smelled of excrement and unwashed bodies.

"Seen enough?" Tching said.

"Yeah," I said.

And then I saw the boy in the blue pajamas, and in that moment I wished that, no matter how complicated it would be, no matter how much red tape or shouting or money it would cost me, I wished that somehow I could take that boy out of that pigsty of an orphanage and out of the tortured country where he was born and across an ocean. I wished I could take him to America.

It's a sucker's dream, I suppose, something soft and sentimental. But as I stood here, under the eaves of this swinish hut in Vietnam, none of that mattered. I just wished I could show that one boy the skyline of New York and the statue in the harbor and the great ocean liners cutting the top of the river on a day bright with spring.

I wished I could explain to him about baseball, or take him with me to the gyms to watch the fighters train, or let him hear a symphony orchestra or watch a Broadway play. Let him eat a hot dog at Nathan's, ride a roller coaster, dive through the breakers at Rockaway. Let him go with me across the country and see the great cornfields in Iowa, the mighty ridges of the Rockies, the cow country of Texas, the clean, flowing streams of Vermont. I would have liked to watch him on his first subway ride, or attacking his first steak, or wearing his first suit, or learning to read.

But I did nothing, of course. I could not look the boy in the face for very long. I guess my feeling, the father of girls, was some secret yearning for a son. Certainly the look in that boy's face was that of a child who wanted, more than anything else, more than clothes, or money, or even food, a father. We walked back to the truck in silence.

We spent the rest of the day here in Son Dong. The hamlet chief, Do Suu Minh, a twenty-six-year-old ex-army officer, ran through a series of charts and graphs that gave detail to what one could see with the eyes. There were 2,600 persons in the hamlet. They produced rice, coconuts, and children.

Only four young people have even the possibility of completing high school, and in the entire history of the hamlet no child has ever gone on to a university. The last time the Vietcong attacked was two months before. They were fought off.

It was difficult to concentrate. I kept thinking about that kid in the blue pajamas and the way he looked running across that field and his deep brown eyes and his fine young smile. In five years the army will take him, and in six years he could be dead. Sitting here, writing this, I realize that I never learned that boy's name. Perhaps if he remains anonymous, I won't have to think of him when I read the casualty reports in 1971. I know it has been said before, but this war is obscene.

January 18, 1966

The Betrayed Defector

Perhaps the party on the colonel's lawn said as much about our troubles in this country as any of the statistics. It was late afternoon, and the sky had turned the color of a bruise, bringing with it rumors of evening. Peasant women in dusty black pajamas trudged the crowded streets, carrying water in gasoline cans from the public fountains. The traffic between town and countryside was continuous. There was no breeze.

On Colonel Dat's lawn, the gentry of Ben Tre were gathered in semicircles, celebrating Tet, the Vietnamese New Year. Ward Just of the Washington *Post*, an old friend, looked around and said, "Jesus, it's Marienbad!" The men had pampered faces and polished fingernails and wore their respectability as if it were a private talisman keeping them permanently from harm. They sucked around the small knot of Americans: pilots; military advisers; Richard Burnham, the USOM representative here in Kien Hoa Province. The women, immaculately groomed, poured ice over beer and fanned themselves in the sticky heat. Fighting speeches were made; but the rhetoric was musty, and no one was stirred.

It was dark suddenly, and fluorescent lights attached to the cypress trees lit up the lawn with their hard blue light. The purr of conversation was punctuated by the sporadic popping of firecrackers, which came with a dull monotony, like the war itself. Too many people were smiling too hard.

Out on the street, their faces bathed in the harsh light from the colonel's lawn, the peasants continued trudging through the night, bound for places where there are no lights and no lawns. There were not, of course, any peasants at the lawn party. That is one reason we are in trouble.

We're in trouble here because of people like Lieutenant Nghia. Nghia is a young man who came over to the government side from the Vietcong several months ago. He is a trim, compact man who looks like Raton Macias, the old Mexican bantamweight champion: a neat mustache, alert eyes, a fine smile. Nghia was a bright kid, and the first people to recognize his existence were the Vietcong. They sent him to the University of Hanoi to study medicine, and after three years he became a battle surgeon. For three more years he shared the life of the Vietcong soldier, slogging through rice paddies, sleeping when possible, moving always at night. But this is a war of attrition, and Nghia finally sickened of the long, slow horror of the war. He decided to come in from the cold.

But when he did, he discovered things that the government

209

propaganda had not mentioned. For one thing, he was not allowed to practice his profession. The bureaucrats in the Ministry of Health said that his qualifications were not sufficient. Nghia did not speak French and therefore could not complete his academic credits at the University of Saigon, which is apparently run like the nineteenth-century Russian court.

This posed a dilemma. Most of those who come over from the Vietcong are young boys who have been drafted into service. But Nghia was a prize: an officer, an intelligent man, a man who had made many friends during his years at war. So USOM gave him a job in the Ben Tre office. He now does some clerical work, some general handyman work, and makes propaganda broadcasts.

This, of course, is a disgraceful situation. There are 620,000 people in Kien Hoa Province. There are five doctors, two of whom work part time and one of whom is attached to the ARVN troops. But because of the smug stupidity of the Saigon authorities, a man who could be saving lives is serving as what John Lardner once called a discless jockey. He is a hunted man who sleeps with a revolver in his hand, and I suspect that he must spend a good part of his time with regret as a companion. I don't blame him if he does. After all, he has been betrayed. There is no other word for it.

It is down here in the delta, away from the perfumed treachery of Saigon, that the roots of the war can be seen with one's eyes. The small details of life here contain all the seeds of the Vietcong rebellion. A paddy farmer's son will be a paddy farmer, and his children will be paddy farmers, too. If he is fortunate, he will receive enough education to avoid being cheated in the marketplaces, but if he is intelligent, a potential leader, a budding poet, or possibly a future surgeon, he has nowhere to go. Except, of course, to the Vietcong.

So we find ourselves as a nation defending the status quo in a situation that begs for revolution. In a country that is 90 percent agricultural, where 45 percent of the land is owned by 2 percent of the people, neither we nor our allies will even whisper the words "agrarian reform." The Vietnamese government refuses even to make the simple promise that farmers now squatting on land in Vietcong territory can take legal title to the land if the VC are driven out. The Vietcong tell the peasants that the government and their American allies are waging war on behalf of landlords, and certainly from the viewpoint of a man to whom land is life, the argument seems a reasoned one.

So we use the silken language of the well fed while talking to the hungry and the dying. We build schools that make a young man literate enough to discover that he is a literate paddy farmer. We should be spending some of our national time, money, and blood on ways of shaking that system to its foundations. We should start 20,000 scholarships for the sons of paddy farmers right now, instead of drafting them into the ARVN to be used as mortar fodder. If we don't do something to force our noble allies to change, then young men will continue to shoot their way into the universities, and this war will last for thirty years. You convince no one with bland pieties about freedom and democracy. Men never fight hard for such things in countries like Vietnam. They do fight for the right to be men.

After the party at the colonel's house, we sat in a restaurant talking about the war. Someone said that poor South Vietnam had no possibility of salvation unless a leader on the style of Magsaysay of the Philippines or Cardenas of Mexico suddenly appeared on the scene.

"You need the kind of man, like Magsaysay, who would get a telegram from a peasant saying he had troubles and would fly to see him at three o'clock in the morning," the guy was saying. "He would knock on a peasant's hut and say, 'I'm the President. What's your problem?' That's how the Huks were defeated. Napalm isn't the only weapon."

The man said a leader should be a man of the people, who thought like the people, who got down on the earth and talked with them in their own language.

"There is one Vietnamese like that," someone said. We stared at him for a long moment.

"He calls himself Ho Chi Minh."

We all laughed, more at the shock of recognition than anything else. Later we found out that a policeman had been shot by the Vietcong three blocks from where we sat. They had waited in his front yard and murdered him, Mafia style. At the colonel's lawn party, they thought the noise of the killing was

firecrackers. I hope the government at least paid for the funeral.
January 18, 1966

This Is a Man Who Loves War

You see him in all the places where the Americans have gone in this country. He is usually about thirty-five, his body trimmer than it has a right to be, his chin fighting the first approach of jowls, the thinning hair disguised by a crew cut. He smokes too much, usually small, precisely cut cigars, and he affects an attitude of cynical bitterness. If he has been here a few months, he has acquired a steady Vietnamese girlfriend; if he has just arrived, he puts in a lot of time in the Tu Do bars, spending his money loudly, smiling a weary smile. He doesn't really care if he ever goes home. He is the war lover.

I was at a table on the raised terrace of the Continental Palace Hotel, on a day brilliant with sunshine, when one of them walked in. There it was: the measured walk, half remembered from old John Wayne movies; the casual flick of the cigarillo butt before climbing the three steps to the terrace; the captain's uniform—he was with the 173d Airborne, Bien Hoa—tailor-made and razor-pressed. He sat at a table next to mine, ordered a scotch and soda, and sat staring out past the potted palms at some point in the middle distance. His face was creased by a wintry half-smile. You have seen it. Clark Gable wore it for the last fifteen years of his life. He turned to me, the polished gabardine rustling as he leaned over.

"Gotta match?" he asked.

"Sure." I handed him the box of wooden matches, a local brand with a dragon for a trademark, and I remembered guys I had known in the Navy who would sew dragons onto the insides of their cuffs the first week out of boot camp. It made them salty. I wondered if the captain had dragons on his cuffs.

"Been here long?" he asked.

"No," I said.

"What outfit you with?"

212

"I'm a newspaperman," I said.

"Writing up the war, eh?" He said it just that way; it was a line of dialogue from a bad war novel. You could tell that from the "eh." He turned and looked into the middle distance. He had put on the I've-seen-terrible-things face again. "Boy," he said, "lotsa luck." I wondered if he was hearing a brass band.

Then the captain slid his chair over and started talking. The war lovers always talk. I suppose that people who truly understand war are like people who have fortunate sex lives or genuine money: They never talk about it. But the war lovers are a special breed. They assume that combat, bravery, the smell of death are things that do not truly exist until they have been translated into words or pictures. They must tell you.

"I've seen some terrible things in this country, fella," he said. I started to laugh. "Have you ever seen a dead man?" he said. I'd seen them, I said. "A lot of good guys are dying in this country," he said. "Lots of good guys." He ordered a double scotch and soda. Across the street kids were firing the last firecrackers of the Tet season. A big one went off, and the captain turned his head in anger.

"If those goddamned kids knew what war was like," the captain said, "they wouldn't be making so much noise."

"Forget it," I said. "They're only kids." They're only kids, and their older brothers are getting shot at, and in a few years they will join them. He drank the scotch quickly and I reached over to light his cigarillo. "What's war really like?" I asked.

"War." He paused dramatically, letting the word hang in the air outside his mouth. It was coming. He reached forward, his gabardines squeaking again, and I wondered for a moment how much he paid the Vietnamese woman who starched them for him. "War," he said slowly, letting the words drop out like freshly minted coins, "war is hell."

The first hours of talk with the war lovers are always the same, and the captain was no different. "We have to stop the Communists somewhere. These people need our help, and we're the only people in the world with enough guts to fight for them. We're gonna win it, too. Boy, if you could see what we've got out there. Napalm, tear gas, artillery, everything. We'll chop them to pieces. These people want to be free."

When the war lovers talk, the abstractions are always wedded to the specific. We shall bring democracy, freedom, liberty, peace, contentment to Vietnam, and we shall bring them by burning women and children and destroying crops and keeping the kill ratio in its proper proportion. "Sure, some people are gonna get hurt," the captain was saying. "This is war."

Most of the war lovers I've talked to are five-drink drunks. The captain made it to seven. Then something soft came into his mouth, and the Clark Gable squint began to droop. I asked him if he was married.

"Yeah, I'm married," he said. He was staring moodily; but his eyes couldn't locate that spot in the middle distance, and he settled for his glass. That's the way Bogie used to do it. Boy, that Bogie. He had class. He knew what hurt meant. "I wonder what my wife is doing," he said to no one in particular. He took out a black elephant-hide wallet with Vietnam stamped on it in gold lettering and brought out the pictures. The war lovers always carry pictures. They want you to know what they've given up.

"That's Agnes," he said, "and that's my kids." A stocky woman in her mid-thirties stared out from the pictures, her eyes lost in the shadows from the hard sun. Behind her was a concrete house of the kind that contractors throw swiftly together around military camps. Three children—two boys and a girl—were posed stiffly in front of her. The boys wore corduroy pants. The captain wasn't in the picture. I suppose he was holding the camera.

"They're older now," he said flatly.

"When did you see her last?"

"See who? Oh, Agnes. Let's see," he started mumbling. "Seven months, I guess. Something like that. She writes to me every week."

The waiter brought another scotch.

"You know something," the captain said. His gabardines were wilting in the midafternoon heat. "You know, I *like* it here. Can you understand that? I *like* it here." He seemed relieved to have said it. "Agnes doesn't understand."

Only the war lovers understand each other. They understand that finally, after twelve years of serving in a peacetime army, they have found the real thing. They've been shooting at tin cans with the most powerful arsenal in human history, and now they can use it on people. No PTA's for them out here. No officers' parties. No worrying about the kids' health or the car payments or whether Agnes can afford a new dress. Now, after giving ten years of their youth, they can do it the way they've only seen it done in the movies. They can be John Wayne, or Clark Gable, or Bogie; they can play fast and loose in the bars; they can enjoy the one luxury war affords the middle-aged: the chance to live again like adolescents.

"I've seen some terrible things, boy," he said.

"I'm sure you have," I said, paying the waiter. I walked across the sun-splashed terrace. The children were still popping their firecrackers. I wondered if the captain had asked to have his tour of duty extended yet. Most of the war lovers do.

January 20, 1966

On the Convoy to Lonely Bong Son

We were awakened at half past four in the morning when the artillery splintered the dark stillness. On the next cot a Japanese cameraman cursed privately, his hand pawing the earth for a lamp which was not there. I struck a match and saw a reporter from Brussels come suddenly awake, the yellow light flickering on his long, bony face. He stood up on the damp ground in his underwear and moved nervously to the entrance of the tent.

"What iss sit?" he said. "What iss happening?"

"Just the goddamned artillery," someone said.

The artillery was hammering from some point behind us, sending its deadly cargo across the great Army base at An Khe to the forest country beyond the far perimeter. Between salvos you could hear trucks moving in the night and the rustle of nylon as men extracted themselves from sleeping bags.

"That goddamned artillery," said Wally Bean, a reporter for *Stars and Stripes*. "Don't those muckers *ever* sleep?"

We dressed quickly in the darkness. Down the road the lights of the convoy were blinking on at the assembly point. Above us the red signals of a patrolling helicopter moved between the clustered stars. We threw water on our faces at an open trough and prepared for the journey to Bong Son.

That morning we knew the peace offensive had ended, that the long lull in the fighting here was over. Perhaps, when the historians sit down to write about this war, the fight for Bong Son will be only a minor detail, a footnote to larger currents, lost in the headlines about the resumption of bombing in North Vietnam. But on this damp morning in An Khe, there were a lot of men to whom this obscure town 300 miles north of Saigon would be the most important fact of their lives. They knew that some of them, no matter how long their luck had held, would die.

"Let's get this show on the road," a major said crankily, waiting for the 73-vehicle convoy to pick him up. "The sooner we get it over with, the better."

"There's no use hurrying, baby," said Captain Jean Coleman, one of the public information officers for the First Air Cavalry, which is based at An Khe. "When you get out there, you'll wish you wasn't."

Then the convoy pulled up, and we climbed aboard. The convoy—carrying men, ammunition, and food—was to travel 80 miles that day, moving east on Highway 19 to Quang Nai, then turning north for 50 miles on Vietnam's infamous Route 1. The destination was Bong Son, where the allies were beginning Operation Masher, covering 450 square miles of territory, the largest single military operation of the war so far. If the convoy made it to Bong Son, its members would be the first Americans ever to travel that far north on Route 1. The French lost three divisions trying to keep it open.

"You got a weapon with you?" asked First Sergeant Edward O. Hoskins, a thin-lipped, hard-eyed twenty-year veteran from New Orleans. I hadn't. He cracked the breech of a shotgun, peered down the blue wide barrel, and showed me how to load it. "If we get hit," he said, "you'd better use this." I am a man baffled by the household hammer, and I hoped my life would not depend on my facility with that weapon.

As we moved toward the Deo Mang Pass, daylight arrived

unobtrusively. The sun hung limply behind the clouds, a damp wet ball. A helicopter churned the air above us, policing the road. The vehicles of the convoy were spread out at 50-meter intervals, emphasizing the peculiar emptiness of the country-side. Hoskins kept his matte-black M-16 trained on the sur-rounding hills.

"It's great ambush country, isn't it?" Hoskins said. It cer-tainly was. Thick foliage crawled upon the face of the moun-tains, creating damp black pockets where dozens of men could squat unseen. The road itself—emptied of all other traffic—pitched and curved and turned erratically, creating blind en-trances and narrow exits. A mined vehicle, a felled tree, a steel wire: any simple device could bring us to a halt and leave the convoy vulnerable to a slaughter. Sitting in the lead jeep, watching the bends in the road, I understood what a relentless companion fear is in a war.

Then suddenly the road straightened, and we were moving quickly down a long slide of road into the flat country. The sky cleared, and the green rice paddies shimmered brilliantly in the sun. Hoskins laid his weapon across his lap and lit a cigarette.

"There were some places in Korea looked like this," he was saying. "That country was pretty in summer. But in winter—I remember one winter when I really thought I'd freeze to death. Guys were falling on the roads with frostbite. You would start a fire and try to get warm, and then someone would start shoot-ing at you and you'd start again. But at least in Korea you had a front. This place you don't. That's why it's so spooky."

At the intersection of Route 1 the roads grew more con-gested. We crossed a railroad bridge into a small village. Chil-dren lined the road. Korean soldiers, stationed in the area, snapped salutes as we went by. Women carrying food on yokes and wearing mollusk hats blocked traffic. The convoy slowed, then halted. Hoskins and I got out of the jeep and stood talking. I asked him if any of the men he went into the Army with were still in it.

"Not many of them," he said. He paused, flipped his cigarette away and looked down at a small Vietnamese kid who was trying to sell us a bottle of La Rue beer. "Times have changed. The Army's changed. Guys get married, and their wives can't take the life. Some guys get killed. You find it hard to have real friends because you know that they can get killed. It's a strange life."

Hoskins seemed anxious to talk more; but then the traffic was unwound, and we were back in the convoy, to make the dash up Route 1 for Bong Son. Hoskins checked his M-16 and searched the sky for the escort helicopter. "You remember how to work this thing?" he asked, indicating the shotgun with his boot. I nodded, and we pulled out.

To see what war has done to this country, a trip up Route 1 is as instructive as any casualty report. Everywhere we passed bombed-out villages, scorched forest areas, the broken rubble of farmhouses, rice fields gone seedy and wild. There were trees with their tops blown off, smashed pagodas, women and children with stricken faces.

In one village, the only inhabitant appeared to be a leper woman whose jaw was gone, squatting at the side of the road, extending a hand with three fingers on it. The doors of the houses were ripped from their hinges, and slogans in Vietnamese painted in rugged slashes across their façades. I suspect they were words of wisdom from the National Liberation Front, explaining to passersby that this village had died for the greater good of mankind. In wars, there is never a shortage of carefully barbered lies.

The road itself was hardly a road at all. The paved top disappeared for miles at a time, and the Vietcong had dug slit trenches through it every 20 feet. The trenches had been filled with dirt by Korean and Vietnamese soldiers; but when we hit the indentations, the jeep bumped and jerked, and we had to hold our steel helmets.

In the 50 miles from Quang Nai to Bong Son I counted seventy-two bridges and every one had been blown up by the Vietcong. Somehow, bypasses of earth piled upon iron culverts had been built, and we were able to go through. Off to our left, the old railroad which once connected Saigon with Hanoi was torn and broken. A section of track would run 100 feet, and then the rails would arc suddenly into the air, as if pried up by some giant animal. Part of the strategy of guerrilla war is to isolate the country from the cities by destroying all means of communication, and the Vietcong had done a thorough job of it.

Finally, after seven hours on the road we could see Bong Son coming near. There were more soldiers on the roads, most of them Vietnamese, and the air began to vibrate with the sounds of helicopters and artillery.

We came into Bong Son, and Hoskins relaxed again. This is another town where the Americans have moved in, and we saw teams of soldiers stringing wires for radio systems and one Vietnamese lettering the words "Cold Beer" on the front of his restaurant.

"Well," Hoskins said, "we made it that time."

We drove down a side road and onto an open field. Tents were billowing in the breeze, and a few miles away napalm skidded and glowed across the top of a ridge. A Medevac helicopter hovered and took off with the wounded. Small-arms fire crackled somewhere to our right, signaling war. The fight for Bong Son was on.

February 1, 1966

Waiting for the Mortars

There were a dozen of us in the tent, sitting on cots, talking softly in the yellow light of the hurricane lamps. Outside, a soft rain was falling, and the tent poles were cold and beaded from leaks in the roof. Occasionally, men would slip in through the flapped entrance, their ponchos slick with rain. They would cook coffee in dark-brown C-ration cans, drink it in silence, and leave. In a corner, a young foot soldier squatted on the damp ground, cleaning his M-16 and whistling stray bars from "Waltzing Matilda." Every ten minutes, a patrolling helicopter would fly low over the tent, billowing its sides, straining the tent pegs. We were expecting to be mortared.

"If Charlie doesn't hit us tonight," said Captain Hank Thorpe, a former University of North Carolina halfback, "he'll never hit us."

"He could hit us pretty easy, too," said Lieutenant James

219

Lawrence of Troy, Alabama. "From that ridge, he could drop twenty mortars in here before we could get to him."

We stepped outside to look around. The moon was gone, vanished with the rain, but away off we could see the long animallike ridge of mountains where the Vietcong were dug in for the night. A flare was dropped, and against its glow you could see the dark insect shapes of the parked helicopters, the squat black outlines of the headquarters tents, unfolding scribbles of barbed wire, and the small knoll where the perimeter was. The rain was heavier.

"I don't like it," Thorpe said. "I don't like it at all."

"Remember," said Lawrence, "the ditch is straight out at the back. If you hear anything, anything that sounds like a mortar round, run back there and get as flat as you can get."

Inside, we drank black coffee, tasting like chemicals from the purified water. Someone started talking about the Ia Drang Valley.

"That was something," someone said. "That was really it."

"Numbah ten thou'," said Thorpe, chuckling.

Operation Masher, the largest single operation of this war so far, was being conducted by the First Air Cavalry Division, with the help of Vietnamese troops and the possible future use of the U. S. Marines. The First Cav. has seen more combat here than any other American unit, has taken the most casualties, and has won the most honors. But in this country, where the phrase "numbah one" means in pidgin English, that something is very good, and "numbah ten" means that something is very bad, the Ia Drang Valley is always thought of as "numbah ten thou'." It was the charnel house by which every future action will be measured.

"I never thought I'd live through it," a young boy named Louis Simpson, from Savannah, Georgia, said. "I never saw anyone killed before, and then there were folks gettin' hit all around. A guy standing next to me got it, an' I didn't. Y' jus' can't figure it."

"The funny thing was that nobody ran," said Lawrence. "I talked to some NCO's later and they said even in Tarawa, Iwo Jima, places like that in the Second World War, they never saw such a field of fire."

"You're wrong," someone said. "One guy ran."

"I forgot about him," Lawrence said. They mentioned his name, with a kind of sympathetic disdain. "He just panicked, that's all."

"But he was the only guy in his platoon who lived," said the boy cleaning his rifle. "Maybe he was smart."

"The thing was, he was so gung ho," said another. "When we'd sit around the camp in Benning, he'd say, 'Man, I can't wait to get me some VC's. Jus' let me get them bastards.' Soon as he seen them, he broke and run."

"Some guys talk to build up their courage," Thorpe said.

"He should of had a lot of damned courage by the time he got here," Simpson said. "He sure did a lot of talking."

"Well," Thorpe said, "he'll live with that day the rest of his life."

All of them would.

That day last November, Lawrence had been leading his platoon into a field of elephant grass when the first shots rang out. "We made one fool mistake," he said. "We were burning houses as we moved into the valley, and if Charlie needed some signs we were coming, those burning houses were all he needed. When we made it up the valley, he had all his guns in position for the ambush. When he opened up, we all went flat, but some of the guys were already dead. We were pinned down and trying to crawl across the field to cover. Then I felt a thump, like someone had hit me with a bat across the forehead. They got me right in the head."

"I thought you was a goner," Thorpe said.

"I reckon I woulda been if I wasn't wearin' my pot," Lawrence said. The bullet had slammed into his steel helmet, and the instant of impact had snapped his head back enough to cause the bullet just to crease the top of his skull.

"I remember when they got me to Clark Field in the Philippines, how they took my pot away," Lawrence said. "I kept yellin', 'Give me the pot. Give me my goddamned pot!' I wanted it for a souvenir. Hell, I'd earned it. But when I woke up out of the morphine, the pot was gone. I reckon some supply sergeant is showin' it to his kids back in the States now."

"Tell him about Humphrey," Simpson yelled.

"Yeah," Lawrence said. "I wake up in the hospital, and Humphrey is there, making a tour. He comes and sits next to me, and some fella from the Associated Press takes a picture. And it goes into all the papers in the states. My pappy starts getting a hell of a lot of pictures, of me and Humphrey, and then I get a letter from him sayin', 'Son, the way you and Hubert are plastered all over Alabama, why he might even carry the state in '72!' "

Everyone laughed. Someone muttered that the war stories should stop. Another guy picked up a cheap paperback called *Dormitory Love.* He started reading: ". . . And as he sunk his teeth into my pearly white shoulder, rivers of love flowed through all of my long, ripe body. . . ." A guy threw a coffee can at him. Men talked about what they would do "on the outside." One wanted to be a press agent. Another said he would be a gigolo, "everything else being equal." Lawrence said he would take over his father's hardware business. The talk drifted, from women, to the lack of mail, to the graduates of West Point (called ringknockers), to women again.

Then we heard the snapping of small-arms fire.

"The light," Thorpe whispered. Men pulled on their boots, grabbed for their helmets, and rushed outside. The rain had stopped. It was dark and very quiet.

"Wait here," Thorpe said. He unsheathed his .45 and disappeared into the blackness. He made a squishing sound in the damp earth as he walked. In five minutes he was back.

"Just a nervous kid," he said. "Thought he saw something and opened fire."

We all breathed easier, but when we got back inside nobody talked much anymore. This night was like most of the nights in Vietnam: men talking about boredom, and survival, and the choices they would all have to make. The conversation would drift and move, but there was no way to forget about the war. We lay on those cots in our shoes, smoking final cigarettes, worrying about the mortars which never came.

February 2, 1966

Men Under Fire

That morning the rain fell steadily across the valley. Soldiers stood in clusters at the edge of the perimeter, the rain trickling down their ponchos, cupping cigarettes in damp hands. The earth around the base camp had turned to mud, the last of the grass trampled by soldiers' boots. We stood on a rise behind a bombed-out farmhouse and looked down at a slow brown river pushing through the rice country to the sea and saw the attack helicopters spitting rockets at the base of the ridge.

"Get them bastards, baby, get 'em real good," said Private James Loughrey of Chicago. "Eat 'em up."

The helicopters were everywhere, darkening the skies like flocks of locusts. This was the day of the big push against a battalion of Vietcong and North Vietnamese troops. Colonel Hal Moore, leading the First Air Cavalry in Operation Masher, explained that the enemy troops were caught on the coastal plain and were trying to escape to the mountains in the west. The helicopters were dropping men at a number of points.

"He's cut off by the sea and the Vietnamese on the east," Moore said. "He can't go very far north because the Marines are there. We're at the southern end, and we have to stop him from going west to the mountains. If we're lucky, we'll nail him and destroy him."

But the Vietcong had been dug into this area (300 miles north of Saigon) for fifteen years. The countryside—when it was not rice paddies—was laced with slit trenches, spider holes, and sniper positions. Progress of the operation had been slow.

"Charlie's lucky," a sergeant said, standing at the edge of a helicopter landing zone in the base camp. The base camp had been pitched in an abandoned cemetery, and a smashed church and untended crosses stuck up on the southern horizon. "He's had time to dig in. He figures he can cut us to pieces during the day and move out at night."

Around noon I boarded a Medevac to go out and look at the field of battle. The Medevacs are engaged in the most dangerous game in Vietnam. Their duty is to remove wounded from the field of battle, and that means they are almost always dropped into the thickest combat.

Three companies of soldiers can be part of the same battle, and only one of them will see actual combat. Because there has not yet been a way devised for men to wage war against each other without having casualties, the Medevacs will always be with the company getting hit.

"You know, of course, that if we have to pick up wounded, you have to get out?" the pilot said.

Of course, I said, and he motioned me in.

Below us, as we climbed, the battlefield took shape. We could see the artillery laid on a line, firing to the north, and then the dirty plumes of the explosions when the shells hit. Off to the left, in the mountains where the Vietcong were heading, a jet sped almost to the green mountain wall, pulled up, and then the napalm skidded and exploded. Again I was struck by the terrible fact that the weapons of war have a special, brutal beauty, like great prizefighters. The napalm burst in a slippery orange mass, brilliant and shocking against the wet dark silence of the forest, and then it was burning its way through the underbrush, sending a long torrent of warm gray smoke rushing down the mountainside.

The crew of the Medevac was unimpressed. There were five of them: two gunners, with .50-caliber machine guns jutting out windows on either side; two pilots; and a medic. On the floor in front of us stretchers were piled; in the corners were the green rubber bags which transport the dead. Away off, we could see the dark surface of the sea and sheets of rain moving inland.

Then suddenly we were dropping swiftly. One of the gunners pointed to an island of land surrounded by the careful oblongs of the rice paddies. It seemed absolutely still from where we were. Then, as we came in we could see men lying down and hear the rap-pap-pap-pap of machine-gun fire. The Medevac hovered, its rotor blades whipping the sandy ground of the landing zone, and we saw men rushing toward us. They had one wounded man and two green rubber bags. We sighed to a stop.

"Afraid you'll have to get off here," I was told. "We'll get you on the next trip."

The wounded man—he was about twenty—had dark curly hair, and the left side of his face was covered with sand where he had fallen. His eyes were fogged over with pain. He kept making small sounds from deep in his chest. "Uh! Uh! Uh!" A pause. "Uh!"

I looked down and saw what had happened. His stomach had been ripped open, probably by mortar fragments. The Medevac medic was working with a field medic to cover the wound. You could see whitish things glistening through the blood from his stomach. His face was draining and he kept saying, "Uh! Uh! Uh!" There was no time to ask his name, or find out where he was from. It didn't really matter. I doubt if the death of men in war can be explained by biography.

Then the helicopter lifted off, churning the ground. Skirls of rain whipped across the open field. Everyone crouched low. There were five of us left after the helicopter left. I asked what was happening.

"They're shooting over there," a young private said. He pointed across the field at a clump of shelled farmhouses and dense scrub. A tall Negro next to me said that the fire fight was just beyond the farmhouses. The medic moved back to the tree line, and the tall Negro started moving, hunched over, to my right. We heard a shot.

"Get down!" someone shouted, and we pitched forward. A furious burst of machine-gun fire came from somewhere close by, and then the scene seemed to explode. Fire from machine guns and small arms pinged and hissed through the air. I was as flat as I could get. Over to my left, a private had his face buried in the sand. We had no cover.

I suspect that fear is the most intense and solitary of the emotions; love is fugitive by comparison. One tries to move forward, thinking that movement will help elude death, but knowing also that to move might be to invite it. We felt the ground shuddering under the concussion of artillery, and still the machine guns hammered. The earth seemed to reel. No one talked. And then, as suddenly as it had started, the firing stopped. We all lay still.

"The —— are gone," the guy on my left said. We rose to a squat. There was still firing on the far side of the village. We were squatting for a few minutes when we noticed the tall Negro.

He was lying still, facedown, his body jerked at an angle. We moved over to him. His body squirmed, but his eyes were still, and rolling backward into his head. I wondered how, back in Saigon, they would list him. One is never, after all, lightly dead, moderately dead, heavily dead; like chastity, death has no degrees.

The tall Negro was from Florida, he was twenty-one years old, he was Protestant, and they took him away later in a green rubber bag.

I left that place on the third Medevac after the one that delivered me. Like all reporters, I was a transient at the war and could leave at my own choosing.

The helicopter climbed away swiftly. I saw the body of one Vietnamese, hit by mortar explosion, his body a wreck. Seven more bodies lay in the rain.

All the way back, I tried to keep my hands from trembling while I smoked, ashamed of my fear. Behind me, the bodies of the dead, washed by the rain, were already becoming a pasture for worms.

February 4, 1966

IV. White Mischief

I N the fall of 1966, Lyndon Johnson announced that he would be traveling to Manila for a conference with all the leaders of "free" Asia. Somehow, I convinced Paul Sann and Dorothy Schiff that I should go with him, along with a plane-load of other reporters. It was like stepping into a novel written by Evelyn Waugh. Absurdity followed absurdity, as Johnson brought his personal touch to the stage of world diplomacy. I never thought I would miss Johnson until I reread some of these pieces; he was the perfect politician for a journalist like me, large, pompous, and boisterous, and to spend some time with him was to be in the presence of a living, breathing human being. By comparison, Richard Nixon is loose-leaf paper. Since he has been President, I've gone to Washington only a few times, and when I have covered him, it was something like covering the actions of the third recording secretary of the National Association of Manufacturers.

I've left these pieces intact, despite repetition and clumsiness caused by haste, because they might provide a sense of a story unfolding and of a writer trying to deal more and more sharply with a single, distant figure. I've done better work than this in my life, but I've never had as much fun.

A South Seas Stopover

As I sat in the hotel in Honolulu, with the telegraph operators punching away furiously, and guys with horn-rimmed glasses and cigars handing out mimeographed copies of speeches, and the Secret Service men checking the exits for Chinese Communists, there were only two real topics of conversation: the tidal wave and Lyndon Johnson. And most of the time it was both.

"You just know what he's gonna do," said a guy from one of the TV networks. "If that tidal wave comes anywhere near here, he's gonna throw open the windows of the Presidential Suite, stand out on the balcony in his shorts, peer out to sea, and holler at the top of his lungs, 'Stop.'"

"And by God," someone else said, "it'll stop."

Out on the beachfront at Waikiki, tidal wave warning sirens were wailing, and someone with a bullhorn was commanding the citizenry to head for higher ground. On the radio, the bulletins said that an earthquake in Peru had caused the expected tidal wave, that it would hit about twelve thirty, and you should be prepared. Instead, you fell off to sleep, to dream of Lyndon Johnson on a beach furious with water and wind, facing Asia with General Westmoreland at his side, while 2,000,000 Boy Scouts cheered him on and Bill Moyers recorded it all on tape.

"Bail, goddammit, bail," he is yelling to the Boy Scouts. "They're closing in on us."

You awake while it is still dark, your tongue feeling as if you had spent the night licking pool tables, trying to get vertical after three hours' sleep, and then stumbling through the hotel courtyard to the press buses. The palm trees look sinister, dripping with morning moisture. The tidal wave, you discover, had never happened, but some of my erstwhile colleagues had gone to face their impending doom at a topless waitress place up the street. The hangovers—moral and physical—were wondrous to behold. Then across the darkened tarmac, onto the plane, and off for Pago Pago. The plane climbs through brooding ridges of clouds, heads out over the great, empty, polished surface of the Pacific, and after breakfast, we all are again unconscious.

When we at last awaken, hours have passed and we have crossed the equator, like tourists lost in a 6B geography book. A popping of ears announces the descent to Pago Pago. It is like everything you have always thought about when you thought about flattening your boss and heading for the tropics: green and lush, with steep mountains, and white breakers hitting reefs, and pastel bungalows tacked to the sides of the hills.

The water is bluer than any Jon Hall movie, with wild birds flying across the valleys, and you felt sure that someone who looked like Thomas Mitchell would come out to greet us, a desperate rummy on the run from civilization, his Panama hat soiled and his ice-cream suit wrinkled, prepared to tell the President of the United States to keep going before the twentieth century ruins the place.

Well, it didn't really turn out that way. The first man I ran into was Sergeant K. Tuufuli of the Samoan police force, a massive man who had spent twenty years in the U.S. Navy. He looked like a gentle menace. "This is a great day for American Samoa," he said. "No other President in history has ever come here, and we will make this a great occasion. Or else."

Tuufuli, wearing a brilliant red sarong called a lavalava, was standing at the entrance to the three main airport buildings, wooden structures based on the traditional architecture of the grass hut. There was a long carpet called a tapa, and the crowd of about 500 held signs saying TALOFA PRESIDENT JOHNSON.

"*Talofa* is what we say for aloha," Tuufuli said. He lit a cigarette and motioned the jackals of the press away from the tapa rug. The heat was terrible, burning into the skins of the city reporters, turning creases in suits into soggy ripples, and forcing at least one TV cameraman to buy a red and white umbrella to place over his camera. Inside, press tables had been set up, and groups of lovely young girls came out with trays of sandwiches and ice-cold lemonade with fruit garlands. They were dressed in the Samoan version of the muumuu, called a puletasi. One young beauty, Miss Faatuina Sue, eighteen, said this wasn't really the way Samoans dressed.

"You know we have television here now," Miss Sue said.

230

"Most of us like to wear the American style, you know." She was looking around at the great spread of Samoans dressed in native costume, the men all heavy, fat-armed and tattooed, adorned with necklaces made of sharks' teeth, most of them smoking filter cigarettes. The colors were gorgeous, violets and reds and splashy oranges.

In the reception line there was one great-looking old man with a purple lavalava, who was wearing a pair of black shoes and drooping socks, apparently uniform of the day for big celebrations. There did not seem to be any middle-aged people. The blooming cinnamon-skinned South Sea beauties seemed to change overnight into the sluggish fat-encased oldsters who were sitting on the grass waiting to see Lyndon Johnson.

"A lot of the young people want to leave," Miss Sue said. "But they can only go to Hawaii. I was there, you know? But you get homesick and come back."

What about the war in Vietnam? Had they been affected in American Samoa?

"Oh, yes, it is very sad. We see it on the television. You know many Samoan boys have gone there and have been hurt or damaged." She spoke English the way people do who have learned it from textbooks, with a kind of translated precision. And when you looked around at those young men to whom fishing, smoking, and lovemaking were the only things they really cared about, you could only regret that even in this isolated place, that awful war had touched people's lives.

Then came Lyndon Johnson among us, dressed in a dark-green suit, Lady Bird with him, dressed in pink, and a flying wedge of officials—American and Samoan—preceding them. There were elaborate ceremonies prepared, all of which put you in mind of a 1930's desert island picture written with the help of Margaret Mead. If Lyndon Johnson were to come permanently to the South Seas, he would almost certainly come as Captain Cook, not as Gauguin.

One official-looking native—"We used to call them a chief," Miss Sue said—even told of the legend of a great white bird who came among the red birds to bring greatness and other vague benefits. Johnson stood on the speakers' platform, nodding and looking like some wonderful grotesque and didn't

231

even seem angry when Lady Bird received a bigger hand than he did.

When it was over, we all piled into a tiny minibus which transformed us into a tortured, sun-wilted gang, and went off to see Lady Bird cut a flowered ribbon opening a new school, which by some accident had been named the Manulele Tausala Consolidated School, which translates into the Lady Bird Consolidated School. A bunch of schoolkids came out and started singing a song in Samoan whose chorus was Lady Bird (Bird, Bird Bird) that even made Lyndon laugh, and she gave them two globes for the school. And then we were all heading back to the airport. Near the entrance Miss Sue and her hostess friends waved and invited us back. Sergeant Tuufuli, that large pragmatist, had other things to do. He was holding back the crowd with a ceremonial spear.

October 19, 1966

Visiting the Folks Down Under

The country that Lyndon Johnson swept through appeared to be the creation of an act of will. From the C-130 coming into the capital, you saw long, rolling handmade slopes, a soft, controlled landscape like that of the Irish or English countryside, with the same persistent rain falling, the same wet grayness washing the houses, and boys playing soccer on open grass. It was as if all those people from the British Isles who had come here in exile had decided that no matter what else happened they would utterly change the wild country's face.

So we discovered ourselves in a place where fish-and-chips stores dot the main streets, and they put butter on the ham sandwiches, and the saloons close at 6 P.M., and grown men tell smutty jokes and giggle at themselves. The houses seem always deserted, as if everyone were secreted in some dark back room, and only occasionally can you see a dusty white face peering from behind a very British lace curtain. It looks like a country

232

of secret drunks, filled with men with rheumy eyes tiptoeing past tearooms, free of sex, public emotion, and disorder.

It was to this country that Johnson came to proclaim New Zealand as part of an emerging Asia. It was a proposition that contained as much logic as saying that Wales was part of Southern California. Yet there he was: standing in a needly rain at Ohakea RNZAF air base, flanked by Prime Minister Keith Holyoake and their wives, facing an audience of schoolboys in short pants, dumpy women, and little girls in wet wool skirts. On the side, a group of Maori dancers shivered in bare feet and beaded skirts, listening to Lyndon talk about his great affection for New Zealand and how threatened it was when he was here in 1942 and how much better it was now.

In the evening Johnson attended a state dinner and the exhausted minions of the press fell into bunks on the ship *Hinemoa,* the only available accommodations in a town which specializes in government, farm instruments, and bad architecture.

We awoke to a breakfast of charred eggs and uncooked bacon and set out again on the trail of Lyndon Johnson. We found him at the National War Memorial, a vast tower that reminded you of the University of Texas. Inside was the Hall of Memories, with the names of great battles of the past on the wall: Gallipoli, North Africa, Palestine, the Battle of Britain, and the North Atlantic. And there were the usual lying sentiments that men carve into marble when the wars are over and the worms have already finished with the bodies.

Outside there was another mob of schoolchildren and some aging members of the Returned Servicemen's Reserve ("sort of like your American Legion," one of them explained).

Johnson arrived to lay a wreath, looking sunburned and fit. He had discarded the green suit of the day before (described by the local press as "unfashionable" and by the White House press corps as "his jolly green giant suit"). He started shaking the hands of the ex-servicemen and stopped to chat with Norman Griffiths, a World War I vet. "Glad to see you," Johnson said. "It's a pleasure to be here." "Hope y'can come back, sir," Griffiths said. ". . . Hope to come back some time for a long stay," Johnson said. "New Zealand's one of my favorite countries." Across the walk, a branch in a pohutukawa tree broke, and three kids fell to the ground. "New Zealand fruit," Griffiths explained, as the President walked off.

After that it was all mob scenes. A mob scene at Parliament, a mob scene on the way to meet the opposition leader, a mob scene trying to get back to Parliament. He stopped at the Wellington City Council Building in the main square to look at some tulips, just escaped the trampling herd of photographers who seemed driven to destroy every last plant, and then looked out in the direction of "Guthrie Bowdon for paint and wallpaper" and said he was glad to be there "and Mizzizz Johnson agrees with me. I want to thank you for your warm welcome and for this beautiful weather. This year we have an election in America, but I know what I'm gonna be doin' next year. I'm gonna be listenin' to Lady Bird and lookin' at tulips." Everyone cheered. A kid raised a Bobby-Kennedy-for-President sign at one point, and a cop pulled it swiftly out of his hands. I asked him where he got the Bobby Kennedy sign (the next day we saw signs reading WELCOME PRESIDENT KENNEDY).

"Me and me mates made it up," he said.

"Kennedy was our man, y'know. 'e really was. Wish it was 'im 'ere todye."

As we set out on the last motorcade, some kids held up a sign saying LBJ RANCH DALLAS TEXAS 8607 MILES. A window had another sign: JOHNSON FOR PRESIDENT, CLARKE'S FOR LOTTERIES. The crowd on Lambton Quay was huge, stopping traffic, and making the press buses ride a gauntlet. Johnson was in and out of the cars, grabbing a bullhorn, shaking hands, waving his little waves, his face beaming. And then it was over. He went back to Parliament for an address, flew back to Ohakea, and grabbed a plane for Australia.

We departed with him, prepared for further mysteries and adventures, certain of nothing, resigned to our fate. We will almost certainly learn nothing about Lyndon Johnson this way, no more than those nice little schoolboys did. We will be pummeled by strangers, have our suits ripped off our backs, watch barbarians trample our typewriters, and listen to the worst prose style since Warren Harding. But this we know: We are in the presence of an original, either the first or the last of a special

234

kind. If we take our opinions of him off the rack, you are entitled to reach for your revolver.

October 20, 1966

Rendezvous in Manila

It all looked very pretty, with lovely girls in white silk dresses
draping the visiting journalists with leis made of sampaguita,
the national flower, and men in embroidered shirts called
barong tagalogs waving small flags, and jet fighters screaming
proudly across the sky. There was a twenty-one-gun salute and
the playing of the national anthems and crowds of children and
an old priest in a white cassock smoking a cigar.

Right off, it looked like a watercolor of politics. But then, five
minutes outside the airport, the car carrying Lyndon Baines
Johnson to the Asian summit conference passed one of those
tar-black eddying creeks, with a crush of iron-roofed shacks
dropping away to the water's edge. It was in the district called
Parañaque, and coming up from its filthy banks were the inhabitants: gnarly women, ten-year-old girls holding infants on
their hips, hard-eyed young boys in sports shirts and shower
shoes, people with sores on their blank-eyed faces, and the
smell of poverty and disease everywhere.

On the seventh day of his journey, Lyndon Johnson had
finally arrived in Asia.

If he didn't know it, the Secret Service certainly did. The car
sped along Roxas Boulevard at 30 miles per hour, and there
were none of the barnstorming stops he had made in Australia
and New Zealand, where he had stopped up to twenty-five
times in a single motorcade to shake hands and exchange plat-
itudes.

In Manila, on the day of his arrival, he passed groups of
schoolchildren, soldiers, ROTC candidates, all spread out one
or two deep, carefully prepared with flags of all six visiting nations.

One vicious slum had been covered with a screen of palm

leaves attached to a wire fence, and off on the left, across Manila Bay, past the great freighters waiting to depart with the cargo of war for Saigon, you could see Bataan. It was just a pale-blue hump-backed shape in the afternoon haze. It didn't look at all like a place where brave men had died, two wars ago.

The caravan stopped finally in front of Luneta Park, a great open sward of green, filled with children and men hawking balloons. Johnson got out of the car, and he, Lady Bird, Dean Rusk, Henry Cabot Lodge, and General Westmoreland walked forward to lay a wreath on the monument to José Rizal, the national hero of the Philippines. Rizal was like José Martí of Cuba: Both were poets; both bravely fought the Spanish colonial system; both were executed. They were the sort of men that South Vietnam has yet to produce.

The ceremony was brief and tasteful, and Johnson got back in the car. He started making the turn toward the Manila Hotel, which would be the headquarters for the American delegation. When the insatiable urge claimed him, he just had to get out and press the flesh. So he stood there on the running board of the car, while the startled Filipino cops started pushing back the crowd and the paper flags waved in the background.

"Let 'em come on in," he said. "Let 'em in." And the crowd surged forward while the photographers on the two open stake trucks snapped away. "This," said one reporter, "is the *Life* magazine cover." And then he was back in again, heading for the hotel. The conference would start in the morning, and Lyndon Johnson needed his sleep.

In some ways, the conference itself is intended to put the world to sleep or at least place all of us in a full doze. The emphasis is on peace, but the group that has been assembled here is not that interested in any negotiations. General Ky stands around, small and dapper like a good bantamweight fighter, smoking filter-tip cigarettes, wearing his half-mocking, half-ironic smile.

He and General Thieu, who made the opening speech on behalf of South Vietnam when the conference was officially opened today, want no part of any coalition government.

Their attitude is let's you and him fight, and they will take our money as long as it keeps coming and will then depart for exile in Paris when, as they must, the war and money come to an end. General Park Chung Hee of South Korea, another great freedom-loving leader of what Johnson calls "the new, emerging Asia" (he took power after a military coup in 1961), is a military man and wants a military solution in Vietnam. He wants a unified military command in South Vietnam and a NATO-like military alliance in the Far East.

The Koreans have two divisions in South Vietnam, on a kind of soldier exchange plan, since we have two divisions in South Korea. To expect independence of attitude from Park is like asking Sandy Koufax to hit home runs. For domestic political reasons, the New Zealanders and the Australians are pushing a hard line on the war, and President Marcos of the Philippines will simply be asking for more money. Thailand has been our client since 1950, is now beset by guerrillas in the North, and is not about to ask the Americans to leave. If peace somehow should come to South Vietnam, we would almost certainly have to start moving the troops over to Thailand.

So, for two days, we shall be following these people around, watching them get in and out of limousines and go in and out of polished wood doors.

There will be bulletins that say nothing and a communiqué that will be couched in sugary generalities. The great American free press will sit still for backgrounders, a form of briefing that makes a mockery of candor and true reporting. A backgrounder is a politician's means to achieving his end regardless of truth.

The press comes into a room, the man—Johnson, Dean Rusk, Henry Cabot Lodge—says what he wants to say, and the reporters collaborate in keeping his name off the story. You end up with a story attributed to a "high White House source," "people close to the President," "the highest authority," and other pseudonyms. If some reporter present decides to do his job and names the source, the great advocates of American freedom bar him forever.

But the main trouble here is not just that the Vietcong, the North Vietnamese, and the Chinese are not here. It is that we are claiming this is an Asian conference when most of the rest of Asia is not here. Japan is not here; Malaysia and Indonesia are not here; Burma is not here; India is not here; Cambodia and Laos are not here. It's a gag, one of those insulting modern fabrications that politicians put together to give the illusion of action.

But out on the street, the feeling is different. In four hours of prowling around Manila last night, I could not locate a single person who thought this carnival will accomplish anything. Perhaps this is because Filipinos are about as cynical about politics as any people I've ever met. But it seems more likely that they have judged the proceedings the way most of us have.

It might be the final judgment of the historians that Lyndon Johnson was the man who finally broke down a country's capacity to believe anything. There isn't much left of words like "freedom," "liberty," and "compassion" when they are debased so viciously as they are being debased here. To talk about ideals when places like that creek in Parañaque still symbolize Asia is to delude yourself. And you can be sure that while we are looking the other way and devoting ourselves to platitudes, the Communists are down there in that creek, hard at work.
October 24, 1966

The Tigers at the Gate

They were all young, wearing slacks, sports shirts, and spoiled faces, and they were standing under the caballero trees in front of the American embassy on Roxas Boulevard, their yellow torches sending blue smoke into the night sky.

Against the curb, army jeeps and trucks formed a screen against the evening traffic, and Filipino soldiers stood everywhere, the oiled blue metal of their M-1's gleaming in the torchlight. You could tell from the violence of the language that this mob of young men was lecturing the United States about peace.

The terrible thing was that their rhetoric was just as exhausted as ours. The imperialists must stop their dirty aggression in Vietnam. Asia was for Asians. Yankee Go Home. The whole bit. The speakers talked in Tagalog, because, as one receptive student explained, "English is the language of Wall Street," and after a while, their juices rising under the harangue of the speakers, they turned and marched on the Manila Hotel. There, in Room 404, trying once more to flog some life out of tired ideas, was Lyndon Johnson.

The kids did not need much to turn them from a crowd of about 600 to a mob. They were angry to begin with because two nights before, the freedom-loving Filipino cops had stopped about fifty buses loaded with antiwar demonstrators at the Manila-Quezon City boundary. Then there was a hassle over demonstration permits. Those who favored the war received permits without difficulty.

The antiwar kids were stalled. It wasn't difficult for the speechmaker to convince the kids that the Philippine government was a U.S. stooge.

One student leader climbed on top of a jeep, and pointed at the great massive hotel, with its green eaves and imperial image, and talked about lackeys and stooges. Then one of his followers rapped on a cop with a placard. The cops went to work on the students, jamming truncheons into their stomachs, pushing at them with their forearms, and then the student leader, Arthur Lim, vice-president of the Student Council of the University of the Philippines, grabbed a microphone and started shouting, "Police brutality, police brutality, police brutality." It was the first time that night that we all felt at home.

Then rocks started arching from the rear of the crowd, and the young men started scaling their placards at the cops, and the guests watching at the hotel entrance began to back away into chandeliered safety. The mob surged forward, fists swinging, bottles flying, the eyes of the kids glazed and angry. Someone grabbed Marvin Parkas, a United Press International photographer, and belted him in the face, and there was another barrage of bottles and rocks before the cops counterattacked.

"Get your hands off me," one kid screamed. "Police brutality, police brutality."

The cops smacked one kid across the skull, and he went down hard with his leg quivering. There were fights everywhere, over a two-block area reaching toward Luneta Park. Soldiers had arrived, using the butts of their rifles, and the cops had started filling the wagons when suddenly, there was a series of about ten shots, snapping the riot off. Prudencion Tam, a student of the Lyceum of the Philippines, had been hit in the neck, and blood was running slowly down the front of his pale-blue sports shirt. After a while, an ambulance came for the injured, and the riot was over.

A mile and a half away, the press taxi and gleaming limousines were turning into the seafront compound run by the American Embassy. This was the site of the Old Manila Polo Club, and its clipped hedges and soft green lawns evoked a time when the arguments in Asia were more simpleminded or at least simpleminded in another way and people like Rudyard Kipling could lecture us about taking up the white man's burden. I suppose that if we hadn't lived those arrogant years between wars, we wouldn't have kids pelting rocks at us outside embassies and hotels. History does eventually extract its penance.

In the compound, we were treated to caviar, hors d'oeuvres, good whiskey, and a pot of chili. Against a wall, Henry Cabot Lodge stood drinking, wearing a wilted, uneasy look, like an executive of an oil company that had just been expropriated. Earlier in the day, he had briefed a select group of diplomatic correspondents who later agreed that they could learn more about Vietnam from the *National Geographic*.

"Hello there." He winced seeing an old Vietnam face. "How have you been?" Lyndon Johnson was expected, and Lodge kept looking at the door, wondering again about what further indignity he would suffer before the evening was through.

General William Westmoreland displayed no such anxiety. He was resplendent in dress whites, his chest beribboned, the hard jaw right out of a John Ford movie, the teeth white and hard. You were sure that William Westmoreland had become a general because he looked like a general, and if we have terrible luck, he might end up running for President.

"Your left hand is the search-and-destroy mission," he had explained, using boxing metaphors, "and your right hand is the pacification program. You can take them out permanently with the right hand, but you can't use it too much or the other man will throw one over it. So you keep him off-balance with the jab. . . ."

It went on like that for a while, as old Asia hands kept coming in the door and the ice clunked dully in the glasses and young Filipino boys moved around the room with glasses on trays, humble and obedient, the way they were before the world changed. The biggest crowd was gathered around Dean Rusk.

Rusk is taller (about six feet two) and more imposing-looking than he is in photographs, although his face seems to have acquired that worn, powdery look that Robert Wagner wore toward the end of his term. His shoulders are broad, and he was smiling a lot and drinking pretty good, and you remembered an interview at the Rockefeller Foundation one afternoon after he had been given the job by Jack Kennedy when people told you that Dean Rusk would be an adventurous, intellectual Secretary of State. Whatever adventure there had been in Rusk seems to have been hammered out of him forever.

October 25, 1966

The Fantastic Journey

We have all just traveled from the absurdity of Manila to the world of bizarre fiction that only Lyndon Johnson could make of a visit to Vietnam. One minute we were plowing through the oatmeal prose of official communiqués, and suddenly we were among the mad dancers, stepping gingerly into a scenario that had everything: peril, secret agents, spies lurking among the potted palms, suspense, pathos, and even romance.

It seems like years have passed since we set out on this fantastic journey, but until today we did not realize just how far the limits of reason could be pushed.

We had been called in the morning, after an evening of struggle with the leftovers of the great Manila conference, and told to appear at the main ballroom of the American Embassy at 10 P.M. for a briefing by Bill Moyers. Those who planned to go to

241

Corregidor or to another outing which Johnson had scheduled at Los Banos had nothing to fear: The buses would wait.

By that time the journey to Vietnam was already in motion. There had been what Johnson had scornfully labeled "speculation" that he would use this visit to Asia as an excuse to visit Vietnam. He would come in, the speculators speculated, get his pictures taken with the troops in time for the November elections, and depart with at least something of value.

But according to a White House source, the first decision at the White House was that there would be no decision. They claim that the trip to Manila was just that. "It was decided finally that no decision about Vietnam would be made until the President talked to General Westmoreland in Manila," the White House source said, pulling a drag on a cigar.

General Westmoreland apparently felt that because stories predicting the Johnson visit had already been printed, it would be a disappointment to the troops if he did not come. He urged Johnson to make the trip. When he finally talked to Johnson in Manila, he assured the President that security would be adequate and appropriate. Johnson set simple terms: He would go if no troops would be called away from their regular posts, if there would be no acceleration around the area he would visit, and if there would be no large-scale military ceremony. Westmoreland agreed to all conditions.

"How much time do you need?" Johnson asked.

"I can do it right away," Westmoreland replied.

By the time we arrived at the American Embassy, Westmoreland was already back in Cam Ranh Bay, already ordering up token detachments of troops for what he explained to his underlings would be a "dry run" for a visit to take place in the next three days by a high civilian dignitary who was probably Dean Rusk. We knew something big was happening when the Secret Servicemen at the door of the embassy's main ballroom refused to allow us to leave after we had checked in.

"There has been, as you know, some speculation about the President going to Vietnam," Moyers said, after all but three of the White House press corps had been assembled in the room, and all foreign reporters, strangers, waiters, and hangers-on had been thrown out. "We are leaving in about an hour from this room."

Yes, the TV people would be allowed to bring some equipment, and all film shot on the trip would be on a pool basis. No, the writers would not be allowed to go back to the hotels to get their typewriters. No one was to leave the room. There was a rumor that twenty or thirty excluded newsmen were outside, and Moyers asked that they be diplomatically removed from the premises. Because of obvious security reasons, no one could write a story now, no one would be allowed to file from Vietnam when we arrived there, and the exact place would not be revealed until we were in the air. Moyers brought in "a highly placed American source," a "White House source," and "a person close to the President," and we killed time asking questions about the conference almost everyone had already forgotten.

At that very moment, the Seventh Air Force was placing eight fighter planes on ground alert at Cam Ranh Bay and eight more at Da Nang. The Thirtieth Regiment of the Korean Army was already moving out into the field to secure the area around Cam Ranh Bay. Three armed helicopters were in the air along with two L-19 FAC observation planes, and Lyndon Johnson was rushing through an already truncated morning schedule.

Then three buses finally arrived, and we all sneaked out the back door of the embassy, past some rather dumfounded gardeners, boarded the bus, and were off. Only Moyers and the Secret Servicemen knew where we were going. We proceeded stealthily, with a mad Filipino bus driver careening around corners, past gasoline trucks and Air Force jeeps, and kids with soda pop bottles, rolling down a road crisscrossed with slit trenches, through the gaudy turf of a street gang called Steady Boys Ltd., past bohios, and mud creeks, and barefoot kids staring from behind palm trees, and young girls covering their mouths against the dust as we clattered along.

Then suddenly we were out of the jungle trails, pulling into a compound you knew was American by the appearance of two young girls with crash helmets heading right at us. They veered away and so did we. We were at the Sangley Naval Station, and a sign on the control tower told us the elevation was eight feet.

We were about as far above sea level as Lyndon Johnson's bed.

Out on the runway was the Pan Am jet. Of course. They had told us we were going by TWA.

At Sangley we were ushered into the officers' mess where lunch was served and a four-piece band played "Red Sails in the Sunset" and we waited for three reporters who had been lost in Manila's maddening crowd for most of the night. The Secret Servicemen were even guarding the men's room, in the event that a secret message might be scrawled on a wet towel and floated down the bay to Western Union.

Finally, the plane was ready, and we climbed aboard for the trip to Vietnam. Air Force One was right behind us, with Lyndon Johnson on board in a multicolored Oriental bathrobe and pale-blue pajamas. He was getting ready to change into the uniform of the day.

An hour and twenty minutes later, we were dropping down to 5,000 feet and we could see Vietnam coming up before us. There were ridges of hills and low hanging clouds, and we could see boats cutting through the water along the shore, and dust rising from freshly cut roads, and long, empty beaches, and there was no indication at all that it was a place where men were dying.

We emerged into thick wet heat and a view of sand dunes, and were ushered into buses from the Fourteenth Aerial Port Squadron. There were screens across the windows and a sign saying no joyriding, and away we went again, down a concrete runway, turning into a wide parade field where two 50-foot flatbed trailer trucks had been draped as reviewing stands and a couple of thousand troops had been assembled. I asked a soldier next to me if the area was secure.

"There are no secure areas, sir," he said grimly. Away off, a greasy column of smoke dripped into the sky. Someone thought it was a napalm strike. It turned out to be Cam Ranh Bay's garbage dump.

A roar went up as a jeep carrying the Pan Am stewardesses arrived, while one of the Secret Servicemen started pushing the reporters out of the way.

Then away down at the end of the runway we could see Air Force One.

"Here it comes," someone said, and he was right.

Lyndon Johnson was in a jeep, squinting for the cameramen, knowing that his visit was staged for their benefit, his face twitching as the muscles tried to set themselves into the patterns that made up compassion and hope and pity, and did not quite obey.

He was wearing a kind of dress jacket, of tan polished cotton, with the Presidential Seal affixed, and he hopped out of the jeep and stepped briskly up on the truck while the band played "Hail to the Chief."

Next to him was General Westmoreland, and next to him were South Vietnamese chief of state Thieu and Premier Nguyen Cao Ky, who was dapper in a three-button brown suit and elevator heels. Dean Rusk's face was flushed, and Henry Cabot Lodge winced.

Below them on the ground, Jack Valenti had removed his blue baseball cap and was staring at Johnson with the sort of emotion you usually associate with unrequited love.

Johnson and Westmoreland went down and climbed into a jeep and went off to review the troops while photographers ran back and forth. "He's gotta turn right here," one of them shouted. "Get the crew ready."

The jeep turned left.

"Now he's gotta come up to the stand again," the same cat shouted, and the jeep turned and went back through the ranks again.

Grown men were running around everywhere, and as I type this, I can barely read my notes. They are streaked with sweat, and not all of it is mine.

Johnson returned and proceeded to award the Distinguished Service Medal and Navy Cross to five young men. Their names were Paul Gorman and Morton Hammer and Clovig Coffman and Charles Morris and John Nolan, and they had done courageous things and come away from death with at least their lives intact.

They were what the war was really about, better men really than those who sent them to this side of the China Sea. Johnson pinned the medal on each of them, while the photographers snapped and pushed and shoved and cursed.

245

"We're very proud of you, son," Johnson said to each, and each said, "Thank you, sir," and then Johnson saluted and went back up on the stage truck.

We endured a speech by Thieu, who injected enough of the PID bit ("poverty, ignorance, and disease") to keep consistent with what he had said in Manila, and then Johnson was at the microphone. You hoped he would rise to the occasion, that here among brave men he would talk with candor and true pity. It didn't happen. He addressed the TV audience in Indianapolis.

"I come here today for one good reason," he said, "simply because I couldn't come to this part of the world and not see you. I come here today for one good purpose: to tell you and every soldier, sailor, airman, and Marine in Vietnam how proud we are of you."

The troops stood by quietly. They didn't applaud the sort of nonsense that Johnson uses on the stump in Iowa, and they didn't swell with pride when he stuck still another medal on Westmoreland's chest (the Distinguished Service Medal). They didn't even stir when he started in with "there are those who may disagree with what we're doing here. . . ."

They cheered for the first time when he removed his jacket and opted for·shirt sleeves. It was the first human thing he had done since arriving.

Then at five twenty (Saigon time) Johnson was finished with the more formal part of the trip and headed for a jeep. He stopped to shake hands and have his picture taken with what he likes to call "Amurrican boys," and then he and Westmoreland were together in the jeep, standing up, two warriors in a rubber-wheeled chariot.

The first stop was the Twelfth Air Force field hospital, a collection of air-conditioned quonset huts which will eventually house up to 400 of the wounded. He walked into two connected quonsets, pinned Purple Hearts on the chests of about thirty of the fifty men lying there in blue pajamas, told them how proud he was of them, and started to go out when one of his damaged charges asked:

"Mr. President, will you have your picture taken with Lieutenant Magee?"

"Of course, son," he said.

Lieutenant Magee was a vivacious redheaded nurse. She was produced from the back of the room, Johnson shook her hand, and then turned and got the wounded kid back. "Hey," he said, "you come back here too and get your picture taken."

Outside, another young kid with a cast on his leg hopped by, and Johnson bent down and autographed the cast. It made a great picture.

Then we were off to Dining Hall No. 2, where Johnson walked through the chow line, loaded a plate with roast pork, bread, potatoes and applesauce, and then headed out for a seat with the men. They had brought medal winners Coffman and Hammer to sit with him, along with some sailors and some soldiers with full field packs and M-16's, and Johnson chatted with them, spearing meat into his mouth with his left hand. A trio played "The Yellow Rose of Texas" while the cameras whirred and everyone boiled in the heat. When Johnson finished eating, he immediately got up to leave. It was six seventeen and almost dark.

Captain Hershel Gober, twenty-nine, of Monticello, Arkansas, sang a few songs first. One was "I Am a Saigon Soldier," and Johnson and Westmoreland stood next to him, chuckling. The second was called "Dear General Westy," the last lines of which are:

> We're out of ammunition
> and almost out of gas
>   If something doesn't happen,
> we're gonna lose our . . .
> job.

Johnson and Westmoreland laughed out loud over those lines.

The final stop was at the officers' club, where the President talked with the young men who are responsible for leading the other young men in war. "This visit has been a very moving experience for me," he said. "It makes a very deep dent on me. . . . You're gonna carry on a two-fisted war militarily with the left hand and diplomatically with the right hand. . . ."

The talk lasted about ten minutes, and then the visit was

over. We all climbed into panel trucks and headed out to the airplane. "General Westmoreland told me that this had been the greatest day since he took command," Johnson said a little later. The last you saw of him, he was staring right at you, the face grim, as if he had just won a karate match with Mao Tse-tung. Away off, the hills were dark, the sky going black, and somewhere beyond them, men were dying.

October 26, 1966

A Most Honored Guest

And so Lyndon Johnson punctuated the great Asian summit conference with a visit among his subjects, bringing to them those special qualities of piety and bombast which they must accept when they take his alms. It turned out to be the only thing about the conference that could not have been done by mail.

The place was the Macalañan Palace, a Spanish colonial structure with a kind of shabby charm which houses Philippine President Marcos, and the occasion was a *barrio fiesta* which was intended as the highlight of the two-day conference. You caught sight of Johnson riding with Lady Bird in a real live donkey cart complete with real-live donkey. He was dressed in a silk barong shirt and a red neckerchief, his face sickly in the light from the yellow bulbs in the acacia trees.

With the reins in his hands as he came down the path, he somehow looked like the sort of man who had helped win the West with a cure for gout. He and the other five visiting heads of state pulled up in front of an unpainted plywood stand where they were to pose for the photographers.

"Goshamighty," Johnson said to Marcos, "this is sure pretty."

"Yes, yes," Marcos said. "And, Mrs. Johnson, you look superb. Very beautiful."

"I just love these things," Mrs. Johnson said. She was wearing one of the local butterfly-shouldered dresses called a balatawang, and Marcos was right. For the first time since she landed among the beauties of the Philippines Lady Bird was holding her own.

Johnson and Lady Bird and all the other heads of state and their women went through the photographing session, while Johnson looked out over their heads at the guests. The crowd seemed to be made up of vaguely corrupt-looking men dressed in barong silk shirts, smoking furiously, and women sitting on chairs in long dresses, fanning themselves in the sticky heat and slapping at the fruit flies. All seemed to be trying to count the number of security men in the house and rapidly losing track.

Then there was a sudden wailing of pipes, and an old-fashioned Spanish procession began, complete with giant white crosses, bamboo flute players, a statue of the Virgin Mary, a choir, a troupe of native dancers and sixteen—count 'em, sixteen—local movie stars. When the movie stars walked by under mobile flowered arches, General Ky pulled a drag on a cigarette and Johnson fumbled for his glasses.

When they finished, everyone tramped across the courtyards of the palace and into a kind of bazaar-styled garden, where stalls dispensed crab and shrimp and pastelles and beer, and into a dining room with a marble floor and the loudest mambo band this side of the Palladium. The place was sweet with the smell of flowers and perfumed women, and Johnson was looking pleased with himself as he sat down at the long main dining table.

He had reason to be pleased, of course. The communiqué had been issued that afternoon, announcing great things for the future of Asia and of Vietnam. Basically, they came down to more of the same, and no one seemed very upset. General Ky had learned the secret formula for dealing with Americans and had made his speech heavy with mystical talk about social reform. The communiqué had also stolen a march on the Communists, by saying that the allies were prepared to withdraw troops six months after "the other side" withdraws theirs to the North.

This, of course, was patently ridiculous. There is simply no way to sit down and list all the Communists in South Vietnam, nor for that matter, all the Northerners. If it came down just to the Northerners, they could easily begin with General Ky. Perhaps the North Vietnamese troops could be relocated North, but they could easily reply that they would agree to do so six months after the Americans leave.

The communiqué attempted to stir the hearts and minds of the South Vietnamese by declaring the following goals: "to be free from aggression," "to conquer hunger, illiteracy, and disease," "to build a region of security, order, and progress" and "to seek reconciliation and peace throughout Asia and the Pacific." These are not even noble thoughts, because they are not, to begin with, thoughts. They are words. Nothing more.

Nowhere did the communiqué even mention the bombing of North Vietnam, and on the possibilities of invading North Vietnam it refused even to be anything like concrete. "The South Vietnamese people have no desire to threaten or harm the people of the North or invade their country," the paper said. The key word is "desire." We didn't desire to bomb them either. But we're doing it.

But as you sat around in the palace, spending a few precious hours of your life watching Lyndon Johnson eat, there was no feeling that the war meant anything at all. The Filipino movie stars played it regal and haughty before Filipino reporters and came on with the foreigners like kids from a model agency. The band hammered away, and people drank too much, and Marcos' lovely wife, Imelda, got up to sing with a thirty-man choir.

Through all of this, no one in the room could keep his eyes off Johnson. There were dance routines where young girls with Malayan faces carried presents up to the chiefs of state, and there was the inevitable chanting of "The Yellow Rose of Texas," and finally they came up and put a flowered crown on Johnson's head.

I'm not kidding. They had a crown on his head, made of flowers, and he leaned away on one elbow the way he does so much, with the crown looking as if he had sent Jack Valenti to get it for him at Neiman-Marcus, and he peered out at the court, watching the dancing girls.

After a while, he took the crown off again and ordered a glass of milk and drank half of it before standing up to leave. When

Johnson got up, they all got up, and they piled into a heavily guarded barge for a trip down a canal to the hotel.

The party kept going, but it was like the gamekeepers playing with the master gone. Out on the street, cops were blowing whistles and the chauffeurs were standing with the limousines. The last thing I saw as I left was a young girl, about ten, with black hair, shoeless, holding a small child, her hand sticking out for a few centavos. I gave her a peso. At least once on this trip, I wanted to feel like Lyndon Johnson.

October 27, 1966

Another Viet?

The helicopter dropped on an angle, its rotor blades pounding the air, while five American-made Royal Thai Air Force jets screamed in tight formation overhead. Lyndon Johnson stepped out of the chopper, to see a vast open square dominated by the black equestrian statue of King Rama V of Siam and a scene that could easily have been staged by Dino De Laurentiis for a movie starring Steve Reeves.

Seven gold motorcycles manned by cops in gold uniforms stood at the ready. The King of Thailand's gold Daimler Benz limousine was waiting alongside a gold Mercedes, and rows of Thai troops from all services stood at present arms. Against the far edge of the square, reporters were eddying around a row of scalloped-edge tents, while a middle-aged Thai in a green uniform handed out Cokes. A cannon started belting a twenty-one-gun salute, "The Star-Spangled Banner" was played, followed by the Thai national anthem, and after that all was silence.

Johnson and the king got into the Mercedes and Lady Bird and the queen got into the Daimler, and the sordid legions of the press got into buses.

The motorcade pulled up before the municipal pavilion, an elaborate, newly built structure with brick-red corrugated iron roofs, adorned with the green seal of Thailand featuring Buddha on top of an elephant, and a platform with a dark wood lectern bearing the Presidential seal in the rear. There were four gold chairs. Johnson got out, followed by the king, a decent-looking little man in a business suit who has no power whatsoever in this military dictatorship. Lady Bird, in a pink dress and white hat, and the queen, all in lavender, got out, and they all went up to endure a speech by the mayor awarding Johnson the keys to the city.

In his prepared text, Johnson was to say, "For we have learned again that we are Pacific brothers, with common interests, with a common destiny." Someone with a memory of the old days when "our little brown brothers in the East" was a favorite phrase of editorial writers must have caught this, and by the time he delivered it, Johnson was talking about us being "Pacific neighbors," which is, of course, as utterly nonsensical as saying that we have common interests or a common destiny.

What was not mentioned in this brief speech—and what will certainly not be mentioned at any other point while we are here—is that Thailand could very possibly become another South Vietnam.

The United States now has 32,000 fighting men in Thailand, which is 9,000 more than we had in South Vietnam in January, 1965. Some 80 percent of all the bombing of North Vietnam and the Ho Chi Minh Trail in Laos comes from six Thai bases. We have Special Forces men here training the Thais in guerrilla warfare. We are building a giant $500,000,000 sea-air base at Sattahip with a landing strip that will accommodate B-52's. We have already poured more than a billion dollars in economic and military aid into the country and are donating more at the rate of $100,000,000 a year.

The results of all this have been predictable. Thailand was the only nation in Southeast Asia to escape the European colonialists in the nineteenth century. They did quit cold to the Japanese in 1941 and become their nominal allies. But the colonial structure so desperately needed by the Communists has never existed here. Now it does.

So now there are as many guerrillas operating in Thailand as were operating in South Vietnam in 1959–60. They are working hardest where the situation is most ripe: in the neglected, desperately poor northeast section of the country. The presence of 30,000 to 40,000 refugees from North Vietnam is not hurting them. The country as a whole also contains some 3,000,000 overseas Chinese whose loyalties are not clear. The government is forcing them to become Thai citizens, as Ngo Dinh Diem did in South Vietnam. But there is some feeling that money for the guerrillas is being filtered through them.

The reason such grim facts will not be mentioned is that the Thais don't want them mentioned. They are rightfully proud of their history of independence, and old Southeast Asia hands among the press corps report that the average Thai reaction to the American presence has been unenthusiastic, if not outright resentful. The trouble is that if they told us to get out now, the guerrillas might indeed make a more serious move for power.

But there was not a hint of that in this city of 2,000,000 yesterday as Lyndon Johnson's own brand of diplomacy moved ever onward.

The rulers drove off together, before a silent crowd, and when they were out of sight, the crowd finally came alive, charging across the square to see the most important person in Bangkok. Miss Universe, of course.

So all you could do, with Johnson gone, was to look for some lines from Kipling.

> The end of the fight is a tombstone white
> With the name of the late deceased
> And the epitaph drear: "A fool lies
> Here, who tried to hustle the East."

Our Pacific neighbors might yet settle our hash for good.
October 29, 1966

Seoul Whistle-stop

At a few minutes before three, Air Force One broke through the gun-metal clouds, trailing jet exhaust behind it, bringing

Lyndon Johnson's road show to Korea. It was never a very edifying country, and it would not prove to be an edifying day.

Johnson was greeted by a twenty-one-gun salute and a band playing "The Yellow Rose of Texas." Against one wall of the airport that once was our major fighter base there were two huge Red Square-style portraits of Johnson and President Park, staring out over a dumpy mob of local Americans, Korean soldiers, schoolchildren with flags, and security men.

At the end of "The Star-Spangled Banner," five jets screamed overhead, leaving a gimmicky trail of fuchsia, yellow, and green exhaust. Then Johnson spoke.

". . . I stand on this hallowed soil of Korea—for whose freedom thousands of my countrymen died alongside yours—confident that we shall redeem their sacrifice, confident that the cause of freedom will prevail." That was all he could bring himself to say about the Korean War. That was all that it meant—a junkpile of empty platitude and generality. Lyndon Johnson had performed the slickest alchemy: He had transformed the scene of a bitter failure of war into a whistle-stop in Iowa.

There was something obscene about it. I can think of no other word. It is obscene to go campaigning in a place where brave men once lay with the lice eating their bodies in summer and their feet rotting and blackening over murderous winters. It is obscene to make a glorious legend out of Korea, when the truth was down in the mud, or in the midst of hammering machine guns in the north, or on those forgotten hills where boys waited for the sound of Chinese bugles at dawn. It is obscene to take the Chosin Reservoir and what happened to young men there and turn it into a throwaway phrase in a hackneyed political speech. Korea was the place where something about America died in the midst of human waves, defectors, prison camps, and false promises.

Johnson turned all of it into a staged punctuation mark for this mammoth exercise in self-aggrandizement. And it must be said that President Park played his own part to the hilt. He knew that Lyndon Johnson requires crowds, and crowds were what he provided.

They were everywhere as we rode into town. The ride is 10 miles from Kimpo International Airport to the center of Seoul, and there were people almost all the way. There were thousands of tough young schoolboys in black uniforms called kyo bok and black worker-style caps called majas, all of them shouting as we went by and looking like inmates of the largest reform school in Asia.

We passed brass bands playing "The Yellow Rose of Texas" and other local favorites, and dozens of posters and drawings of Johnson. The posters must have pleased him. Among the better ones—"Welcome the King of Kings," "The World Marshal" (with a picture of Johnson with two guns out, wearing a cowboy suit), "Leader of the Time, Be Long," "Texas Bull—We Like," and "We Like Big Shot of World."

And then there were the people themselves. You have never seen a crowd until you have seen an Asian crowd, and when you have seen an Asian crowd, you have seen an organism never far removed from a mob. Johnson, of course, could not resist it. When the motorcade was halted about halfway to town to let the press buses catch up, Johnson was up and out of the car, shaking hands with kids. Off to the right were rice fields, with shoots drying on neat rows, and the terrible Korean hills climbing away to the northeast. Johnson saw the fields and plunged right into them, walking down an embankment, surrounded by children. Now he could come home and say, "I have walked in the rice fields of Asia. I have scraped the mud of Asia off my shoes."

When he got back to the car, a Secret Serviceman scraped his shoes.

At every stop the crowd swelled and moved, and you could no longer see individual faces but swatches of black for the boys, and navy blue for the schoolgirls, and bright blue for factory girls, and bright yellow where a band was. There was something dangerous about it as we got closer to the main square and a lot about it that was distasteful. Whatever it is that drives Lyndon Johnson, that part of him that requires the faces of strangers to look at him in awe is vaguely disgusting.

When the motorcade finally halted at the city hall, the mob had grown to well over a million. They were at every window, on the hills looking into the square. They eddied and swirled while down in front of us, beneath the huge Oriental speakers' stand, the Korean Army MP's were working the crowd, plunging in after dissenters, holding their rifles high. Once they needed a hole and simply kicked their way into the crowd. In seconds, it had filled.

Park made a speech, and Johnson made another speech, all filled with pieties about Communism and developing countries and the rest of it. And then it was over. Johnson was driven to a park where he picked up a helicopter. It was dark when he took off, and the mob was scattering down the back streets, dropping their American flags behind them. In South Vietnam at that moment, young men were dying the way their older brothers died in Korea, and you felt that fifteen years from now, some politician would be running this game in Saigon, looking for votes of support for some other war in some other country, which will be fought, of course, by other young men. Until this stop, in this special country, I had not realized how contemptible this whole journey has been.

November 11, 1966

The Return

The last we saw of him, Lyndon Johnson was gazing into the remains of a monster bonfire in Anchorage, Alaska, his eyes glazed, his features worn, surrounded by members of the electorate. Just as we had expected Lady Bird to go to Vietnam and ceremonially uproot a tree, we had expected Lyndon Johnson in Alaska to chew us a sealskin coat. But now he was beyond ceremony, the juices cooled, and all of us could finally go home.

We will have no easy time. We who journeyed with him know what is coming. We cannot escape by fleeing on the shuttle to New York.

For Lyndon Johnson will almost certainly begin his assault as soon as he has one decent night's sleep. He will tell us how he has walked through the rice fields of Asia (after a six-and-a-half-minute dalliance by the side of the road outside the Seoul airport). He will remind us that he has been with our fighting

256

men in Vietnam (after two hours and twenty-three minutes in Cam Ranh Bay, a sort of Mr. Roberts backwater of the war). He will tell us that he has walked through the jungles of Southeast Asia (after one hour and five minutes in the Malaysian hills, surrounded by 140 armed men).

It will all be outrageous and shot through with mad laughter, but it is all beyond our control now. All you are left with are the fragments of the journey itself.

It can be safely said, for example, that of all the people around Johnson the only one who is consistently impressive is Bill Moyers. He is still listed as press secretary, but it was obvious on this trip that he is considerably more than that.

You have an image of him in the disordered swamp of Manila, where the Filipino assistant press secretaries were selling tidbits to the Filipino reporters, and the freeloaders had descended on the press bar in a great cigar-smoking horde. There was confusion at every point. And then Moyers was walking into the room, pulling on a cigar, answering questions quickly and accurately before they were half asked, heading for the front of the room with a trail of us after him. He was order walking into chaos.

Only once did he lie, which is a fantastic average for a government press agent. That was the afternoon of the final communiqué, when Moyers leaked portions of it to the wire services. He said later that he had only done this to force the Filipinos to release it, that they wanted to hold it until after that night's *barrio fiesta,* to force the press to attend. Actually by leaking a portion of it, he could use the wire services to emphasize what he wanted emphasized. It was an untruth, but still a good average for a long journey. Moyers is a bigger man than his job and is obviously one of the few restraining forces on the man he serves.

You were struck also by the overwhelming number of Texans who worked on every level of the trip. If you had any doubt that this is the first Southern Presidency in recent times, they should have been dispelled when the drawls and twangs started bouncing off you at every level from secretary to Secret Serviceman.

Their conduct is seldom lovely, though, because they seem to consider themselves part of some new ruling class. One night in Seoul, we were eating dinner in the hotel restaurant when one of the Texans started operating his walkie-talkie at the next table, playing the big man for his Korean hostess. A floor show was in progress, and a *Life* photographer very properly told this operator to shut off his toy.

"Hew the hell yew think yew toakin' tew?" he shouted.

"You," the photographer shouted. "Shut that thing off, or go outside and play with it."

The operator stormed out, came back with two huge sides of beef in business suits and started yelling about how he was gonna tell Bill Moyers and how he was gonna tell Marvin Watson. I don't know about Watson, but Moyers would have fired him on the spot. It was indicative, though, of the sort of men who follow Johnson around that when the photographer left, the two sides of beef went after him. He almost certainly would have ended up a casualty in the hotel parking lot if a couple of reporters hadn't stepped out, too. These people don't commit mayhem if the odds are even.

At any rate, it is good to be back. After two and a half weeks with the Teeming Asian Masses, one can only look forward with expectation to writing again about that product of twenty centuries of Western civilization, the Patrolmen's Benevolent Association. It will be at least one way to take your mind off the real world.

November 3, 1966

V. Pols

I LIKE politicians. Someone once said that there was only one way to look at a politician, and that is down. But I don't agree. Some of the best people I know are politicians, as they say, and much of my journalism has been about them. I'm particularly fond of old pols, and their crusty skepticism about ideals has always acted as a rein on my own sometimes rampant otherworldliness. The Democrats are easily the best company, because they usually come from the old school; the best of them (and Meade Esposito, the Brooklyn boss, is a good example) still operate political clubs based on the supply of services, and they do it with some style and personal grace. I've never met any Republicans with whom I feel easy, although I'm sure they exist somewhere. They always seem as if they had just come from a board meeting or are on their way to dinner with Herbert Brownell. But even Republicans seem exciting when you place them side by side with the Communists.

I was a Kennedy Democrat for a long time because I admired the Kennedy ability to meld the best of the old politics with the best of the new politics and infuse the result with some idealism. There is no room here to argue the merits of the Kennedy administration, so I won't attempt that complicated task (John F. Kennedy was elected in such a simple time that he and Richard Nixon could argue about two hunks of rock called Quemoy and Matsu and the existence of some popularity poll that showed the United States was slipping). But I liked the idea that Robert Kennedy could make impassioned speeches about the war and racial injustice, and still manage time to go to the funeral of Charlie Buckley; Kennedy was trying to carve out a constituency among the liberals and Charlie Buckley, the Democratic boss of the Bronx, was part of the liberal demonology. Robert Kennedy didn't care; for him, Charlie Buckley was a friend of the family, and that was that.

Looking back now, the sixties were a time of tremendous political passion, and the reasons were complicated. The assassination of John F. Kennedy was a major factor; his killing was a kind of martyrdom that made everything that followed subject to terrible scrutiny. At times, Lyndon Johnson seemed a man possessed by ghosts, as his personal style, his mannerisms, his personal history were continuously compared to that of the murdered prince. The war in Vietnam exaggerated everything even more. Before the country could even begin to reassemble after the assassination, we found ourselves moving into a land war in Asia. Johnson had been elected in 1964 as a peace candidate, and the next four years struck many people as an example of how *all* politicians lie. The war in Vietnam also underlined some grave doubts about the American political system; what good was the Constitution, after all, if a single man could send a half million troops to Asia without a declaration of war by Congress? How could we talk so easily about being a democracy when the choice of the political candidates themselves was left to several thousand people at a national convention? How could we talk about justice when black people were going hungry while millions of dollars were spent each year on dog food?

Some people began to think about saviors, and as the country became more and more unraveled, I became one of them. I still thought then (as I no longer do) that the country could be put together if we only elected the right man, and for me that man was Robert Kennedy. I met him after he had become a Senator from New York, and I liked him enormously. I liked the dark, brooding black Irishman in him, and I thought his passion about the poor was genuine. We became friends. Along with Jack Newfield, Allard Lowenstein, and a few others, I was one of those who urged him, during the dark winter of 1967, to run for President. He didn't then, and his natural constituency among the young moved to Eugene McCarthy; when he finally announced in March, most of them never came back. I couldn't really blame them.

I thought Robert Kennedy could have won the nomination in Chicago, and the time I spent at that disastrous convention convinced me of it. Instead, he was murdered. I was there that night, and an account of what happened is here. Eugene McCarthy apparently did not want the nomination or was not willing to sell a portion of his ass to get it, and we ended up having to make a choice between Hubert Humphrey and Richard Nixon. I went to the Olympics instead.

But I learned several things in my brief association with Robert Kennedy (and that friendship was a lot more complicated than I am indicating here). After that second Kennedy assassination, I began to understand that it was a mistake to invest all of one's hopes, political or personal, in one human being. Human beings die, and you are left then to clean up the mess. The era of man-on-the-white-horse politics now seems over, and we are better for it, and the Kennedy myth, the need to believe in Camelot, the delusion that one can move the clock back to November 21, 1963—all that went off the bridge that dark midnight at Chappaquiddick.

The other thing I learned was the danger of too much intimacy with a politician. Robert Kennedy was my friend, and it had to affect the way I functioned as a reporter. I've never been able to be that intimate with a politician since then and probably never will again. John Lindsay, a pol whose courage I admire, has been mayor of New York for five years, as I write, and I've never even had a drink with him. That is probably the way it should be.

But if the Kennedy time is over, there are still politicians around to write about. It is difficult not to like pols like Robert Wagner. Several weeks after my piece on him appeared in print, I found myself sitting next to Wagner at a formal dinner. He just sailed along as if nothing had ever happened, as if I had never written a word (he did tell me he saw the piece), an old pro to the end. (Mario Procaccino won the Democratic primary that year, with Herman Badillo running third behind Wagner; Badillo lost by the margin of votes that went to Norman

Mailer.) I even found things I liked about George Wallace: a kind of Cagneyesque spunk and a fondness for soda pop. I liked him even more when he threw a girl named Ja-Neen off the plane later in the campaign, and she turned up a year later under arrest for soliciting.

But Richard Nixon is something else. He seems to me more a bundle of technique than a man of any real convictions; it is difficult to think of him naked. I write about him a lot in the newspaper columns, but I have no real confidence about who he is. And yet there is a real American story in him, and it says something about my carelessness as a journalist that I have never seriously tried to find out what it is. Life, in this case, is too short.

Waiting for Bobby

"I think I hear a plane," said a beautiful little girl with long, tanned legs and a dazzling smile. "Don't you hear a plane, Mary Lou?"

"Sounds like a car to me," Mary Lou said.

They were behind the fence, staring at an empty white platform. The sky was black, and you could feel the California breeze blowing down the great valleys from the grapevines and the olive orchards, and you remembered that this was William Saroyan's town. It had changed a lot from the days when he could write with such total innocence about Western Union boys, and barbershops, and Armenian wild men, and the exploits of the Assyrians. But when you looked around at the cops and the children and the young girls with the red-white-and-blue hats, and saw a dog and some musicians and some old-timer with a drum borrowed from the Elks, you had to feel that much had remained the same.

"There's the plane now!" someone shouted.

And the plane came in from away off to the right and landed, silver in the dark, and taxied as close as it could to the waiting area. The ramp was pushed to the front exit, the door opened, and a stewardess came out, and you could see movement in the cabin, and then the first people came down the ramp. Staffers, reporters, cameramen with clumsy harnesses on their shoulders —they were the foot soldiers in every political campaign. The crowd cheered wanly as the men came out. Cigarettes were lit. Men pulled notebooks from pockets and started writing down words from the signs and posters: SOCK IT TO 'EM, BOBBY and GET OFF A DROWNING HORSE—VOTE FOR RFK and BOBBY, YOU HAVE OUR VOTE.

And then there was a roar, and the lights of the TV cameras came on, hard and blue, and Robert Kennedy was standing at the door of the plane, in a gray suit, smiling in that odd, almost shy way he has, and there was a surge from behind the barriers, and as he stepped out onto the tarmac, he was engulfed.

"I touched him. I touched him," this girl was shouting to a friend. "I won't wash this hand for a week!"

An old woman with a lined face and gray hair was standing to the side, trying to get close. Her eyes were watery.

"I voted for his brother, and I'll vote for him," she said. "God bless him. God bless him."

And in the center of the mob, Kennedy was smiling and trying to keep his feet and keep moving, trying to get to that small white stand and make his speech and then take the motorcade into town and get some sleep. They wouldn't let him. Whatever it was—the need for ratification, the need to verify that the man they had seen on TV or in photographs really existed—they all wanted to touch him. Finally, he broke through and got up to the stand and was introduced and started to talk. He talked about the things he talks about at every stop: the need for Americans to be decent to each other, the need to replace welfare handouts with decent jobs, the need to end the war in Vietnam and begin the task of rebuilding the cities. They had heard it all on television before, but they listened respectfully and applauded when he mentioned the war.

"That is why I run for the Presidency of the United States," he said. "That is why I come here to *ahsk* for *yoah* help."

It was over, and they exploded and rushed forward again. The staff members drifted over to the waiting limousines. The reporters boarded the press buses. And Robert Kennedy finally made it to the open limousine.

"They're beating the hell out of him," said Richard Dougherty, the novelist, who heads the New York bureau of the Los Angeles *Times*. "The schedule has been insane. He had a seventeen-hour day yesterday. He's punchy."

"He looks all right to me."

"Take a closer look."

Kennedy arrived twenty-five minutes later at Del Webb's Towne House, a hotel-office building in downtown Fresno, and I saw what Dougherty meant. The lobby was filled with young telephone operators who had just finished a strike meeting in a downstairs room. About a dozen Mexican-Americans were there, and some flustered room clerks. Kennedy walked into the lobby, and the telephone operators all rushed to him, squealing incongruously, while behind them a rerun of *The Dean Martin Show* played without watchers. Kennedy shook hands with all of them, but you could see the fatigue in his face, a great wash of it, and he made no speech and indulged in no small talk. He started to go into the elevator, and then stopped, and smiled, and said, "Gosh, I almost forgot. Good night."

The girls all squealed again, and he was gone.

"You know, he's really a *hunk*," said one of the phone operators, a small blond girl named Tina Dunbar.

"What did you expect?" said her friend, Mercedes Morales. "Of course, he's a hunk."

"I always thought he had buckteeth."

"That's just the photographs."

Upstairs, Robert Kennedy undressed slowly, took a shower, and went to bed. That was the way a man campaigned for the most important political office on earth. He hurtled across the continent on airplanes, visiting strange towns, staying in a monotonous series of hotels. Kennedy's wife, Ethel, was back at their home in McLean, Virginia, trying to keep some normalcy in a family that includes ten children (an eleventh is expected) and, as of last count, four dogs, two horses, one kitten, and various salamanders, frogs, and lizards that belong to the children. She would travel with Kennedy when she had time, presiding over Kaffeeklatsches with considerable charm and vivacity, visiting various leagues for women voters, not infrequently inviting with her presence the question: How can a nice girl like that marry someone who is ruthless? She would even fly on airplanes, a means of transportation she despises (with good reason: Her parents and one brother have died in plane crashes).

Even as Kennedy slept, the mechanics of the campaign went on. Down the hall, in Room 1414, two young men named Adam Walinsky and Jeff Greenfield started opening their typewriter cases. Walinsky is thirty-one, Greenfield, twenty-four, and they were Kennedy's speech writers. The next day Kennedy would address students at Fresno State College and then

265

move on to a town-hall meeting at the Biltmore Hotel in Los Angeles. He needed speeches for each stop.

"How has it been going?"

"It's still fantastic," Greenfield said. "But it's hard to figure states. There really is a difference in, say, Indiana and California."

"There sure is," said Walinsky.

"In Indiana he got the crowds, too," said Greenfield. "Just as big as anywhere else. But there was silence. They listened, they applauded politely. But it was hard to tell what they were thinking."

"You're ahead, then," someone said. "You want people to listen to what he's saying."

"Boy, that's true," Greenfield said.

"It's strange," someone said. "From a distance it's hard to figure Bobby's campaign. The reporters are writing the crowd story and not bothering too much with what he's saying."

"That's starting to change," Walinsky said.

"It better."

Walinsky stripped to shorts and undershirt and started making notes on a yellow legal pad. Greenfield excused himself and started answering a wad of phone messages that had been waiting for him when he checked in. The speech for town hall was to concern some of the human uses of technology and Greenfield was checking with some of the idea men from the universities around Los Angeles.

"Right, right," he said. "Yeah, it's been very useful. . . . Yeah. . . . Right. Right. . . . Well, it's just that you have to say what's true. Twenty years ago we said we were going to build a defense system and we built one. We can do it with the cities, too. . . . Right. Right. . . . Yeah. . . . OK. We'll be in touch."

Someone knocked at the door. Greenfield hung up and answered it. A girl from the Kennedy staff wanted to know when the speech for town hall would be ready. She had to mimeograph it and give copies out to the press.

"The Senator will read it at seven thirty," Greenfield said. "You should have it at eight fifteen, latest."

Walinsky was asleep. Greenfield started writing ideas on his yellow pad. They looked as exhausted as the candidate.

In Room 1701, the local Kennedy-for-President campaign had set up a press room and bar. The cameramen, who had no more work that evening, were throwing the whiskey down pretty good, and some of the local politicians were standing around talking about California politics. After a while, Frank Mankiewicz came in.

"Everybody OK?" Mankiewicz said. He is Kennedy's press secretary.

"Yeah, yeah," everyone mumbled.

"We'll have the town-hall speech on the plane to Burbank tomorrow," Mankiewicz said. "There'll be a press room at the Biltmore, so you can all file, and we'll have about three hours before going on to San Diego."

Mankiewicz talked for a while with a drink in his hand. The local reporters and those who had just picked up the campaign plane wanted to know about Indiana. It would be very tough, Mankiewicz said. The governor of Indiana was entered in the primary as a favorite son, and there was a chance that this first direct confrontation between Kennedy and his rival for the Democratic nomination, Senator Eugene McCarthy, would be inconclusive.

"What happens then?" some asked.

"You just keep going."

Later Mankiewicz talked for a while in his room on the fourteenth floor. He had not bothered to unpack his suitcase.

"It's a very strange contest," he said. "Three weeks ago, we knew what kind of fight we were going to have. But then Johnson withdrew, and Humphrey hadn't yet come in, so we don't know how it's going to turn out."

"The campaign seems diffuse," someone said. "At least, from the distance."

"You might be right," Mankiewicz said. "There is a hell of a lot of uncertainty about where it should go. And it's very early."

"Forget it," the visitor said. "Why don't you hit the sack?"

"Yeah."

The next morning the luggage was piled in the lobby of the hotel as we waited for Kennedy. A crowd of curious bystanders

267

stood in the lobby, and Kennedy's staffers checked off the names of those who would be making the whole trip—Los Angeles–San Diego–San Francisco–Denver–Nebraska–Washington. Then the trucks were loaded, the reporters all headed for the press buses, and Robert Kennedy came out into the sunlight.

He looked rested and fit, as if those hours of sleep had pumped some secret fresh supply of blood into him.

"Hey, Bobby!" yelled a Negro girl who worked in one of the offices in the building. "We're with you, Bobby!"

"Hello," he said. "How *are* ya?"

The motorcade went through Fresno and stopped in front of Fresno City College, where a thousand young people had jammed the street. Kennedy was not scheduled to speak at this college, but he got out and climbed up on the back of the limousine and someone handed him a bullhorn and he started to talk. When he *ahsked* them for their help, the kids cheered.

"What about the *Pueblo*?" one kid shouted from the audience.

"I think we should keep doing what we're doing," Kennedy said. "I'm less interested in getting the *Pueblo* back than I am in getting back those eighty-two men. We can only do that by discussing it with the North Koreans."

"Do you think President Johnson will support you for President?" another voice shouted.

Kennedy smiled broadly.

"You'll have to ask him personally about that, I'm afraid."

"Who will the Republican candidate be?"

"Well," Kennedy said, "I happen to know. I do. I have his name, but he doesn't know it yet." They all laughed. "But I think if we're lucky, it will be Richard Nixon."

There was more banter back and forth, and Kennedy looked as he always does with young people: relaxed, at home, in the company of friends. And the California kids—those incredibly healthy-looking and confident kids—seemed at home with him. The motorcade resumed. Two of the students, who had been watching from behind a wire fence, turned and made running dives into the swimming pool.

The rest of the day was more complicated. At Fresno State, a mile from Fresno City College, he had another warm reception, which only grew hysterical at the end when he tried to get to the car. The town-hall speech was something else: The audience was made up of businessmen and professional people, and Kennedy—for a variety of reasons—is not well regarded by businessmen. Or, at least, that is what the columnists have been writing all along.

"You know," said John Lindsay of *Newsweek,* as we descended into the airport at Burbank for the drive to the Biltmore, "maybe businessmen really *like* Kennedy. Maybe some columnist started all this a long time ago, and they've all been rewriting each other ever since. They've been wrong about everything else this year. Maybe they're wrong about businessmen, too."

"I don't know," someone said. "I think they're just afraid of him. He just doesn't *look* like a businessman. George Romney *looked* like a businessman and *was* a businessman."

"He doesn't look like a columnist, either."

At the town-hall meeting in the Biltmore, Kennedy went over like a pitchman for the National Association of Manufacturers. He seemed to disarm the audience with a self-deprecating humor; he asked that businessmen consider using their talents, energy, and techniques to help solve the problems of the big-city ghettos; he answered questions from the floor when it was over.

"You say you want to abolish welfare," one questioner said, "and bring business into those areas where government has failed. How are you different from a conservative?"

"I think that something should be *done,*" Kennedy said.

"What have you done to deserve to be President?"

"Well," he said, "for one thing, I've cut my hair. . . ."

The applause was deafening.

At San Diego, we were in Hysteria Country again: young girls straining to touch him, children being crushed, police wearing worried faces, and then the standard stump speech— asking for help, asking that all citizens, young and old, black and white, work together to build a new America.

"He's a fink like the rest of them," one young kid said.

"Why?" an itinerant journalist asked.

"He's not talking about revolution. He just wants to put Band-Aids on the problems. He doesn't want to destroy the system."

"What's the system?"

"Finks like you."

It was true, of course: Kennedy was not interested in handing out guns to every college sophomore and sending him forth to battle with the gendarmerie. He thought it was possible to straighten out the country without destroying it first. That was unacceptable to some of the student radicals, especially in California, where student politics had begun. At the airport in San Diego, members of the newly formed Peace and Freedom Party handed out mimeographed sheets of paper, quoting from *Mac-Bird*, Barbara Garson's scurrilous play that accuses Lyndon Johnson of murdering John F. Kennedy, in some vague collusion with Robert Kennedy. The sheets quoted the following lines from *MacBird*:

> We must expose this subtle Bobcat's claws;
> He even now collects the straying sheep
> And nudges them so gently toward the fold.
> O sheep, awake and flee this fenced corral.
> He's just like all the rest. They're all alike.

Not many sheep were fleeing the fenced corral, and if they were, they were heading for the gentle tutelage of Gene McCarthy. But the bitterness was there, and the anger, and we saw it that night when Kennedy brought his campaign to the crowded auditorium of the University of San Francisco. This is a Catholic school, where Bill Russell, the six-foot-ten center for the Boston Celtics, once played basketball, and is located only a few blocks from Haight-Ashbury. The audience was a curious meld: scrubbed sons of the middle class, Catholic nuns looking like lost survivors from a Hollywood convent movie, hippies with old army clothes and hairstyles as implacably casual as the hedges at Versailles, black nationalists in shades and denims, middle-aged liberals who still believed that decency in America was possible.

When Kennedy got out of his limousine, a group surged forward, spitting, trying to hit him, waving signs—symbols of all the hatred and viciousness that come so naturally to some Americans. They were the champions of the left, self-styled revolutionaries, on the side of the angels; they looked like Klansmen.

"Fascist pig!" one paper revolutionary shouted.

Robert Kennedy smiled icily at him.

Then he was inside, and when he came up on the platform the audience congealed; it was no longer individuals, it was the mob in the pit, screaming, endowed suddenly with an animal quality that reminded me of the conservative audience that had shouted down Nelson Rockefeller four years before at the Republican Convention in San Francisco. They were all the same, Barbara Garson said, and she was right; the far left and the far right were equally petrified at the prospect of free and open discussion.

Kennedy sensed this immediately and threw away the prepared speech he had in his pocket. The only way to meet an audience like this was to confront it directly. He said he would answer questions from the floor. They were disarmed, and Kennedy received a loud, long, standing ovation.

"Why did you work for Joe Kennedy?" someone shouted.

"Joe Kennedy? Yes, I worked for Joe Kennedy. Joe Kennedy is my father."

One kid stood up, wearing crossed gun belts (empty), a large harvest of hair, beardless. He asked a long, involved question that no one understood.

"Whatever you want to do," Kennedy said, laughing, "I'm with you."

A woman in the balcony asked whether he thought he should be running for President, and Kennedy recited his involvement in civil rights, as Attorney General, in the Berlin crisis, the Bay of Pigs, and the Cuban missile crisis. "In the last analysis, the question is whether we can preserve the peace. I think I can make my contribution, my best contribution, running for President." At another point, he said he wanted to keep the United States from "being involved in any future Vietnams."

271

"Victory for the Vietcong!" shouted one young kid with glasses who was in another balcony, behind Kennedy, and was obviously stoned.

"Victory for the Vietcong?" Kennedy said. "No, I don't agree with that."

"Victory for the Vietcong!" the kid shouted.

"How about shutting up, you rude bastard!" a Negro boy shouted back at the kid. Everyone's attention was changed when a five-year-old boy, with a bright dazzle of blond hair, came to the platform and reached up. Kennedy seemed puzzled. The boy stuck out his hand, and Kennedy shook it. "That's about the nicest thing that's happened to me all night," Kennedy said. And the audience laughed. At the end, he had answered every question, even when the audience didn't like it (he didn't believe in an amnesty for young people who had fled to Canada and Europe to beat the draft, mainly because many other Americans had decided to face the music; if they did not believe in the draft or the war, they should be prepared to go to prison for their beliefs). The young paper revolutionaries probably hadn't changed their minds, but at least Kennedy was no longer an abstraction to be hated at a distance. They had seen him. They had never seen Lyndon Johnson.

That night on the plane for Denver, everyone tried to relax. About twenty reporters were left. Lindsay and I entertained ourselves with the personals column of the LA *Free Press* ("Professional man, tall, dark, handsome, forty-three, planning divorce. Seeking well-built girl, married or single . . ."). In the back of the plane, Walinsky and Greenfield worked on another speech. Mankiewicz chatted in the aisle with the reporters.

"That was pretty hairy back there," someone said.

"I thought he handled it well," Mankiewicz said.

"But it's so goddamned demeaning."

"So is politics," Lindsay said.

"You know, the British could have held three general elections in the time since this started," someone else said. "We've got six more months of this mania."

This was the center of the hurricane. In other places, in Indiana, in the cities that slipped by in the darkness beneath us, in

Washington and New York, other men were working at the complex business of getting a man elected. Some were the old pros of the New Frontier: Pierre Salinger, round and intelligent, smoking the perpetual cigar, was in Washington, supervising the over-all press campaign; Theodore Sorensen, John F. Kennedy's chief speech writer, was fashioning a general approach to the rhetoric of the campaign; Richard Goodwin, who had worked for John Kennedy and Lyndon Johnson, had just left the McCarthy campaign to join Kennedy's entourage in Indiana. Fred Dutton, secretary of the Cabinet in JFK's administration, who is one of the most intelligent men in American politics, was emerging as Kennedy's chief adviser on the campaign trail. Walinsky and Greenfield were carrying the burden of the day-to-day speech writing, a burden that was crushing because the TV camera was eating up material from politicians as ruthlessly and remorselessly as it does to TV comedians. The campaign would take millions of dollars, and Kennedy's brother-in-law Steve Smith was directing the complex business of financing it. In college campuses and smoky hotel rooms all over the country, men were bringing their energies and ideas to bear on the fortunes of one man: Robert F. Kennedy.

But on this evening, as the plane moved across the high reaches of the Rockies toward Denver, Robert Kennedy was just tired. He came back, drinking a bourbon, dressed in shirt sleeves, his necktie askew, and sat down to talk with us.

"That was pretty good back there," he said.

"For a fascist pig, you did all right," one itinerant said.

"Yes, as one fascist pig to another."

"How do you think you're doing?"

"It's all uphill," he said. "So much has happened . . . just in the last two weeks. . . . Indiana is very tough."

"Are they listening to you?"

"You just don't know," he said. "I'm trying to be as direct and honest as I can be. But it's complicated. Governor Branigin is very popular. He's a good man, and he'll get a lot of votes."

"Do you think that Indiana might just be a zero at the end?" someone said. "That you and McCarthy won't prove anything, after spending a lot of money?"

"That's a real possibility," Kennedy said. The plane wobbled

273

in some weather, but Kennedy didn't bother with his seat belt.

"How do you think Hubert will do?"

"He'll fight," Kennedy said.

"What does that do to your campaign?"

"It's hard to tell," he said. "He'll have a lot of professional support. The big city bosses, the regular organizations, George Meany."

"I think it's got to help," someone said. "You'd have an opponent again. It takes two to make a fight."

"That's true."

The talk went on like that through the night. At two thirty in the morning we landed in Denver. There were no brass bands or balloons. Just a group of those men who were working for him because they loved his brother and hated the way he died. Some were there because they didn't like the way their country was going and hoped that Robert Kennedy could change it. Some were there, I suppose, because if they worked for a President, they could make money, pull strings, be close to the sources of power. Robert Kennedy wondered about all of them but knew he could question none of them.

"I need all the help I can get," he said. And turned to the waiting limousine, for the long ride through the darkened streets of another town, to sleep in a room in another hotel where men would stay up through the night at typewriters. It was grueling and terrible, a strangely out-of-date way for a great nation to choose a leader. But it was the only way we had, and no one understood that better than Robert Kennedy.

July, 1968

America in the Eye of the Telescopic Sight

At the long rented tables inside the door of Kennedy-for-President headquarters, three middle-aged ladies wearing Kennedy hats were selling bumper stickers and posters. It was the afternoon after Nebraska, and you arrived expecting elation, perhaps even euphoria; instead, the three middle-aged ladies sat there rather glumly, staring out at the bright clean sidewalks of Wilshire Boulevard and the plump, suited figures of other ladies shopping at the Broadway across the street.

"What's the matter?" I asked one of them, a blue-haired lady nervously shuffling bumper stickers. "I thought you'd have a party going here."

"Oh, no," she said, smiling metallically. "We're just beginning. The real one is just beginning."

She was right, of course, Indiana, the District of Columbia, and Nebraska were important enough; Kennedy could not have afforded to lose any of them. But the real fight is in California. This is the heart of the new United States, and if he cannot win convincingly, Hubert Humphrey will be the next President of the United States.

"The other ones were just the preliminaries," a young USC graduate said. "It's sort of like the heavyweight elimination. You can't afford to lose any of them, but the last one is the big one."

Away down Wilshire Boulevard, in Beverly Hills, McCarthy-for-President headquarters had seemed like a West Coast version of Walter B. Cooke's. One lovely little girl sat behind a table covered with literature, and her face was so wasted and forlorn that you felt like taking her to a Laurel and Hardy movie just to give her some perspective.

"It's so . . . unfair!" she said.

Kennedy headquarters was something else: It had a kind of motion and fury to it, played against a background of jerky shabbiness. The walls were painted red, white, and blue, adorned with posters of the candidate. People were dashing everywhere: the three middle-aged ladies were the somber window dressing for a jumble of hammering typewriters, clattering mimeograph machines, ringing telephones, blasting TV sets, radios tuned to the all-news channel. Young girls with impossibly white teeth and Kennedy hats gathered up clusters of posters and signs to take to the airport to greet the candidate. They walked across a floor littered with a compost of cigarette butts, crushed coffee cups, discarded press releases, balled carbon paper, and crusts of Danish pastries. They were pretty, but they were like all the chicks you ever saw around a campaign headquarters: clean, straight, smart, and oddly sexless; in the sack, they probably hollered for the Candidate.

The men in Kennedy headquarters were something else. All the younger guys seemed to have been pressed from the same mold at the Rent-a-Volunteer-with-Pragmatic-Compassion Works. They wore gray suits on the street, and in the office hiked their shirt-sleeves halfway up the forearm, in case a photographer from *Look* dropped by. They all had horn-rimmed glasses. They all had tight law-school mouths. They all smoked thin panatella cigars. And they were all pricks. That is, they were almost without exception rude, bursting with self-importance, quick to hang up telephones, incapable of returning calls, and for most purposes unconcerned with anything except the technical processes of politics.

With a few exceptions, Kennedy had nothing to do with enlisting these people. Most of them, I'm told, have come out of the Jesse Unruh operation in California. Unruh does not run a machine, in the old sense of that word, but in Democratic politics in this state he has the best organization. The trouble is that the guys who work for him now feel they are working for a winner at last, after the Pat Brown and Pierre Salinger disasters. And they feel that they can win without any outside help. The major organizational problem Kennedy has in California has been caused by the Unruh men who answer the telephones; hundreds of people who wanted to work for Kennedy were told by Unruh's people to forget it, they had enough help. These potential volunteers have gone to work for McCarthy or the Peace and Freedom Party or stayed home. (I haven't heard of anyone joining up with Hubert the Soul Brother.)

My brother Brian and I were standing around when one of the volunteers came over. He was one of the few fat guys in the place and stuttered a little.

"You going to the airport?" he said.

"Yeah."

"Can you take two riders?"

"Sure."

"Why not?" I told Brian. "We're going out there anyway." A few minutes later the fat guy came back with a girl and a pile of posters.

276

"You can squeeze in some more people, can't you?"

"No."

The guy looked miffed. We went and got the car, and the fat guy and his girl and his hats and his posters all piled into the back. We started for the San Diego freeway and the airport. After two blocks the fat guy said, "Roll the window up, will you?"

"Can I smoke?" I asked.

"Let him walk," Brian said.

"Just don't want to get a cold," the fat guy said.

I rolled the window up. The girl was quiet, and the fat guy started talking about how terrible it was that Kennedy was late after all the planning they had done. I rolled the window down.

Kennedy was expected at American Airlines Gate 44, and all the way to the airport a disc jockey who sounded like 1958 Bruce Morrow announced the arrival time every ten minutes. I expected 10,000 people. There were about 100 there when we arrived. They were clustered around the gate, with the press off in the waiting area on the side. About 60 Kennedy girls in tight white blouses and plastic boaters were rehearsing a song while a woman's voice led them on from some mysterious loudspeaker. The song kept repeating a line that talked about "conscience with a capital K." It sounded like a song constructed by Jimmy Van Heusen for the Ku Klux Klan.

All the little girls were white, except for one pretty black chick with blue eyes (sorry, Rap), who was brought up to the front for the photographers. A black guy and his wife and six-year-old daughter leaned over the fence to see Kennedy. The man carried a Kodak. I asked him why he was there.

"Bobby's my man," he said. "I want my daughter to see him too."

"We never saw President Kennedy in the flesh," his wife said. "And so we want the little girl to see Bobby."

The little girl watched the cameramen, who were banging and tripping each other with cameras and wires. As usual they reminded me of the CBS reporter who once said, "If I ever have a retarded child, God forbid, I won't worry. I'll just enroll him in the cameramen's union." Then a middle-aged woman came to the front, trim, neat, bright-eyed, in a white dress a couple of inches above the knee, looking as if she drank Tanqueray in the summer and Chivas Regal in the winter and subscribed dutifully to the *New York Review*. She started dancing, cold sober, and I realized she was the cheerleader. She started singing again about conscience with a capital K, and all the Kennedy girls did their best, while the reporters and photographers stared dully at them and I wondered if there were any girls in California with flat chests and cavities. They weren't at the airport.

After a while a squad of the pricks arrived carrying clipboards and folders, smoking those goddamned small cigars, wearing the tight mouths and the horn-rimmed glasses. They started pushing the crowd around and making Terse Announcements about how Kennedy would first make a statement to the press and then would walk through a kind of gauntlet of Kennedy girls "so you can all see him." Then they started arranging the reporters with the TV guys in front, followed by a few lonely magazine reporters, and the local newspapers somewhere around the candy stand in the next terminal. The crowd was growing bigger now, with people standing up on the stairs to the left and a few cops drifting around the edges.

About seven thirty the plane arrived, and the crowd had grown to about 1,000. Those reporters who had not been given a week off by their bosses trailed off first, limp and pale, toting typewriters. The cameramen crashed forward, a wall of them, and the girls' choir came on about the conscience with a capital K, and you could hear screaming and shouting, and there was Kennedy, with tired lines around his eyes, blue-gray suit, his lips moving into the cluster of microphones, and I decided to get the hell out of there.

I made it just in time: The line of girls was pushed forward, some women screamed, the black guy was wobbling with his daughter on his shoulder, and the cameramen were committing various acts of mayhem as they shot film they must have known would never be used. Another mob was in the rotunda near the escalator. One of the pricks pushed a TV reporter, and the TV reporter gave him a good shove back. More screaming. A little girl fell.

"I touched his hand, I touched his hand," said one of the long-haired California girls.

278

"I'd hate to tell you where I touched him," her girlfriend said, all teeth and innocence.

And then we were down the stairs and moving fast along the shiny corridor between the horizontal escalators that they use to move people in LA. Kennedy did his best to smile while people leaped around him, and then he was outside, climbing into the convertible, while the press buses loaded, and we went off behind him to Valley College in Van Nuys.

The trip took us north on the freeways, heading for the blue ridge of mountains that separates LA from the San Fernando Valley. Mayor Yorty had provided two motorcycle cops and a station wagon with two more to follow the press buses. We didn't know until later that the Van Nuys cops had received a call from some terrified citizen saying that his brother was going to shoot Kennedy.

We got off the freeway at Burbank Boulevard and passed into a neighborhood of town houses, clotheslines, gas stations, kids on bikes. A sound truck had plowed the route earlier, warning the residents that Kennedy was coming. The reception from knots of scattered people was warm. The kids on the bikes kept up with the motorcade all the way to the college. I saw one Nixon sign, one sign that simply said ECCCH!, and about fifty Kennedy signs. At one point, a lone man in a sleeveless undershirt stood out in the street under the trees and shouted, "Booo." That's all he said, and you wondered what the hell his kids thought of him.

There were cops blocking traffic at the college, and they stopped a black reporter in a Volkswagen in front of us and made him park three blocks away. They couldn't let us do anything else. We parked and started running through the cool evening after the twin red eyes of the press bus. It was beautiful: kids on an overpass, someone yelling into a bullhorn, and Brian and me running through the tennis courts on the trail of the candidate. And all around us young college kids were running, too, in the direction of the great ugly brown building where Kennedy was scheduled to speak.

The motorcade stopped at the front door, and the McCarthy signs started waving high. Kennedy tried to get out, and the cops started rapping people with bats held at each end. I was on

279

the side beside a hedge of pine trees as we all tried to get into the gym behind Kennedy.

This was impossible. When Kennedy was through the door, they slammed it behind him and locked it.

"It's all right, it's all right, there's a loudspeaker."

"What about the press?"

"Go around the back."

A guy fell on the ground beside me, and a girl stepped on him, and we cleared some room. "I lost my shoe!" he said. There seemed to be nowhere to move, so Brian and I started to crawl under the pine trees. A big dark-gray dog stared us in the eye.

"The hell with it," I said. We ran around to the back, and the door there was locked, too. Three football players arrived and started crashing with their fists against the door. It looked certain that we'd be arrested if we stayed with them. That, or torn limb from limb by the people charged with feeding them. We went around to the front again and finally convinced a cop that we were supposed to be on the inside. We stepped through, followed suddenly by the football players. Another beautiful evening in the only life I will ever have.

Kennedy was already talking when we came into the gym. There were about 8,000 young people in the place. The McCarthy kids were in the stands flanking the speaker's platform, and down in front, seated on the floor, were some of the kids from the Peace and Freedom Party, who looked like the McCarthy kids before they cut their hair.

Kennedy was talking about welfare and the need to give citizens jobs. It was a familiar theme, and Kennedy himself seemed a bit bored by it. The formal speech was repetitious and ragged and was not really what these young sons and daughters of the middle class had come to hear. They wanted to hear about Vietnam and true change in the American system. Kennedy was not giving that to them, though he was applauded loudly and often. He talked about how great numbers of Americans were hungry and humiliated, "how some of them might have wanted husbands, some of them might have wanted fathers, and we have only given them checks." He talked about what a disaster the welfare system was, how demeaning and ugly it was. He started building then, throwing the prepared speech away. He talked about the law passed by Congress last year that will cut off vast numbers of children from even the humiliating subsistence of welfare. "Those children have a choice between starving to death or moving," Kennedy said. "I've seen them, in the state of Mississippi, with their bellies swollen and their faces covered with sores. . . ." He enumerated and exploded some of the myths about the poor. "It is simply not true that the poor do not want to work," he said. "It is far more likely to be children of favored families rather than the poor. . . ."

Then there was a question period, and Kennedy was better than he ever is with prepared speeches. Some of the kids were nasty and bitter, and after one particularly snotty question Kennedy said, with a tired voice, "What we need in the country is to cut down the belligerence. If we let this hatred and emotion control our lives, we're lost."

"It's our lives!" one of the Peace and Freedom kids yelled.

Kennedy talked about the draft, as he always does with college audiences, and tried again to say to them that if they really oppose the war, if they were against the draft, they should follow their consciences on the matter. "But you also have to face the consequences of your actions," he said. This never goes over well, because most of these kids have grown up believing that there are no consequences to their actions. (Joel Oppenheimer once explained why he can't take potheads seriously: "The drinker pays with a hangover. The junkie pays with a big habit. The pothead never pays.")

Kennedy's line of argument infuriated the Peace and Freedom kids. They shouted and booed and interrupted both questions and answers. "You fascist pig!" one kid said (seriously). Others threw tantrums, like nine-year-olds being asked to clean up after a birthday party. They looked as if they wanted to kill somebody, and they were in the same ugly mood when the evening ended and Kennedy made his way outside to the convertible.

A group of them stationed themselves on the school overpass, and as Kennedy's car started moving they unleashed a barrage of small stones, pebbles, apple cores, and other debris. This was

281

in the name of social and racial justice, of course. Kennedy was not hit, but he slid down into the seat. Fred Dutton, of Kennedy's staff, was hit on the head. The kids were ranting on the overpass, and I tried to get up there. The cops sealed it off. Kennedy's car disappeared into the quiet side streets, heading for the Ambassador Hotel and some sleep.

I don't believe that those young people were just an obscure case, hardened up by the barbarities of Marxist prose. No. They were the truest children of the Johnson era, because if the past few dirty years have taught us anything, they have taught us how to hate. Hatred on the left is even more vile and disgusting than hatred on the right, because it clothes itself in the rhetoric of decency. All those people sitting around the West Side getting their hate-Bobby rocks off are not much different from the George Wallace animals; they just think that their hatred is purer. They've made Kennedy into Savonarola and McCarthy into Francis of Assisi, and when the primaries are over, the hatred will go even wider, hitting Humphrey and Rockefeller and Nixon, too.

I think Kennedy is a decent man; he is the only politician now functioning on a national level who presents at least the possibility of bringing us back from the brink of race war; personally, he is the only politician I know who has never lied to me. He'll have my vote, no matter how many potential Walt Rostows now are attaching themselves to his campaign. But it would be self-deception of the worst kind to believe that any single man will save America. Kennedy alone will not do it; McCarthy can't, and Nixon would only push us into a seething caldron, like Mexico about 1917. It's too late for fairy tales, especially when we tell them to ourselves. I enjoy funny hats, balloons, campaign songs, and the rest of it. But 562 American men were slaughtered in Vietnam last week. They are what politics is about this year. The smug, pampered, self-righteous kid who takes rocks into the darkness of an overpass and pelts a candidate with them is only a step away from picking up a Mannlicher Carcano with a telescopic sight. He is what politics is about in 1968, too. The cold dumbness of the pragmatists killed those kids in Vietnam. The Cocktail Party Left with its

nasty little sophistries and its thrill at the prospect of violence put the rocks in those kids' hands. I'd like to see America saved, but that's not going to happen until all of us, the left even more than the right, begin to deescalate our capacity for glib hatreds. Politics used to be our national clown show; but it has become an ugly confrontation between armies of opposing haters, and if it keeps going that way, we're doomed.
May 23, 1968

Two Minutes to Midnight: The Very Last Hurrah

It was, of course, two minutes to midnight, and the Embassy Room of the Ambassador Hotel was rowdy with triumph. Red and blue balloons drifted up through three golden chandeliers to bump against a gilded ceiling. Young girls with plastic Kennedy boaters chanted like some lost reedy chorus from an old Ray Charles record. The crowd was squashed against the bandstand, a smear of black faces and Mexican-American faces and bearded faces and Beverly Hills faces crowned with purple hair. Eleven TV cameras were turning, their bright-blue arc lights changing the crowd into a sweaty stew. Up on the bandstand, with his wife standing just behind him, was Robert Kennedy.

"I'd like to express my high regard for Don Drysdale," Kennedy said. Drysdale had just won his sixth straight shutout. "I hope we have his support in this campaign." There was a loud cheer. He thanked Rafer Johnson and Rosey Grier (cheers) and Jesse Unruh (timid cheer) and Cesar Chavez (very loud cheers), and he thanked the staff and the volunteers and the voters, and the crowd hollered after every sentence. It was the sort of scene that Kennedys have gone through a hundred times and more: On this night, at least, it did not appear that there would be a last hurrah. Kennedy had not scored a knockout over Eugene McCarthy; but a points decision at least would keep his campaign going.

"I thank all of you," Kennedy was saying. "Mayor Yorty has

283

just sent a message that we have been here too long already" (laughter). "So my thanks to all of you, and now it's on to Chicago. . . ."

I was at the rear of the stand, next to George Plimpton. Kennedy put his thumb up to the audience, brushed his hair, made a small V with his right hand, and turned to leave. The crowd started shouting: "We want Bobby! We want Bobby!" Plimpton and I went down three steps, and turned left through a gauntlet of Kennedy volunteers and private cops in brown uniforms.

We found ourselves in a long grubby area called the pantry. It was the sort of place where Puerto Ricans, blacks and Mexican-Americans usually work to fill white stomachs. There were high bluish fluorescent lights strung across the ceiling, a floor of raw sandy-colored concrete, pale dirty walls. On the right were a rusty ice machine and shelves filled with dirty glasses. On the left, an archway led into the main kitchen and under the arch a crowd of Mexican-American cooks and busboys waited to see Kennedy. Against the left wall, three table-sized serving carts stood end to end, and at the far end were two doors leading to the press room, where Kennedy was going to talk to reporters.

Kennedy moved slowly into the area, shaking hands, smiling, heading a platoon of reporters, photographers, staffers, the curious, TV men. I was in front of him, walking backward. I saw him turn to his left and shake the hand of a small Mexican cook. We could still hear the chants of "We want Bobby" from the Embassy Room. The cook was smiling and pleased.

Then a pimply messenger arrived from the secret filthy heart of America. He was curly-haired, wearing a pale-blue sweat shirt and blue jeans, and he was planted with his right foot forward and his right arm straight out, and he was firing a gun.

The scene assumed a kind of insane fury, all jump cuts, screams, noise, hurtling bodies, blood. The shots went pap-pap pap-pap-pap, small sharp noises like a distant firefight or the sound of firecrackers in a backyard. Rosey Grier of the Los Angeles Rams came from nowhere and slammed his great bulk into the gunman, crunching him against a serving table. George Plimpton grabbed for the guy's arm, and Rafer Johnson moved to him, right behind Bill Barry, Kennedy's friend and security chief, and they were all making deep animal sounds and still the bullets came.

"Get the gun, get the gun."

"Rafer, get the gun!"

"Get the fucking gun!"

"No," someone said. And you could hear the stunned horror in the voice, the replay of old scenes, the muffle of drums. "No. No. Nooooooooooooo!"

We knew then that America had struck again. In this slimy little indoor alley in the back of a gaudy ballroom, in this shabby reality behind the glittering façade, Americans were doing what they do best: killing and dying, and cursing because hope doesn't last very long among us.

I saw Kennedy lurch against the ice machine, and then sag, and then fall forward slowly, to be grabbed by someone, and I knew then that he was dead. He might linger a few hours or a few days, but his face reminded me somehow of Benny Paret the night Emile Griffith hammered him into unconsciousness. Kennedy's face had a kind of sweet acceptance to it, the eyes understanding that it had come to him, the way it had come to so many others before him. The price of the attempt at excellence was death. You saw a flicker of that understanding on his face, as his life seeped out of a hole in the back of his skull, to spread like a spilled wine across the scummy concrete floor.

It was as if all of us there went simultaneously insane: A cook was screaming, "Kill him, kill him now, kill him, kill him!" I tried to get past Grier, Johnson, Plimpton, and Barry to get at the gunman. The Jack Ruby in me was rising up, white, bright, with a high singing sound in the ears, and I wanted to damage that insane little bastard they were holding. I wanted to break his face, to rip away flesh, to hear bone break as I pumped punches into that pimpled skin. Budd Schulberg was next to me; I suppose he was trying to do the same. Just one punch. Just one for Dallas. Just one for Medgar Evers, just one for Martin Luther King. Just one punch. Just one. One.

Kennedy was lying on the floor, with black rosary beads in his hand, and blood on his fingers. His eyes were still open, and as his wife, Ethel, reached him, to kneel in an orange-and-white dress, his lips were moving. We heard nothing. Ethel smoothed his face, running ice cubes along his cheeks. There was a lot of shouting and a strange chorus of high screaming. My notes showed that Kennedy was shot at 12:10, and was taken out of that grubby hole at 12:32. It seemed terribly longer.

I don't remember how it fits into the sequence, but I do have one picture of Rosey Grier holding the gunman by the neck, choking the life out of him.

"Rosey, Rosey, don't kill him. We want him alive. Don't kill him, Rosey, don't kill him."

"Kill the bastard, kill that sum of a bitch bastard," a Mexican busboy yelled.

"Don't kill him, Rosey."

"Where's the doctor? Where in Christ's name is the doctor?"

Grier decided not to kill the gunman. They had him up on a serving table at the far end of the pantry, as far as they could get him from Kennedy. Jimmy Breslin and I were standing up on the table, peering into the gunman's face. His eyes were rolling around, and then stopping, and then rolling around again. The eyes contained pain, flight, entrapment, and a strange kind of bitter endurance. I didn't want to hit him anymore.

"Where the fuck is the doctor? Can't they get a fucking doctor?"

"Move back."

"Here comes a doctor, here's a doctor."

"Move back!"

Kennedy was very still now. There was a thin film of blood on his brow. They had his shoes off and his shirt open. The stretcher finally arrived, and he trembled as they lifted him, his lips moved, and the flashbulbs blinked off one final salvo and he was gone.

The rest was rote: I ran out into the lobby and picked up my brother Brian, and we rushed to the front entrance. A huge black man, sick with grief and anger and bitterness, was throwing chairs around. Most landed in the pool. The young Kennedy girls were crying and wailing, knowing, I suppose, what the guys my age discovered in Dallas: Youth was over. "Sick," one girl kept saying. "Sick. Sick. What kind of country is this? Sick. Sick." Outside, there were cops everywhere and sirens.

The cops were trying to get one of the wounded into a taxi. The cabby didn't want to take him, afraid, I suppose, that blood would sully his nice plastic upholstery.

When we got through the police barricades, we drove without talk to the Hospital of the Good Samaritan, listening to the news on the radio. The unspoken thought was loudest: The country's gone, Medgar Evers was dead, Malcolm X was dead, Martin Luther King was dead, Jack Kennedy was dead, and now Robert Kennedy was dying. The hell with it. The hatred was now general. I hated that pimpled kid in that squalid cellar enough to want to kill him. He hated Kennedy the same way. That kid and the bitter Kennedy haters were the same. All those people in New York who hated Kennedy's guts, who said "eccch" when his name was mentioned, the ones who creamed over Murray Kempton's vicious diatribes these past few months—they were the same. When Evers died, when King died, when Jack Kennedy died, all the bland pundits said that some good would come of it in some way, that the nation would go through a catharsis, that somehow the bitterness, the hatred, the bigotry, the evil of racism, the glib violence would be erased. That was bullshit. We will have our four-day televised orgy of remorse about Robert Kennedy, and then it will be business as usual.

You could feel that as we drove through the empty LA streets, listening to the sirens screaming in the night. Nothing would change. Kennedy's death would mean nothing. It was just another digit in the great historical pageant that includes the slaughter of Indians, the plundering of Mexico, the enslavement of black people, the humiliation of Puerto Ricans. Just another digit. Nothing would come of it. While Kennedy's life was ebbing out of him, Americans were dropping bombs and flaming jelly on Orientals. While the cops fingerprinted the gunmen, Senator Eastland's Negro subjects were starving. While the cops made chalk marks on the floor of the pantry, the brave members of the National Rifle Association were already explaining that people commit crimes, guns don't (as if Willie Mays could hit a home run without a bat). These cowardly bums claim constitutional rights to kill fierce deer in the forests,

287

and besides, suppose the niggers come to the house and we don't have anything to shoot them with? Suppose we have to fight a nigger man to man?

America the Beautiful: with crumby little mini-John Waynes carrying guns to the woods like surrogate penises. Yes, the kid I saw shoot Kennedy was from Jordan, was diseased with some fierce hatred for Jews. Sam Yorty, who hated Kennedy, now calls Kennedy a great American and blames the Communists. Hey, Sam: You killed him, too. The gun that kid carried was American. The city where he shot down a good man was run by Sam Yorty. How about keeping your fat pigstink mouth shut?

At the approach to the Good Samaritan Hospital the cops had strung red flares across the gutter and were stopping everyone. A crowd of about seventy-five people were on the corner when we arrived, about a third of them black. I went in, past those black people who must have felt that there was no white man at all with whom they could talk. A mob of reporters was assembled at the hospital entrance. The cops were polite, almost gentle, as if they sensed that something really bad had happened and that many of these reporters were friends of the dying man.

Most of the hospital windows were dark, and somewhere up there Robert Kennedy was lying on a table while strangers stuck things into his brain looking for a killer's bullet. We were friends, and I didn't want him to die; but if he were to be a vegetable, I didn't want him to live either.

We drove home, through the wastelands around LA and the canyons through the mountains to the south. When I got home, my wife was asleep, the TV still playing out its record of the death watch. Frank Reynolds of ABC, a fine reporter and a compassionate man, was so upset he could barely control his anger. I called some friends and poured a drink. Later I talked to my old man, who came to this country from Ireland in flight from the Protestant bigots of Belfast forty years ago. I suppose he loved John Kennedy even more than I did, and he has never really been the same since Dallas. Now it had happened again.

"If you see Teddy," he said, "tell him to get out of politics. The Kennedys are too good for this country."

I remembered the night in 1964, in that bitter winter after John Kennedy's murder, when Robert Kennedy appeared at a St. Patrick's Day dinner in Scranton, Pennsylvania. He talked about the Irish, and the long journey that started on the quays of Wexford and ended in the Parkland Hospital. He reminded them of the days when there were signs that said NO IRISH NEED APPLY (and it was always to his greatest dismay that so many sons of Irishmen he came across in New York were bigots and haters). Bob told them about Owen O'Neill, an Irish patriot whose ideals had survived his martyrdom. Men were crying as he read the old Irish ballad:

> Oh, why did you leave us, Owen?
> Why did you die? . . .
> We're sheep without a shepherd,
> When the snow shuts out the sky.
> Oh, why did you leave us, Owen?

Why did you die?

I didn't know. There was some sort of answer for John Kennedy, and another for Robert Kennedy. But I had learned that I knew nothing finally, that when my two young daughters present the bill to me in another ten years, I won't have much to say. I sat there drinking rum until I was drunk enough to forget that pimpled face cracking off the rounds into the body of a man who was a friend of mine. Finally, easily, with the sun up, I fell asleep on the couch. I didn't have any tears left for America, but I suppose not many other Americans did either.
June 13, 1968

The Last Mayor of New York

The big red, white, and blue campaign truck was parked in front of Korvette's on Fulton Street in Brooklyn, with one lonely blue balloon hanging from a plain pipe rack over the speaker's platform. The balloon bobbed pathetically in the soft early-summer breeze, while a young man with a bullhorn split the air with his pitch. "Come and listen to the dy-*nam*-ic Wagner team!" he shouted, with the kind of mindless enthusiasm you associate with Army lifers. "Stick around for Bob Wagner! He'll be here in *five* minutes, folks, the last real mayor New York ever had! Right here to *Brooklyn,* folks, right here to *Fulton Street!* Bob Wagner! The last real mayor New York ever had!"

It went on like that for a long time, like something written by a bad imitator of Tom Wolfe, the hyperbole rolling out over the afternoon shoppers like excited glue. People stopped in shock at the noise, looked up at the guy with the bullhorn, saw the lone blue balloon, and moved on. Then, a half hour later, Robert Ferdinand Wagner was among us again.

"Good ta see ya," he said, moving into the crowd. There were about 150 of them, and Wagner moved through them lumpily, smiling wanly, stopping to sign random sheets of paper or cardboard boxes from the department stores. Wagner didn't seem to mind. He had, after all, been to this place before, moved through a thousand similar crowds, had heard a thousand other pitchmen, had shaken perhaps a half million hands. If you were a professional politician, there was no other route to take, and this was the part of the craft that most resembled the operation of a drill press: It was dull and usually predictable, and Wagner's blocky face described it all.

The eyes were tired and watery, the eyes of a man who had just emerged from a dark afternoon saloon into the bright sunlight. There were swollen pouches beneath the eyes, forced into relief by the high sun, and wrinkles laced the neck, and the mouse-colored hair was thinner now. The skin still had that blotchy freckled texture we remembered: a true New Yorker's skin, ravaged by the air and the night, skin that always made the newspaper photographs look as if they had been printed from mozzarella engravings. Wagner seemed bored; he knew that this primary would not be won on the corner of Lawrence and Fulton streets: victory would come if the regulars trooped dutifully to the polls on June 17. And yet he also knew he must go through the motions.

Immediately, Wagner showed his great strength. It was the same strength he had shown on the first of the TV debates with his Democratic opponents. He looked like the incumbent. And he looked like the incumbent because for so many years he *was* the incumbent. From 1954 to 1965 he was part of our lives in this town, the hundred and second mayor of the city of New York, the man in whose company we had spent 4,380 days and nights. *This is Maya Wagneh.*

"Welcome back, Mr. Mayor," a heavy lady with furry hair shouted.

"Good to have you home."

"You got my vote. . . ."

The people talking were mostly middle-aged, and most of them were white, but sprinkled through the crowd were the faces of tired middle-aged black men, too. They received Wagner with that peculiar kind of reserved warmth which is at the heart of the New York style. They would not jump up and down for Robert Wagner; they have done that for only a very few politicians, and all of them are dead. But they did not heckle him. He was, after all, one of them: the sort of New Yorker whose sins were always minor, whose triumphs were always muted.

They liked Robert Wagner because they knew him. In the years when they were getting to know him, they were all a little bit younger, a little bit more hopeful, perhaps even a little bit more happy. "Some of it is nostalgia," Wagner would say later. "You know, in the political game it takes a long time for people to get to know anybody. They know the mayor; they know the governor; they know the President. And for better or for worse, they know me."

You cannot begin to understand why Robert Wagner should be the odds-on favorite to win the Democratic primary unless you understand that New Yorkers are the most sentimental people in America.

"I just wanna mention why we're in this battle," Wagner said. ". . . It's so we can win the election in November and give this city back to the people. . . . We have to bring the people of this city together again. We don't want our people to be separated; we don't want the ugliness of recent years. And another thing, we want the dirt cleaned off our streets. In all my years I've never seen the streets as dirty as they are now. We

wanna see the streets of the city of New York clean again. . . .
We want a police department that is free of politics, a police department that works for all the people of this city, a government that works for all the people of this great city, whether they are on Park Avenue or right here on Fulton Street. We wanna see the cop back on the beat. . . . We're gonna win this election, friends, and then we're gonna have the kind of city that we can be happy to hand down to our children. . . ."

Then he was finished. It was a stump speech, but not much different from what Wagner had been saying all along. He was the Great Conciliator. It was dull, almost lifeless. But he finished to warm applause.

The shill with the bullhorn announced breathlessly: "He's gonna commence a walkin' tour among you!" And while Wagner and his running mates, Congressman Hugh Carey and State Senator Seymour Thaler, signed more autographs and started moving slowly through the crowd, another shill grabbed a horn to shout: "Dis is truly da team of da future."

The team of the future?

Well, it's possible that Carey and Thaler have a future, and Wagner might indeed be elected mayor again. But the astonishing thing is that Wagner has such a long past. Go to a newspaper morgue to look at the clips. There are millions of them. Literally. Drawer after drawer. Envelope after envelope. Millions of words, all dead and forgotten, the clips flaking in the hands.

The clips will tell you that he is deaf in one ear, color-blind, played squash in college, liked swimming, and was born on April 20, 1910. He grew up in a house at Lexington Avenue and Eighty-seventh Street, among the politicians of Yorkville. His mother died when he was nine. And his father, Robert F. Wagner, Sr., showered him with affection. The father broke into politics in a Tammany club, served in the state legislature, and in 1926 was elected to the United States Senate for the first of four terms. Wagner, Sr., authored the Wagner Labor Relations Act, helped pass major Social Security legislation, and championed civil rights.

He loved and spoiled his son and never remarried. The boy

was brought up a Catholic (his mother's faith), went to Loyola, the Taft School, Yale (with the class of 1933), the School of International Relations, the Harvard School of Business Administration, and then graduated from Yale Law School in 1937. Six weeks later he was elected to his father's old seat in Albany.

He didn't do much in the legislature, and when the Second World War broke out he joined the Army Air Corps. He spent most of 1942 making speeches in war plants. Then he went to Europe, handling judge advocate duties and planning bombing raids. When he was discharged in 1945, he was a lieutenant colonel, with a Bronze Star, six battle stars, a Presidential unit citation and the Croix de Guerre. By this time he also had been married to the former Susan Edwards—on St. Valentine's Day in 1942—and was the father of Robert F. III (another son, Duncan, was born in 1947).

His rise in New York politics started when he came home. Mayor William O'Dwyer and the Tammany organization immediately recognized his potential: Robert F. Wagner, Jr., was a veteran, a quiet, affable man, and the son of a famous liberal father. The organization began to build him the way old-time fight managers build up pugs. First, O'Dwyer made young Wagner a member of the City Tax Commission and swiftly moved him up to chairman. But that was to be a brief stay: the idea of a buildup is to keep your boy out of trouble, keep him moving breezily. Wagner moved on to become head of the Department of Housing and Buildings. This department was a sinkhole, packed with inspectors on the take and various other Tammany hacks. Wagner did not stay long; O'Dwyer moved him up to chairman of the City Planning Commission before the muck could really touch him.

By 1949 O'Dwyer had decided to run again, and Wagner went after elective office for the first time since his return from the war. The post was that of Manhattan borough president. O'Dwyer and Tammany wanted him, and Wagner won easily.

Almost immediately, the Wagner style showed itself. One of his father's favorite political maxims was: "If in doubt, don't." He followed the advice in 1950, when he took office as borough president; he still follows the advice. The Manhattan borough president's office then contained one of the largest collection of

293

political meatballs assembled in one place since Boss Tweed's day. They were all Tammany hacks, and some of them were friends of gambler Frank Costello. At first Wagner said that he didn't care much about their Tammany affiliations, as long as they got the work done. But the news about the friendships with Costello bothered him. He did what he was to do hundreds of times later: he appointed someone else to do the job. This time it was a Republican lawyer from the Citizens Union. The meatballs refused to be investigated. They went to court and challenged the legality of the investigation. They won. New York lost. But Wagner came out of it looking the way he always looks in memory: the decent man who tried his best and occasionally did not win.

By 1953 he was the Democratic candidate for mayor. His sponsors were Ed Flynn, the boss of the Bronx, and a man named Carmine De Sapio. Then, as now, nobody really disliked Wagner. Nobody thought he was dishonest. And he had the Name. He beat Vincent Impellitteri in the Democratic primary and went on to win the election easily.

For the next twelve years, Robert F. Wagner was the mayor of the richest city in the world. But it is difficult to say that he actually *ruled* it. Ask people who now support Wagner what he *did* during those twelve years, and the answers come rather slowly. Well, er, uh, he made the north-south streets in Manhattan one-way. He banned all private traffic from Manhattan during one big snowstorm. He put cops in the subways at night after one particularly brutal knife killing. He, uh, beat the bosses in 1961. Well, actually, there's also what he *didn't* do. He didn't have a subway strike or a sanitation strike or a big teacher's strike. Listen a little longer and you might think that from January, 1954, to December, 1965, there was no racism in New York, no anti-Semitism (black or otherwise), no crime, etc.

The facts are that the Wagner years were rather dreadful as far as government was concerned. Start anywhere. There were, to be sure, far more units of housing built under Wagner than under John Lindsay; there was also an unprecedented amount of graft in the awarding of contracts to specially approved builders and contractors. In 1961, Wagner promised to hold the line on rent control; by the end of the last term he had managed to decontrol all apartments renting for more than $250, the very five-, six-, and seven-room apartments most needed by the middle class of New York City.

On TV these days, Wagner is attempting to tell Democratic voters that he will somehow stop the spiraling crime rate. In fact, it spiraled under Wagner himself, as it will spiral under the next mayor, whoever he is. In 1964, felonies in New York increased 8 percent, robberies went up 17.1 percent, thefts went up 23.9 percent, assaults increased 13.9 percent, forcible rapes went up 28.1 percent, and murders went up 16.1 percent. Juvenile delinquency cases handled by Children's Court rose 163 percent over a ten-year period. The crime rate rose in every year of Wagner's administration and is still rising. When Wagner took office, there were an estimated 20,000 heroin addicts in the city; when he left office, there were about 75,000. Robert Wagner did not cause the increase in crime, but he really can't keep giving the impression that crime did not exist when he was mayor or that crime will go away if he is elected again.

Wagner presided over the exodus of the white middle class from the city. The 1960 census showed the city's population falling for the first time (by 1.4 percent). During his twelve years, the city lost 80,000 manufacturing jobs and 800,000 middle-income families. He stood by meekly while Robert Moses bulldozed his way all over the city, building highways that carried the middle class out of town, putting together a World's Fair that made money for a number of Wagner political backers but that lost the city milliions and was one of the most pathetic exhibitions of rotten taste seen in this country for years. While he occupied City Hall, air pollution tripled, the traffic on the streets started slobbering to a halt, and the subway system—in one typical year—was plagued by several thousand fires and 10,000 delays while old cars and decrepit roadbeds rotted under its passengers.

There was great inefficiency. In 1961, the year of Wagner's greatest political triumph, a street sign cost $3.90 in the Bronx and $12.15 in Manhattan. Each borough had its own asphalt producing plant, so that asphalt cost $5.82 per ton in Queens and $21.07 per ton in Staten Island. From 1955 to 1960, the city was overcharged $176,599.59 on rock salt. In 1960, the Transit

Authority burned weeds on 200 acres of its property at a cost of $20,000; it could have done it with chemicals, causing no air pollution, for $14,000. In 1959, $200,000 was spent to rehabilitate the athletic field at Franklin K. Lane High School in Brooklyn; they did such a good job that the field was ruined and had to be closed completely. In January, 1960, Wagner's grocery bill at Gracie Mansion was more than $2,400 a month, with an additional $600 for meat; the police commissioner took over the mayor's commissary, and by December the bill for groceries *and* meat was down to $491 a month.

And then the other little beauties started to pile up. Broadway Maintenance Corporation, charged with maintaining the city's streetlights, parking meters, and air-raid sirens, beat the city out of $2,000,000 through what the State Investigation Commission called "extensive irregularities." These included charging $7.90 for changing a single 15-cent light bulb. The SIC made its charges in the fall of 1960; on June 30, 1961, Wagner announced that the city was renewing its contract with Broadway Maintenance.

The Board of Education was also in fine shape. In May and June, 1961, the SIC found deterioration in 98.6 percent of all public schools. The results: One hundred Board of Education employees were investigated for taking bribes from school contractors; one school engineer was indicted; the head of the board's School Construction Bureau was suspended for accepting gifts and fees from businesses under contract to the board; the school superintendent admitted that he had some high school vocational students build him a boat and that he bought material at wholesale prices for his home from firms doing business with the schools. The entire Board of Education had to be abolished at a special session of the legislature. Today Wagner is against "too much" community control because it might lead to "chaos."

There were other beauties: the Title I scandals; the rioting in Harlem in 1964 (the worst in the city since the Second World War), which was blamed by Deputy Mayor Screvane on "the Communists"; the government by committee (at one point there were almost 200 committees trying to govern the city, none of which did much work); the deficit financing which wrecked the city's credit rating. We don't have the room to detail everything, but we remember them.

One of the great puzzles about Wagner remains his political beliefs. In general, of course, he is a New Dealer, a programmatic liberal of the old school. But his ideas about government remain vague. Some of his friends say that the reason is that he is basically a shy man, not given to pompous rhetoric. Others say that he simply has no ideas at all, that he is a technician who does his best to keep people from getting mad at him and at each other. (Certainly his own rhetoric has not changed much. The first sentence of his Brooklyn stump speech is not very different from the first sentence of his 1953 campaign announcement: "We believe we are embarking today on a crusade to return the government of the city of New York to the people.")

One way to try to discover his political philosophy is to deal briefly with his curious relations with Carmine De Sapio of Tammany Hall and the old Lehman-Roosevelt reformers.

In 1954 Wagner was describing De Sapio as a man of "complete integrity." On April 26, 1957, he said that De Sapio "had set an example of undivided allegiance to the principles of good government—of government devoted exclusively to the needs and the welfare of the people." De Sapio was a "stalwart friend of decency, honesty and integrity in government" and Wagner was "proud to call him my good friend." On May 14, 1959, Wagner called De Sapio "the best leader the Democratic Party has had in New York." By August 2, 1961, however, Wagner was saying: "I say De Sapio and his boss-ilk must go and the Democratic party must be given back to the people. At long last the master boss of all, De Sapio, has come out of the back room where he has been pulling the strings and has joined the battle publicly. I hope he has the guts to stand up in the open from now on."

The reasons for Wagner's turnaround were complicated. For many years, he had wanted to follow his father's steps to Washington. He ran for his father's old seat in 1956 against Jacob Javits but was beaten in the second Eisenhower landslide. Then, in the summer of 1958, the New York State Democrats had to pick a candidate for the other Senate seat. Wagner was already thinking about the Vice Presidential slot on the 1960 ticket, a position he could only hope for if someone other than John F. Kennedy received the nomination. Kennedy and Wagner, both Eastern Catholics, could not run together. But if the Presidential candidate were a Midwesterner, like Stuart Symington, or a Westerner, like Lyndon Johnson, Wagner had a chance. He was also under great pressure from the growing reform movement in New York City, a movement that was increasingly aiming its guns at De Sapio. Then-Governor Averell Harriman was running for reelection in 1958 and wanted a liberal. So did Wagner, both to respond in some way to the reform movement and to establish broader liberal credentials for 1960.

But De Sapio took over the convention in Buffalo, through Monroe Goldwater (a law partner of Boss Flynn's) and Percy Gale (husband of De Sapio's secretary and director of the Bureau of Real Estate, which was then under investigation for corruption). De Sapio rammed through the nomination of Manhattan District Attorney Frank Hogan and humiliated Harriman and Wagner. Wagner never forgot this. In 1961, his newfound friends in the reform movement were to claim that this Display of Raw Power Turned Him Away from Bossism. Actually, Wagner has always been a shrewd pol. Some friends claim that the series of scandals in his administration were caused by De Sapio appointments; this will never be completely known, because so much of the record is fogged. Does a businessman make a fast buck because a political leader forces him to do it? Or does he get larcenous because he sees a city adrift in lethargy and indecision?

At any rate, Wagner turned on De Sapio with a Display of his own Raw Power in 1961. His achieving the Vice Presidency was precluded the year before by the nomination of John F. Kennedy. There was no chance of beating Nelson Rockefeller and no Senate election ahead for three years. Wagner had to run for mayor to maintain a power base. But he couldn't run with the increasingly large liability of De Sapio around his neck. He conceived a beautiful piece of politics. He decided to run against his own record. He attacked the people who had initially put him in power, blamed all of his own shortcomings on them, was rewarded when all five county leaders rallied behind Arthur Levitt in the Democratic primary, and won the nomination and the election easily.

But the third term was a period of lethargy again. The arrival of Robert Kennedy in 1964 began to diminish Wagner's power. The anti-boss campaign had not endeared him to many Democratic legislators in Albany, many of whom came from regular clubs, and financing the city became tougher. Wagner's wife, Susan, was sick with cancer. There were stories that Wagner had begun drinking heavily. He looked tired and defeated. New York was sliding into the urban crisis, and Wagner's tools were already outdated when he took office. The reformers had helped destroy the good things with the bad in the old machine system. Susan Wagner died in March, 1964. In June, 1965, with tears streaming down his face, Wagner announced that he would not run for a fourth term.

A month after dropping out, in Cardinal Spellman's private chapel at St. Patrick's Cathedral, he married Barbara Cavanagh. His handpicked candidate, the very capable Paul Screvane, lost in the primary to Abe Beame; John Lindsay became the hundred and third mayor, and Robert Wagner disappeared into private law practice. He served as ambassador to Spain for seven months, and in February he came home.

After his arrival and his decision to run for mayor again, the crowded primary started losing characters. Congressman Jack Murphy was to drop out. So was Norman Frank. But the rarest display of Wagner's own power came in Brooklyn, where County Leader Meade Esposito was backing Congressman Hugh Carey, a respectable liberal Kennedy Democrat. Esposito and Carey both understood the realities: It would cost more than a million dollars just to get Carey's name known in the other five boroughs. Even then, Wagner was likely to win. They pulled out. Carey joined the ticket as candidate for president of the City Council. Esposito threw the Brooklyn organization behind Wagner, and the Man Who Slew the Bosses became, at fifty-nine, a candidate of a boss.

The Wagner campaign is being run from the Biltmore, where thirty offices have been rented. The personnel are mostly middle-aged. There are no jumping children in the halls of the Biltmore. Most of the campaign workers see little of Wagner, who spends most of his noncampaigning time in an upstairs office.

"There must be some reason why people are so anxious to see us," Wagner said the other day. "And that's really the only way to find out how people feel, going out there in the field. Some people have been kind enough to say that it's better than 61.

"I know people in all groups, and I always try to approach them without feeling that you have to be antagonistic or that you are one-sided. You know, there are always problems, and some of them are more complicated than before. But the mayor twenty-five years from now will be saying that that fella Wagner had it easy. You know, looking back, we think LaGuardia had it easy. The old-timers downtown tell you that LaGuardia used to answer his own mail every morning. Sure things change and get more difficult. But they couldn't have changed that much in three and a half years."

Wagner is opposed to decentralization as a concept of government and shows little interest in the idea of strengthening the borough president's office and expanding the City Council, two moves that would be a start toward easing New Yorkers' alienation.

"People say that the mayor is the mayor," he said. "If he has the burden and the responsibility, then he should have the authority. All of our citizens can play a role. The city government has a function to perform. I want greater participation, but if you only have three, four percent of the people in some areas making the decisions, then you're going to have trouble. I don't plan to preside over the dismemberment of the city."

There was more, but we've heard it before, over and over. Then Wagner had to leave. A few nights before, I had watched him film a TV commercial on the street where I live in Brooklyn. It was all about how unsafe the streets had become, and how few cops were on foot patrol anymore, and how he wouldn't allow "my Barbara" to go to the Sanders Theater alone. The Sanders is on my corner, and four cops are among my neighbors, and there hasn't been a mugging in that particular area for years. But poor Wagner didn't know that. He didn't know anything about my neighborhood. He didn't know why we were laughing when he recited the commercial into the TV cameras or why we thought he was a liar because at the moment there were a dozen cops on the corner directing traffic. Wagner lives in the country of politics. Not in Brooklyn or Manhattan or Islip. He lives in the country of politics, where his father's portrait is on all the walls and the real estate guys kick in to the campaign chests and Harry Van Arsdale speaks for the workingmen to promise, in effect, that four more years of Wagner will certainly keep the blacks out of the construction unions. In the country of politics, there are men who go out and buy shopping bags bearing the candidates' names, and people who hire sound trucks and advertising agencies and printers and paid volunteers. They take polls for a living and canvass voters and count the vote in the regular clubs. Wagner has lived there all his life, and he is among us again, promising to reward us all with a new passport to the years when we all were more innocent and we all knew the name of the district leader and the sound trucks were festooned with hundreds of balloons. There was only one lonely balloon on that sound truck in Brooklyn—a small symbol, perhaps, that the old pros have forgotten how to do their jobs. But in this election, I wouldn't mark it as an omen.

June 16, 1969

Wallace

I. "SURE, I'M FOR WALLACE"

It was a half hour from closing time at the Brunswick Billiard Parlor, a dark, green-walled place squashed under the flaking portico of the Capital Hotel on West Markham Street in Little Rock, Arkansas. The pool tables were empty green rectangles at the back of the room. In one corner, three men in sport shirts sat at a plastic table. They were drinking Schlitz from bottles while an old Hank Williams tune drifted from the jukebox. At the bar, munching sardines and crackers, a tall, lean man named Jim Lewis stared at himself in the mirror. He was wearing a plastic boater adorned with a Wallace-for-President bumper sticker.

"Sure, I'm for Wallace," he said, washing the sardines down with a beer. "There ain't no one else but Wallace. He's the one, the only one who's really sayin' he's gonna change things in this country."

"You don't care for Humphrey or Nixon?"

"Just a couple of phonies. Couldn't change a gah-dam thing. . . ."

"What kind of change are you looking for?"

"Everythin'," said Jim Lewis, who is a carpenter. "Get these long-haired scum in the colleges straightened out. Stop the gah-dam knee-groes from riotin' an' lootin'. Stop taxin' us to pay people for not workin'. Let our boys win that war in Vietnam. Hell, any plain fool knows what we gotta change."

"What makes you think Wallace can change all of that?"

Jim Lewis slowly turned his head and squinted the way John Wayne has squinted in every movie he's ever been in. "George Wallace can do it," he said firmly, "because George Wallace is his own man!"

Around the corner, two blond hookers walked past the Trailways bus station, waving at cruising automobiles. Humphrey headquarters was deserted and forlorn, and Nixon headquarters looked as if it hadn't opened at all. A green 1967 Chevrolet convertible pulled up at the corner. The two hookers went over and talked to a pair of crew cuts inside. After a minute of bargaining, they climbed in, and the car pulled away down West Markham Street. The car bumper carried three Wallace stickers. As they passed the Marion Hotel, one of the crew cuts saluted the building with a toot of the horn. Upstairs in his sixth-floor suite, George Corley Wallace slept the sleep of the just . . . or at any rate, one of the just who had pulled down a large and holy score. He was assisted in his serenity by the guns of the Secret Service.

II. ON THE TRAIL

At seven thirty in the morning, the seedy, high-ceilinged lobby of the Marion Hotel was confused and noisy. Luggage spilled onto the sidewalk, while crews from the three networks checked and rechecked their precious cargo of cameras, film, and cable; they received no help from the black hotel staff. Secret Servicemen with discreet blank shades and tiny identification pins in their lapels scrutinized every strange face. The Wallace staff, born in parochial campaigns in Alabama, struggled bravely with the problems of the big time. Luggage was lost; some staffers searched for it while others called ahead to Springfield, Missouri, to see what the problems would be at the next stop.

"Gah-dam, Jess," one staff member complained. "I told you to get this straight fo' you went ta bed lass night."

"How could I, Bill? You know I did my best."

"The best ain't good enough, Jess."

The male staff wore blue college-style blazers with Wallace crests sewn onto the breast pockets. Most were middle-aged, with deep lines of erosion on their faces; a few were younger, decent-looking kids from prep schools or law offices who didn't seem to care what the campaign was all about, but who acted happy to be in on it. The Wallace girls wore maroon blazers, no makeup, and a look of faintly disguised unhappiness. One of them passed out a revised schedule; there were no advance copies of speeches, because Wallace delivers the same speech everywhere. As we were about to leave, the elevator doors opened and a girl walked out. She was dressed from head to toe in a shiny silver cowboy suit. She smiled, and her capped teeth and silver-blond hair must have jolted the hangover sacs at the backs of various skulls. She looked like Candy Mosler, the great Texas lady who had beaten a murder rap in Miami a couple of years ago: a face purchased in stores and a body saved from age by tender care. She was wearing a Wallace cowboy hat.

"Who the hell is that?" I asked.

"That," said Bob Greene of *Newsday*, "is the girl from the Dodge Rebellion."

"The girl from the *what?*"

"You know, the Dodge Rebellion commercial on TV. She comes on and says I want *you* for the Dodge Rebellion, and then she tries to sell you a Dodge Charger. She's doing the same for ol' George."

It was truly beautiful: George Wallace had found his La Pasionaria, and she was wearing a silver cowboy suit. A couple of days later I realized that the girl from the Dodge Rebellion (whose name is Janeen Welch) was to be one of the pinnacles of good taste in the campaign.

On the campaign plane, Wallace sat in the front compartment with his advisers, while the press suffered in the rear. Most campaign planes have a kind of boozy familiarity to them; if the trips are long, the stewardesses serve an unlimited supply of drinks and sandwiches; reporters walk the aisles or write advance stories which are taken in hand by a representative from Western Union for filing at the next landing. There is no liquor on the Wallace campaign plane. You can bring your own on board, of course, but if you have neither the time nor foresight to make such an arrangement, you must settle for a can of Dr. Pepper or Coke and perhaps a box of Crackerjacks.

Occasionally, Wallace walks down the aisle to visit the john or talk with reporters from Alabama. He spends much of his campaign time blasting the press, but he's friendly enough on the plane. "Yawl keep hittin' it," he'll say. "Just get the name right." And he'll stand there smiling, clutching a cigar in a horn holder, a small, round-headed man with the air of a dandy about him. He wears his suits cut tight, with highly polished shoes, carefully trimmed fingernails, a handkerchief making a white arrowhead in his breast pocket. He looks a lot like a caricature, with his Vitalis-sleek hair combed straight back.

Black eyebrows dominate his small, Cagney-like features and have a way of making him look Satanic when he lowers the head and looks up from under them. The back of his neck was raw on the day I first met him, as if he had just come from a barbershop, and he reminded me of a good bantamweight named Pappy Gault who came out of South Carolina in the early fifties. Wallace, of course, was a fairly good amateur prizefighter in the thirties, and he won several amateur titles (people who remember him say that he lacked skill but had plenty of animal courage).

At ten thirty-five we touched down in Springfield, Missouri, in the middle of flat, dry country. There were about 150 people waiting at the airport for a glimpse of the candidate; overhead, a small plane flew back and forth trailing a Wallace-for-President banner. The small crowd cheered the girl from the Dodge

Rebellion when she came down the ramp, and then they cheered even harder when Wallace emerged.

"Let's go right to the fence," he said, and the Secret Servicemen flanked him as he walked with small, precise steps over to see some of the people who hope he will be the next President of the United States.

"Sorry we late," he said, shaking hands as he moved. "Sorry we late, real sorry bout that. Good to see you. Hope yawl come on downtown with us. Good to see you. How are you, son, good to see yawl. Sorry we late."

The people looked at him in the way that would become so familiar in the days that followed. There were older people with bad teeth and glazed eyes, men with hard, calloused hands, mothers with children in their arms. Some had hand-lettered Wallace-for-President posters; others had bought their emblems (hats, bumper stickers, and buttons which are sold, not given away, and bring in about $7,500 a day to the Montgomery headquarters alone). "You're gonna be the next President, George, you really are. . . . We're with you, George . . . give 'em hell, George. . . ." They loved him and wanted him.

Wallace finished at the fence and walked to a waiting Ford. A group of air national guardsmen stood in front of a hangar housing dark khaki helicopters. Wallace threw them a snappy military salute, shook hands with the local cops, and climbed in for the trip to Springfield.

The Wallace car moved through flat, scrubby country, past scattered billboards advertising farm equipment, and into Kearney Street. The Wallace campaign does not try to arrange motorcades; they are too dangerous, they cannot be milked for contributions, and if the crowds aren't large, Wallace could be compared unfavorably with the other candidates. And yet there were small clumps of people waving at him along the way, as he went past the McDonald's hamburger place, the Colonel Sanders Southern Fried Chicken store, past the Homemade Chili Parlor, the Tastee-Freez, the Safeway, past all those old white houses with swings on the front porches and the grass out front trimmed neatly, where the people who hate the twentieth century continue to exist as if Tom Sawyer still lived up the street.

He stopped on West College Street, in front of Frank's Barbershop, and talked for a while to some of his local campaign managers. The reporters walked through an alley between Heer's Department Store and the Evans Drugstore. There were uniformed men from the Sheriff's Department everywhere, and Secret Service types glommed the crowd. We entered the public square, and there before us, 15,000 strong, cheering and shouting, were the Wallace people.

"Are you for Dixie, yeh, yeh, are you for Dixie, oh, yeah. . . ."

A country music band with electric guitars was jamming on a flag-bedecked flatbed truck while two singers named Mona and Lisa Taylor, part of Wallace's traveling crew, shouted into the microphone. Mona and Lisa were wearing red, white, and blue dresses and silvered hair, two skinny girls who seemed to be trying to remember all the moves the McGuire sisters made on the *Ed Sullivan Show* years before; dentists and beauty shops in Alabama hadn't helped them much, but the crowd didn't care. They were there to stand up for America.

"I been a Democrat all my life," said Ed Higgins, a florid, heavyset plumber, "but this last year I begin to wonder if I been making a mistake. We had Roosevelt; we had Truman; we had President Kennedy. Now we got Johnson. And it still hasn't made a darn bit of difference. Nobody respects anybody anymore. These goddam protesters don't respect nobody. They want people just to give them things. They don't want to earn anything. People around the world, they don't respect us anymore either. We been suckers too long, and I think this man can stop that and make people respect us again."

High up behind Ed Higgins, a cop with field glasses stood on the roof of the Betty Day clothing store, watching for people whose lack of respect for George Wallace might lead to murder. In one section, fenced in by Wallace supporters, a group from the Black Students Association carried signs reading: WALLACE IS A RACIST; ONE HITLER WAS ENOUGH; DON'T LET GEORGE DO HIS THING TO EVERYBODY ELSE; SUPPORT WALLACE AND HELP THE BLACK REVOLUTION.

"Look at those animals," said Mary Hearne, a fortyish housewife wearing rimless glasses and a flowered dress. "They always talk about free speech and civil rights, and then they come in here to try to spoil this."

"Are you for Wallace?" she was asked.

"Of course I'm for Wallace. You can't even walk the streets of this country without some black animal robbing or raping you or some of these students with their hair and all causing some kind of trouble. That has to stop."

Such talk was general in this crowd and common to all the crowds Wallace attracted in the next few days. I wanted to find out something about the Wallace people and discovered, of course, that there was little mystery to them. They were my own people, lower middle-class people who worked with their backs and their hands, who paid dues to a union that was remote to them, people who drove a cab or tended bar one night a week to make ends meet, people who went hunting with the boys on vacations, people who handed their infant children to their wives while they applauded the candidate. Most of them seemed to make about $125 a week and were struggling to pay off GI loans on their homes. They told you about a world filled with enemies: Walter Cronkite and Huntley and Brinkley; long-haired protesters and Chinese Communists; the New York *Times,* Fidel Castro, Russians, people with beards, New York, pot smokers, anarchists, pinkos. It's a strange world, filled more with fear than with hate, but containing enough hate to make it dangerous. Most of them say, for example, that they do not hate Negroes; they just wish that Negroes would shut up and go away.

They want change; the America they thought was theirs has become something else in their own lifetime, and they want to go back. Some of them have even been supporters of Robert Kennedy (a phenomenon first noted by Paul Cowan in the *Village Voice*), because they saw him as an agent of change; whatever America is in 1968, they want to change it, and their instincts are true enough to tell them that Humphrey and Nixon will change nothing. So they have rallied to George Wallace, mainly because he says to them that change is simple. Just change the man at the top and we can all return to a year like 1910, when there were harvests in the fall and feasts in the spring, when kids went swimming in the old swimming hole and played baseball and football and respected God, Flag, and Country. Most of all, they want to return to a time in America when you lived in the same house all of your life and knew everybody you would ever care to know on the street where you were born. Dismiss these people as racists and bigots if you will, but you would be a bit too glib. A lot of the people attracted to George Wallace are just people who think America has passed them by, leaving them confused and screwed-up and unhappy.

"There's some days when I get up and read the paper and feel like I'm gonna go out of my goddamn mind," a farm implement salesman named James Quigg told me in Springfield, Missouri. "When is all of this gonna end?"

I didn't know, and he didn't know, and poor Mrs. Hearne in her flowered dress and rimless glasses standing in the public square didn't know either. Mrs. Hearne just seemed certain that if her candidate were elected President, it would all go away.

"This is the greatest country in the world," she was saying. "People used to be happy here. I'm telling you. Maybe in the Depression we didn't have much money, but nobody starved. And we made our own fun. We read books to each other or played Monopoly at night, and once a month we all went to a show. Kids today got too much. They don't do anything for themselves. And ever since this civil rights business started, people have been unhappy."

She turned from me suddenly and started jumping clumsily and waving her small red hands in the air. Wallace had climbed to the speaker's stand, and the square exploded with a huge, somewhat terrifying roar. Wallace placards bobbed in the air; clenched fists shot out at the sky; the band played "Dixie."

And we were awash in defiance and an oddly touching and pathetic kind of hope.

III. THE SPEECH

Everywhere that Wallace went the Speech was sure to go. In Little Rock and Milwaukee, in Springfield, Illinois, and Springfield, Missouri, in Cincinnati and Charleston. Only a phrase or two would change, and only the audiences were different. Wallace would stand before a cluster of microphones and cameras, his hands shifting from one pocket to another or stabbing the air for emphasis, and the Speech would come rolling out—cocky, defiant, loaded with innuendo, sarcasm, and country humor. The audiences were almost always filled with His People, and they would sing the national anthem and recite the Lord's Prayer and fill the plastic boaters with dollar bills when the Wallace girls came around, and some even signed the automated pledges for larger amounts which would be billed to them long after the candidate had left town, even after his campaign had been settled forever at the ballot boxes. But they were willing to give, because they were true believers and because when that was settled, they could hear the Speech.

"I want to talk to yawl about dissent," Wallace says. "I believe in dissent. I myself am a dissenter. I agree with the right to oppose the war in Vietnam and the right of dissent." The audience is quiet, unsure of what's coming. "But I do not agree with your right to advocate and work for a Communist victory in Vietnam! There's a difference between dissent and treason! [Roar from the Crowd] And any good cabdriver here in Springfield [Milwaukee, Columbia, Charleston] knows that! [Big-Roar] So I promise you when I'm elected President and someone waves a Vietcong flag or raises blood, money, or other things for the enemy, we're gonna throw him under a good jail someplace!"

To visitors freshly arrived, his views on Vietnam seem surprising; the popular image of Wallace, at least in the east, would lead one to believe that he is a super hawk who is fully prepared to unload the hydrogen bomb on the yellow vermin of Southeast Asia. But he actually says something quite different.

"Now about Vietnam," he says, "I don't think we should have gone in there alone in the first place. We should have gone to our Western European allies and the non-Communist nations of Southeast Asia, and if we decided to go in there at all, we should have told them we would not carry the military and economic burden alone. That they would have to share equally, and if they were still not interested, I would cut off every dime of foreign aid and make them pay back every cent they owe us datin' back to World War One. [Big Applause] So I would go to the Joint Chiefs of Staff, and I would ask them, 'Can we win this war with conventional weapons?' And if they said yes, I would make full use of this country's conventional weapons to quickly end this war and bring our boys home." This always brings a roar from the crowd. Wallace never says what he would do if the Joint Chiefs told him the war was not winnable with conventional weapons. Some of his aides say that he would pull out "and the hell with it."

A lot of what he says on other issues is reasonably mild. Even on law and order (or as he says it, "Lawn Awduh"): "The other two candidates—before the conventions I used to say they wasn't a dime' worth a difference between 'em, especially on Lawn Awduh. Now I say they's not a dime' worth a difference between them and me . . . and I'm the original!" Wallace is against increased welfare spending and poverty programs which he feels are essentially used to bribe slum dwellers. But he is also against creating a national police force. "I said face-tiously that we oughta turn the country over to the police for two years," he will say. "Well, you all know what I mean. I mean that we should give the police and firemen just two years of being able to enforce the law, without the Supreme Court standin' on their necks, and we could straighten this country out. We don't need new laws. All y'have to do is enforce the laws you got and if they [Read Blacks] don't obey them, then throw them under a good jail someplace." This always brings a roar, and he follows it this way: "You know, if you were to be mugged or beaten or molested on the way home from heah to-night, the person that did it to you would be free before you got to the hospital. [Laughter] And on Monday they'd be charging some policeman with a crime!"

Wallace reserves his most withering scorn for those members of the federal bureaucracy who are charged with enforcing fed-eral guidelines on desegregation, open housing, and equal op-portunities. These are the guideline writers, a contemptuous breed of Americans who are only slightly worse than their allies in perfidy, the pointed heads Who Can't Park a Bicycle Straight. These people have clogged the country's laws with so much bureaucratic verbiage that "the anarchists and sedition-ists" have been running amok on the streets of America.

"Ramsey Clark doesn't have enough time to weed out the anarchists and the seditionists," Wallace says, "because he's too busy running around the country enforcing these guidelines. They got guidelines that tell you when to get up in the mornin' and when to go to bed at night. [Laughter] We're stranglin' on guidelines. And you know who writes the guidelines? Some pointy-head who can't park a bicycle straight. They all come from the multimillion-dollar tax-exempt foundations. I'm talkin' about Rockefeller, Ford, Carnegie, and Mellon Foundations who are making fortunes on tax loopholes, while the little man is bangin' his head against the wall tryin' to pay his taxes. When I'm elected President, we're gonna close those loopholes and we're gonna ask the Congress to raise the individual tax exemption from six hundred dollars to a thousand dollars." This brings a big round of applause, especially from the tired inhabitants of the not-very-posh suburbs who might literally be going crazy trying to pay taxes. Wallace follows up with the fate awaiting the guideline writers under the Wallace administration:

"You know, these guideline writers go around the country with their briefcases filled with guidelines havin' themselves a good ol' time. But when I'm elected President, I'm gonna recall all them guideline writers and take their briefcases and throw them in the Potomac! [Big Roar of Laughter and Applause] And then I'm going to send them all out to private industry and have them do some honest work for a change!"

That's pretty much it. On the surface, at least, Wallace is just another descendant of the old Southern populist tradition: anti-big government, anti-Establishment. It is a position that has always had its touch of paranoia, and in Wallace's case the paranoia comes out in deep suspicion about the press (especially the Washington *Post,* the New York *Times,* and the Baltimore *Sun*) and a severe case of anti-intellectualism. But this should not be very surprising; at this point in 1968, George Wallace probably expresses the deepest sentiments of the majority of Americans a hell of a lot more than does Eugene McCarthy or, for that matter, Humphrey and Nixon. Wallace and the black and radical militants also share some common ground: local control of schools and institutions, a desire to radically change America, a violent distrust of the power structure and the Establishment.

311

In this year's election, the only one of the three major candidates who is a true radical is George Wallace. "There's more of us," he tells every audience, "than there are of them." And, of course he's right.

The only problem, of course, is that the masses, those cabdrivers, beauticians, steelworkers, ironworkers, and construction men so beautifully romanticized by generations of dreamy socialists, are really an ugly bunch of people. If the campaign of George Wallace has its ugly and racist aspects, it is because George Wallace is the creation of the people.

IV. ENVOI

There was a night in Milwaukee when the good white lower-middle-class burghers came out by the thousands to see ol' George at the auditorium. They came as if it were a church social: well-scrubbed, smelling of underarm spray, the girls wearing their skirts longer than in any other town in America. There were children and old people among them, but there were also a lot of the urban young. These were not the kids who worked for Kennedy and McCarthy, and they certainly weren't the kind of kids who become hippies. They were street kids, tough street kids, who drink beer every Friday and Saturday night and get their muscles off in lieu of their rocks by beating each other senseless on the sidewalks or in the cafeterias when the saloons close. They were carrying Confederate flags and Wallace hats, and if you are given to writing sonnets about how youth will save us all, I wish you had seen them there that night.

Just before Wallace arrived, while the band was playing "Your Cheatin' Heart," a group of Father James Groppi's NAACP commandos and their followers came into the hall. The place shook with boos and jeers.

"Out, you black bastards, out," some of the finer young Wallace men shouted. A few white girls from Marquette University were with the commandos, and the Wallace men yelled, "Can't you get any white cock, baby? Those boogies must do you real fine." About ten of the commando girls started dancing on chairs, while the rest stomped the wooden floors and clapped their hands, and one beery Wallace kid started slamming his folding chair, groaning: "Niggers! These goddamn niggers!" He looked as if he would cry.

The MC asked everybody to stand up, and they all started singing the national anthem. The commandos kept clapping. Then the MC called for the Lord's Prayer before the pitch for funds, but the commandos stayed on the attack.

"Oh, Jesus, those black bastards," one of the young Wallace men said. "They don't even have no respect for God."

Still it went on, and you hoped that Wallace would soften the Speech, that he wouldn't talk much about Lawn Awduh or running over an anarchist with your car; you thought, if he did that, if he eased off, then there might be some secret place in his character where responsibility still lived. If he made the Speech intact, there could be dead people in the auditorium before the evening was over.

But Wallace was implacable.

". . . I tell you that when I'm elected President, and some anarchist lies down in front of my car . . . it'll be the last car he'll ever lie down in front of. . . ." The place roared. The young Wallace thugs started moving toward the commandos and down from the side mezzanines, and then suddenly it was over. Father Groppi led his group out, calmly and orderly. "We made our point," he said. "We wanted to make the point that everyone in America doesn't buy Wallace's racist garbage. It was a useful evening."

And as Groppi and his people marched out, the audience stood and booed and cursed and yelled about niggers and tramps and other things. You wished that Groppi was right about America, but after all we've gone through these past few years it is more likely that the people shouting filth and abuse were the real America. Ladies with flowered dresses, confused salesmen, men eating sardines and crackers late at night in bad saloons: all of them lusting for some terrible vengeance, some bloody catharsis that would make everything the way they think it once was in this country. George Wallace is not the cause of the disease; he is only a symptom. And before this year is out, we might discover just how much company we have in the cages of the damned.

October 26, 1968

Richard the Third-Rate

The features had not changed much in eight years. The face had made its deal with the man who wore it, and the nose and the plastic teeth and the neat ears had ceased all struggle to become something else. Only the jowls seemed different—trimmer, devoid of their earlier sickbed blueness.

The key to how much Richard Nixon has changed, how much he has managed to control his own vagrant passions in eight years, lay in his eyes. Once those eyes would glitter in dark panic when someone refused his proffered hand, when Eisenhower's pink skull nodded in command, or when he first saw Jack Kennedy stride across the floor of a television studio. In 1960, the eyes revealed fear and unease and ill-disguised envy.

That was behind him now as he stood in the chill autumn brightness of a Nassau County afternoon. The eyes betray nothing today, and neither does Nixon. He is no longer from any special place, from neither California nor New York nor even Washington. He inhabits the country of politics. And on this afternoon the button eyes were searching the far reaches of the crowd, counting perhaps, while the mouth stretched into a series of toothy horizontals and the hands shot up into a triumphant V. "Thank you, my friends, thank you. . . ." The serene voice came from some distance, dripping with confidence and triumph and self-righteousness.

Richard Nixon stood there on that platform with the defeated shell of Nelson Rockefeller beside him, a lily-white sea of strangers cheering, and you knew that Richard Nixon's candidacy, his style, his rhetoric and his very life were a masterpiece of schlock.

I suppose we have had nothing like him since Warren Harding. Nixon had been going around the country these past weeks talking and talking and talking and saying nothing, badly. Every time he talked and said something emptily and badly the American people cheered, and his rating in the polls rose. He knew that nothing he said could really matter to the people who were listening to him. He needed no masterpiece of prose, no daring issue, nothing that might disturb a Midwestern editorial writer. He just had to be there to be cheered by people who do not truly love him, but who at least respect the telling quality of great schlock art, its ability to endure. For Nixon had discovered the one great secret about America. It was a first-class nation with a third-rate people, and he was the champion of the third-rate. Jack Kennedy had taught him that lesson about himself—that he was third-rate—and he no longer cared.

". . . and here's the man who's going to unify the country," said Nelson Rockefeller. Nixon stepped to the microphone. You could hear them all cheering from the corners of the shopping center and you could remember all the other times you have seen him performing the same routine. The times had caught up with him. There is no new Nixon; there is only a new America. And it doesn't care much anymore about excellence or justice or the rights of human beings. It just wants things to be quiet.

"This administration has set a record for striking out for America in the last four years," Nixon was saying. "They have struck out on peace abroad. They have struck out on peace at home. They have struck out on stopping the rise of crime. They have struck out on stopping the rise in prices. . . . [Cheers, Applause, Rockefeller's Crafty Grin] They've been up at bat long enough. I say let us get up and we'll hit a home run!"

That's it. Baseball and a shopping center on Saturday afternoon and the plea for help from Decent America. Nixon gets that in at every stop, the pitch to all those Decent Americans who don't riot or picket or take drugs or call the cops "pigs" or complain or burn draft cards. They wash their cars on Saturdays and respect the flag and pay their bills and live in the suburbs. At night they watch TV in their undershirts, and they think Richard Nixon is just fine.

"What do you think of all the things Nixon did in the old days?" one of them was asked, a man who was standing at the edge of the crowd carrying a NIXON IS THE ONE sign.

"What things?"

"Well, Alger Hiss and Helen Gahagan Douglas and the rest."

315

"Never heard of them," he said. "He was Eisenhower's Vice President; he knows what he's doing."

The Nixon fan was thirty-three years old, and he was a chemical engineer. To millions of people his age, the old tawdry Nixon has no meaning at all. He is one of those millions who, in a Chicago delegate's phrase, "can't remember the bad Nixon and can't remember the good Humphrey." He is just Richard Nixon, intoning warnings about the decay of the Republic, the permissiveness of the society, and the need for a new home run hitter.

For many of us, Nixon has been with us forever: slandering Helen Gahagan Douglas, hounding Alger Hiss with the grim ferocity of a Protestant Savonarola, linking Hiss to Adlai Stevenson, and intimating that Stevenson, Truman, and Acheson were "traitors." He was always doing something in those years that seemed at least vaguely disgraceful, like taking $18,000 from a group of California businessmen and then going on television to talk about his wife's "Republican cloth coat." He was Joe McCarthy's friend and the hatchet man in Eisenhower's two campaigns, which were among the most vicious campaigns of this century (because of Eisenhower, not Nixon). Nixon was everywhere: getting spat on in Caracas, going through a silly platitude contest with Khrushchev in that kitchen in Moscow, talking in the TV debates with Kennedy about the "bad language" that Harry Truman had used about the Republicans and Jack Kennedy cutting him dead with a smile. He lost the election without grace, although only by 113,000 votes, and then he lost again in the California gubernatorial race of 1962.

Finally, there was the famous press conference when we all thought he must have been flipping out or half in the bag, and all the columns said that he was politically dead. And then the long, slow comeback, building the organization he had never had, enduring the trials of the rubber chicken circuit and all the mushy garrulity which one must live with in the company of Republicans.

Along the way he learned some secrets about America and particularly about the Republican Party. In San Francisco in 1964, when the rank and file booed Rockefeller and nominated Goldwater, Nixon discovered that Republicans were really just

316

bigots of the country-club variety. They respected money and success and despised failure. They wanted the trains to run on time, and you did not have to promise them much to excite their passions. But it was absolutely necessary to be successful.

So Nixon ran after success in private life with the same rigid determination he had shown in the early years of his public career. He joined the New York law firm of Mudge, Stern, Baldwin and Todd and helped pull that old but sagging concern out of the doldrums. The rubber chickens came back to roost as clients and the firm started to boom.

Almost from the beginning Nixon prospered. Fletcher Knebel of *Look* magazine reported that Nixon's tax returns from 1963 to 1966 showed an average gross income of $200,000, about three-quarters of it from the law firm and the rest from royalties, speeches, real estate, and investments. He moved into a twelve-room apartment at 810 Fifth Avenue in Manhattan, a co-op that cost $135,000 to purchase and about $10,000 a year to maintain.

By the time he arrived on the podium in Miami Beach this year money had cured him of his old terrors. He had never believed very much in anything, and during those years when most men's personalities and viewpoints are being formed, he was in Washington. Nixon had done what Hubert Humphrey was also doing in the years after 1960. He had paid those dues which a politician must pay to go after any real power: to party chairmen in a thousand counties across the nation, as well as to the fat cats in the party's national structure.

But Nixon had always been an empty man, so the process only changed him for the better, adding ease and comfort and a kind of dull confidence to his exterior. After the assassination of Robert Kennedy, he understood that the Presidency was his for the taking. In such a contest he knew that the American people would always take the safe-looking man.

So there is little to discuss about traveling with Nixon. He already travels like a President, with his own party and a group of pool reporters on one plane and the scriveners of the press in separate planes behind him. He does nothing that is not calculated. Every stump speech is the same as every previous stump speech: the need for law and order, the need for peace, blah,

317

blah, blah. He assures his audiences that there is nothing wrong with them, that they really shouldn't believe what the intellectuals and the media and the other knockers are telling them about themselves.

"There is a growing attitude," he will say, "that many opinion molders, community spokesmen, and political leaders are promulgating, that each person has a right to decide what laws are good and what laws are bad and that he should break the laws he doesn't like and obey the laws he does like. This kind of attitude is one which inevitably creates a tendency toward lawlessness across the country. The role of poverty as a cause of the upsurge of lawlessness in America has been grossly exaggerated. If the conviction rate was doubled in this country it would do more to eliminate crime than a quadrupling of the funds of any governmental war on poverty. . . ."

Some of Nixon's eastern defenders say that his alliance with Strom Thurmond and his choice of Spiro T. Agnew were just exercises in practical politics, that he is not really like that. But there is nothing in the record to support such wishful thinking. Nixon is a rightist. Not the Birch Society type—he has publicly attacked the Birchers—but the country-club type. He is one of those soft children who think you can always win by talking tough and you will never really have to fight very hard. He has played the law-and-order bit with the same innuendo-filled approach as George Wallace. His program for "peace and tranquillity" would give direct block grants to the states for enlargement of police forces. He would pass strong wiretapping bills for government use only, pass legislation to overrule Supreme Court judgments, such as the Miranda and Escobedo decisions on confessions, fire college faculty members who aid or abet rioters, expel student rioters and ban their organizations from the campuses.

He doesn't say much about Vietnam, claiming that he does not want to imperil the peace talks in Paris; more likely it is because he senses that Americans are tired of the war, tired of talking about it or hearing about it or even seeing it on TV. He might have a better chance of ending the war than Hubert does, but his past record of Johnson-like vanity and anti-Communist paranoia does not afford much hope. It was, after all, Richard

Nixon who said in Saigon in 1964, "There is no substitute for victory in South Vietnam."

There is no hope either that Nixon will do anything at all to repair the various ruptures that have occurred in recent years. It seems unlikely that he will move to normalize our relations with Cuba, since the chairman of the Cuban Americans for Nixon Committee is Dr. Emilio Nuñez-Portuondo. The Nixon people have proudly described Portuondo's ties with the UN and his father's role at the time of the Declaration of Independence from Spain. They don't mention that he was Batista's Foreign Minister, one of the brains of the pre-Castro government and a founder of the White Rose, a counterrevolutionary organization composed almost entirely of former Batista police and army officers.

Among those serving on Nixon's committee of economic advisers are Robert T. Stevens and Roger Milliken, two of the most antiunion businessmen in the country. Milliken, head of the Deering Milliken Corporation, closed his Darlington, South Carolina, manufacturing company plant in 1956 because its 550 employees voted to join the Textile Workers Union of America. Stevens has been waging a five-year battle against unions which have tried to organize his J. P. Stevens & Company, Incorporated. At latest count, 111 former Stevens employees were still out of work because of their union activities.

Nixon's panel of Republican Congressmen, who are charged with advising him on major policies, are almost entirely members of the conservative wing. They include Senators Tower, Texas; Baker, Tennessee; Hruska, Nebraska; Mundt, South Dakota, and Representatives Arends, Illinois; MacGregor, Minnesota; May, Washington; and Morton, Maryland. All but one of these men voted against the Economic Opportunity Act of 1964. All voted against the Appalachian development program. All but two voted against the antipoverty program in 1965. Three voted to kill the program in 1966, and six asked for reduced appropriations in 1968. It goes on.

Yet there should be little surprise if Richard Nixon is the next President of the United States. He is the candidate with whom the most people would feel the most comfortable. He is a man with no beliefs, no private life of any mystery or gaudiness, a man who is beyond roots, beyond true passion, a convenient cipher whom millions of people seem determined to choose as President. He is the best symbol we now possess of all the terrible things that have happened to us in the past five years. We have passed so much time in the company of hate, we have committed so many foul and unholy acts, that as a nation we no longer care what anyone else thinks about us. We are at last shameless and alone like Richard Nixon.

November 17, 1968

VI. Fighters

I N some important ways, prizefighters are the best people I know. They make their living with controlled violence, and yet they are the gentlest of men. It is as if the violence had been hammered out of them, as if men so completely involved with receiving and administering pain were not interested in using it to prove their *machismo* or to settle arguments. There have been bullies who called themselves prizefighters, but they were usually not very good in the ring. If we look at those who send young people out to fight wars, they are usually people who have had little experience with war itself. Lyndon Johnson flew one combat mission, was fired at, and ran back to Washington. Hubert Humphrey never served, and neither did Mendel Rivers. Richard Nixon was a glorified supply clerk. It seems to work that way with street violence; the people with the biggest mouths generally can't fight. Prizefighters, who know about fighting, are quiet and casual and never look for trouble.

José Torres is one of my three closest friends. He won the fight with Wayne Thornton, referred to in the following article, beating Thornton so badly with body punches that he was bleeding for two weeks afterward and had to retire from boxing. José defended his title three more times, then lost it in a close decision to Dick Tiger. He fought Tiger again, lost an even closer decision, and a riot followed. He fought twice more, scoring knockouts, but in his last fight, he was knocked down by a fighter named Charlie Green, who once was his sparring partner. He got up and knocked out Charlie, but that was the end of it. He retired the next day, and now writes an excellent weekly political column for the New York *Post*. He'll probably end up in Congress.

When I went to interview Patterson, he was making a comeback against Eddie Machen. He beat Machen and kept fighting, losing a title fight to Muhammad Ali, then losing a disputed decision to Jimmy Ellis in Sweden, in a fight which everyone thought he won. He retired for a few years, but as I write, he is embarked on a comeback and has won three straight knockouts. We remain friends, but I wish he would quit.

I never did find out what happened to Toluco.

The Lost Hero

The first time I ever saw him practice his craft, I thought José Torres would be the greatest prizefighter of his time. I also thought (with what strikes me now as almost unbelievable innocence) that he would become a hero: an authentic, minted, solid-gold hero, perhaps the last one that the dying sport of boxing would ever have.

That was almost eight years ago. In the years since then Joe and I have become close friends, and he has become the light-heavyweight champion of the world. No one can ever take that from him; it's in the record books, printed in agate type, a permanent testament to the fact that, for a while at least, José Torres was the best 175-pound fighter in the world.

This month he is scheduled to defend his title against Wayne Thornton, the leading contender, and it should be a good fight. It will be held outdoors in Shea Stadium, and there is always a special excitement about an outdoor fight in New York City. Joe has his title, but somehow—perhaps because life is more complicated than a scenario—the rest of my hopes for him didn't work out. Joe became a champion all right. But he never did become a hero.

I first saw Torres one night at the St. Nicholas Arena in the early winter of 1958. I arrived early, bought a balcony ticket, and stood for a long time under the small marquee, watching the Puerto Ricans of New York come up out of the subway at Sixty-sixth Street. The Puerto Ricans never quite look comfortable in New York; their soft Caribbean faces do not blend with the harshness of the city. But this night, despite a driving winter rain, it looked as if New York were their town, that Santurce and San Juan and Caguas were just stops at the other end of the subway lines.

They talked excitedly, rapidly, in their clipped staccato Spanish, their eyes moving quickly at the prospect of the planned violence inside, and you could hear the name over and over and over again. "Torres," they said, "Torres, Torres, Torres."

This was the old music of the fight racket, and it was only appropriate that the Puerto Ricans were making it. There were few nights that belonged to them in the fifties: They were the scorned people of the city. Despite their American citizenship, they were considered immigrants, and they were demeaned because they knew no English, because they were poor, because they inhabited the slums and committed a bit more than their share of the crime. They emptied the city's garbage and swept the city's floors, and for most of them the golden dream of America was just another cynical joke.

And then, like the Jews, the Irish, the Italians before them, they had turned to the fight racket. In the richest city in the richest country on earth they began to bleed for a living. They fought for the same reasons everyone before them had. They wanted passports to the world where waiters called you by your first name, and you drove a long shiny car and kept $300 suits in the closets, and you were loved, and not hated, by strangers.

Before the war they had produced a few good boxers, but since then, there had been only a dreary line of club fighters. Until this night they hadn't seen one of their own who could have been a champion. There were few nights that belonged to the Puerto Ricans that year of 1958, but the night José Torres knocked out Frankie "Kid" Anslem was one of them.

When I walked into the St. Nick, the old arena was throbbing with the kind of excitement I remembered only dimly from evenings during the war, before television killed most of boxing. I smelled wet wool and cigars and men who worked all day with the sweat running down their backs and then drank beer as the sweat dried. Sitting next to me in the $1.50 seats was a small, round-faced man who told me he came from Playa Ponce, Torres' hometown on the south coast of Puerto Rico. We bought each other beers and squinted into the haze toward the dressing room at the far end, waiting, like everyone else in the hall, for Torres to appear. When he did, the place exploded.

"Chegui! Chegui! Chegui!" they chanted, using Torres' nickname (a contraction of José Luis), and as he stamped his feet in the rosin in a neutral corner, he gave a small wave to the crowd.

"*Matalo,* Chegui!" a guy yelled, "Kill him, Chegui!" And Torres, brimming with youth (he was twenty-two) and the knowledge of what he could do, heard him and smiled back. He had a fine smile.

At the bell Torres came out with his hands held high against his face in the peekaboo style made famous by Floyd Patterson (who was then the heavyweight champion and Torres' stablemate). But Torres was no copy of anyone. Like Patterson he was essentially a counterpuncher, making his man miss and reacting with volleys of punches. But his hands were even faster than Patterson's, his jab was a punch, not a flick (Patterson seldom used the jab anyway), and even more important, he had a sense of the dramatic that the heavyweight champion lacked. Torres was not only interested in winning; he wanted to win spectacularly.

So Torres used the pauses in a fight the way some jazz musicians use silence—to heighten an effect. He would be moving slowly, controlling the rhythm of the fight, punching lightly, intimidating Anslem with shoulder feints, and then—suddenly, dramatically—his hands would lash out, in three-, four-, and five-punch combinations, startling the crowd, bringing the fans to their feet, making them scream for more.

In the ninth round Torres unleashed a five-punch combination that ended with a hammering left hook to the jaw, and as the referee counted Anslem out, the guy next to me hugged me in joy and shouted in Spanish that José Torres, a boy from *his* hometown, would be the next middleweight champion of the world.

The Puerto Ricans were proud to be Puerto Ricans that night, and as we streamed out into the street, I saw an old man with snowy mustaches reach up and pull down a fight poster from the wall, rolling it in his hands as he pushed through the crowd, tears streaming down his seamed face. It was as if we had not been in the St. Nick at all; we were really on a sound stage in Hollywood and it was *Golden Boy* all over again, and in a year we would all march through Yankee Stadium on a night thick with summer and triumph and tell each other that we had seen the newly crowned middleweight champion of the world back when he had won his eighth professional fight.

It was all too neat, though, all too simple. For José Torres it didn't work out that way at all.

He boxed once more at the St. Nick, knocking out a Canadian light-heavyweight named Burke Emery. He fought a few times in Sunnyside Gardens, won the semifinal to the first Patterson-Johansson fight the following summer, and then disappeared from New York. I read in the Spanish-language papers that he fought a draw with Benny "Kid" Paret in San Juan, that he decisioned Randy Sandy in New Jersey, and then he dropped from sight completely. The hero had vanished; the excitement had ebbed; José Torres was the champion of nothing.

I was a newspaper reporter in 1960, working the city side for the New York *Post*, and I had forgotten about Torres until one night when I was drinking beer with some friends at a bar in Brooklyn.

"Hey," someone said, "whatever happened to that guy, the middleweight? You know, the guy fought just like Patterson, only better?"

"Torres?"

"Torres, yeah. Torres. José Torres. Whatever happened to him?"

No one could say. I don't remember much of the rest of that night's conversation, but all that weekend I kept wondering about Torres. On Monday afternoon I decided to go down to Fourteenth Street to visit the Gramercy Gym, where Torres trained, to see what had happened to the lost hero.

I found the entrance of the gym at the right of a tiny open-front candy store and climbed the two flights of squeaking wooden stairs. Torres was at the side of the ring. He was wearing a blue sweat shirt and black trunks, and he was having his hands taped. I introduced myself.

"Hey," he said, "man, you're the first newspaperman I seen in a year and a half. Stay here. Don't move. We talk when I'm through."

Torres seemed older than I had remembered, with thicker features, a flatter, broader nose, heavier through the body. He had grown a thin, wispy mustache. In the ring he looked as good as he ever had. Snorting, he threw punches with speed and variety, shifting from body to head and back, handling his big, heavyweight sparring partner as if he were a welterweight.

He was being trained then by a perceptive young man named Joe Fariello. When Joe came down to the floor to work the heavy bag, I walked over to Fariello, introduced myself and told him that Torres looked fine.

"Pete," he said, "this guy isn't the fighter he was. Can't you see it?"

I told Fariello that Torres still looked to me like one of the best middleweights around. Fariello shook his head. He could see that Torres had lost something that was not apparent to me or to the young fighters in the gym who were watching Joe with admiration. To Fariello, he just was not the fighter he had been.

After the workout, Torres and I went into the dressing room, and he talked in grammatical but thickly accented English. Yes, he said, he had been inactive now for a long time. He had been training now for a month, but not very hard. There were no fights coming up.

"Why not?" I asked. I couldn't believe that no promoters wanted to use the fighter who had been the hottest New York boxing attraction since Rocky Graziano.

"Cus," Joe said. He said it simply, undramatically, as if it were a commonplace. "Man," he said, pulling on a pair of sharply creased gray trousers, "this is a complicated SOB."

He certainly was. Cus was Cus D'Amato, Torres' manager, close friend, and admirer and one of the most controversial men in boxing. For years he had run the Gramercy Gym, handling amateur fighters and about a dozen professionals. Most of the latter happened to be deaf and dumb, and he was thought of as a kind of freak, "the Deaf and Dumb Manager." Then in 1948 a young kid named Floyd Patterson climbed the two flights to the Gramercy Gym. He was the kind of kid every manager dreams of, a kid who could win the heavyweight championship of the world. And that was the way it had worked out.

But Cus had become much more than a fight manager. He saw himself as the savior of the fight racket, which he claimed had fallen into the hands of television, hoodlums, and the International Boxing Club. D'Amato began feuding with just about everyone in boxing, and in the long, terribly complicated aftermath he seldom let Patterson fight. Because Torres was part of D'Amato's stable, he had been hurt by the feuds. D'Amato would not let him take the fights he desperately needed to mature as a boxer.

Joe and I left the gym together, and as we walked along Fourteenth Street, Puerto Ricans of all ages stopped to talk to him. They were obviously fond of him, but also wondering and puzzled—as I was—about his inactivity. "*Ola,* Chegui, when you gonna fight, man?" "Soon, soon," he said, "it will be in the papers. Look in *El Diario.*" But Torres didn't seem to believe what he was saying.

"Come on," Joe said, breaking away from a small knot of Puerto Ricans and heading for the subway. "We'll go to *El Barrio.*"

El Barrio means the Neighborhood, and for New York's Puerto Ricans it is equivalent to the Lower East Side for the Jews and the West Side docks for the Irish; it is where the strangers in a big town can feel at ease among their own. It is a huge slum, running roughly from 96th Street to 130th Street, and from Fifth Avenue to the East River, with isolated pockets of Italians and Jews scattered in between. Puerto Ricans had been living there for thirty years, and when the great postwar migration began, most of the newcomers went to *El Barrio* first. Walking its streets, you realize how much of a Latin-American city New York has become: *Bodegas* (grocery stores) stand hard by the offices of *abogados* (lawyers), and bars sell *cerveza* (beer). We stopped at a small open-front store under the Park Avenue railroad tracks and ate *chicharrones* (cracklings) while Torres talked about his life.

He was born on May 3, 1936, in Playa Ponce, Puerto Rico, the second of seven children, and he had started fighting in the streets. "Every time there was a fight," his older brother Andres told me later, "we knew it was Chegui. He loved to fight, and the bigger the guy the better he was."

José started boxing with gloves after he went into the Army in 1954. "Man," he said, "I hated the Army. I got flat feet, you know, since I was a kid, and when we went out on those marches, I always felt like I just walked from Korea. I heard I could get out of that stuff if I start—start*ed*—boxing, so I did. We also got better food, and I could save my money that I was paying in the cafeteria to stay alive. With the money I save, I pay off the guys who need money so I don't have to stand any watches either." Torres started laughing. "Oh, man, I was a *bad* guy!"

Torres went on to win a flock of Army titles, including the All-Army championship, and later, after his discharge, most of the other amateur titles. He lost only one fight in the amateurs, in the finals of the 1956 Olympics in Melbourne. And as a pro, his record was even better.

"You know what's funny?" Torres said to me that first day. "I'm twenty-four, I never lost a professional fight, and now I'm starting my comeback. It doesn't make much sense, does it?"

After that afternoon Joe and I became friends. We were about the same age, both single, and we ran the night side together—to places like the Broadway Casino and the Caborrojeno Club in the Bronx, to dance halls where the pachanga and the mambo blared into the night, and the great gold-skinned girls, dancing big-hipped and saucy, kept all of us awake as long as we had hours to squander. Joe neither drank nor smoked (and still doesn't), but his hours were erratic. "If I have a fight, I train," he would say. "If I don't, the hell with it." For Joe there were too many laughs to be had and girls to meet and dances to dance to worry much about other things.

Joe was then engaged to a girl named Ramona Ortiz, a plump, soft-spoken girl who lived with her mother on Smith Street in Brooklyn. They had been engaged for six years when I met Joe, and it looked as though it would be a long engagement. One Sunday, when we all were at her house for dinner, she took me aside. "Pete," she said, "what does Joe tell you? When do we get married? I can't wait forever, you know."

"Joe said he wants to get married next year," I lied. "Just as soon as he gets some money."

"But how will he get some money," she said, "if he never fights?"

I couldn't answer that one.

D'Amato was holding Torres back for a lot of complicated,

personal reasons that I don't believe anyone really understood, but to the public it was beginning to look as though Joe was afraid to get into the ring. They began calling him a coward. Joe was sick over the accusations. "How can I show I got heart if I don't ever get any fights?" he asked me.

The weeks became months, the months stretched into almost a year without a fight, and then Joe called me one morning. "Pete," he said, "I got a fight." "I don't believe it," I said. I asked him where and with whom. "Puerto Rico," Joe said, and then he started laughing hysterically. "With . . . Gene Hamilton!"

Joe had fought Gene Hamilton before. He had fought him, in fact, in his first professional fight, knocking him out in one round. Hamilton had not improved much since then. He had not won a single fight in his last eleven.

I went to the fight, which was held at night in the Ponce ball park, and it was even worse than I had expected. Joe carried Hamilton for a few rounds, but the referee stopped it in the fourth, and the small crowd booed. Some friends of mine across the ring asked me what had happened to the great fighter I was touting. I couldn't answer. I knew that *I* could beat Gene Hamilton. All I could think was that Joe was back in the amateurs.

The next day Torres and I took a walk along the beach. There was a threat of rain, and we sat for a long time in a breezy waterfront bar. A kid came in selling the San Juan papers, but Joe didn't want to read them. He stared at his soda, talking very softly. "Pete, this isn't what it's supposed to be like," he said. "After last night I feel like quitting. Get a job. Drive a truck, anything. I feel like a bum."

"What the hell, Joe," I said.

"But, Pete, this is my town. This is the first time I ever fought here. And it's like last night. That was a disgrace."

"Don't worry about it, Joe," I said. "It will come out all right. Just don't worry."

It was raining lightly as we walked back. A girl in a starched white dress smiled at Joe as we passed her. He kicked a tin can down the empty street. He never saw the girl.

Torres and I became closer friends in the next year. D'Amato began letting him have a few fights in places like Boston, Houston, Elizabeth, New Jersey. I had a small apartment on the Lower East Side, and after a while Joe moved in because it was easier to get to the gym from there. He began to work his way through my library. That first year he read all of Hemingway, some of Conrad, *The Brothers Karamazov, The Great Gatsby.* He started helping me on assignments, a newspaper series on *El Barrio* and drug addicts and the boardinghouses of the West Side, and I started helping him to learn the craft of writing. Manolo Rodriguez, the sports editor of *El Diario*, encouraged him too, and one morning Joe came in with ten copies of the paper.

"Look at this," Joe said. There was a story about Puerto Rican migrant farmers in New Jersey, and the byline was "por José Luis (Chegui) Torres." He kept writing for the paper on a sporadic basis after that, and Manolo told me that he was good enough to work as a professional.

One night we went to a party on Atlantic Avenue in Brooklyn, a house party celebrating the birth of someone's son. The music was punishingly loud, the bathtub stacked with iced beer, and there was a roomful of good-looking girls. The word got around that Joe was a prizefighter. And for some reason, probably because I was fatter than Joe, they thought I was a wrestler. Joe began to introduce me as Count Erik von Hamill and told the girls that I had once annihilated twenty-three Chinamen in Singapore and had followed that up by challenging him. "When I beat him," Joe said, "we became friends."

The girls listened in awe. As the night went on, Torres and I both started eying a young girl in a beige dress, who was accompanied by her mother. "Her mother is a dragon," Torres said, "but, oh, man, look at *her!*"

"Come on, Torres," I said, "you're engaged. You're in training. You're the idol of the Puerto Ricans and all that. Do you have to have all the broads in the world?"

"Oh, man, look at her do that mambo!"

"Joe! Stop. Go into the kitchen and say ten Hail Marys and come back."

"Oh, *man!*"

"Joe! Get me a beer!"

I started dancing with the girl. Her name was Ramona Negron, and a year later I married her.

Meanwhile, Joe and his Ramona finally decided to get married. The wedding was held in a church in Red Hook, and I was one of the ushers. Cus was the best man. The wedding reception was at Cus's new apartment on Fifty-seventh Street. One of the guests was Obdulio Nuñez, a Puerto Rican middleweight who was then rated ninth in the world. I talked a bit with Nuñez. He liked Joe, he said. He was Joe's friend. But underneath the conversation I also felt that Nuñez considered Joe a phony. "Man, he can't keep fighting palookas. The people, they think he can't fight anymore. This Cus is ruining the guy." While Nuñez talked, Joe was standing on a chair, singing, in a light baritone, *"Una Copa Más,"* a drinking song.

Cus kept promising Joe big fights. They mentioned Joey Giambra, Joey Giardello, Chic Calderwood, Willie Pastrano. Something always happened. Cus blamed "my enemies." And Joe kept fighting nonentities. Finally he came to Cus one evening and said that he was going to retire. I was with him.

"Joe, how can you quit when you're this close to victory?" Cus demanded.

"Victory, promises, title shots that don't happen, I heard all that, Cus," Joe said. He was more agitated than I had ever seen him before. "I want to fight. Fighters fight. That's all there is to it. Either I fight good guys, or I quit."

"Joe, what the hell happened? Who have you been talking to?"

Joe hadn't been talking to anyone. The night before he and I had gone to the Spanish Golden Gloves at the St. Nicholas Arena to watch some of the fighters from the Gramercy Gym. Halfway through the evening, Torres, along with some other fighters, was called to the ring to be introduced. And then the chant started. *"Cobarde! Cobarde! Cobarde! Cobarde!"* In the St. Nick, where Joe had had his biggest nights, he was having his worst. He was being called a coward in public. He left the place in tears.

Cus finally agreed to make some matches with name opponents. "I think you've finally become mature," he told Joe.

Joe's first big comeback fight was against his friend Obdulio Nuñez for the Puerto Rican middleweight championship. In the seventh round Joe hit Nuñez with a vicious right hand to the jaw. He was out for seventeen minutes. It had been Joe's best fight in a couple of years.

Then Joe signed to fight in Puerto Rico against Florentino Fernández, a broad-shouldered Cuban who was a murderous puncher with a left hook. Florentino had gone fifteen rounds with Gene Fullmer and almost had the NBA champion out in the last round before losing a decision.

I couldn't get away from New York that week. The night of the fight I stayed home, waiting for Joe's call. He always called when he was fighting out of town. The phone rang a little after one.

"Pete," he said, "I got knocked out."

"Knocked out?" I couldn't believe it.

"Yeah, in five rounds. The referee stop the fight. I'm sorry, Pete."

"Joe," I said, "you don't have to be sorry for anything."

A week later I saw the films of the fight. Florentino caught Joe in the first round with his hands down, and Joe never got over the punch. He took a fierce beating for the rest of the fight, until the referee stopped it, with Joe still on his feet against the ropes. I never worried about Joe's heart again.

I went to Europe the following September and worked there for fourteen months. Joe started fighting again. In a letter he told me that now he would fight no more bums, "because I have to find out once and for all whether I am really a fighter or a fraud." He won decisions over Don Fullmer, Wilbert McClure, José Gonzalez, and Gomeo Brennan, all good fighters.

He was also getting friendly with Norman Mailer, who had come up to the gym with me one day. Joe was impressed with Mailer, and Mailer was impressed with Joe. "He's really not like Patterson at all," Mailer said to me one night, after I had returned from Europe. "He's really one of us. He's alive."

Torres had changed in the year I was away. He met me at the plane and drove me to a restaurant in Bedford-Stuyvesant, telling me all the time what had happened since I'd left. Although he still was friendly with D'Amato, Torres had acquired a money man, a Brooklyn real estate operator named Cain Young. I went with Joe the next morning to see Young at his office in Bedford-Stuyvesant. Young, a dark-skinned Negro with horn-rimmed glasses, was a bit frosty and distant. He called Torres "José" and Joe called him "Mr. Young." Mr. Young liked to talk about money. He had made a lot of it, and occasionally he would preface a story about, say, a promoter, with a remark like, "I don't know how much education *he* has, and I got my degree by going to NYU at nights, but he strikes me as being pretty *dumb*. The people in boxing are just not businessmen."

With Young's backing and D'Amato's approval, Torres decided to move up a class to the light-heavyweights. The middle-weight division was so confused that he doubted that he would ever get a title shot, but light-heavyweight champion Willie Pastrano was ready to fight for money. Torres was first matched with Bobo Olson, who was ranked fourth in the division, although he was about finished as a fighter. Torres knocked him out in one round. Then, suddenly, Torres was signing to fight Pastrano for the light-heavyweight championship of the world, with Cain Young guaranteeing Pastrano $100,000.

Perhaps Joe wasn't the fighter he might have been the night he fought Pastrano last year, but he was good enough. He outjabbed Willie, trapped him in corners, and mauled his stomach. At the end of the second round, after Pastrano had absorbed a savage body beating, Joe was jigging in his corner. He knew he had the fight won. In the sixth round he knocked Pastrano down with a terrible left hook to the kidneys. Three rounds later the referee stopped the fight. The ring was stormed. Mailer got in, and so did a lot of people, leaping over the working press. Torres was carried out on the shoulders of the fans. In the dressing room Cain Young even smiled.

After the fight we all went to Toots Shor's, a promise Joe had made me three years before when we had visited the place and the bartender had looked Joe up and down, as though he doubted he had money. Later we went to a huge party at Mailer's house on the top floor of a brownstone in Brooklyn Heights, overlooking the bay, with the skyline of Manhattan beyond. On this night, it did resemble Truman Capote's "diamond iceberg." The party itself was as good as the fight. A three-piece combo blasted rock 'n' roll; a bartender dispensed whiskey and beer and chile con carne. People like James Baldwin stood next to people like Danny Perez, one of Joe's sparring partners. Torres arrived at two forty-five, dressed in a Chesterfield coat and looking as if he had just left a concert, and people mobbed him, carried along on a wave of talk, cigar smoke, and triumph.

Mailer was elated. He had won $600 on the fight and was determined to spend three times that amount on the party. "He's a champion," Mailer said. "Joe's a champion."

Somewhere around six, Cain Young whisked Joe away. He never had time to say good-bye.

The night after the fight my wife and I went over to visit Torres. "I still can't believe it, Pete," he said. "You know, it's strange. It's like it happened to someone else. I woke up this morning. 'I'm the champion,' I say, 'I'm the champion.' But it doesn't seem right. I was excited. I couldn't go back to sleep. But something strange . . . it still doesn't feel right."

Joe went upstairs to pose with his wife for a photographer, and I sat in the living room with my wife, Young, and Torres' father, who seemed irritated. A couple of days later he was to leave for Puerto Rico ahead of time, "because I can't talk to my son alone." The night of our visit he became more irritated when Young began to talk.

"I'm gonna make thirty thousand dollars for José in the next three weeks," Young said. "I got him the championship, and now I'm gonna make him some money with it. A lot of money. It was me, you know, who advised him to become a light heavyweight. I told him—"

He was starting to talk about how he went to NYU at night when my wife and I got up to leave. Joe said in Spanish that he would call me the next day, and we could talk alone. He had a lot of appointments to keep. "Everyone wants something," he said. "Where the hell were they a couple of years ago?"

For a while after the Pastrano fight, Joe went through the motions of acting like a hero. He went to 110th and Lexington Avenue and sang the Puerto Rican anthem to a crowd of almost 2,000 Puerto Ricans. He walked the streets shaking hands with strangers and buying ice cream for small children. In *El Diario*, the Puerto Ricans of New York read that he was signing to do a radio program, that he had become a public relations man for an airline, that he was going to appear in a series of beer commercials. For a while Joe was earning $2,000 a week on endorsements alone. But still he didn't feel that his life had turned out the way he thought it would.

"There's something wrong," he said to me one night. "I don't know what it is."

I think that in his heart Joe did know what part of the matter was. He had become the champion, but somehow he had never become a hero. Any fighter with some ability, some luck, and a manager with connections could win a championship. And when Torres had finally mastered the politics of boxing, he won his crown. But the momentum had ended long ago, and though Torres was still a fine fighter, he was not the brilliant boy he was that night a long time ago in St. Nick's. That peculiar spontaneity which is the true measure of heroes had been lost somewhere.

In the year after the fight, Torres fought only once, a sluggish ten-round charity fight with heavyweight Tom McNeely, Jr., in San Juan. Joe had trained only eight days for the fight and looked it. The day after the fight he was hospitalized with an infection of the pancreas that kept him in bed for five weeks, and he did not box in a gym again for seven months. By then the radio program was gone, his face had disappeared from the beer posters, the Puerto Ricans were sneering at him again, and because he wasn't defending his title, the boxing commissions were already threatening to take it away from him.

Finally, Torres signed with Wayne Thornton, the No. 1 contender. I suspect that when they fight in Shea Stadium, it will be the best fight of the year, and maybe when it's over, if Joe wins, he will have back a little piece of what he once was. If he loses, he tells me, he will retire.

Not long ago I talked to Joe in his training camp in Hyde Park, New York. It seems incredible that he is thirty now. But the evidence is in everything he does. His eyes are a little sadder, he doesn't laugh as much, and he works in the gym with the fierce concentration of a fighter who has suddenly become an old pro. He looks bigger and stronger than he ever has, and the punches still come in volleys. But now he is a pro working at a trade, and I wish more than anything else that nothing had ever become entangled and life had been simpler for Joe. He boxes for money. He doesn't look at all like the young man who always seemed to be leading his own private parade. Only José Torres knows exactly how much he's lost.

"Remember what it was like, Pete—before?" he told me that day. "You didn't know it, and I didn't know it, but we were kids then. Whoever thought we could run out of girls? Or music? Or laughs? Boy, that was a time!"

He cuffed me distractedly. Then he pulled on a pair of light gloves and went over to punish the heavy bag.

May 21, 1966

Floyd's Fight to Save His Pride

Tiny blisters of sweat broke across Floyd Patterson's brow as he began the daily ritual that has been most of his life for the past fifteen years. Once again he was in an improvised ring in a training camp, and a padded leather helmet was being strapped to his head, his hands were being taped, someone was smearing his face with Vaseline and jamming a white rubber gum shield in his mouth. The big training gloves were pulled on while he gazed out at a roomful of strangers, all waiting to watch him fight. Then the sparring partner was ready, a bell rang, and Floyd Patterson was boxing again.

"When you're training," he said later, "everywhere you go, things are the same: only the names of the places are different."

The name of the place this time was Ronneby, a resort town on the south coast of Sweden, 300 miles from Stockholm, where, on July 5, he will box Eddie Machen in a twelve-round fight that will determine the future of both men.

For Patterson it could be the most important fight of his life, but it has nothing to do with money. In eleven years as a professional, he has grossed $8,000,000 with his fists, and the money left after taxes has been saved or cautiously invested. By most standards he is a rich man and allows himself a few extravagances. He owns and flies an $11,000 Cessna, drives three expensive automobiles, owns a $2,000 motorcycle. He has a $100,000 home in Yonkers, New York (which he is about to sell because of racial incidents involving his daughter) and another home in Rockville Centre, New York. He has set aside money for his four children's education, invested in an integrated housing project with baseball star Jackie Robinson, and bought a piece of a hotel in the Bahamas. For Patterson, the money he can earn from prizefighting is no longer of prime importance. What is important is his pride. He wants to erase the image he fears he will leave behind when he retires: that as heavyweight champion he was an elaborate fraud with no ability to take a punch, a fraud whose true measure could be found in the total of four minutes and sixteen seconds he lasted in two fights with Sonny Liston.

"If I were a wise man," he says, "I would retire now. But I'm not a wise man, I'm like everyone else: I want that one more chance. Just one more. That means fighting Clay, and then Liston again. Then I could retire."

And so Patterson, who was the youngest man ever to win the world's heavyweight title and the only one ever to regain it, was back in a training camp in Sweden. He was boxing a light-heavyweight named Greatest Crawford, moving in the familiar patterns, his hands held high against his face, the jab coming straight, bobbing and weaving under punches, grunting when he threw them himself. To a visitor who had followed his career from the days in the late 1940's when he was the best amateur fighter in the United States, his hands seemed as fast as they always had been, the punches coming in swift volleys, raking the sparring partner's belly, and moving to the head as the crowd gasped. He sparred two rounds and then began the manual labor of boxing: smacking the heavy bag, sweating through sit-ups, turning the tiny speed bag into a staccato blur, being pounded for a round with a medicine ball, skipping rope, and then the day's work was over. The 200 people in the large hall broke into loud applause, shouting, "Welcome, Floyd," and he turned and smiled at them, said good-bye, and walked back into the dressing room.

While Patterson showered, a crowd of almost 500 gathered outside the large, white-frame building, standing in clusters, talking in respectful tones about the former champion, some of them carrying placards welcoming him to Ronneby. For Patterson it is like this all over Sweden. When he walks the streets of big towns like Stockholm and Goteborg, he is besieged by autograph hunters and tailed by photographers; in the small towns like Ronneby, people stop him on the country roads and invite him home for dinner. "You might say I'm a kind of one-man Beatles," he said after signing almost 100 autographs and setting off for a walk in the country. "The thing about Sweden is that they seem to like me for *me,* for Floyd Patterson the man, not just Floyd Patterson the fighter. I got just as warm a welcome here after Liston knocked me out the second time as I did in 1960, when I came here for the first time after beating Ingemar [Johansson]. If they like me in defeat, they must really like me."

Patterson's popularity in Sweden is a unique sports phenomenon. He had lost to, and then soundly thrashed Johansson, the first Swede ever to hold the heavyweight crown. These fights, plus his Olympic victory at Helsinki in 1952, made him a familiar name in Scandinavia. Further, in a perverse switch of loyalty, Swedes who were irked by Johansson's tax-avoiding move to Switzerland quickly became Patterson fans.

Now he was in a borrowed automobile, dressed in a light-blue jacket, gray workman's pants, and heavy black boots, driving the back roads of the Swedish countryside. It was late afternoon, and the slanting rays of the sun broke across fields of heather, and pale washes of green, and small lakes, and Patterson talked easily.

"I love boxing in many ways," he said, "but there are two sides to it, too. There is the bright side where a young boy who has nothing can come along and become famous and earn a lot of money, and that is the good side. But then there is the dark side too." He turned into a main road, leading to the town of Karlskrona, about twelve miles from Ronneby.

"The name that keeps coming back to me is Jimmy Carter," he said. "I trained with him at camp once, when I was just coming up. He was the lightweight champion of the world then, and I was nothing; but Jimmy Carter impressed me as a humble, nice man, and you just couldn't help liking him."

A car came past, and the driver honked at Patterson, smiled, and waved. "Hey," Patterson shouted in reply as he went by. "Well, Jimmy Carter had a beautiful home and a nice wife, and you couldn't tell me that he would end the way he did. The next time I saw him was in Oceanside, California, where I was training for the Roy Harris fight in 1958. I could see right away that something had gone wrong. He had no more family, no home, no money, and he didn't look good. It shook me."

He pulled into Karlskrona, parked the car, and got out. People looked at him and smiled. A middle-aged woman giggled nervously and searched through her purse for a piece of paper he could sign for her. A crowd gathered, and for ten minutes Patterson signed autographs.

"You see," Patterson said, "that's what happens to too many fighters. Boxing gives a hungry youngster something to belong to, it establishes him, it gives him money, it gives him a chance to live with class. It happened that way with me. But ninety-nine out of one hundred who come up from the gutter go back to it. For them, it was all in vain. Some guys just get jobs on the docks, and other guys say, 'Well, I had a taste of the good times.' Is that what it should be? A man works at something for fifteen, twenty years and can only say he has had a *taste?*"

Patterson turned into the main square of Karlskrona, a wide, cobblestoned plaza with the city hall at one end and a flower market in the center. A man with wiry, tattooed arms came over and stood in front of Patterson and raised his hands in a picture-book imitation of a fighter.

"Me Svedish fighter," he said.

"Oh, yeah?" Patterson said, smiling. "That's fine." They shook hands.

"I think of Sugar Ray Robinson, the best fighter I've ever seen," Patterson said. "He's forty-three, forty-four years old now and still fighting. I think of Joe Louis, who can walk anywhere in the world with respect, and how much did he take out of boxing? Especially in proportion to what he gave? You know who makes the money out of boxing?" He paused to emphasize the answer to his own question. "The crooks. C-r-o-o-k-s. They go to college and become lawyers and start signing papers for you and sitting back, and all you have to do is go out and do the fighting. You bleed. And who makes the money? Them—not you. That's why I call all the shots for myself. Not a cent of my money is invested until I've investigated every possible angle, read up on the subject, and thought of all the ways it could go wrong.

"Poor Sonny Liston," he said, smiling at the irony of saying that about the man who had humiliated him twice. "I've thought of him often. I was never so certain in my life that a man would wind up broke, and sure enough, after the Clay fight, it came out that he was cut up more ways than a loaf of bread. But I'm just as certain of another thing: No one around him will wind up broke."

In the evening, after dinner, Patterson sat on a wicker chair on the porch of the large Victorian mansion called Villa Vera, where he lives alone. Across the road was a white building where the sparring partners sleep. Beyond that was the gym. A visitor asked what had happened in Yonkers with his daughter. Patterson explained that a writer had come up to camp a few months before to write a magazine article. On the day the writer arrived, Patterson received a phone call from his wife, saying that the children at school had been calling his daughter names again. The writer included all this in his story. "When the article came out," Patterson said, "there was a lot of bitterness in the neighborhood. I had criticized the neighborhood and in a way the local Catholic church. The priest wrote me a letter, which wasn't exactly nasty, but wasn't exactly warm either. So I wrote him back in the same tone."

Patterson, a Roman Catholic, then went to see the priest. "I realized that I might have been wrong in my bitterness, because the church had actually bent over backward to be nice to my girl," he said. "But these things kept going on, with other kids calling her nigger, and chocolate drop, and Sambo. Anyway, the priest said something that I don't believe he understood. He said Negroes were pushing themselves too hard, with sit-ins and demonstrations and whatnot, and that this pushing was doing them more harm than it was good. That the Negro was losing a lot of white men who sympathized with him, who were his friends."

Patterson's brother, Raymond, a twenty-year-old heavyweight who has won five of his eight fights since turning professional, came up the road and asked Floyd for the keys to the car. Patterson gave them to him, and told him to drive slowly.

"Well, I answered him," Floyd said. "I said that many white people don't understand the *purpose* of the black man's fight. It's not a fight for *friendship;* it's a fight for equality. As long as I can sleep in the same hotels as you, as long as I can eat in the same restaurants as you, as long as I can read in the same libraries and swim in the same swimming pools and watch movies in the same section as you and vote with the same rights as you, then we can consider friendship. I mean, it stands to reason that if we are seeing each other in all these places, we're both of us gonna say, 'Hey, don't I know you from somewhere?' Then we can be friends. Right now it's not a question of friendship."

It was early the next morning now, the best part of the day, and Floyd Patterson was dressing. Gray light crept through the blinds. He pulled on heavy black boots and walked out. There was a smell of dew and cut grass, and the countryside was empty. He talked of retiring, something he had promised to do if Eddie Machen defeats him decisively. "I definitely don't want to live in the city," he said. "I'll live in the country somewhere. But when I retire, I retire. You won't see me up on a stage singing or something.

"I'd like to live on a farm," he said, "away from prejudices of all kinds, and away from the fastness of life, and then I would tone down my life so that it would be very slow. I'd want to take two hours to dress and an hour and a half to eat breakfast. And then I'd like to take a handful of kids—kids of eight, nine, ten, eleven—and train them, like I trained the kids in Greenwood Lake for two years. I'd even like to adopt some kids, and the kind of kid I would adopt would be the scrawniest, ugliest kid I could find, because those are the ones no one else wants. But nothing is settled, not even where we'll live, as long as I'm fighting."

He has fought only once since losing to Liston, against an unrated Italian named Sante Amonti, whom he knocked out in eight rounds in Stockholm. To some observers he did not look good, but he feels it was a good fight. "I needed the work," he explained. But now, walking in a small lane in the countryside of Sweden, a long way from the Bedford-Stuyvesant section of Brooklyn, you realize in a way why he struck some people as the strangest of all modern heavyweight champions. As a prizefighter, he is a gentle man who does not really like violence and who has not even attended a fight other than his own since Rocky Marciano beat Ezzard Charles in 1954. He never ran with the Broadway crowd, or sang songs on TV, or played the traps in a Harlem nightclub. More than any other fighter, though, he has been true to his calling. Most of his life has been spent like this: walking, running, boxing, and training in silence. Now, growing older, he seems for the first time to be tiring of it all.

"The worst thing is the waiting," he said softly. "All my life I've been waiting, and now I sit back, and I'm twenty-nine years old, and I'm still waiting. When I was in the amateurs, I couldn't wait until it was time for a fight and I could find out how it ended. Then I couldn't wait to find out the results of my first professional fights, right on up to the championship. Then I couldn't wait to find out what would happen with Liston. And now, here I am, still waiting. I'm almost thirty years old. My kids are growing up, life is passing me by. But at least I've got something to wait *for.* There are millions of people in this world who are waiting for things they will never get, or they cannot get. I would do it all over again. But I'd cut down on the waiting."

June 27, 1964

A Beautiful Party While It Lasted

MEXICO CITY

Nobody knew what had happened to Toluco. At the boxing commission, the secretary said that they had no record. The promoters at the Arena Mexico didn't know: They heard he

343

was still hanging around the slum in Tepito, drinking a lot, but they didn't know what he did for a living, and they had no phone number or address. The old managers never returned the calls: If you were a fight manager and you once had a piece of Toluco López, you had to end up hating him. Toluco had vanished.

And yet, in those places where hard drinkers talk about fighters, it was as if Toluco were still around, still the best fighter Mexico had produced since the Second World War. One afternoon, I stopped in the Pulquería Casita on Avenida Melchor Ocampo. There were about eight good drinkers in the place, and we were talking fighters. The new kid, a bantamweight named ChuChu Castillo, was very good: smart, tough, brave, but not a real puncher. A flyweight named Alacran Torres had moxie but no chin. They didn't know what to make of Mundo Ramos.

"He's very big," one drinker said dryly. He didn't say anything else.

The older fighters didn't move them that much either. Joe Medel, a very good bantamweight, was too old and should retire, and I remembered that I had seen his sixth professional fight on TV in someone's house in Mexico in 1956. Another night, Tim Lee and I watched a featherweight named Pajarito Moreno cream an American import; Pajarito took the American out with a right hand to the elbow, and the fans whistled and jeered and would have torn the tanker apart if they had reached him. In the Pulquería Casita, they sneered at Pajarito: a good puncher, they said, but the heart of a mouse. Raton Macias was a kind of choirboy; Joe Becerra. . . .

"*Ola, pendejos,*" one huge guy said. "There was only one fighter."

They all looked at him.

"Toluco."

They all smiled at the same time, the way men do at the memory of a great meal or a beautiful evening. The bartender poured a round.

I just wish you had seen Toluco when he was one of the three or four best prizefighters in the world. That would be about

1957 to 1962. He was a bantamweight and then a featherweight, so he never fought in New York, a town which prefers great big slow men to classy small men. But in Mexico City, and all the smaller towns here, and occasionally in Los Angeles, Toluco would climb into rings and show what the phrase "a hell of a fighter" was all about.

He could do everything. He was square-shouldered, with a flat, neat Indian face, hard white teeth, and straight black hair that glistened under ring lights and was cut square in the back. He was a good boxer, who came at you behind a left hand that was a punch and not a flick: His right hand was devastating; he could double up hooks, and work your kidneys inside, and slide away from you and stop for a fraction of a second to ram the right hand home. If he staggered you, you were finished, because Toluco would be on you, the black hair straight up, the feet set, and punches coming in furious combinations. Toluco liked to knock people out. It gave him more time to drink.

And that was his problem. Toluco was a drinker, and a dancer, and a guy who liked women. Managers hated him. Once, on the day of a big fight in Mexico City, one of the sports papers ran a cartoon, five columns wide, of a fight manager at the end of a street lined with cantinas and whorehouses. "Toluco!" he was yelling. "Toluco!" Another time, he was stopped in the ninth round in a fight in Acapulco. Everyone was shocked, and we waited for the papers to see what had happened. Nothing cosmic: Toluco, like all good drinkers, had suffered an attack of diarrhea in the seventh round. In 1964, after he had been fighting for ten years, he boxed a kid named Lalo Guerrero in the Arena Mexico and lost a close decision. The next day, the sports papers, *Esto* and *Ovaciones*, ignored the result. Their headlines were: TOLUCO OPENS BANK AC-COUNT. They even had pictures of him and the bank manager depositing the check.

The managers hated Toluco for being Toluco: for being a fighter who could have been a great champion, who could have banked a quarter of a million dollars, and who didn't do that at all. Toluco didn't care. The promoters in the States were always leery of him. They didn't know if he would show up, and if he did show up, they didn't know whether he could stand. Ten years ago, Americans still wanted their fighters to be Boy Scouts.

So Toluco took his paydays where he could. He didn't train very much because he liked to do his training in the ring, where he was being paid. He would fight every two weeks, do most of his training in the first three rounds, and then go on to take his man out. Look at his record in an old (say, 1965 or 1964) *Ring Record Book*; he had about 125 fights, and I think he lost only about 15 of them, most of them at the end, when his legs finally betrayed him.

The men in the Pulquería Casita loved him. They didn't care that he lost a fight here or there. He was *macho, muy macho.* He was the fighter they wished they could have been: the fighter—who would drink until four in the morning, take home some member of what the Mexican papers call *la vida galante,* listen to her tell him that for Toluco there would be no charge, and the next night climb into a ring before 18,000 people, slightly bleary-eyed, and still be the toughest, smartest, and bravest fighter in the world. If he trained better, no one would ever have beaten him. But then he would not have had the booze, the women, or the laughter.

I asked them if they knew what had happened to Toluco. One said he was up in Los Angeles. Another said he was working as a bouncer in some *mariachi* place near the Plaza Garibaldi. Another said he was working for some gangsters down near the produce market. The *mariachi* joint sounded the best. That night, I took a cab down to the Plaza Garibaldi.

The streets were wet from the afternoon rain. There was a traffic jam, and I had to walk from San Juan de Letran. Mariachis stood around smoking dark cigarettes in the wet night air. Cooking smells came from the covered market area. I went into the Tenampa Club and ordered a beer. The place was very crowded, and the *mariachis* were singing, as they always are, about unfaithful women, and guns, and Jalisco.

"Está aquí Toluco López?" I asked the bartender.

"Toluco López?" he said. *"El boxeador?"*

"Sí."

The man shrugged. No, Toluco was not in the Tenampa

Club. But he would ask. He went into the back. After a minute, he came back. No, he said, they had not seen Toluco for a couple of years. And the last time he was there, the bartender said, they told Toluco not to come back. He looked very grim: Whatever he had done, Toluco must have been terrible.

I walked down the street to the Guadalajara del Noche. Four mariachis were standing outside. I talked to one of them, a fat guy with a great Zapata mustache and scuffed boots. "Excuse me," I said, "but does Toluco López work inside?"

He looked at me for a long moment. And then he smiled. "Aaaah," he said. "Toluco."

He turned to the other three and said that this character was looking for Toluco. They came awake, and they all smiled. No, the fat one said, they had not seen Toluco for a long time. About two years ago, when he retired, there was a big party for him at the Tenampa Club. All the whores in the capital were there. The boxing people came. A lot of big shots came. The party started at four on a Friday afternoon, and ended Saturday night. People went home to sleep and came back. There were three mariachi bands going all the time, and the cops kept all the tourists out. Toluco got drunk six times in two days, and they let him sleep on the main table while the party went on around him. Then, when the boss of the Tenampa started asking who would pay, they woke Toluco up for the last time.

"It was very bad," one of the mariachis said.

Toluco woke up shouting that the party was going on forever. The manager said they had to end it then, because there was no room for his customers and there were 200 drunks in the place. Toluco flattened the manager. Then he flattened two of the waiters. Then he flattened a bouncer. The cops arrived, and he flattened four of them before they carried him out. He didn't go to jail. They took him down to Tepito and released him.

Was he still there? I asked. The fat guy shrugged. He didn't know. They saw him around Plaza Garibaldi once in a while. He was a little fat guy now, always laughing. Did they think I could find him? Perhaps. I thanked them and said I would try.

"If you see Toluco," the fat one said, "tell him he was the best fighter I ever saw."

"I will," I said, and walked back to Bellas Artes to find a taxi.

347

I didn't go down to Tepito to look for Toluco; I remembered that old cartoon, and I didn't have the time. But I wished that I could see him fight again, even on film, and I was sure there was no film, and it would never be 1956 again. Toluco was gone, vanished, disappeared, and would stay that way, except in the minds of people who once saw him work. They were fortunate, and even if prizefighters don't mean much anymore, I wish I had been at that final party.

July 25, 1968

VII. New York

I'M a New Yorker, of course, but the relationship has always been a difficult one. Several times I've left the city, swearing that I would never be back. I've lived in Mexico, Puerto Rico, and Europe and worked well in a few other places. I've always come back to New York. It has become a city that is in my blood, deeply entwined in my personal character, and now, in my mid-thirties, I know that I'll never be able to live anywhere else. I don't mean to give the impression that living in New York is like being sentenced to life imprisonment. If the choice is a big city, New York is clearly the best, the most exciting, various, and enriching, and I would include the current darling of some Americans, London, in that judgment.

The city is not what it was, of course, but then neither is America. Heroin is eating at the city's heart, and much of the street crime can be traced to that infection. A welfare system that was begun in a spirit of compassion has become a disaster and a disgrace. The city treasury is empty, so there is no money for the amenities that make city life tolerable to the middle class. Much of the middle class has bought the suburban lie, heading out of town with a sense of relief, believing, in some touching way, that heroin, race, and poverty can be abolished by a shift in geography. And yet, as we moved into the seventies, I began to sense that New York would survive, might even become a better city than it ever was. It would not be a task for sprinters; the baton had been handed to the long-distance runners. All of the following pieces were written for *New York* magazine, and if they are marked by any single emotion, it is hope. New York is too good a town to be allowed to die.

New York magazine grew out of the old Sunday *Herald Tribune*, and it is the magazine in which I feel most comfortable. Clay Felker is one of the great editors, one who respects writers, helps them through difficulties, and allows them time and room in which to develop. Jack Nessel, who works with Clay, helped me with all these articles, with great humor and a craftsman's care. The articles themselves have been a means for me to develop the themes of the newspaper column or to deal with subjects I seldom write about in the newspaper because of the limits of space.

The article called "The Coming Revolt of the Lower White Middle Class" grew out of a conversation with Felker and is one of the most important I've written. At the time of publication, the subject had not been treated in any major magazine; after publication, all the major magazines did stories, and the politicians started to listen. There has even been a number of novels published about white working-class people, and the film *Joe* is a large success. After the article was published, Pat Moynihan called me from the White House to tell me that the President was impressed by it and that it had been reprinted for perusal by the Cabinet; somehow, I might have been responsible for the clobbering the Republicans took in the 1970 Congressional elections, when they misread the complaint of the white working class. The predicted revolt did come, in the nomination of Mario Procaccino, in the election of "law-and-order" candidates around the country, in the reelection of Sam Yorty in Los Angeles, and finally in the hard-hat rioting in New York. It seems now to have calmed down, as the Nixon economic policies have hurt a lot of these people into second thoughts and the more virulent stage of black nationalism seems to have passed. My own feeling is that the calm is only apparent and temporary and that the white working class will be heard from again.

In the piece on the Puerto Ricans of New York, I tried to put together several journalistic techniques: the heavy job of research with the personal point of view. I brought my own knowledge of the subjects to the mass of available statistical

350

facts, adding personal reporting to fill in the gaps, or to flesh out the statistics. Throughout the sixties there had been a lot of talk about the "New Journalism," although it was never quite clear what was new about it. From the time of Defoe, through Addison and Steele, Stephen Crane, the Hearst and Pulitzer stars of the first thirty years of the century, to the great New Yorker reporters like A. J. Liebling and Alva Johnson, journalism had been a personal form. Most of these writers knew that "objectivity" was a quite difficult, if not impossible, standard to meet. Richard Rovere, in his book on Senator Joseph McCarthy, had reminded journalists how false standards of "objectivity" had allowed McCarthy to put lies into circulation, simply by uttering them ("Senator McCarthy charged today . . ."). In the sixties, after a long dull stretch in which reporters had been satisfied to clerk the facts, there was an alteration in the form. But it was not really "new." It was merely a return to the tradition.

My feeling is that one man was reponsible for the change: Norman Mailer. When his piece about the 1960 Democratic Convention ("Superman Goes to the Supermarket") appeared in *Esquire,* it sent waves of excitement running through the city rooms of New York. Mailer had taken the form, exploded it, opened it up, above all, *showed us its possibilities,* and after that it was quite difficult to start a story in a newspaper with words like "Police today were hunting in 13 states for the killer of. . . ." Mailer changed American journalism with that first article; when his great piece about the first Patterson-Liston fight appeared a few years later, the change was total.

This is not to say that Mailer was alone at the time; he was just the best, the man with the largest imagination and the finest sense of possibilities. Gay Talese was already writing rich, solid personal pieces in *Esquire;* Jimmy Breslin had been working the mine for ten years in magazines like *True* and *Sport.* As the decade moved on, a small army of good writers began to break out in the pages of the magazines, in the New York *Herald Tribune,* and in the *Village Voice.* Tom Wolfe came along like an out-of-control stock car, his head alive with a complete vision of another America, brilliant and dazed at the same time, anti-intellectual, yet drawing on the resources of cultural anthropology and even symbolic logic; Wolfe was an original of some daz-

351

zling, spectacular kind, and he ruined more prose styles than any other writer except Kempton. Larry King, David Halberstam, John Corry, Lewis Lapham, and others clustered around *Harper's*, which was edited then by Willie Morris. The *Voice* found and nurtured writers like Joe Flaherty, Vivian Gornick, Ron Rosenbaum, and others and made room in its pages for novelists like Edward Hoagland. *New York* had its own stable: Wolfe, Breslin, Gloria Steinem, and others. Jack Newfield came out of Bedford-Stuyvesant to the *Voice* to try to make a language that could express rage and compassion at the same time; and Tom Buckley made the pages of the *New York Times Magazine* come alive with his beautifully researched and written articles from Vietnam, New York, Palm Beach, or wherever else he might move. Newspaper writing seemed increasingly dull, conservative, and unimaginative, with honorable exceptions like Mike Royko in Chicago, Nick Von Hoffman in Washington, Marty Nolan in Boston, Gerald Nachman in Oakland. I suppose there were rivalries at work, petty professional hatreds going on among these writers, but I never saw anything like that. If anything, there was a spirit of fraternity and generosity; the nasty little feuds of New York literary society did not seem to infect the journalists. They appeared to understand, as the ex-wife of one of the writers once put it, that writing was not football or even chess; it was golf. It was you and the ball. Sometimes you failed, sometimes you were better than you thought you could be. The joy was in the attempt at excellence. And in some odd way, Mailer's huge presence in the room freed everyone else. He was the acknowledged genius, and it was stupid and futile to engage in a rivalry with another writer when Mailer was better than the both of you.

This is not to say that everybody was brilliant or a genius or even a good journalist; some writers had never learned their craft, had never covered fires at three o'clock in the morning or gone off to cover homicides under the strict and level gaze of a tough city editor. There was great danger that the journalists would ignore the facts of a situation in favor of the sweet feverish embrace of style. Self-indulgence was the most frequently committed sin. The extraordinary thing was that the sin was not committed more.

For me, the line between journalism and other writing began to disappear. I still wrote "newspaperman" on my passport, but it did not seem such an unusual act to write a novel or to write screenplays. It was all writing, done to the best of my abilities, and whether it was good or bad, whether it was important or trivial, those were judgments to be made by others. My column shifted back and forth from reporting to polemics, but the prose got harder and more direct as fiction allowed me an outlet for deeper, more obsessive, more private concerns. I found myself being less self-consciously literary in the daily journalism, hoping for a certain ruthlessness of statement and sometimes succeeding. A part of me yearned to be off in that cabin in Utah that Dylan was singing about, where I could write long books about things I knew and felt deeply; the other part wanted the action of New York and the immediacy of daily journalism. The choice would eventually have to be made; but I had learned that much of life was a lottery, and in the end, the choice might not be mine.

eral schemes (guaranteed annual income, negative income tax, demonstration cities, national welfare standards, etc.).

But if these suggestions—some major, some minor—would be incorporated into a candidate's platform, and then put into effect, they might go some of the way toward saving the city. The way we are going, the city will end up a place where executives land on rooftop helipads, to deal in talent and money, while the poor besiege them from the streets and the whole angry mess is ringed by hostile white suburbs. The hour is late, *compadres,* and the only action permissible should be drastic.

DECENTRALIZE THE CITY ITSELF.

That is, break up the five boroughs into five separate cities, with five separate governments. I first heard this idea from Assemblyman Al Blumenthal, and the more I think about it, the more sense it makes. One of our problems is that the city itself is dominated by Manhattan, which is only one of the five boroughs and not even the largest. The mayor lives and works in Manhattan. The headquarters for all major government agencies are located in Manhattan. The bulk of the office work available in New York is in Manhattan. The three daily newspapers act as if the other four boroughs do not exist, except at those moments when crisis erupts (for example, in Ocean Hill-Brownsville). New Yorkers outside Manhattan feel, with some justification, that the mayor simply doesn't have the time for them.

Some of the larger advantages of this scheme would be psychological. Most New Yorkers feel that the city is simply too large, that we are prisoners of some malevolent, uncontrollable fate or at the mercy of strangers. But if this city were five cities, the problems themselves would be decentralized. If Ocena Hill-Brownsville becomes an educational battleground, resulting in a strike, the largest unit affected by the strike would be the City of Brooklyn. If the garbage men in Queens have a beef with the City of Queens, that's a problem for Queens. This is not a question of ignoring the problems of other citizens. It is deciding whether "community control" means what it implies: that local

White Paper from a Native Son

From now until November, about a dozen otherwise sensible men will engage in that quadrennial suicide rite known as running for mayor of New York. To do so, they must weave a verbal tapestry of hope, goodwill, and blandness, where the trick is to say nothing well, offend no one, and pray for the intercession of the gods. All this is to be done before an audience that largely feels the whole thing is a waste of time. That audience is convinced that New York is doomed.

New York is, to be sure, an increasingly nasty, expensive, uncomfortable and joyless town at best, and a violent and fearful one at worst. And yet it does not really have to be this way. The following is a White Paper from a Native Son, offered to any and all candidates free of charge. It does not pretend to solve all our problems or replace combinations of more massive federal schemes (guaranteed annual income, negative income tax, demonstration cities, national welfare standards, etc.).

But if these suggestions—some major, some minor—would be incorporated into a candidate's platform, and then put into effect, they might go some of the way toward saving the city. The way we are going, the city will end up a place where executives land on rooftop helipads, to deal in talent and money, while the poor besiege them from the streets and the whole angry mess is ringed by hostile white suburbs. The hour is late, *compadres,* and the only action permissible should be drastic.

DECENTRALIZE THE CITY ITSELF.

That is, break up the five boroughs into five separate cities, with five separate governments. I first heard this idea from Assemblyman Al Blumenthal, and the more I think about it, the more sense it makes. One of our problems is that the city itself is dominated by Manhattan, which is only one of the five boroughs and not even the largest. The mayor lives and works in Manhattan. The headquarters for all major government agencies are located in Manhattan. The bulk of the office work available in New York is in Manhattan. The three daily newspapers act as if the other four boroughs do not exist, except at those moments when crisis erupts (for example, in Ocean Hill-Brownsville). New Yorkers outside Manhattan feel, with some justification, that the mayor simply doesn't have the time for them.

Some of the larger advantages of this scheme would be psychological. Most New Yorkers feel that the city is simply too large, that we are prisoners of some malevolent, uncontrollable fate or at the mercy of strangers. But if this city were five cities, the problems themselves would be decentralized. If Ocean Hill-Brownsville becomes an educational battleground, resulting in a strike, the largest unit affected by the strike would be the City of Brooklyn. If the garbage men in Queens have a beef with the City of Queens, that's a problem for Queens. This is not a question of ignoring the problems of other citizens. It is deciding whether "community control" means what it implies: that local citizens will have the power to deal with immediate, local problems, hoping that the larger society will take care of itself.

There would be problems involved, of course, and some of them might be insoluble. There might be a terrible distortion caused by wealth, with schools in Queens bidding to attract the best teachers, the best sanitation services, etc. Some borough-wide services, such as subways, would obviously need to be placed in the hands of a supra-local agency like the Port of New York Authority, with financing and maintenance shared by the four boroughs which use the subways (no trains to Staten Island, of course). The schools, the police, the firemen, and the Sanitation Department really should be in the hands of the local city governments, so that community control would be a fact. The present system of having borough presidents really doesn't work, because the borough president must, in the end, come to the mayor and the City Council to accomplish anything. Remember, through most of this city's history the five boroughs were *not* one city; perhaps our grandfathers made a grave mistake in uniting them.

SPREAD THE TAX BASE THROUGHOUT THE ACTUAL METROPOLITAN AREA.

It seems apparent that for the next ten to twenty years there will not be enough money available to New York City from the collection of individual taxes. This is a poor city: One million people are on welfare, and another million earn less than $5,000 a year. Before anyone can talk about improving the city, it is necessary to talk about where the money will come from. It is not coming at more than a subsistence level from the federal and state governments. The most obvious solution is the creation of a Metropolitan Tax Area, which would include New York City; Westchester, Rockland, Nassau, and Suffolk counties; and parts of New Jersey.

At present, this really is one unit, the dread megalopolis, and for tax purposes it should be considered one urban area (with local government determining the uses of revenue). It is disgraceful that people in New York City find their state taxes being spent to stock beaver dams in the Adirondacks or to build highways in the boondocks.

But even more unacceptable is the presence in New York City of armies of Hessians who arrive every morning from the suburbs, earn their money among us, and then depart for the world of the barbecue pit and the two-car garage. These people depend on New York but refuse to help make it grow. They clutter it with their automobiles every day but refuse to share the responsibility of easing its problems.

There is a small tax being levied on some of these people now, but it is not enough. If the tax base were spread into the real metropolitan unit, they could not escape, at least not as long as they earned their money in New York City. Some of them might even be convinced of the merits of leaving the suburbs and coming home again, while potential escapees might be convinced to stay.

TAX ALL RELIGIOUS INSTITUTIONS, PRIVATE SCHOOLS, PRIVATE HOSPITALS, AND TAX-FREE FOUNDATIONS.

If the commuter is forced to pay, then the loopholes in the city itself must be sealed. Religious institutions own billions of dollars' worth of real estate and pay no taxes. In a city starving for land, you can find small groups of nuns, for example, rattling around in huge empty convents, which remain open only because they are tax-exempt. Private and parochial schools, which contribute heavily to the fragmentation of the city and the alienation of large groups of the poor, contribute practically nothing in taxes. As long as the private hospitals get their tax-free ride, nothing serious will be done to improve the public hospitals.

As for the foundations, they were started as a tax dodge and remain a tax dodge. Some of them do good work, I suppose, but more and more they are functioning as a shadow government, based on nontaxable wealth. They should have no right to exert as much influence as they already do, but they have no right at all to do so without paying taxes.

LEGALIZE GAMBLING AND HARD DRUGS.

The reason for the success of the Mafia, as all New Yorkers know, is that the Mafia provides services which are not available elsewhere. The result is a crime rate that seems to be going out of control. Millions of New Yorkers live with the nagging fear of the mugger or the burglar. The mugger and the burglar usually have one thing in common: the need for money to buy drugs. Specifically, heroin.

Since heroin is illegal, the Mafia and its agents supply it. The junkie pays outrageous prices and steals, burgles, shoplifts to get the price of his daily supply. He can do nothing else. But most heroin addicts could get through the day holding down a job if their supply were certain; there is a tolerance level to heroin, and it is possible for some junkies, especially older ones, to function.

One obvious solution is to legalize junk—that is, to make heroin, or at the very least methadone, available to certified heroin addicts through city-run clinics, at nominal cost. This would place the city in open rebellion against the federal government, I suppose, but what the hell, we have nothing to lose but our crime rate. The Mafia would get out of the racket because the profits would dry up. We would have a chance at *containing* the present addict population, because pusher-addicts would not be forced to infect more and more young kids to keep their businesses going. And we might force the federal government to change the heroin laws immediately (obviously the major drawback to unilateral action would be a flooding of the city with every junkie in the United States; but we have almost every junkie anyway, so it wouldn't make much difference).

One detective in the Manhattan district attorney's office told me recently that institution of the British system of treating addicts would cut crime in the city by 70 percent. We have debated the British system for more than ten years, and while we have debated, our addict population has risen from 25,000 to more than 100,000. It's time to stop debating and do something which is not timid.

(Obviously marijuana should be legalized. The cops who are now running all over town trying to find out what people smoke could be used for better—or worse—things, and the city's coffers could certainly make better use of the tax revenues from pot than the dealers are making of their profits.)

I still don't understand our puritanical ideas about gambling. Why is it moral to place a bet out at Aqueduct and immoral and illegal to place a bet in a store on your corner? We do have a New York State lottery, which has been mildly successful, but we really should have off-track betting just as soon as it is possible to set up a workable system. These parlors could handle racing, of course, but also take bets on basketball, pro football, boxing, and other events. It works perfectly well in England and could certainly be made to work here.

I would go one step further and legalize the poor man's lottery: numbers. The numbers racket employs about 5,000 people in Harlem alone, with the gross running, according to some police estimates, to about $5,000,000 a week. Obviously, none of this money is taxable. And of course those 5,000 people who work in numbers are technically outlaws. They don't pay taxes because their income is illegal. They don't appear to have jobs, so they find it impossible to obtain bank loans, mortgages, or credit. And the big money does not stay in Harlem, where it is produced and where it belongs; the mob guys take it out of Harlem and invest it elsewhere.

(One minor benefit of legalizing numbers would be a certain increase in respect for the police. Every cop in Harlem knows about numbers, and the racket could not exist without active or passive collusion with the police.)

CONTROL OR DESTROY THE AUTOMOBILE.

In 46 B.C. or thereabouts, Julius Caesar found it necessary to ban all wheeled vehicles from the streets of Rome during daylight hours. We are rapidly approaching the point where we might have to do the same.

Our town is basically a nineteenth-century structure and has never really learned how to deal with the automobile. The automobile is poisoning our air, a situation which might eventually be cured by conversion to electric cars. But worse even than the air pollution is the fact that the auto is destroying our nerves. You can't get anywhere in midtown with a car, and the constant stopping, starting, screeching, and cursing keep building and building. I often wonder how much the car contributes to the suicide and murder rates, driving ordinary citizens to the edge of desperation, even to insanity.

We cannot and should not build a freeway system, Los Angeles-style. Robert Moses caused enough trouble when he built those highways leading out of the city; they became the escape routes for the middle class. More highways or freeways would only destroy what is unique about New York. But there are at least some patches we can make on the present system.

First, the cost of a license should be raised to $150, unless a citizen can prove that his livelihood depends on the automobile.

We have an adequate system of public transportation in this town, and it should be used. (I said adequate; if it were used by more people, thus bringing in more revenue, it might be a hell of a lot better.) If a citizen can afford the car, he can afford the license fee; the poor don't own many cars, so they would not be hurt the way they are hurt by the sales tax. (The guys who picked up phony Jersey or Connecticut licenses would face a mandatory year in jail, if caught.)

We could set up toll booths at all entrances to the city, and charge $3 for a car bearing only the driver, $2 if he is carrying a passenger, $1 if he has two passengers, and nothing if the car has a minimum of three passengers plus driver. Anything to stop those people who drive into town alone every day.

Second, the island of Manhattan should ban all private vehicles during daylight hours, at least from Ninety-sixth Street to the Battery. Taxis and buses would be allowed to use the streets, along with those trucks whose owners can prove that deliveries cannot be made at night. Such a ban would not really affect the New Yorker, because most of those cars seem to be from New Jersey or the Long Island suburbs; if those people must come to Manhattan to shop, let them use the Long Island RR, the Hudson Tubes, and the subways. Or consider moving back to the city itself.

Third, all alternate forms of urban transportation should be encouraged. Gypsy cabs should be licensed. If there are not enough taxis, then license more, and abolish the ugly, excluding tradition of the taxi shield. The entire taxi industry should be given help to construct a computerized system allowing citizens to call taxis to their homes, places of business, and saloons (the computer should be able to find out, for example, the location of cabs going to Brooklyn or the Bronx at three in the morning or the location of Black Pearl cabs going to Harlem or Bedford-Stuyvesant). The dreadful problem of trying to get to Kennedy Airport during the day should be solved by the airlines themselves: they should be forced to build a high-speed monorail between midtown and the airports, perhaps traveling down the center islands of the highways. One possible way of easing the horrors of truck traffic could be the use of freight trains in the subways, especially at night.

The way we are going, we shall have to put every building in the city on stilts and use the surface area for driving and parking. Personally, I'd rather go back to the horse. I like the way they sound at night.

LEARN HOW TO REALLY WASTE MONEY.

I mean, implementing Michael Harrington's notion that a city should spend some money on projects that don't actually accomplish anything tangible. For example, I have a thing about fountains. Rome is another city being choked to death by the automobile. But its continuing splendor is based, for me at least, on its fountains. You can walk those streets, assaulted by noise and gasoline fumes, and suddenly make a turn into an absolutely lovely little oasis with a burbling fountain, spray dampening your face, and a peculiar kind of peace permeating the place. Why can't we put some of our fine sculptors to work building fountains? I don't mean in front of the Seagram Building, but down on Avenue B. In the middle of Times Square. In the South Bronx, Red Hook, Long Island City. Not just massive fountains, but fountains of every size and shape.

In addition to fountains, of course, there could be more money spent to put bold and colorful murals on the sides of buildings in the slums (this is being done now on a small scale). Why can't some of our fine designers—the Milton Glasers, Bob Gills, Jerome Snyders, Herb Lubalins—be commissioned to spruce up slum streets? Who knows what changes in mood might be accomplished by, say, painting the fire escapes fuchsia?

NATIONALIZE THE SLUMS.

The slumlord has been made the archvillain of the housing problem. But a lot of the problems are not really of his making. Many slumlords bought their buildings years ago. They are rent-controlled. But while the cost of repairs, maintenance, and real estate taxes have gone up, the slumlord's income has not. He stops providing services; he doesn't replace the broken window; he lets the garbage can rust away; he puts 40-watt bulbs in the hall. And then he hides behind some corporate façade, hoping for the day when his building is included in a slum clearance program and he can get some of his money back.

Now the fact is that many of the slum buildings in this city are still structurally sound; sure, they are old, but so are the mansions on Fifth Avenue. They don't really have to be torn down (especially some of the true architectural gems in Bedford-Stuyvesant and Fort Greene), but they could be reconditioned. If the slumlord does not agree to do the job (with help from the state and federal government), then the City of New York should become the Landlord of Last Resort.

As the landlord, the city could then begin to do a real rehabilitation job in the slums, an urban renewal program that is not Negro removal or a program that destroys neighborhoods. There have been some experiments by private enterprise on reconditioning the interiors of buildings, using prefabricated units. Apparently the process is still too expensive, but if the city could guarantee Alcoa a minimum of 75,000 apartments a year, the cost could be drastically reduced (or should be). The actual construction work would be done by men in the neighborhoods themselves, and those men would be guaranteed full union books and future jobs in the construction industry. All reconditioning would include the extermination of rats and roaches, the twin symbols of slum living. The only real demolition would take place on the avenues, so that backyards could be opened up for playgrounds, malls, and other uses (free automatic laundries, fountains, meeting halls, day nurseries for working mothers, etc.).

The city could also set up, with federal help, housing banks, which would allow the tenants of the reconditioned buildings to convert those buildings into co-ops (a kind of Urban Homestead Act). No money down for people who have lived there for a certain period of time, and nominal sums to people who want to move into those buildings. That would allow the city eventually to get out of the landlord business and would give the tenants a real stake in the maintenance of the buildings (and a chance to build equity). Since the poor have more children and thus produce more garbage, some of our industrial designers should be able to come up with a smokeless system for incineration; we still can't depend on the Sanitation Department.

363

Civil servants are one of the crucial elements of an urban middle class. Yet for various reasons (especially the abolition of the old Lyons Law), we allow our 325,000 civil servants to live outside the city limits. No reason can be good enough. If a man is a New York City policeman, he should live in New York City. If he sells you a marriage license at City Hall, he should not be allowed to live in Rahway. The civil servant who lives outside the city lives in fear or contempt of the people who employ him—namely, the citizens of New York (one explanation, by the way, of why he is seldom civil and provides few services). If he wants to earn his money from us, he should live among us.

UPGRADE PUBLIC HOUSING FOR THE POOR, AND LIMIT THE BUILDING OF LUXURY HOUSING.

Obviously, there are some areas of the city which are so far gone that no amount of rehabilitation can save the buildings. But if the solution is public housing, we should never again sanction the building of the red-brick rabbit hutches which have passed for housing in the past twenty-five years. We should begin with the architects, since most of New York's public housing could not pass a second-year architectural design examination at Pratt Institute. I believe that every piece of public housing should be passed on by a committee of the American Institute of Architects, just as candidates for judgeships are considered by the bar associations; but I would make the decisions of the AIA binding. In addition, the city should somehow start attracting the best architects available, instead of the long string of hacks who have been responsible for the design of our new instant slums. I think a lot of the good architects would welcome the challenge, and if their creations don't conform to our present zoning laws, then we should change the zoning laws.

The architects should also be given the opportunity to design complete communities: housing, but not just housing. There should be schools, shopping centers, and space for smokeless industry, as well as the usual assortment of recreation areas (is Arthur Ashe fated to be the last Negro tennis player, as well as the first?). If a neighborhood has been cleared to make way for the housing, then the people of that neighborhood should have first crack at the apartments and the jobs. And neighborhood institutions, such as saloons, should be carefully replaced, down to the last mahogany bar and the last chased mirror.

For at least four or five years we should severely limit the building of luxury apartment houses. Nothing infuriates a poor person more than to see the buildings going up almost daily on the East Side while nothing happens in East Harlem. He looks in the paper for a decent five-room apartment and discovers that such apartments start renting at $400 a month. These buildings are constructed like fortresses, destroy the neighborhoods which they invade (and New York is nothing if not a network of neighborhoods), and prevent their inhabitants from knowing anyone else in the city. But worse, the real estate interests and the construction unions don't really have to worry very much about the rest of the city. If the only building going on in the city were building for the poor, the construction establishment would figure out some way to make a buck out of it. Even if we passed a law forbidding the use of red brick for the rest of the century.

MAKE NEW YORK CITY HISTORY A MANDATORY COURSE
IN THE CITY'S HIGH SCHOOLS.

Our kids learn world history and American history, but any knowledge they gather about their own city comes strictly by accident. If they learned more about this town, and how it got this way, and where we all came from, it might create an almost nationalistic bond among the next generation of New Yorkers. (A city of 8,000,000 people is really a city-state, larger than a number of countries.) The history of New York would teach a kid about every immigrant group that ever came to this country; it would teach him about American politics; it would teach him about every American war from the Revolution to Vietnam; it would teach him every variety of sin and every attempt at virtue. Such a course, honestly taught, might teach him absolute cynicism, but it might also teach irony, which is the only ultimate weapon for survival the New Yorker owns.

MAKE NEW YORK INTO A TRUE CONVENTION CENTER.

This could be done over the next eight years. First, we should determine to make an all-out drive to have the 1976 Olympics held in New York City, an idea I picked up from Mike Scott, a Brooklyn Reform Democrat. That will be the two hundredth anniversary of the American Revolution, and this city was the first capital of the Republic. The basic site of the Olympics could be out near Marine Park, where large areas are now lying fallow, mainly because of inadequate transportation. Again, a monorail could connect the Olympic site to midtown Manhattan. And the buildings themselves, which must include housing for more than 7,000 athletes, could subsequently be turned into public housing.

With the Olympics as the goal, we could begin to rebuild many wasted areas of the city. For years, Congressman Ed Koch has been asking that the West Side waterfront be turned into a kind of Fisherman's Wharf, with nightclubs, dance halls, and restaurants. A subway shuttle could make the area more accessible, and there is some room under the West Side Drive for parking. If this kind of area were built up, nobody could possibly complain, because very few people live over there. The out-of-town dentist, joining with his fellows, would have a place to visit other than the joints around Times Square and the East Side saloons.

And Coney Island could be built into a real resort. There are buildings rotting away there now, only feet from the sea, and the only solution the city seems to imagine is to use the land for public housing. Instead, they could make it into a vital area of the city. Two things are necessary: first, the construction of a convention center, broken into at least several halls like the new Madison Square Garden; second, the licensing of gambling casinos in whatever hotels are built on the seafront. I mean casi-

366

nos in real Las Vegas style: slot machines, craps, roulette, whatever might be your pleasure. Every day, planeloads of highrollers leave New York for Las Vegas, to deposit their money in the state of Nevada. Why should it be that way? Why can't New Yorkers have the whole thing—gambling, floor shows, people like Sinatra and Don Rickles and Johnny Carson, and the rest—without having to spring for the airplane fare and travel across the continent? The reason nightclubs have died in New York is that they cannot afford the big talent. The big talent plays in Vegas because Vegas can pay them. If I thought I could spend a Saturday night gambling into the dawn while watching Dean Martin in the lounge and drinking when I feel like it, I would go to Coney Island on the next subway. New York always has managed to get by on the myth it composed about its own "class." But we haven't had many top performers in town for more than ten years. If we got them back, we would feed our own self-image again and might feel a little better about ourselves. Besides, we could use the money, even if we have to make Meyer Lansky a consultant to the City Planning Commission.

In short, the convention hall would attract the hotel guests, and the gambling would keep them there. See you at the Nathan's Hilton.

BUILD A NEW ATHLETIC STADIUM IN THE BRONX.

You might think this is not crucial. But the football Giants and the Yankees are now threatening to leave New York, and if they do, we would be poorer for it. I think there should be public hearings on the subject, to discover whether the only problem is the dilapidated condition of Yankee Stadium. If it is, we should build a new stadium, like the Astrodome, which would also help attract convention business. It took this town almost ten years to recover from the loss of the Dodgers and the Giants, and we should not let it happen again. But the Giants and the Yankess are now making noises about going either to Westchester or to Jersey (the Westchester Giants? the Secaucus Yankees?). Well, we have the Anaheim Angels already. If they are really going to the suburbs because their white middle-class fans are going there in large numbers, then that should be put on the record. And anything we can do to keep them here should be started now, before they start shopping around.

COME TO TERMS WITH MODERN TECHNOLOGY.

The black kid attending a New York City public school is being somewhat cheated when his school does not carry courses on black history and culture, but he is being absolutely cheated if he is not taught early to use the tools he will need in the 1980's and 1990's. Instead of memorizing the date of the founding of Jamestown and the implications of the Dred Scott decision, he should be learning the uses of computers. Every scientific journal I look at says that the day is coming when the man who does not understand the uses of computers will be the equivalent of a functional illiterate. And as much as that vision of the future might frighten the humanist, it is a future that must be dealt with, controlled, and made to serve us. If it doesn't, the computers and the people who understand them will rule us.

Technology is a fact of life on the West Coast, but it hasn't even begun to be used here. It is now possible to build a forty-story greenhouse in a place like the South Bronx where most of the city's supply of fresh fruits and vegetables could be grown. This would eliminate some of the brutal traffic from the suburban truck farms and would also lower the prices of food for the consumers. It is possible for outfits like Con Edison to use the sea for power, instead of carving into the heart of Storm King Mountain or fouling the atmosphere with old-fashioned fuel-burning methods.

TURN THE STREETLIGHTS AROUND.

This is last, but not least. Can anyone explain why our streetlights hang out over the streets, when every automobile has its own lights? I could understand this if we were still driving around in horse-drawn carriages. But we really need the light on the sidewalks. The muggers hang out in doorways, not in traffic.

None of the above suggestions alone could cure our illnesses, and some are admittedly minor cures. But perhaps combinations of them, along with some of the programs now in operation, might move us in the right direction. Our problem is not just escalating welfare rolls, or corruption in the poverty programs, or simply an increase in violence and bitterness. It is a meld of those problems and a lot of other things, too. Most important, it is a surrender to lethargy and the spirit of defeat. The town could still work, if a lot of people—and especially the next mayor—would break open the ice pack of dead ideas. If *we* don't save the town, nobody else will.

March 3, 1969

Coming of Age in Nueva York

Here, examine the baggage, with the great jets screaming in behind us and the glossy girls staring from the counters of the San Juan airport and the signs blinking at us from every space and the horde of strange cold faces coming through the arrival gates and the cold wind of New York starting to blow within them across the darkened airfield. Quickly: while the children run to the candy machines and the girl from Trans Caribbean argues with the passengers on the outgoing flights and the cop lolls against the wall swinging the bat of authority and you check the ticket again and hope that nobody knows that you have some pages of La Prensa *in your shoes and some* yames *for your aunt in Brooklyn. Quickly: it is getting cold.*

The luggage: new undershirts bought in the Pueblo supermarket on the road to Bayamón. Some slacks, and shirts, and the suit bought for Belen's wedding two years ago to that guy from Caguas who left her later. That luggage, and the other kind. The way the flags of the Popular Party blow in the sea breeze in spring over the tar-paper roofs of La Perla; children playing in those mud streets; tourists with peeling faces gawking over the walls of the old city; the sea beyond, foaming at the shore, and then green, and then turning dark blue away out where the Atlantic conquers the Carib-

369

bean. Up in the hills, the road turning, chickens cawing in the damp morning, an old jíbaro with a lined face walking on home-made sandals with a machete on his hip, the flamboyant trees exploding against the hillsides, a flock of white birds against the blue roof of the sky. That luggage: nuns in white habits walking along the Avenida Ponce de León, and the tourist ladies in bikinis on the beaches of the Condado, and the Cuban whores along the water-front in San Juan Antiguo, and the way the sidewalks in El Fanguito were made with rubber tires and there was no electricity and no toilets and you drank water from a common pump. One summer the ticks came like a plague and attached themselves to the skins of children, and the public health people sprayed and made everyone sicker. That luggage: the yellow eyes of old men; women gone crazy with the spirits; the man who used to wear silk suits in the afternoons and play piano in the bands and who was found dead one morning with a needle in his arm. That luggage: but the sweet part more than the bad, with the sun climbing in the sky, and the sound of laughter, and the distant swelling roar of the sea, and music.

New York, mon. Check the luggage. I've got some Don Q in the overcoat, and when I sit down, I'm going to start drinking. It's dark out, but I've made this trip before. I don't want to see the swells around El Morro, or the lights of fishing boats, or the garish light-blinking spread of San Juan. I don't want to see it vanish behind me. I might never see it again.

The Puerto Ricans came to New York to live better. It was as simple as that. It was a trickle at first, in the 1920's and 1930's, because the ticket on the Bull Line cost more than a man could earn in a year, and the trip was long and dangerous and the city was a mean, hard place then, if your skin was dark and your language was Spanish. Some of the earliest worked on the Brooklyn piers, unloading bananas, with the spiders large enough to play baseball with and the old Bull Line captains keeping the men in line. A few drifted into the South Bronx and the Lower East Side, to the places that were being abandoned by the Jews and the Irish who were starting to make it. But most went to East Harlem, *El Barrio*, where 110th and Lex was the center of the world, and you could buy *plátanos* at the Park Avenue market and rice and beans from people you knew.

They came here because the island they left behind was the sinkhole of the Caribbean, with a life expectancy of thirty-two, a place where the American rulers would sit around the palace in white duck while *jibaros* died in the mountains from yaws and parasites. Even today, with conditions changed radically from the dark years of the 1920's and 1930's, the population density of Puerto Rico is eleven times that of the United States, unemployment runs at a constant 13 percent, and the per capita income is still only about $1,000 a year. New York might have been a strange and alien place to those early arrivals, but it was better than dying young.

And then the migration started to build. Puerto Ricans were different from others who had come to New York from the slums of Europe. Most important, they were citizens and had been so by act of Congress since 1917. So they were not immigrants; they were migrants. They fought in the First World War and all the wars after, and if there were large numbers of Puerto Ricans then who wanted independence from the United States, it was only because the United States had treated them so shabbily. The *independentistas* followed in the footsteps of Muñoz Rivera and later followed a brilliant man named Albizu Campos, who died finally of heartache and insanity. Muñoz's son, Luis Muñoz Marín, made the journey in those years, and sat around the Village writing poetry and socialist tracts and enjoying himself more than he ever would again.

And through all those years, before the explosions of the years after the Second World War, the dream remained the same: to come to New York, make money, learn a trade, and go home to Puerto Rico. Muñoz Marín went back and became the most important politician in the history of the island. For others it wasn't so easy. I remember once, a few years ago, sitting around one afternoon in Luis Cora's barbershop in East Harlem, talking to a man who had settled in New York in 1921. He was a seaman who had given up the sea because his wife was lonely, and who had come to New York because he had no job back in Puerto Rico.

"I always thought I would go back," the old man said. "But it was too expensive, too long a trip. I finally went in 1958, with my son, who paid for the airplane ticket. In three days I was ready to come home. I had been away too long, and I was a New Yorker, not a real Puerto Rican anymore. It was sad."

A Puerto Rican was something strange and exotic in those days. There weren't enough of them to be a threat to anybody, not enough of them to be identified as a group. The word "spic" came later (most common theory: from the phrase "No spik Inglis"). It came with the wave after the war. It came with the airplane.

And it was the airplane that changed everything. The ships started shifting to freight (and I knew a woman who had been torpedoed in one off the Bahamas during the war and lived to put double locks on her home in Williamsburg and lose a husband to alcohol). The airplane changed it all. The hustlers moved in with the charter flights and created a kind of airborne steerage, with shaking aircraft, packed with women and screaming children, skimming out over the Atlantic, pushing against the headwinds of the north, moving on, leaving it all behind, heading for New York. A lot of the planes never made it, falling into the sea with their cargoes of people doomed to hope, until the charter flights were banned and the big lines took over.

Every day the planes unloaded, and the people were pathetic to look at. Their suitcases were cardboard, tied with rope, holding everything they possessed. They did not understand the cold; they had seen snow only in the movies; they arrived in January in sports shirts, with vague addresses scribbled in pencil on the backs of envelopes and hardly any money. The cold overwhelmed a lot of them. "After that first winter," a friend told me, "I was never warm." Somehow they would make it from the airports to town, and there were jokes among them later, when they had the luxury of laughter, that the Puerto Ricans were the only people in New York who knew how to get to Idlewild by public transportation.

There was no place to go except to the slums, of course: to the dark spiky landscapes of fire escapes and mean streets and doors covered with metal. There was never enough heat, and they plugged towels into the cracked windows to keep out winter, and bought a hundred thousand miles of felt tape to tack around doors, and made blankets from leftover clothes, and carried drums of kerosene up to the stoves in the parlor, and kept the gas ovens going at night. It was never warm enough, and every time you picked up a paper then and saw a headline that said SEVEN PERISH IN TENEMENT BLAZE, you knew it was Puerto Ricans and that they had died of the cold.

That New York cold killed a lot of them. The cold that made a man a "spic" instead of a man. The cold that sent women off to work in sweatshops for more money than their husbands were making cleaning the slops in the cellar of the Waldorf. Myths were growing up then, in the late forties and early fifties, especially after the outbreak of the Korean War brought jobs and the Puerto Rican trickle became a flood. They were here to go on welfare. They had come here because Vito Marcantonio, the old leftist Congressman, had bought their votes. It didn't seem to matter that the Puerto Rican migration coincided almost exactly with the increase or decrease in jobs or that the Puerto Ricans had arrived at a time when automation was starting to eliminate the jobs which were traditionally the first rung on the immigrants' ladder. The myths grew up, part of the New York cold, part of everything that is mean-spirited and ungenerous in us.

The cold broke things apart among those who were not prepared to resist it. I remember one man I knew in East Harlem, sitting alone in his kitchen, while platoons of roaches scurried across the walls, his wife gone off, the house smelling of feet and long-burned bacon, talking quietly over a can of Schaefer about how it had all gone wrong. "We should not have come here," he said. "This is an evil place. There is no respect, not for people, not for fathers." His daughter had not been home for two nights. She was fifteen, and he didn't know what to do about her. He talked about her, and about how he would like to go back to Puerto Rico, and how if he could find his wife, he would bring her back with him and they could put the thing together again. His tone said that his mouth was lying. The city had broken him, and he sat there while a parakeet he had bought for his wife's birthday whistled in the other room. It was August, and the cold came through the rooms, damp and threatening and triumphant.

But the Puerto Ricans have done what all the immigrants did. They have endured. They turned out to be long-distance runners, not sprinters, and now they are a very important part of this town. There are, to begin with, their numbers. The latest count shows that there are 1,586,397 Puerto Ricans in the United States (up from 855,724 in the 1960 census), with 977,832 of them in New York (up from 629,430 in 1960). In 1950, Puerto Ricans were only 3 percent of the city's population; today they are almost 11 percent. About one-third are second generation. One recent set of figures showed that there are 244,258 Puerto Rican students in the public school system, an increase of 75 percent over a ten-year period.

The Puerto Ricans have spread to all parts of the city (although Richmond still does not have any sizable population). Brooklyn now has the most—a symbol, I suppose, of the trend of migration; in this town a lot of the old immigrants went from the Manhattan slums to the Bronx and on to Brooklyn. The Puerto Ricans, who once were most heavily concentrated in East Harlem, were forced into the slums of the South Bronx by the swinging ball of urban renewal and are now making it into the greener glades of Brooklyn. In addition, the number of Puerto Ricans outside the city has increased from 30,000 to 51,200, a 70 percent jump. Suffolk County, with its Puerto Rican population increase of 4,700, leads the other sixty-two counties in the state.

More important is the fact that the Puerto Ricans have been accepted. It has been a long time since I have heard the word "spic" around this town. (The Spanish-language papers continue to use the word *boricua,* which derives from the pre-Spanish name for the island, Borinquen. A lot of the second-generation kids just refer to each other as "PR's".) In my white-middle-class neighborhood, the Puerto Ricans open grocery stores and put starched collars on their children in the mornings before sending them off to school.

The Puerto Ricans have followed the old routes: Some 10,000 of them run small businesses in this town, and some are expanding into larger things. There are people like José Rojas, who is now the president of Puerto Rican Steel Products Incorporated at 4 Whale Square in Brooklyn. He and eight others have started their own steel plant, with the help of private business interests and the United Puerto Rican and Spanish Organizations of Sunset Park. Or someone like Pablo Morales, who got a $2,000 loan from the Banco de Ponce several years ago to buy a truck and now owns five trucks in his own garage on Westchester Avenue and Southern Boulevard in El Bronx. The Puerto Rican banks themselves are an important part of the story, ever since they were allowed to operate in New York after changes in the state banking laws in 1961; Banco de Ponce now has four branches in the city, as has the Banco Popular, and the Banco Crédito is now breaking into this lucrative market.

The Puerto Rican Homeowners Association has plans to build a $2,700,000 low- and middle-income housing development in Brooklyn, and the Puerto Rican Community Development Project has instituted programs which in one year led to 402 members of the community's receiving high school equivalency diplomas. Everywhere the mood is one of energy and movement; it is a long way from the desperate days of the early arrivals, when you would see thin, shivering girls in spring coats in winter walking Fourteenth Street with guys in plastic-visored yacht caps, going to S. Klein on Christmas Eve to buy their kids the scraps. The great Puerto Rican neighborhoods are still solid blocks in the town: East Harlem, the South Bronx, Williamsburg, Red Hook, the Lower East Side. But there are Puerto Ricans scattered now throughout the city, in Bay Ridge and Corona and Inwood and out into the suburbs. They've purchased through grief and work and endurance that special thing which the sociologists work so hard at dehumanizing: mobility.

That mobility has freed the first brigades of the emerging Puerto Rican middle class in this town (with the same set of conflicts over loyalties to those left behind which afflicts the black middle class). But there are still hundreds of thousands living in desperate situations, and the Puerto Ricans are in fact still at the bottom of the city's economic ladder. One recent study (by Leonard S. Kogan and Morey J. Wantman) estimated that the median annual income for all city families was $6,684. The Puerto Ricans earned $3,949, nonwhites $4,754, and whites $7,635. The Puerto Ricans had gained only $49 in two years, while whites gained $927. Puerto Ricans receiving relief rose more in percentage than any other group—from 29.5

percent of the welfare rolls in 1959 to 33 percent in 1967—they are now about 35 to 40 percent. Some estimates state that some 40 percent of the city's Puerto Ricans are receiving some form of public assistance, most of it supplementing the low wages paid to Puerto Rican fathers.

In East Harlem last year, according to Herbert Bienstock, the regional director of the Bureau of Labor Statistics, 36.9 percent of Puerto Rican workers were unemployed or subemployed. The general rate was 33.1, indicating that blacks there fared slightly better. In Bedford-Stuyvesant, 29.7 percent of Puerto Ricans were unemployed, compared to 27.6 percent of the blacks. In Harlem itself, 12 percent of the Puerto Ricans are unemployed, and 8 percent of the blacks.

In some respects, the situation is not encouraging at all. White-collar employment of Puerto Rican men actually declined from 17 to 12 percent from 1960 to 1965, according to Richard Lewisohn of the Economic Development Administration, while—in the familiar pattern—white-collar employment of Puerto Rican women increased (from 18.7 percent to 24.9 percent). In a report released last year by the federal government's Equal Employment Opportunity Commission, we learned that only .9 percent of those employed in radio-TV and newspaper white-collar jobs were Puerto Ricans. (On the three major New York dailies, only 2.5 percent of *all* employees were Puerto Rican or of Latin background.) In the banking industry, only 5.1 percent of white-collar employees were Puerto Rican. The government queried 4,239 firms with 100 employees or more, or with more than $50,000 in federal contracts; some 1,926 firms did not employ a single Puerto Rican in a white-collar job. A survey by the State Human Rights Commission showed that of twenty-five of the city's forty-one major advertising agencies, only 1.6 of their 18,000 employees were Puerto Rican.

Some of this can be attributed to the problem of education. An analysis by the Puerto Rican Forum shows that of those Puerto Ricans who finish high school, 90 percent have been getting a general diploma, 8 percent a vocational degree, and only 1.2 percent the academic diploma leading to college. In the elementary schools, there is still an insistence on teaching kids in

English, which they sometimes do not know, with the result that ordinarily bright kids are stunned and humiliated before they have much of a chance to learn anything at all.

Another factor is that the Puerto Ricans are the youngest people in the city, with a median age (according to a 1966 City University study) of 19.1, compared to 38.6 for whites and 26.1 for nonwhites. This indicates a group in flux, and the educational statistics at present might be quite misleading; there might be an explosion of academic diplomas any year now. It is one indication of the way the Board of Education sees the students, however, that despite the fact that blacks and Puerto Ricans make up more than one-half of the city's public school population, only 30 of the more than 900 schools are named after distinguished blacks and only 5 after Puerto Ricans.

And yet, just because the Puerto Ricans are so young and just because they are starting to make their move, we have to deal with their presence in a rational way. Anyone who understands New York will understand that their presence is a good thing for us, perhaps the most fortunate piece of luck we have had since the end of the Second World War.

To begin with, the Puerto Ricans have brought an element of stability to New York. When the white middle class started its mass stampede to the suburbs, lamming like units of a defeated army across the frontier, the Puerto Ricans stayed on. They stayed on because they had to stay on. You simply do not have a choice if you can't ever imagine yourself having $2,000 for a down payment on a house. They stayed on, too, because they wanted to. More than the white middle-class refugees, the Puerto Ricans understood early that this could be a mean and nasty and vicious town, but it was also a great one.

"I tried living in the country," my friend José Torres, the former light-heavyweight champion of the world, once told me. "It was beautiful. There was grass and trees and clean air and birds. People were friendly. It was healthy. The schools were not crowded. The trouble was that I started going crazy. I needed noise."

Noise. Not the noise of jackhammers and ripped sidewalks and coughing trucks. What Torres means is the noise of streets, to be able to walk along Smith Street in Brooklyn and hear people shouting back and forth at each other in greeting and guys coming out of saloons on Saturday afternoons to stop friends and whisper *piropos* to girls ("Ah, *mi vida,* it must have been a fine and splendid mother to have produced such a beauty as you"). The noise is at a party in my friend Cocolo's house on Dean Street, the bathtub packed with ice and beer, babies crying in the kitchen, the table groaning with *pulpo,* and arguments in English and Spanish over the Mets and Mario Procaccino and the cost of cigars and Fidel Castro and the best way to seduce a Swedish girl. Cocolo has hit the number for the third time that year, and all his friends are there, and his relatives. "Hey, you better eat all this stup, mon, because you doan hit the number three times in a year every year." Cocolo is beaming, and on his wall he has a picture of Jack Kennedy and a poster from the O'Dwyer campaign and a smaller picture of Robert Kennedy, and later in the night, all of us slowed by beer and food, and the children asleep, and not much more to travel to daylight, Cocolo points up at the picture of Bob Kennedy and says, "Hey, mon, you explain this goddamn country. What kine of a sum of a bitch would shoot that guy? Huh? You explain that to me, mon." And the other three guys start to sing, because they've seen this happen before, and they don't want Cocolo, who is thirty-eight years old and weighs 240 pounds, to start crying all over again.

That kind of noise: and nights in Otero's on Smith Street, eating *pernil* in the back room, and talking boxing at the bar, and how one night we all came in late and the place was empty and Junior, the bartender, had a big bandage on his face. "What the hell happened?" someone said. "You get in a fight with your girl?" And Junior said, no, it wasn't a fight, it was a car accident. Pedro Ortiz, the meanest-looking man in Brooklyn, leers: "Hey, Junior, you don't have to lie to us." And Junior gets mad and goes into the back room and comes back with the door from his car, the whole goddamn door, smashed and crumpled, and everyone starts to laugh, and Pedro Ortiz falls off the stool, and we order another round.

That's what José Torres means by noise. Noise and life. Travel around a little and look at it: the Jefferson Theater, with the children crying in the audience and guys selling ice cream right in the middle of the movie, and a great comic like Johnny El Men making jokes on the stage about being a Puerto Rican in New York. Move around: to the Broadway Casino, or Carlos Ortiz's place in the South Bronx, or the Club Caborrojeño, and make a Saturday night. Who's on? La Playa, or Tito Puente, or El Gran Combo, with the music thundering down, the musicians making bad jokes, the lights sly and romantic, the girl singers with impossibly narrow waists above implacable swelling hips. And on the dance floor, girls with soft fleshy faces doing hammering mambos with their shoes off, series after series, the guys weaving baroque steps around them, the floor itself starting to groan from the pounding, the single guys lined against the walls, the people from the community clubs sitting in private parties at the tables, an occasional older woman chaperoning her daughter or niece. Ten years ago, Torres and I spent a lot of time in those places, and maybe he would have been a better fighter and I would have been a better writer if we had stayed home. I doubt it. We certainly wouldn't have had as much laughter.

The problems remain terrible. Nine out of ten Puerto Ricans over the age of twenty-five have never finished high school. There are still large sections of the community which do not read or speak English, which depend for news and information on the Spanish radio and TV (UHF) stations and upon *El Diario-La Prensa* (the other Spanish-language paper, *El Tiempo*, is a right-wing sheet directed to the community of Cuban exiles and other non-Puerto Rican Spanish-speaking people in the city: *El Tiempo* supported Mario Procaccino over Herman Badillo in the Democratic primary). There are still many Puerto Ricans working for unconscionably low salaries in sweatshops and factories run by gangster unions; a union like the International Ladies Garment Workers Union still does not have real representation of Puerto Ricans at its highest level despite the overwhelming number of Puerto Ricans in its rank and file. Narcotics remains a poison, with some communities, like Hunts Point in the Bronx, practically devastated by the problem. Heroin addicts were practically unknown in Puerto Rico itself until those who were contaminated started coming home from New York. The Puerto Rican street gangs, which were so prominent in the 1950's (the Enchanters, the Dragons, the Latin Gents, etc.), have largely disappeared, not because of especially enlightened social workers, but because a junkie doesn't have much time for gangbusting. ("It's not cool anymore to be in the hitter's bag, man," one kid told me last year.)

In the 1950's and early 1960's, there were still so many broken marriages that they seemed to a casual outsider to be almost a majority. Every day's issue of *El Diario* carried stories of guys who would visit their estranged wives and throw wives, kids, and selves out the fourth floors of tenements. The pressures were intolerable: Women who worked and made more money than men offended the Puerto Rican male's occasionally exaggerated sense of *machismo;* the resort to welfare was humiliating; the disgraceful conditions of the tenements themselves did not exactly make for the most encouraging belief in a happy and rich future. But that seems to have lessened with the breakthrough the Puerto Rican men made into the town itself. If a man does not feel he is being supported by his wife, he can find it a lot easier to live with her, whether he is a Puerto Rican or not.

The younger generation of Puerto Ricans are also making the whole thing move in another way. They don't feel sorry for themselves; they have been here all their lives; they have a sense of what must be done and how to go after it. Some are starting militant Puerto Rican organizations, like Barrio Nuevo in East Harlem. Others are going the college route. Many of them have been made aware of the obscene distortions in American life which let blacks, Puerto Ricans, and poor whites fight unjust wars while the children of the middle class have the luxury of protesting it from the sanctity of the college campus. Some have gone into a rather romantic, nostalgic Puerto Rican independence bag, which might work if the Puerto Rican in Puerto Rico could only believe it was the best thing for him. (The various independence parties have never fared well at the polls in Puerto Rico, which, if it ever gives up its present semicolonial commonwealth status, would more likely opt for becoming a state.) Increasingly, the younger generation is political, and if that has set up a generation gap of sorts, it is only because the Puerto Ricans are finally part of something larger.

380

For one thing, they have a sense of laughter now that just wasn't there fifteen years ago; I think of the group of Puerto Rican high school girls on the F train, coming back from Coney Island singing: "We all live in a yellow submarine, eating rice and beans, eating rice and beans . . ."

The young people are throwing over some of the things their parents believed in. The ones I've talked to are not terrified of Communists (despite all the horror stories passed on to them about Fidel). They certainly don't listen much to the spiritist heresy, in which *brujas* (witches) can be hired to cast spells, or win women, or whatever else one might want, at a price and with the purchase of the right herbs at the *botánica*. Religion itself doesn't seem very strong anymore, either. Some 85 percent of the Puerto Ricans in Puerto Rico are Catholics, but until very recently the church there was run by outsiders, by Irish bishops or Spanish bishops, by anyone but Puerto Rican bishops. In New York this meant that not many Puerto Ricans ever went to church, and those that "got religion" generally ended up in a more lively, less authoritarian, but somewhat more puritanical form of Christianity like the Pentecostal.

The younger people seem more interested in specifics. I remember going to a meeting in East Harlem the day after the 1967 riots took place. Ted Velez and Andrew Segarra and Torres and a lot of others had worked long into the night trying to cool the riots, and this meeting, in a school auditorium, was held to try to make sure that that trouble would not flare up again. There were representatives from the city and from the police to listen to the grievances of the young people who had done most of the fighting and bottle throwing. Their initial grievance, as it had been in other circumstances in other sections of the city, was with the Tactical Patrol Force. The TPF, these kids felt, was an armed guard of cops from outside the district, cops who could not possibly know who was who in East Harlem, who probably did not know much about Puerto Ricans, and who had reacted brutally and without sensitivity to the first outbreak of trouble. That was predictable. But when that had been cleared out of the way, they got down to the real issues. One kid got up, his voice laden with emotion, and said very loudly: "All right, to hell with that for a minute. I want to know *why* in the goddamn hell you can't get the garbage off a Hundred and Twelfth Street? Just get the garbage, and we'll believe you." It is a measure of how the bureaucracy cannot seem to unwind itself that in August of this year there was almost a second East Harlem riot. It was over the failure of the Sanitation Department to pick up the garbage on 112th Street.

When there was trouble on the Lower East Side the year before last, I went down there to talk to the people on the streets. One guy ran up to his apartment. "I got to get our demands, mon." The demands were again familiar: get the TPF out of the neighborhood; clean the garbage more frequently ("We got big families, mon, and we make more garbage"). But the demands that interested me were the ones that seemed most Puerto Rican. One was "a place to play dominoes." The other: "dancing once in a while."

Politically, the Puerto Ricans are certainly on the move. The near victory of Herman Badillo in the Democratic primary has probably removed "the Puerto Rican thing" the way John F. Kennedy's 1960 victory changed the myth about Catholics running for President. This was not supposed to be the year for a Puerto Rican, and Badillo was supposed to have been better off running for the controller's office or as president of the City Council on somebody else's ticket. When he almost won (he lost by 38,000 votes), he established himself *and* the Puerto Ricans as an important political force in New York. On the other hand, there still remains a problem of apathy to be overcome. The Puerto Ricans are still the hardest people in the city to get registered, because of a combination of factors (distrust of politicians, uneasiness about the language, and fear of anything resembling an agent of the government are some of the factors; among older Puerto Ricans, there is still some feeling that they aren't from New York, that their political candidates are an airplane ride away).

The streak of conservatism in the Puerto Ricans also seems to be widening as more of them make it into the middle class. Many of them join regular Democratic clubs, because they see those clubs as the safest way to make it politically; a man like Tony Mendez, the regular boss of East Harlem, remains a powerful man politically, and some of the less radical or adventurous younger Puerto Ricans don't want to take any chances on blowing a career by playing Don Quixote. Rivalry among Puerto Rican politicians is rather strong and sometimes leads to bizarre situations: Next year there will not be a single Puerto Rican serving on the City Council, despite the fact that there are more Puerto Ricans here than in San Juan. In those councilmanic districts where a Puerto Rican might have been elected, Puerto Ricans ran against each other and non-Puerto Ricans slipped through the seams.

Despite that, the Puerto Rican community seems more together now than it has ever been. "Up until a couple of years ago," a pretty young schoolteacher from the Two Bridges district told me, "I was ashamed to say I was a Puerto Rican. I would say I was Spanish, or something like that. Today I'm ashamed for being ashamed. We PR's are really going to take this town."

They might just do that—politically, at least—and it might not be such a bad thing. They have already added things to New York which have made it a better place: their music and their food and their sense of the outrageous. No matter where you want to go, if you travel with a Puerto Rican cabdriver, he'll take you there; he'll say: "Hey, I don't know where it is, but you show me, mon, and I take you." The rocky decade with the marriages seems over, and the stable family unit is there again, the way it is in Puerto Rico. There is still a feeling among those who came here from Puerto Rico that they don't really belong to this town, but in that sense they belong nowhere. My friend Johnny Manzanet, who is a boxing commissioner now, once said to me: "You know, I sit here in New York, and I'm homesick for Salinas; I go home to Salinas and I'm homesick for New York. I don't know what the hell I am."

What seems to be forming is a special breed: the New York Puerto Rican. One who listens to La Lupe and the Beatles, who reads the *Times* and *El Diario*, who can move around the East Side pubs and still make it up to the Broadway Casino. He is a baseball fan, because of Orlando Cepeda and Roberto Clemente and a dozen other stars who came up from the island; but he probably does not look for the score of the Ponce-Caguas game anymore; he more than likely roots for the Mets (I have yet to meet a Puerto Rican who cared for pro football or rooted for the Yankees). But he no longer needs to go to prizefights to identify vicariously with heroes. He seems to be breaking down between two New York cultural traditions, with a touch of the third: the Puerto Rican with the can of beer in a paper bag playing dominoes on the street is the Irish Puerto Rican; the guy selling the beer in the *bodega* is the Jewish Puerto Rican; the guy starting to move into numbers and narcotics in East Harlem is the Mafia Puerto Rican. Ah, give me your tired, your poor. . . .

Here, compadre, *put the luggage in the rack. I'll be in the bar having a scotch and soda. It will be warm soon enough. I have to tell my friends about snow, and the lights of Broadway, and the way the kids wear their hair in the East Village, and that crazy night I spent at the Electric Circus with the newspapermen. That, and hard afternoons looking for work, and the time we had to grab the landlord and push his face against the wall to make him listen to the rats scratching behind us. That, but the good things too: the-aters, and the Big A, and fight night at the Garden, and hanging around the corner on DeGraw Street, and playing ball in the week-end leagues in Central Park, and the great shows coming through at the San Juan and the Puerto Rico. That, and how the skyline looks coming across from Jersey at night, and the way the girls swagger down Fifth Avenue on the first warm day of spring. It will be warm soon enough, and I want to see the pastel houses in the sun and the palms blowing in the breeze and the dead calm before the hurricanes. And music.*
November 24, 1969

The Revolt of the White Lower Middle Class

They call my people the "white lower middle class" these days. It is an ugly, ice-cold phrase, the result, I suppose, of the missionary zeal of those sociologists who still think you can place human beings on charts. It most certainly does not sound like a description of people on the edge of open, sustained, and possibly violent revolt. And yet that is the case. All over New York City tonight, in places like Inwood, South Brooklyn, Corona, East Flatbush, and Bay Ridge, men are standing around saloons talking darkly about their grievances and even more darkly about possible remedies. Their grievances are real and deep; their remedies could blow this city apart.

The "white lower middle class"? Say that magic phrase at a cocktail party on the Upper East Side of Manhattan and monstrous images arise from the American demonology. Here comes the murderous rabble: fat, well-fed, bigoted, ignorant, an army of beer-soaked Irishmen, violence-loving Italians, hate-filled Poles, Lithuanians, and Hungarians (they are never referred to as Americans). They are the people who assault peace marchers, who start groups like the Society for the Prevention of Negroes Getting Everything (SPONGE), the people who hate John Lindsay and vote for George Wallace; presumably because they believe that Wallace will eventually march every black man in America to the gas chambers, sending Lindsay and the rest of the Liberal Establishment along with them. Sometimes these brutes are referred to as "the ethnics" or "the blue-collar types." But the bureaucratic, sociological phrase is "white lower middle class." Nobody calls it the working class anymore.

But basically, the people I'm speaking about *are* the working class. That is, they stand somewhere in the economy between the poor—most of whom are the aged, the sick, and those unemployable women and children who live on welfare—and the semiprofessionals and professionals who earn their way with talents or skills acquired through education. The working class earns its living with its hands or its backs; its members do not exist on welfare payments; they do not live in abject, swinish poverty or in safe, remote suburban comfort. They earn between $5,000 and $10,000 a year. And they can no longer make it in New York.

"I'm going out of my mind," an ironworker friend named Eddie Cush told me a few weeks ago. "I average about eighty-five hundred a year, pretty good money. I work my ass off. But I can't make it. I come home at the end of the week, I start paying the bills, I give my wife some money for food. And there's nothing left. Maybe, if I work overtime, I get fifteen dollars or twenty dollars to spend on myself. But most of the time, there's nothin'. They take sixty-five dollars a week out of my pay. I have to come up with ninety dollars a month rent. But every time I turn around one of the kids needs shoes or a dress or something for school. And then I pick up a paper and read about a million people on welfare in New York or spades rioting in some college or some fat welfare bitch demanding—you know, not askin', *demanding*—a credit card at Korvette's . . . I *work* for a living and *I* can't get a credit card at Korvette's. . . . You know, you see that, and you want to go out and strangle someone."

Cush was not drunk, and he was not talking loudly, or viciously, or with any bombast, but the tone was similar to the tone you can hear in conversations in bars like Farrell's all over this town; the tone was quiet bitterness.

"Look around," another guy told me, in a place called Mister Kelly's on Eighth Avenue and Thirteenth Street in Brooklyn. "Look in the papers. Look on TV. What the hell does Lindsay care about me? He don't care whether my kid has shoes, whether my boy gets a new suit at Easter, whether I got any money in the bank. None of them politicians gives a good goddamn. All they worry about is the niggers. And everything is for the niggers. The niggers get the schools. The niggers go to summer camp. The niggers get the new playgrounds. The niggers get nursery schools. And they get it all without workin'. I'm an ironworker, a connector; when I go to work in the mornin', I don't even know if I'm gonna make it back. My wife is scared to death, every mornin', all day. Up on the iron, if the wind blows hard or the steel gets icy or I make a wrong step, bango, forget it, I'm dead. Who feeds my wife and kid if I'm dead? Lindsay? The poverty program? You know the answer: nobody. But the niggers, they don't worry about it. They take the welfare and sit out on the stoop drinkin' cheap wine and throwin' the bottles on the street. They never gotta walk outta the house. They take the money outta my paycheck and they just turn it over to some lazy son of a bitch who won't work. I gotta carry him on *my* back. You know what I am? I'm a sucker. I really am. You shouldn't have to put up with this. And

386

I'll tell ya somethin'. There's a lotta people who just ain't gonna put up with it much longer."

It is very difficult to explain to these people that more than 600,000 of those on welfare are women and children; that one reason the black family is in trouble is that outfits like the Iron Workers Union have practically excluded blacks through most of their history, that a hell of a lot more of their tax dollars go to Vietnam or the planning for future wars than to Harlem or Bed-Stuy, that the effort of the past four or five years was an effort forced by bloody events, and that they are paying taxes to relieve some forms of poverty because of more than 100 years of neglect on top of 300 years of slavery. The working-class white man has no more patience for explanations.

"If I hear that four-hundred-years-of-slavery bit one more time," a man said to me in Farrell's one night, "I'll go outta my mind!"

One night in Farrell's, I showed the following passage by Eldridge Cleaver to some people. It is from the recently published collection of Cleaver's journalism: "The very least of your responsibility now is to compensate me, however inadequately, for centuries of degradation and disenfranchisement by granting peacefully—before I take them forcefully—the same rights and opportunities for a decent life that you've taken for granted as an American birthright. This isn't a request but a *demand.* . . ."

The response was peculiarly mixed. Some people said that the black man had already been given too much, and if he still couldn't make it, to hell with him. Some said they agreed with Cleaver, that the black man "got the shaft" for a long time, and whether we like it or not, we have to do something. But most of them reacted ferociously.

"Compensate him?" one man said. "Compensate him? Look, the English ruled Ireland for seven hundred years, that's hundreds of years longer than Negroes have been slaves. Why don't the British government compensate me? In Boston, they had signs like 'No Irish Need Apply' on the jobs, so why don't the American government compensate *me?*"

In any conversation with working-class whites, you are struck by how the information explosion has hit them. Television has made an enormous impact on them, and because of the nature of that medium—its preference for the politics of theater, its seeming inability ever to explain what is happening behind the photographed image—much of their understanding of what happens is superficial. Most of them have only a passing acquaintance with blacks, and very few have any black friends. So they see blacks in terms of militants with Afros and shades or crushed people on welfare. Television never bothers reporting about the black man who gets up in the morning, eats a fast breakfast, says good-bye to his wife and children, and rushes out to work. That is not news. So the people who live in working-class white ghettos seldom meet blacks who are not threatening to burn down America or asking for help or receiving welfare or committing crime. And in the past five or six years, with urban rioting on everyone's minds, they have provided themselves (or been provided with) a confused, threatening stereotype of blacks that has made it almost impossible to suggest any sort of black-white working-class coalition.

"Why the hell should I work with spades," he says, "when they are threatening to burn down my house?"

The Puerto Ricans, by the way, seem well on the way to assimilation with the larger community. It has been a long time since anyone has written about "the Puerto Rican problem" (though Puerto Rican poverty remains worse than black poverty), and in white working-class areas you don't hear many people muttering about "spics" anymore.

"At least the Puerto Ricans are working," a carpenter named Jimmy Dolan told me one night, in a place called the Green Oak in Bay Ridge. "They open a grocery store; they work from six in the mornin' till midnight. The PR's are willin' to work for their money. The colored guys just don't wanna work. They want the big Buicks and the fancy suits, but they jus' don't wanna do the work they have ta do ta pay for them."

The working-class white man sees injustice and politicking everywhere in this town now, with himself in the role of victim. He does not like John Lindsay, because he feels Lindsay is only concerned about the needs of blacks; he sees Lindsay walking the streets of the ghettos or opening a privately financed housing project in East Harlem or delivering lectures about tolerance and brotherhood, and he wonders what it all means to *him*. Usually, the working-class white man is a veteran; he remembers coming back from the Korean War to discover that the GI Bill only gave him $110 a month out of which he had to pay his own tuition, so he did not go to college because he could not afford it. Then he reads about protesting blacks in the SEEK program at Queens College, learns that they are being paid up to $200 a month to go to school, with tuition free, and he starts going a little wild.

The working-class white man spends much of his time complaining almost desperately about the way he has become a victim. Taxes and the rising cost of living keep him broke, and he sees nothing in return for the taxes he pays. The Department of Sanitation comes to his street at three in the morning, and a day late, and slams garbage cans around like an invading regiment. His streets were the last to be cleaned in the big snowstorm, and they are now sliced up with trenches that could only be called potholes by the myopic. His neighborhood is a dumping ground for abandoned automobiles, which rust and rot for as long as six weeks before someone from the city finally takes them away. He works very hard, frequently on a dangerous job, and then discovers that he still can't pay his way; his wife takes a Thursday-night job in a department store, and he gets a weekend job, pumping gas or pushing a hack. For him, life in New York is not much of a life.

"The average working stiff is not asking for very much," says Congressman Hugh Carey, the Brooklyn Democrat whose district includes large numbers of working-class whites. "He wants a decent apartment, he wants a few beers on the weekend, he wants his kids to have decent clothes, he wants to go to a ball game once in a while, and he would like to put a little money away so that his kids can have the education that he never could afford. That's not asking a hell of a lot. But he's not getting that. He thinks society has failed him, and, in a way, if he is white, he is often more alienated than the black man. At least the black man has his own organizations and can submerge

389

himself in the struggle for justice and equality or elevate himself, whatever the case might be. The black man has hope, because no matter what some of the militants say, his life is slowly getting better in a number of ways. The white man who makes seven thousand dollars a year, who is forty, knows that he is never going to earn much more than that for the rest of his life, and he sees things getting worse, more hopeless. John Lindsay has made a number of bad moves as mayor of this town, but the alienation of the white lower middle class might have been the worst."

Carey is probably right. The middle class, that cadre of professionals, semiprofessionals, and businessmen who are the backbone of any living city, are the children of the white working class. If they are brought up believing that the city government does not care whether they live or die (or how they live or die), they will not stay here very long as adults. They will go to college, graduate, marry, get jobs, and depart. Right now, thousands of them are leaving New York, because New York doesn't *work* for them. The public schools, when they are open, are desperate; the private schools cost too much (and if they can afford private school, they realize that their taxes are paying for the public schools whose poor quality prevents them from using them). The streets are filthy; the air is polluted; the parks are dangerous; prices are too high. They end up in California, or Rahway, or Islip.

Patriotism is very important to the working-class white man. Most of the time he is the son of an immigrant, and most immigrants sincerely believe that the Pledge of Allegiance, "The Star-Spangled Banner," the American flag are symbols of what it means to be Americans. They might not have become rich in America, but most of the time they were much better off than they were in the old country. On I Am an American Day they march in parades with a kind of religious fervor that can look absurd to the outsider (imagine marching through Copenhagen on I Am a Dane Day), but that can also be oddly touching. Walk through any working-class white neighborhood and you will see dozens of veterans' clubs, named after neighborhood men who were killed in World War Two or Korea. There are not really orgies of jingoism going on inside; most of the time

390

the veterans' clubs serve as places in which to drink on Sunday morning before the bars open at 1 P.M. or as places in which to hold baptisms and wedding receptions. But they are places where an odd sort of know-nothingism is fostered. The war in Vietnam was almost never questioned until last year. It was an American war, with Americans dying in action, and it could not be questioned.

The reasons for this simplistic view of the world are complicated. But one reason is that the working-class white man fights in every American war. Because of poor educations, large numbers of blacks are rejected by the draft because they can't pass the mental examinations; the high numbers of black casualties are due to the disproportionate number of black career NCO's and the large number of blacks who go into airborne units because of higher pay. The working-class white man (and his brothers, sons and cousins) only get deferments if they are crippled; their educations, usually in parochial schools, are good enough to pass Army requirements, but not good enough to get them into the city college system (which, being free, is the only kind of college they could afford). It is the children of the rich and the middle class who get all those college deferments.

While he is in the service, the working-class white hates it; he bitches about the food, the brass, the living conditions; he tries to come back to New York at every opportunity, even if it means two fourteen-hour car rides on a weekend. But after he is out, and especially if he has seen combat, a romantic glaze covers the experience. He is a veteran; he is a man; he can drink with the men at the corner saloon. And as he goes into his thirties and forties, he resents those who don't serve or bitch about the service the way he used to bitch. He becomes quarrelsome. When he gets drunk, he tells you about Saipan. And he sees any form of antiwar protest as a denial of his own young manhood and a form of spitting on the graves of the people he served with who died in his war.

The past lives on. When I visit my old neighborhood, we still talk about things we did when we were eighteen, fights we had, and who was "good with his hands" in the main events at the Caton Inn, and how great it was eating sandwiches from Mary's down near Oceantide in Coney Island. Or we talk about the

Zale-Graziano fights, or what a great team the Dodgers were when Duke Snider played center field and Roy Campanella was the catcher, and what a shame it was that Rex Barney never learned how to control the fast ball. Nostalgia was always a curse; I remember one night when I was seventeen, drinking beer from cardboard containers on a bench at the side of Prospect Park, and one of my friends said that it was a shame we were getting old, that there would never be another summer like the one we had the year before, when we were sixteen. It was absurd, of course, and yet it was true; the summer we were seventeen, guys we knew were already dying on the frozen ridges of Korea.

A large reason for the growing alienation of the white working class is their belief that they are not respected. It is an important thing for the son of an immigrant to be respected. When he is young, physical prowess is usually the most important thing; the guy who can fight or hit a ball or run with a football has more initial respect than the guy who gets good marks in school. But later, the man wants to be respected as a good provider, a reasonably good husband, a good drinker, a good credit risk (the worst thing you can do in a working-class saloon is borrow $20 and forget about it or stiff the guy you borrowed it from).

It is no accident that the two New York City politicians who most represent the discontent of the white working class are Brooklyn Assemblyman Vito Battista and Councilman Matty Troy of Queens. Both are usually covered in the press as if they were refugees from a freak show (I've been guilty of this sneering, patronizing attitude toward Battista and Troy myself at times). Battista claims to be the spokesman for the small homeowner, and many small homeowners believe in him; but a lot of the people who are listening to him now see him as the spokesman for the small homeowner they would like to be. "I like that Battista," a guy told me a couple of weeks ago. "He talks our language. That Lindsay sounds like a college professor." Troy speaks for the man who can't get his streets cleaned, who has to take a train and a bus to get to his home, who is being taxed into suburban exile; he is also very big on patriotism, but he shocked his old auditors at the Democratic Convention in Chicago last year when he supported the minority peace plank on Vietnam.

There is one further problem involved here. That is the failure of the literary/intellectual world fully to recognize the existence of the white working class, except to abhor them. With the exception of James T. Farrell, no major American novelist has dealt with the working-class white man, except in war novels. Our novelists write about bullfighters, migrant workers, screenwriters, psychiatrists, failing novelists, homosexuals, advertising men, gangsters, actors, politicians, drifters, hippies, spies, and millionaires; I have yet to see a work of the imagination deal with the life of a wire lather, a carpenter, a subway conductor, an ironworker, or a derrick operator. There hasn't even been much inquiry by the sociologists; *Beyond the Melting Pot,* by Nathan Glazer and Pat Moynihan, is the most useful book, but we have yet to see an Oscar Lewis-style book called, say, *The Children of Flaherty.* I suppose there are reasons for this neglect, caused by a century of intellectual sneering at bourgeois values, etc. But the result has been the inability of many intellectuals to imagine themselves in the plight of the American white workingman. They don't understand his virtues (loyalty, endurance, courage, among others) and see him only through his faults (narrowness, bigotry, the worship of *machismo,* among others). The result is the stereotype. Black writers have finally begun to reveal what it means to be black in this country; I suppose it will take a working-class novelist to do the same for his people. It is certainly a rich, complex, and unworked mine.

But for the moment, it is imperative for New York politicians to begin to deal with the growing alienation and paranoia of the working-class white man. I really don't think they can wait much longer, because the present situation is working its way to the point of no return. The working-class white man feels trapped and, even worse, in a society that purports to be democratic, ignored. The tax burden is crushing him, and the quality of his life does not seem to justify his exertions. He cannot leave New York City because he can't afford it, and he is beginning to look for someone to blame. That someone is almost certainly going to be the black man.

This does not have to be the situation, of course. If the government were more responsive to the working-class white man, if the distribution of benefits were spread more widely, if the government's presence were felt more strongly in ways that benefit white communities, there would be a chance to turn this situation around. The working-class white man does not care if a black man gets a job in his union, as long as it does not mean the loss of his own job or the small privileges and sense of self-respect that go with it. I mean it; I know these people, and know that they largely would not care what happens in the city, if what happens at least has the virtue of fairness. For now, they see a terrible unfairness in their lives and an increasing lack of personal control over what happens to them. And the result is growing talk of revolt.

The revolt involves the use of guns. In East Flatbush, and Corona, and all those other places where the white working class lives, people are forming gun clubs and self-defense leagues and talking about what they will do if real race rioting breaks out. It is a tragic situation, because the poor blacks and the working-class whites should be natural allies. Instead, the black man has become the symbol of all the working-class white man's resentments.

"I never had a gun in my life before," a thirty-four-year-old Queens bartender named James Giuliano told me a couple of weeks ago. "But I got me a shotgun, license and all. I hate to have the thing in the house, because of the kids. But the way things are goin', I might have to use it on someone. I really might. It's comin' to that. Believe me, it's comin' to that."

The working-class white man is actually in revolt against taxes, joyless work, the double standards and short memories of professional politicians, hypocrisy, and what he considers the debasement of the American dream. But George Wallace received 10,000,000 votes last year, not all of them from red-necked racists. That should have been a warning, strong and clear. If the stereotyped black man is becoming the working-class white man's enemy, the eventual enemy might be the democratic process itself. Any politician who leaves that white man out of the political equation does so at very large risk. The next round of race riots might not be between people and property, but between people and people. And that could be the end of us.

April 14, 1969

Letter from the Fever Zone

The only thing I remember with fondness about that fierce and muddled week was the sight of the Popsicle man, caught in the surging crowds beside the offices of the Carnegie Endowment for International Peace, his face beaded with perspiration, his eyes glazed in the thick summer heat, not listening to the rage or the obscenity, unaware of the helmeted police on their bronzelike horses, oblivious to the tides of roiled blood and sullen anger. The young moved around him, feinting moves toward the United Nations across the street, screaming at the cops, or snarling defiance, and that man stood among them, plying his poor trade. After a while, the young dispersed and went off into the city, and the Popsicle man turned his cart around and vanished with them. The difference, I suppose, is that he was going home.

There were people like the Popsicle man working all over the city during that week in May when America seemed finally to have come to the end of one particular road. They were islands of normality around which the riptides of change moved in their inexorable way, and watching them, I felt a peculiar kind of envy. In my own odd way, I had been caught up, I was part of the rage and the abstract currents, I had embraced the apocalypse with which, as a writer, I had played such casual games through the previous five years. Much had come unraveled in those years; I feared the wildness and wanted to see it controlled, and yet I had never really thought it all through. Public events hammered at me and my friends with a relentless consistency; they broke into our bedrooms, into the hours we once spent drinking together and talking about baseball or boxing.

395

Marriages broke up: Private alliances seemed impossible; in New York, the level of private generosity and trust seemed to fall as the quotient of spite and smallness rose.

So it was possible to envy people who still seemed to have located positions in the world which did not involve considerations of politics and ideology. They lived somewhere outside the fever zone. They worried about money and children and dirt in the streets, but the blame was never placed on people who could actually control those conditions. Those targets were too elusive. I would drink through long evenings in Brooklyn bars and come away wondering what I would be thinking if I had never left. I had come from there, from the bars and churches of Brooklyn, and there were parts of me that had been forever formed there. But I had left, and moved through other parts of the world, and moving around had changed me and made me someone else. Some of them envied me; they would talk to me about how great it must be to live the way I lived, going to great cities, following the famous and the powerful around and writing about them and, on top of all that, getting paid for it too. They—firemen, cops, construction workers, bartenders—would say such things at late hours of the night—friends still, because of personal history, but aware of gulfs and distances. And I would mumble something or other about how that's just the way it turned out, and how a good cop is just as good as a writer, and go over and play the jukebox and come back to talk about Muhammad Ali. And then at closing time, we would drift back to our own slices of the earth, to conjure our own visions of gain and loss before sleep grabbed us all.

I don't mean in any way to sentimentalize the Popsicle man or the friends I have in Brooklyn. They have their own private cargoes of unhappiness and rage, I am sure, and more than most people, I suppose, I am uneasy with glib judgments because as a writer for a daily newspaper I have made so many of them. But what struck me during the week after President Nixon's announcement that we had invaded Cambodia was the way one's reaction to events can be shaped by proximity to those events. Newspapermen have always been strange animals, because they have so much in common with the people they cover; police reporters begin to see the world through the eyes of cops, and talk a lot about "collars" and "squeals" and other kinds of police jargon; society reporters start out as observers of the scene and end up as part of that scene themselves. People who make politics and social change their central themes run the same risks. Today, with politics moving so thoroughly through everything, it is even more difficult to make a life which has a sense of privacy at its core.

On the night of April 30, I took a girl to see *Borstal Boy* at the Lyceum Theater. I had seen it a couple of years before at the Abbey Theater in Dublin, and this time it seemed even better; it is a play that moves the observer on a basic human level, that forces us through art to feel something about one other human being. We came out of the theater and went home, and when I called the *Post,* I learned that Nixon had sent troops into Cambodia. I tried to sleep, and couldn't, and went out and took a cab down to Sheridan Square to get the *Times.* And there it was, an invasion whose only authority was Nixon's military title of Commander in Chief. I went into the Lion's Head and had a beer. My friends were in a state of disbelief; they had wanted to talk about basketball, Willis Reed, Wilt Chamberlain. Suddenly, it had hit all of us that something dark and terrible had happened. We talked for a long time, and then I went home again. It wasn't until I lay back to sleep that it occurred to me that I had just lost more than four hours of my private life arguing about distant events when I could have been sharing a bed with a fine sweet girl.

The full impact of what had happened did not hit all of us until the next morning, when we could read the speech in detail. And here it was not any longer a question of *what* Nixon had done, but the reasons he gave for doing it. The speech was full of defensive, wormy reasoning, all about the need to prove that America was a first-rate power, and that somehow one proved one's power in the world by beating up midgets. It was as if Joe Frazier had become the heavyweight champion of the world by beating up Arnold Stang. Even worse, it sounded like the reasoning of a man who had lost contact with the world. That day, people talked darkly about the possibility that the President was losing his grip, in prime time, with his manhood stored in silos in Kansas.

On Saturday, I went to a block party in Brooklyn, where people stood in the bright sun on President Street, drinking beer, watching their children run free. We drank canned beer and talked about the Panther rally in New Haven and how nonviolent it seemed to be, but it kept coming back to Cambodia. Before the afternoon was out, the word had come in that we had once again bombed North Vietnam, after an eighteen-month interval. The news ran through the party like a particularly poisonous fog; we left the block, with its promise of community and life, and went home. My daughters were with me, and the oldest, who is seven, wanted to know why all of us were so upset and angry. It was difficult to explain to a seven-year-old; the only consolation, in some odd way, was that I still did not have a son. To have a son in America now is to run the risk of raising him to die in Asia. On Monday, May 4, sometime during the afternoon, sitting at home, I turned on WINS and heard the news about Kent State.

The rest of the week was a journey through the fever zone. The Army of the Young was everywhere, chanting "Avenge Kent State, avenge Kent State," marching through streets, gathering in a dozen places at once, seeming to burst with anger and the threat of violence. I found myself spending most of my time slogging along with them, too old to be part of them, too angry myself to be their enemies. They were younger than any of those I had seen at demonstrations in the past (or I was older, it is still not clear), and there was a growing hardness about them that was not immediately understandable. It wasn't until Tuesday when I saw my brother Joe, who is sixteen and goes to Fort Hamilton High School, that it began to come clear. These were no longer just the children of the affluent on the march; it was not a simple case of credit-card revolutionaries; a lot of these young people were the children of the working class, the younger brothers and sisters of the people I had grown up with, and they had moved out beyond their parochial visions of the earth into something larger. They no longer identified with a neighborhood, a church, a nationality, a softball team, a high school, or even, I suppose, a family. They had moved into the fever zone, and marching with them up Lexington Avenue in the direction of the United Nations, I found them rather saddening. Renata Adler, in the preface of her book *Toward a Radical Middle,* correctly placed those of us who are in our mid-thirties in the generation that is between generations. We had lost much through growing up in the fifties, but we had our consolations too; we had been able to sort out the degrees of violence because we remembered the Second World War. On that Tuesday, May 5, some police on horseback ran up against a crowd. The less inflamed kids could warn the others that a cop on horseback was not Kent State; we could say that Kent State was still not Auschwitz.

But that still did not excuse anything; to understand was still not to forgive, and there was something instinctively wrong with the idea that violence was relative. My brother Joseph is sixteen, that means that there has been an active American war going on in Indochina since he was ten. Forty-three thousand young Americans had been killed, and Cambodia said to him that they would still be dying when he was in his twenties; that was the one unacceptable thing. Many of those young people (it is impossible anymore to talk about them as the Kids) are people driven close to anarchy and even murder by the inability or unwillingness of their government to stop a vile and distant war.

So they marched around a lot, as if they might stay alive simply by showing themselves physically. One sign at Wall Street said: MR. NIXON, FOUR ARE DEAD: ONLY SIX MILLION LEFT. That was the threat: could the government impose its policies in Indochina without killing off an entire generation? The young could not be isolated the way the government appeared to have isolated the blacks (in unwitting collaboration with some black separatists). There were too many of the young. They all had parents in the middle classes, and they all had brothers and sisters, and, despite all the media concentration on the Generation Gap, they were still talking to each other. The guardsmen who killed those students at Kent State were killing the children of the Silent Majority.

I knew something about this because I had seen it happen in my own family. When my father was a young man in Ireland he was a member of Sinn Fein, the Irish revolutionary organization, but as he grew older, he became more and more conservative (though never racist); my mother, in the tradition of fine Irish women, grew more radical and more outraged; she cast one of the few votes that Mailer and Breslin received in Bay Ridge, and when I talked to her the day after Kent State, she said: "God forgive me, but I can't even talk about that son of a bitch Nixon without getting sick." In our family, which is large and sprawling, we had agreed long ago that we would keep politics out of general conversation; it led only to anger and meanness. But after Kent State, it even touched my father. The day after the killings, when I phoned him, he was talking about going back to live in Ireland. "The country has had it," he said, and for that moment at least, I understood what he meant. Even if he had become an American.

But deep in the fever zone that week, it became impossible to make any very clear distinction about anything. None of us knew what was happening in Washington; since Nixon's election I had been there only once, and that was for the November 15 Mobilization; there was nobody to call, and the newspapers provided little really hard information. We were left to wander among the young, moving from Wall Street, up Broadway, through the NYU and Columbia campuses. The split in the two nations was at first glance obvious. On one side, people who wanted to stop the war and end racism in America; on the other, people who believed that you must support the President, defeat the Communists, and deal with our other problems at a later date.

The problem was that it had become increasingly difficult to make a complete embrace of the left. To do so, it seemed necessary to accept everything or nothing; accept the Panthers, Young Lords, Young Patriots, Weathermen, RYM I and II, SDS, and all the rest. Accept the notion that exploding bombs in public buildings was going to effect real change. Accept the notion that "Free Bobby Seale" or "Off the Pigs" were ideas. Accept the notion that no one should have the right to speak at public meetings unless he had received approval from the Crazies. That was too much to accept. Many good men had spent too much energy fighting the simplicities and iron totalitarianism of the right to accept it on the left. And yet there were apologists for the left who believed that *everything* the young did or said was right, which was of course absurd, and a further belief that all of the young had acquired precocious wisdom.

For years, I had tried to stand aside from all of that; I thought that there was nothing more comic, in one sense, or repulsive, in another, than to see middle-aged men masquerading as seventeen-year-olds; to see Timothy Leary in his buckskin suit walking among the young as if he were their peer was some modern perversion of the Dorian Gray myth, and you could not really sympathize with it in even small ways. It was outrageous that Leary was sent to jail for smuggling marijuana or whatever the hell it was, but the lunatic asylums also had their share of casualties from the days when Leary had set himself up as a prophet of LSD. There were many things about the young that moved me and made me feel something close to love, but I never felt that because of that feeling I had to smoke grass when I didn't like it, or listen to the Mothers of Invention when I really despised their music, or join in a commune to show my commitment (I had, after all, once lived in a commune; we called it the United States Navy).

And wandering around that week, I felt myself becoming a private battleground. I still believed in the life of reason. I wanted the country to survive as a free nation, and not become a totalitarian state. I thought of myself as a democratic socialist, but I was not prepared to give up the democracy in order to get the socialism.

And yet I knew that cold reason was one of the factors that had brought us to where we were that week in May. Walt Rostow, Henry Kissinger, McGeorge Bundy, and all the rest were men who believed in reason. They had constructed reasonable theses about our interests in Southeast Asia, and when you listened to them, they always seemed to be logical. The problem was that their reason was abstract; it was a technique in search of an idea, and when you examined the consequences of their reasoning, you discovered that it involved blood and mutilation and the burning of villages and the destruction of acres of the earth. What some people thought of as clear thought was only a windowpane: on the other side of the windowpane, people were dying.

So I tried to understand the way the young felt, as the week moved on its dark way to its major events: the assault on peace demonstrators by the construction workers in downtown Manhattan and the demonstration in Washington scheduled for Saturday. The student strikes were spreading across the country, in the first general strike of students in the nation's history. But although that might have impressed students, some of us were uncertain about its real value and troubled by other questions raised by the strikes. A student strike, after all, is not the same as a general strike of post office workers, defense plant workers, or the men who labor for General Motors. It does not cripple the economy, it will not bring a government to its knees, and it could be thought of by some segments of the population as just a glorified form of playing hooky. It also raised serious questions about the rights of some students.

I have to assume that *all* students don't want courses that are supposed to have "relevance," that most debased and overused word. Some might want to be medieval scholars; some might want to learn more about Chaucer; some might have been moving toward some large and private insight into the seventeenth century. Most scholarship is a private act, it cannot really be done by crowds, and during that week, I wondered what had happened to those young people who had gone to universities in order to expand and develop their private selves and whether the events of the week had broken something in them that might be irretrievable. I understand the feeling of some members of the left that there is no sense in being the greatest expert on Melville if there is no country left in which to think about white whales. But to resist the totalitarian instinct is also to resist the sin of pride; too many of the people on the far left have convinced themselves that they are the only just men and can therefore legislate for everyone else. It is the same sin committed so grandly by the men who have ruled us for the past seven years, and it is not more attractive because you agree in general with most of the goals of the sinners. One longs for a country where people would respect each other and act toward each other in a spirit of ordinary, casual decency. That week in May, and at the Bryant Park rally a few weeks before, there was not much hope left that such a simple state of affairs was ever going to happen.

There were hints earlier in the week of what was to happen on Friday. If you understood those hints, they filled you with even more anxiety than the possibilities of the cops pulling a Kent State in New York. I remember writing an article for this magazine last year in which I tried to warn about the growing anger of the white working class, how that class had been largely ignored in the past ten years and how if their needs were not dealt with in real ways, then the next round of rioting might be between people and people instead of between people and property. That was written before Nixon and Agnew started pandering to those people with an almost grim determination. A lot of us had tried to deal with the white working class from a position of sympathy; I knew them well enough to know that they were not all racists, not all beer-drinking bullies. But Nixon and particularly Agnew went after them in the ugliest way possible. Agnew did not choose to speak directly to their fundamental decency, to use the power of the White House to move them into positions where they could begin to understand some of the other people with whom they must share America.

Instead, Agnew inflamed them. More than anyone else in the country, he appealed to their basest emotions, fanned their fears, flattered their prejudices. If Agnew had said that people with long hair can still be great Americans or reminded them that every nineteenth-century American hero had long hair, then some small move might have been made to help those quite alienated people understand something about a democracy and even their own children. He didn't do that or anything even vaguely resembling that: He talked about separating rotten apples; he invented a media conspiracy; he fed the right wing what it had always lacked—a quite large dish of respectability.

So on Wednesday, walking up Broadway with a crowd of demonstrators, I was not really surprised when beer cans, soda bottles, and clumps of asphalt started flying from the high stories of a building being erected at the corner of Maiden Lane. Those construction workers were only doing what the Vice President had asked them to do. I remember running up to the inspector who was leading the police patrol and asking him when he was going into the building to make arrests. He told me to do my job, he would do his. At the end of our brief shouting match, he called the marching young people "bums"; that was no surprise, either, since the President of the United States had used the same term a few days earlier. The police made no arrests that day, and no arrests the following day, when the same construction workers unleashed an even more powerful barrage, injuring people who were just walking by.

So on Friday the construction workers felt free to come down from the buildings and beat demonstrators in the name of the United States. They came with the authority of the President and the Vice President, wrapped in the flag, acting as if it were Iwo Jima, knowing that the police would do nothing about it. They were Agnew's constituency all right, which accounts for the particularly vicious and cowardly way they went about beating people; there were few cases of one man fighting one other man with his hands; it was always five grown muscular men kicking and stomping 123-pound students. A friend of mine, who is a Wall Street stockbroker and a former Marine officer, found three construction workers kicking one high school kid; he spun one of them around, dropped him with a punch, and then was jumped by about six of them and kicked to the ground. In the new American spirit.

I don't sneer at the construction workers because they love this country; it has been rather good to them, although someone should explain to them that their 7.9 percent unemployment rate has been largely caused by the war in Vietnam. The left didn't help in the attempt to win them over when it tolerated and then encouraged the waving of Vietcong flags at peace rallies, as if the peace movement could ever win by calling for an NLF victory instead of the withdrawal of American soldiers from someone else's civil war. But the construction workers have all grown up since the Second World War, too; they believe in "patriotism" and its symbols of flag and national anthem, but they have also been altered by the way the government has altered the general design of our nation. We find ourselves allied with right-wing movements all over the earth; we have never intervened in a country where a right-wing government has taken over; we have come to value size and power over everything else (which is why pro football has passed baseball as the national sport and why the only division in boxing that draws crowds is the heavyweight).

In Vietnam, where we have been asked to root for the upper-dog, where there are 450,000 American troops combined with 1,100,000 armed South Vietnamese to fight a combined force of 110,000 Vietcong and North Vietnamese, we see the new concept this country has of itself and a partial explanation of what happened that Friday at City Hall. The government's choice of violence as a solution to its problems has been used now as an excuse for more violence by the left and the right; combine that with the *macho* instinct in the construction workers and in Richard Nixon (see the Cambodia speech), throw in the construction workers' twenty-year history of breaking the laws against discrimination, add the inexcusable failure of the police to intervene, and you have the City Hall riot. On the whole, our police are a rather well-disciplined force; but at City Hall that day, they acted like the Southern police of the early 1960's, standing by and letting the poor red-necks do to the niggers what they couldn't risk doing themselves.

Most people went to Washington that weekend in a state of fear and came away in a mood of depression, futility, and some small hope. The speeches at the Ellipse were largely boring and predictable, sets of slogans buttered together, and most of the young people there didn't seem really to care very much. They were there because they agreed with the speeches, so it was the convinced lecturing the convinced. But there was another mood to the crowd, which was younger and somehow calmer than the crowd in November. In November, the crowd had roared to its conclusion with everyone singing "Give Peace a Chance" while one group went over to the Justice Department to get tear-gassed. This was different because there wasn't as much music, no real desire to be victims (Kent State had changed that), and because the Nixon people had been trying so hard to defuse it. In November, Nixon had hidden in the White House bunker, watching a football game. This time he had made a bizarre early-morning visit to some demonstrators and talked to them (not with them) and got the headlines he wanted. The weather was thick and muggy, in a way that only Washington can be, there was not enough water, and more than anything else, there was a feeling that demonstrations were not enough any more. They had become formalized and ritualized. The same people helped put them together, and the same people attended them. You went to Washington and stayed in the same hotel as the last time, and drank with the same people as the last time, or sought out the same place for your sleeping bag as the last time. It just wasn't enough.

I came away from Washington, though, with some small hope. One was in the growing idea among young people that one of their immediate tasks would be to place some iron into the Congress. For the first time since Eugene McCarthy went to New Hampshire there were stories about young people cutting their hair and shaving their beards and trying to transform the system. They wanted to flatter the Congress, if necessary, rather than frighten it, in the hope that Congress would fully recognize that even beyond Vietnam, there is a major crisis in this country over the uses of the Constitution. If Congress would take back its power to declare war and then cut off the monies from any other foreign adventures, then there would be a possibility of saving the country as it has existed. It would be a constitutional crisis of a major order, but there might be a country left when it was over, instead of a swatch of real estate ruled by tanks. This was one small indication that at least some students seem willing now to make the move from ideology to politics. They seem bored now by the increasingly meaningless rhetoric of the far left, which reads like arguments between religious sects rather than an attempt to move other people to action. They might even be bored by slogans, and if there was any slogan they might accept, it would be "Constitution or Revolution."

The other hopeful sign in Washington was that nonviolence is not as dead as we had been led to believe. In fact, it might suddenly be stronger than ever. Time after time it appeared that some groups were building to an explosion, and time after time the Mobe marshals would successfully intervene. At one point, in front of a line of buses and police on Pennsylvania Avenue, they formed a line between police and demonstrators, their eyes and lungs seared by tear gas, and held on, accepting the momentary pain, until the police relaxed and the spark was extinguished. Later in the night, there was some violence, but not many took part. I thought about a conversation I had heard a few days before, after someone had kicked in the window of the

Daily News Information Service on East Forty-second Street. A black kid in his late teens was talking to a soft white girl wearing a Red Cross armband. The black kid said: "Look, you nonviolent people fight your way and leave us violent people alone." It seemed funny then; as I watched the massed nonviolence of most of those people in Washington, it seemed absurd.

Leaving Washington on Sunday, I was going through Georgetown, saying good-bye to some friends, when I saw a tall, pregnant young woman in a red dress. She was wearing white socks, just like any pregnant young woman from Bay Parkway, and suddenly the girl with me recognized her. It was Lynda Bird Johnson. She turned and went into a friend's house, leaving the world behind her.

We drove out to the airport shortly after that, and I wondered about Lynda Bird and what it must be like to stand around on the street and have the currents of anger and rage swirl around someone you do not know and how strange it must have been to grow up in the White House. I wondered if she had any real privacy, now that she had no connections with real power, and then, as the sky darkened, I remembered a lot of trips I had made to that airport in 1967 when I lived in Washington and how much of my own private life had been left in wreckage. We had become a strange and barbarous and occasionally wondrous people, but it was becoming terribly difficult to create a sense of life for oneself that provided solace and consolation and refuge.

In politics, the only hope for people like me and my friends was to try to carve out a position that was not based on self-deception or lies or that did not include the commission of crimes. By crimes, I don't mean breaking the law; some laws are unjust and can only be changed through challenge. I mean crimes against other human beings; I mean needless cruelty or making assumptions about strangers that are based on stereotypes. There must be a way to carve out that position without worrying about being called "liberal" or "Uncle Tom" or whatever other term of hatred the credit-card revolutionaries have devised that month. Renata Adler calls the position the Radical Middle, and it is a position that is at least acceptable to those of us who are not prepared to write off large sections of the population. One could still hope for a society based on decency without calling every cop a "pig" or by succumbing to wholesale paranoia. It would not be easy, because it is never easy to adopt a political position that asks for an understanding of complexity.

The terrible thing somehow is the growing feeling that no matter what political position you move toward, the need for privacy might be beyond reach. I don't think there are any of us who do not long for strong houses with libraries filled with old books, a sense of continuity and time worked into the leather and the wood, the consolation of silence, the private communication of feeling between two humans, the moment when your child learns to read, lemons spread on a white table in the weekend sun, a piece of the earth that you alone possess.

Those things seem to be increasingly difficult to obtain. Someone always calls you at two o'clock in the morning to tell you about assassinations, burning buildings, and public murder. In the week after Cambodia, living in the fever zone, bombarded with news of burning and destruction, battered by the AP wire and the telephone, knowing that young men were dying in still another country, seeing the father of one of the dead Kent State students breaking down on television, knowing that the men who rule us were apparently intractable, nothing seemed more important than silence and privacy. I flew back to New York in the mauve dusk, thinking about my two daughters and wishing, despite everything, that I had a son.

May 25, 1970